£6·00

ML

THIRTEENTH CONGRESS OF THE
UNIVERSITIES OF THE
COMM

The Congress Symbol

The upper part of the logo is intended to suggest: B for Birmingham; 13 for 13th Quinquennial Congress; St. George's Cross for England; and, in the coloured original (see front cover), red, white and blue for the Union Jack and Britain.

Designed by Kilvington & Associates, who also designed the Congress Handbook upon which the design of this Report's cover is based.

For a list of ACU publications, see end of volume.
Reports of some previous Congresses are also available.

TECHNOLOGICAL INNOVATION: UNIVERSITY ROLES

The Report of Proceedings of the
Thirteenth Congress of the Universities of the Commonwealth
Birmingham, August 1983

THE ASSOCIATION
OF COMMONWEALTH UNIVERSITIES
JOHN FOSTER HOUSE, 36 GORDON SQUARE, LONDON,
ENGLAND WC1H 0PF

1984

Editor of Congress Proceedings
T. CRAIG, MA

Assistant Editor
EILEEN A. ARCHER, MA

Price £6
Printed in Great Britain by Hobbs the Printers of Southampton
Copyright © The Association of Commonwealth Universities, 1984
ISBN 0 85143 087 2

FOREWORD

This Report contains
- summaries or short versions of the papers presented by the speakers who introduced each of the discussion sessions held during Congress week. Mention is also made of several other papers circulated during the Congress;
- summaries of the discussions that followed the presentation of the papers;
- a commentary by each of the five Topic Chairmen on the nature and outcome of his own group's meetings.

The editors are greatly indebted to the five Topic Co-ordinating Chairmen who (within certain broad guidelines) not only organised the Topic discussions but also collected and collated for this Report the texts that appear in the individual Topic sections.

Speakers and rapporteurs were asked to provide for inclusion in the Report texts within specified maximum lengths and in some cases it has been necessary, in the interests of balance, to edit the original text so as to bring it within the suggested format.

Also included are the full texts of addresses given at the opening of the Congress, at the first plenary session, and at the banquet which brought the Congress to its close.

The Preface contains an overview of the Congress as a whole—its planning and organisation, and the major events and other meetings associated with it.

CONGRESS ORGANISING COMMITTEE

Rt. Hon. Lord HUNTER OF NEWINGTON, *Chairman*

Dr. C. W. L. BEVAN (from 26.3.81)

Dr. S. A. S. GALADANCI (until 31.10.82)

Professor D. W. GEORGE

Sir DOUGLAS LOGAN

Sir ALEC MERRISON (from 4.11.81)

Dr. C. R. MITRA

Professor R. W. STEEL (until 4.3.81)

Professor T. H. B. SYMONS

Dr. J. STEVEN WATSON

Sir HUGH W. SPRINGER, *Secretary General, ACU* (until 30.9.80)

Dr. A. CHRISTODOULOU, *Secretary General, ACU* (from 1.10.80)

Mr. H. HARRIS, *Secretary, University of Birmingham*

Mr. A. J. PRIOR, *Assistant Secretary, University of Birmingham*

Mr. T. CRAIG, *Editor of Congress Proceedings (Assistant Secretary General, ACU)*

Mrs. Blanche GUBERTINI, *Personal Assistant to Secretary General, ACU*

CONTENTS

PREFACE

The thirteenth in the ACU's series of quinquennial Congresses of the Universities of the Commonwealth took place at the University of Birmingham from 14th to 20th August 1983. The series began with the 1912 Congress in London, out of which the Association of Commonwealth Universities (the Universities' Bureau of the British Empire as it was first named) was born, and has continued without interruption except during the two world wars. After world war II the decision was taken that Congresses should be held alternately in Britain and another part of the Commonwealth; and thus the 1958 Congress was held in Montreal, the 1968 Congress in Sydney and the 1978 in Vancouver.

A General Meeting within the week before or after the Congress is required by the Association's Statutes, and around it is arranged a Conference of Executive Heads of member institutions; it is customary also for the Council to meet before or after the Congress in the same country. For the first time all three meetings were held in the same venue. The Council assembled in Birmingham on Wednesday 10th August and inaugurated its meeting with a formal dinner following a reception given by the Vice-Chancellor of the University of Birmingham. On the 11th it held its business meetings.

ACU Conference of Executive Heads

The members of the Conference (224 participants with 145 members of families) gathered during Thursday 11th August and were welcomed by the Chancellor of the University of Birmingham, Sir Peter Scott, with a reception followed by an informal supper. On Friday the members of the Conference spent a day of intensive discussions on *Higher Education on Trial: Commonwealth Perspectives* prompted by consideration of the principal findings and recommendations of the Leverhulme Study Programme into the Future of Higher Education as summed up in the final report *Excellence in Diversity*. After meeting in plenary session to hear Mr. C. J. E. Ball (Warden of Keble College, Oxford, and Chairman of the Board of the National Advisory Body for Local Authority Higher Education) present the report, the meeting divided into four groups: *Governing the system*, under the chairmanship of Professor D. A. Bekoe (Ghana); *Financing universities*, under the chairmanship of Professor G. D. Sims (Sheffield); *Managing universities*, under the chairmanship of Professor Lim Pin (National, Singapore); and *New structures of courses*, under the chairmanship of Professor A. Wandira (Makerere); and came together in a final plenary to review the day's discussions.

The statutory General Meeting was held on Saturday 13th August, the main items on the agenda being the Secretary General's quinquennial report on the activities and affairs of the Association; the Honorary Treasurer's report; the report of the Working Party on the Future Policy of the ACU; and a report by Sir Roy Marshall (Hull) on the work of the Commonwealth Standing Committee on Student Mobility. Consideration of the latter led to the adoption of resolutions for transmission to the Commonwealth Secretary-General urging Commonwealth Heads of Governments to support measures encouraging staff and student mobility.

The Conference's programme included a reception and concert arranged by the Trustees of the Barber Institute; and ended informally in a day's visit to Badminton on Sunday 14th August by kind invitation of their Graces, the Duke and Duchess of Beaufort.

Preparations for the Congress

The Congress Organising Committee was appointed by the Council at its meeting in Delhi in February 1980 with the Rt. Hon. Lord Hunter of Newington (then Vice-Chancellor of the University of Birmingham) as Chairman, the other members being: Dr. S. A. S. Galadanci (Sokoto) who left in October 1982; Professor D. W. George (Newcastle); Sir Douglas Logan (Deputy Honorary Treasurer, ACU); Dr. C. R. Mitra (Birla ITS); Professor T. H. B. Symons (Honorary Treasurer, ACU); Dr. J. Steven Watson (St. Andrews) and Sir Hugh W. Springer (then Secretary General, ACU). Professor R. W. Steel (University College, Swansea) served from May 1980 to March 1981 when his place was taken by Dr. C. W. L. Bevan (Wales and University College, Cardiff). Dr. A. Christodoulou, who succeeded Sir Hugh Springer as Secretary General on 1st October 1980, served as its Secretary from that date. Sir Alec Merrison (Bristol) joined the Committee in November 1981.

The Committee held its first, third, fouth and fifth meetings in London, while its second was held in Hong Kong in March 1981 during the Executive Heads' Conference of that year. The Council at its meeting in the Caribbean in April 1982 also discussed arrangements for the Congress.

Arrangements for the meetings at Birmingham were undertaken by staff at the University of Birmingham under Mr. H. Harris, the Secretary, and Mr. A. J. Prior, Assistant Secretary. Over a three-year period many meetings took place between them and the Association's secretariat. The programme of tours and outings for families of participants in the Congress was organised by the Ladies' Committee under the Co-ordinator, Mrs. Eleanor Davis. A special programme for children was organised by the Guild of Students of Birmingham University under the direction of its permanent secretary, Mr. Ian McCrae, in co-operation with Mrs. Davis and the Ladies' Committee.

A preliminary notice of the dates and places of the meetings and an outline programme were sent to member institutions in April 1981 with a request for suggestions for topics for discussion at the Congress and Conference. In June 1982 members received formal invitations to be represented by up to four participants each at the Congress and by executive heads of universities at the Conference, and notification of the topics to be discussed. Invitations to both meetings were sent also to the executive officers of the Commonwealth inter-university bodies associated with the ACU.

Membership of the Congress

The total number attending the Congress as official delegates was 578 (comprising 489 nominated by 224 member institutions together with 89 representatives of other organisations and specially invited guests), about 265 of whom were accompanied by one or more members of their families. The overall total attending was 891.

Her Royal Highness, The Princess Anne, Mrs. Mark Phillips, Chancellor of the University of London, graciously consented to be the President of the Congress. The Vice-Presidents of the Congress included the Chancellors of the United Kingdom universities, Ministers of the Crown in the United Kingdom, High Commissioners in London of other Commonwealth countries and dignitaries of the County of the West Midlands and the City of Birmingham. Other representatives included the executive officers of national and regional university organisations in the Commonwealth, the chairmen of various University Grants Committees and equivalent bodies, and representatives of a variety of other Commonwealth, non-Commonwealth and international organisations involved with university education, including university representatives from European countries and the USA.

11

The Congress

Members of the Congress and their families assembled on Sunday 14 August and were accommodated in halls of residence of the University of Birmingham. The meetings were held on the University's campus.

The Congress was opened in the Great Hall of Birmingham University on Monday 15 August with a formal ceremony at which the Council of the Association processed in academic robes accompanied by the Lord Mayor of Birmingham, the Chairman of the West Midlands County Council, the Chancellors and Vice-Chancellors of the universities of Birmingham and Aston in Birmingham and the Chairman of the Congress Organising Committee. Addresses of welcome were given by the 1982–83 Chairman of the Association, Sir Alec Merrison, and the Chancellor of the University of Birmingham, Sir Peter Scott. The opening address was given by H. E. Mr. Shridath S. Ramphal, the Commonwealth Secretary-General, under the title of *Must Technology be a Flawed God?*

After the formal opening the first plenary session was held under the chairmanship of Sir Alec Merrison. The Chancellor of the University of Aston in Birmingham, Sir Adrian Cadbury, gave the keynote address on the overall Congress theme *Technological Innovation: University Roles*. The five topics under this theme—*The social consequences of technological innovation*, *The contribution of universities to integrated rural development*, *University/industry partnerships*, *The development and transfer of technology* and *Continuing education*—were then discussed in groups on Monday afternoon, Tuesday morning and afternoon and Thursday morning and afternoon, after hearing lead speakers drawn from universities throughout the Commonwealth and elsewhere. On Friday afternoon the second plenary session of the Congress, at which the chairmen of the five topics—Professor Sir Bruce Williams (Director, The Technical Change Centre), Professor R. W. Steel (former Principal, University College of Swansea), Sir Henry Chilver (Vice-Chancellor, Cranfield Institute of Technology), Sir Denys Wilkinson (Vice-Chancellor, University of Sussex) and Dr. J. H. Horlock (Vice-Chancellor, the Open University, UK)—gave summary reports of the discussions, was followed by the closing session at which Professor E. A. Marsland, the Vice-Chancellor of the University of Birmingham, said how pleased the University had been to be the host, and Dr. H. E. Duckworth, President and Vice-Chancellor Emeritus of the University of Winnipeg, expressed the thanks of the participants to all who had contributed to the success of the meetings.

The chief social events of the meeting were the day-long visit to the Ironbridge Gorge Museum, when participants were taken to see the world's first iron bridge and various museums and sites associated with the industrial revolution; a reception given by His Worship the Lord Mayor of Birmingham; a reception given by the University of Aston in Birmingham; a visit to a performance of *Twelfth Night* at the Royal Shakespeare Memorial Theatre at Stratford-upon-Avon. The last event of the Congress was the customary banquet on Friday 19 August (preceded by a reception given by the West Midlands County Council and attended by its Chairman, Sir Stan Yapp), at which the ACU's Chairman, Sir Alec Merrison, presided and the toast 'Universities of the Commonwealth' was proposed by Sir Zelman Cowen, Provost of Oriel College, Oxford, and former Governor-General of Australia. Distinguished guests present included the High Sheriff of the West Midlands, the deputy Lord Mayor of Birmingham, the Chairman of the West Midlands County Council and several high commissioners. Sir Zelman was introduced by Professor D. E. Caro, Vice-Chancellor and Principal, University of Melbourne, and Sir Alec responded to the toast on behalf of the universities.

There was a special daily programme for the families of participants which included visits to a variety of historic houses, museums and cultural centres around Birmingham.

The Association is much indebted to the University of Birmingham and to its staff, of whom special mention can be made here of only a few: the Vice-Chancellor, Professor Marsland, for his unfailing generosity and cheerful ubiquitous presence; Mr. Harry Harris, the Secretary, who guided the whole operation from its inception to final fruition; and, through him, all his staff and especially Tony Prior, the chief local Congress administrator; and not least Mrs. Eleanor Davis and the Ladies' Committee over which she presided, whose special efforts provided a memorable series of events and experiences for accompanying spouses.

Mention must also be made of an innovation at this Congress when the Guild of Students of the University organised some of its members into a brigade to help with all aspects of the running of the Congress, from welcoming participants on arrival, carrying luggage, baby-sitting, and generally caring for all involved.

To all of them we record our deepest gratitude.

November 1983

A. CHRISTODOULOU
Secretary General

ACKNOWLEDGEMENTS OF SUPPORT

Generous assistance towards registration fees and travel costs of executive heads from the least developed countries was provided by:—
The British Council
The Canadian International Development Agency
The Commonwealth Foundation

The universities of the United Kingdom supported the Congress financially through arrangements made by the UK Committee of Vice-Chancellors and Principals.

The generosity and help of the following to the Congress is warmly acknowledged:—

The Lord Mayor and Council of
  the City of Birmingham
The Trustees of the Barber
  Institute of Fine Arts
Their Graces the Duke and
  Duchess of Beaufort
Cadbury Schweppes plc
Dale Services
The Ironbridge Gorge Museum
  Trust
Lloyds Bank plc
Midland Bank plc

National Exhibition Centre
National Westminster Bank plc
The Royal Shakespeare Theatre,
  Stratford-upon-Avon
Stanford & Mann Ltd.
UNESCO
University of Aston in
  Birmingham
Waterford-Aynsley (UK) Ltd.
West Midlands County Council
Allenways Coaches

OPENING OF THE CONGRESS

Monday, 15 August

Sir ALEC MERRISON (*Vice-Chancellor of the University of Bristol and Chairman of the Association of Commonwealth Universities*): We have arrived at the moment for the formal opening of our great five-yearly Congress of the Association of Commonwealth Universities; *formal* because we have already in the last few days been able to renew and refurbish old friendships which form so much of the firm foundation on which the success of our Association is built. And it is on those friendships and on new ones which will be formed in the coming days that so much of our work together rests and will continue to rest.

For certain it is that whatever difficulties beset the dealing of one nation with another no such difficulties stand in the way of the easy commerce of universities and academics throughout the world. This happy situation finds its expression in so many ways: by the world-wide conferences of scholars in particular fields to which, in one way and another, our universities play host; by the extensive system of international fellowships and scholarships, not least those administered by this Association; by the opportunities for study afforded to young people in countries other than their own, curtailed to some degree by unwise national decisions but still vigorous.

Those of you who have attended one of our Congresses before will know that they are unique in their sheer variety—the variety in the people attending, the variety of their interests and the variety of their home backgrounds give us all an oppportunity to *learn* which we can get in no other way. Happily they give us, too, the opportunity to enjoy ourselves, which we certainly shall.

But one cannot have a great Congress without great burdens falling on the host university. All of us who have been privileged to see the enthusiasm and efficiency with which our colleagues in Birmingham have set about ensuring the success of this Congress are filled with both admiration and gratitude—but not surprise! Everything this great University tackles it does well and we are the beneficiaries of this simple fact.

The Congress in its formal sessions and in the more informal business and activities of this coming week will be dominated throughout by the serious purpose of our universities working together, and working together in an environment which is for us

15

all changing ever more rapidly. Our universities have played an important part in helping the societies in which they find themselves to come to terms with change, both through the research that we do and also through the fact that we are entrusted with the education and training of the ablest young people in our societies. But there is no doubt that we can do more and equally there is no doubt we can do better. During this week we shall be trying to learn what in fact we may do. We are privileged to welcome to our opening session the Secretary-General of the Commonwealth, His Excellency Mr. Shridath Ramphal, who has contributed so much to Commonwealth understanding.

But now it is a pleasure to be able to express our gratitude to the Chancellor and Vice-Chancellor of this great University for the extraordinary work that the University has done for us and the extraordinary welcome they have given us.

After Sir PETER SCOTT (*Chancellor of the University of Birmingham*) had welcomed the members of the Congress on behalf of the University of Birmingham, the Commonwealth Secretary-General gave his opening address.

TECHNOLOGY: A FLAWED GOD?

H. E. Mr. SHRIDATH S. RAMPHAL (*Commonwealth Secretary-General*): Invitations to do the honours at conferences vary between opening and closing the proceedings. I am never quite sure which I should welcome more. The one seems to say with impatience 'let's get over with the frills early so that we can get down to serious business'; the other seems to say with resignation 'now we've done our serious business, let's hear what you have to say'. On the whole I prefer the former; vanity at least allows the illusion that there is a chance to influence the proceedings. So I am pleased as well as honoured, Mr. Chairman, that you have asked me to be with you this morning.

And it is not a formality that I begin with a word of contratulation to the Association of Commonwealth Universities on the theme of the thirteenth Congress and on the care and perspicacity with which the topic discussions have been prepared. The nature and out-turn of your consultations on university roles in relation to technological innovation can be of great significance in the determination of the right policy patterns not only by universities, but by governments, by industry and perhaps even by the Commonwealth collectively. Sir Adrian Cadbury's address later this morning will begin a process of discussion among our most learned, caring and experienced Commonwealth citizens that is of wide and urgent import. I wish you well and commend you for engaging them.

Your theme and discussion topics raise issues of importance to universities world-wide. That is often the case with the major issues that spark Commonwealth discussion. It could hardly be otherwise, since the Commonwealth is so much a microcosm of the world. But as you approach the question of responses to the challenge of technological innovation it is pertinent to ask whether the Commonwealth connection that facilitates your discussion might not itself facilitate your response. Are there practical arrangements that Commonwealth universities can make to enlarge the gains to people throughout the Commonwealth's forty-seven countries from technological innovation? Can your camaraderie in discussion take concrete shape in co-operative action?

This Congress, I believe, will fall short of its true potential if you merely examine the role of universities generally in relation to technological innovation without specifically asking what Commonwealth universities separately or together can do to facilitate performance of the roles you identify. Neither the erudition nor the realism you will assuredly bring to your discussions will do justice to this occasion unless each helps you to identify in practical terms what Commonwealth universities, what you, can and should do in facing up to the challenge of technological innovation.

The question of student interchange, of student mobility, is one area in which we need to translate Commonwealth sentiment into Commonwealth policy. This Congress is infused with the value of sharing. It epitomizes all that is good in the long and distinctive tradition of educational interchange which has been such an important feature of the Commonwealth. Most of you have benfited from scholarships, awards, study visits, exchanges, attachments, visiting lectureships and professorships, and thus bring to bear on your work within your respective countries an appreciation of the social, economic and political complexities of a wider world shaped and tempered by study overseas. You are better people because of it and the Commonwealth is stronger because of you.

I believe passionately in the interdependence of our world community. If I were asked to single out the one objective to which I have devoted myself above all else during the last eight

years as Commonwealth Secretary-General, I would say it has
been to try to persuade governments and peoples to acknowledge
the reality of interdependence and its concomitant implications.
An interdependent world requires more, not less, educational
interchange. I have found few things more disturbing therefore
than the barriers created to student flows through fee increases,
quotas and other impediments in a number of Commonwealth
countries, some with a long tradition of access to their educational
institutions. By the same token I have been greatly heartened by
the vigorous opposition of the academic world to these barriers,
and the slowly-dawning realisation in political circles that the long-
term costs to national and international development of limited
student mobility may outweigh any short-term financial savings.

For the Commonwealth itself this is a matter of the utmost
importance. A significant reduction in educational interchange
within the Commonwealth has serious implications for the future
character, if not indeed the future, of the Commonwealth itself. I
do not say that lightly. I have a rather unique opportunity to meet
with Commonwealth leaders and to share with them their hopes,
and sometimes their concerns, for the Commonwealth itself. I tell
you that there is a deep anxiety that if we do not fairly quickly
find ways of strengthening educational interchange within the
Commonwealth, not necessarily by returning in all respects to old
ways, but certainly by endowing educational interchange between
Commonwealth countries with a special place in our educational
systems, the Commonwealth connection will itself be in danger of
impairment.

Equally in danger of impairment is the quality of education
itself. I do not need to tell this gathering of the benefits which
accrue from interchange to both sending and receiving countries.
Your Congress is particularly well equipped to pronounce loudly
and clearly the value of educational interchange. Of all Commonwealth gatherings it is perhaps best able to spell out the practical
benefits to be derived by receiving and sending countries alike. I
know that many of you individually, as well as through your
institutions, have raised your voices in protest against short-sighted
policies and have done all that you can to promote and foster this
cherished Commonwealth tradition. I thank you warmly for your
efforts and urge you to continue them. We have begun to climb
back; but your awareness and commitment are the best guarantors
of success.

And there is another respect in which the Commonwealth
umbrella under which you meet imposes a special obligation and
could give your consultations a significance not easily achieved at

the wider international level. I refer to the question of small states. There are, of course, small states outside the Commonwealth; but we have in the Commonwealth community a high proportion of the world's smallest societies. Twenty-five Commonwealth countries, more than half our members, have populations of under one million; 17 of them, more than a third, have populations of under 300,000. Many are island communities. Small states are not just scaled-down versions of larger states; smallness can be a factor in its own right; quite often a problem factor.

Small may sometimes and in some contexts be 'beautiful'; but our smallest states are unquestionably disadvantaged in the matter of tertiary education. When you address the question of the role of universities in relation to technological innovation in the context of a state of, say, 300,000 people or less you are obliged not to contract but to widen your enquiry. 'What technology?', of course, becomes a pertinent question; but, even more to the point, 'what university?'. Such necessary questionings will inevitably lead you into exploring a range of co-operative measures at the regional, inter-regional and Commonwealth-wide level in supplementation of the resources of these very small states. For them, a part of the challenge of technological innovation is innovation in the role of universities, innovation that emerges out of the traditional springs of university improvisation and perhaps out of technology itself.

As you enter on your discussions, therefore, I ask you to be mindful of the small state dimension and consciously to expand the range of your responses to accommodate these special cases. Otherwise you run the risk of not being at Birmingham as relevant as you can be to very many Commonwealth countries.

And I commend you, too, on the choice of Birmingham as the venue of this Congress. I do not know whether venue was matched to theme or the other way around; or whether a kindly fate brought the two together. But they are surely well conjoined. Birmingham, after all, is something of a symbol (shared, it is true, with Manchester) of the industrial revolution. In that right alone it is an ideal centre for your appraisal of the potential and prospects of the new technological revolution whose implications for human history might be as primordial as were those of the revolution that had its beginnings in Britain's industrial midlands.

The industrial revolution changed the course of human history; but not always, or at least immediately, for the better. For one thing it was a revolution that widened social and economic inequalities within the new industrial societies and between those societies and all others. William Blake's 'dark Satanic mills' remain the prevailing image of both the human and physical environment at home that the process of industrialisation generated. It was a revolution that had itself to be reformed before its full potential for improvement of the quality of life of people generally could be realised. It was not, some would say still is not, an unmixed blessing. It carried with it a great propensity for enlarging human disparities. It tended to make the few much more than the many, a tendency curbed in time at home by the great movements for reform—reform of which this magnificent campus itself bears witness—but a tendency which was left unchecked abroad in relation to disparities between industrial societies and others. That tendency produced in time the developed and developing societies, and the counterpart to the process of reform at home, so far an unfulfilled counterpart, is the story of the struggle of the developing countries—the non-, or under-, industrialised countries—to redress the legacy of inequality between nations that was the product of that earlier revolution. Are such imperfections inevitable?

Let me remind you (in caricature) of Hephaestus, the Greek god of fire and metalworking in the pantheon of classical gods in Olympus:

Hephaestus was one of the ugliest somewhat deformed and most irascible of the gods. In spite of the antipathy of the other gods to him, however, Hephaestus was eagerly sought after for his technological skills because he was an architect, a smith, an armourer, a chariot-builder and an artist. He fashioned delicate works of art, furnished weapons, and provided transportation in the form of the golden shoes with which the gods moved through the air. In short, he was a central and indispensable part of the workings of Olympus. Entrusted with the development and maintenance of many key technologies, Hephaestus was responsible for keeping society running smoothly and perfectly. Yet he was, ironically, the only imperfect member of the pantheon of classical gods.

Must technology always be a flawed god?

This is the setting, the historical, contemporary, intellectual setting, in which you have to consider the role of universities in relation to technological innovation. It is a new revolution taking the industrialised countries to another kind of development, full of possibilities for their post-industrial society; full of challenges for social organisation, and human life generally—and not without its hazards. But what does it hold for countries that are still pre-industrial and for the newly industrialising? Different implications, it is clear. Already these differences emerge in the initial responses of people to technological innovation. In the rich industrial societies the question increasingly asked is 'how do we cope with the crisis of leisure likely to arise in post-industrial societies?' In poor countries, as your discussion topics rightly reflect, the question is whether technological innovation can contribute to redressing the enforced idleness imposed by the crisis of poverty. Paradoxically, for the rich (at least in this sense) the prospect may be crisis; for the poor, the prospect could be hope.

But, of course, in another and perhaps more realistic sense the reverse may be true. One of the questions that need to be asked and answered by our generation is whether the technological revolution will have the same propensity as the industrial revolution for widening disparities within nations and between them. The reforms already rooted in industrial societies will go a long way to ensuring that the gains from technological innovation are fairly shared in post-industrial societies. By the same token, the absence of reform in relations between industrial societies and others will almost certainly enlarge the danger of the new technological revolution widening even further the disparities between rich and poor nations, between developed and developing countries.

And what about the newly industrialising countries—those who have just begun to turn the corner of development? Are all the gains in catching up, so hard won by them, to be virtually wiped out as science and technology help those already industrialised to a great leap forward and a widening of the gap once again?

'Knowledge itself is power', Francis Bacon asserted in timeless wisdom nearly 400 years ago. Today knowledge (or technology) is inducing rapid social change globally and almost instantaneously, because of human mobility and telecommunications. What issue does the attendant danger of unleashed power raise? For me, the overriding issue is whether the new technological revolution will be an equalising element in human relations or a factor of further distortion and contradiction. Will it be harmonised to human needs and managed for the greatest human good or be allowed to serve mainly selfish adversarial ends, maximising its gains for a few, mindless of its adverse implications for many?

As you consider the role of universities in relation to technological innovation you will find it necessary, I believe, to make assumptions about this. What will those assumptions be? Are there good reasons to think that we can do better in the 1980s than in the 1780s? In the 21st century than in the 19th? I believe that there are some reasons for so thinking; but it would be naive to ignore that there are strong countervailing forces, and that at the moment these are in the ascendency.

But, first of all, the element of hope. This surely must lie in the fact that man who long ago perceived his oneness (however much our tribal instincts opposed our insights) has begun to recognise that we can no longer deny our inseparable humanity with impunity. At an altogether new level of awareness we have begun to admit that, for all the differences of power and wealth that separate human beings, man's essential condition is one of mutual dependence; that we all need each other to some degree not merely for survival but for making the world on a day-to-day basis a tolerably just, peaceful and habitable place. Interdependence is not a new word or a new concept; but it has a new relevance, a new insistence.

Most of you have seen a print of the first photograph of earth taken from space—taken in 1966 as the lunar orbiter turned its camera away from the stars and aimed it back to planet earth. For the first time over a decade and a half ago man, through his journeying into space, saw the planet as we had for half a millenium known it to be, one whole. Not much later man himself stood upon the moon and saw the earth rise over the horizon. 'Planet earth', Barbara Ward exclaimed for us all, 'is a small place'. The miracle machines of modern communications have brought into focus the global village that our world community is—a village we shall soon be able to 'shuttle' from and to as we commute in space.

'Heaven', wrote Robert Frost, 'gives its glimpses only to those not in a position to look too close'. Perhaps earth-bound man has been too close to discern his oneness; but there are glimpses of our future global society here in our technologically-aided present. We talk of 'balkanisation' in pejorative terms—the axiomatic nonsense of a fragmented region; for how long can we fail to see a 'balkanised' world that is the glimpse from space. And have we the will to use these glimpses actually to shape the future closer to fulfilment of man's needs? The technological revolution has put the future within our power to save or destroy. But in truth the future depends less on space probes than on the 'close encounters' here on earth, the relationships which we allow, or encourage to develop, between the world's nations and peoples, the attitudes, the habits, the perceptions that lie behind those relationships.

We know, for example, that while man's science can transform the world to make it a more prosperous and habitable place for all its people, human frailty can turn that very potential of science to global destruction. Once more, as in the early eons of his existence, man faces a primary challenge of survival—only this time, in strange reversal, the danger lies not so much in the power of a hostile and untamed environment to destroy him, but in the dominion his genius has vouchsafed him over his environment. In the result, we must now make the future possible, if we are to have a chance of making it tolerable for all people.

And the processes must go together; we cannot, for example, defer facing up to the challenge of development while we pursue the problems of disarmament. We cannot ask the poor to remain poor while we persuade the rich to give up their games of war. As we look to the future we dare not forget that for everyone now alive on this planet the future begins today—a fundamental truth I urge you not to ignore as you engage your topic discussions.

Over a century ago the Russian political thinker, Alexander Herzen, balancing future aspirations with present needs, reminded us that: 'Each epoch, each generation, each life has had, and has, its own experience, and the end of each generation must be itself'. 'Would we condemn today's human beings', he asked, 'to the mere sad role of caryatids supporting a floor for others one day to dance upon? Or wretched galley slaves who, up to their knees in mud, drag a barge with the words "Future Progress" on its prow?' The answer, of course, is: 'No'. The future cannot properly be constructed upon an unacceptable present. The task facing us is one of compelling urgency: an immediate response to current emergencies that cannot await the promise of the future, and planning today for those longer-term changes that can only be agreed and installed over time.

My point is that your appraisal of the prospect for technological innovation, even for the role of universities in relation to it, cannot ignore the relevance of the world's response to this task. What we do now about development and about disarmament provide a scenario that you cannot avoid this week—if only by making it your major premise that there must be an enlightened human response to both challenges if technological innovation is to serve maximum human good.

World military expenditure this year is around 650 billion dollars—1.2 million dollars every minute, day and night, all year round. Eight hours of that expenditure—one working shift—could eliminate malaria world-wide and improve the lives of some 200 million people. Two days of world military expenditure is the equivalent of one year's budget of the United Nations and all its specialised agencies—and all of them are starved of resources.

But the arsenals are not starved of stockpiles. The bomb that fell on Hiroshima on 6 August 1945, 38 years ago last week, was one single crude, primitive, atomic device. It killed, to date, 20,000 people. Its successor weapons are more than one hundred times more powerful, more lethal; and there are between 50 and 60 thousand of them—mostly in the primed and targeted war-heads of the super-powers. That is how our world, at the height of its scientific accomplishment, uses some 20% of its research and development resources. People—the end victims of this accumulation of destructive power—are only slowly beginning to know what is being done in their name.

After three years of study the UN Governmental Expert Group on the relationship between disarmament and development concluded that the world can either pursue the arms race or move consciously to a more sustainable international economic and political order; but that it cannot do both. In opting for the arms race we are opting against a comprehensible future, while deceiving ourselves that we are acting to secure it.

Improving the climate of international security—securing peace otherwise than by preparing for war—is therefore one element of the action immediately needed if technological innovation is to have a chance to improve our world. The other lies in the international economic domain, the area that has traditionally been the preserve of the North-South dialogue—the issues on the international economic agenda.

I don't need to tell university leaders that the world economy faces today a crisis of major proportions. It is a crisis of contraction: contraction of financial flows, contraction of economic growth, contraction of international exchange. Its outward and visible symbols are deepening poverty, mounting unemployment, massive debts and payments deficits, collapsed commodity prices, a casino-like quality to currency markets and rising barricades of protectionism. Its human impact is the shattering of the assured prosperity of the rich, of the new-found confidence of those who have begun to glimpse real development, and of even hope of better times for the poorest. Its political fall-out could be an era of instability that alters the political geography of the world and unleashes conflicts of apocalyptic dimensions. The signs of such calamities are all around us.

In the history of science, technological innovations generated locally appear to have depended on several factors: a long-term investment in science and technology for human development; a strong foundation, of the highest quality, in science education especially in schools; a complex infrastructure for scientific research and technological development; a sustained political and administrative commitment towards the advancement and promotion of science including technology; and, finally, political realisation that only steady progress over a long time-scale can transform a society from a technology-absorbing to a technology-generating one.

And we can go on. Countries, universities, need to identify, establish and maintain centres of excellence in specific areas of

science and technology, not only for promoting scientific advancement and technological innovation but also for acquiring the
universal knowledge necessary for the training of skilled manpower
and for the development of a philosophy of life. In the industrialised
countries such centres proliferate; consuming more than 95% of a
multi-billion global enterprise (1980: US$150 billion) while the
developing countries have a minuscule fraction of less than 3%.
The industrialised countries spend 1·5–3% of gross national
product on research and development while the developing
countries spend less than 0·5%.

Do we really believe that responding to these requirements
and redressing these disparities are simple matters of policy for
governments or universities? Of course they are not. They are
conditioned and largely foreclosed by the disparities between
nations. The former cannot be addressed, or at least addressed
satisfactorily, unless the latter are redressed. That is why the issue
of development is your concern; the question is not only how
can technological innovation contribute to development, but how
without development will technological innovation even begin to
contribute?

At the start of the eighties it is both simplistic and facile to think
that the progress of the poor depends on the prosperity of the rich.
That is why in the Brandt report, while we acknowledge that 'the
poor will not make progress in a world economy characterised by
uncertainty, disorder and low rates of growth', we recognise that
'it was equally true that the rich cannot prosper without progress
by the poor'; that 'it will not be possible for any nation or group
of nations to save itself either by dominion over others or by
isolation from them. On the contrary, real progress will only be
made nationally if it can be assured globally'. Our conceptual
framework is 'mutual interest in change': the joint interests of rich
and poor countries in the kind of changes—and they are fundamental changes—that we recommend in the world economy. 'We are
looking', the report says, 'for a world based less on power and
status, more on justice and contract; less discretionary, more
governed by fair and open rules'. Must you not look for such a
world as well, if there is to be a role for universities in responding
to the challenge of technological innovation for the vast majority
of Commonwealth countries?

That perception is in fact unavoidable; the approach need not
be timorous. Already developments in many fields are calling
for measures of global management. In food, in energy, in the
environment, in population, in finance, in global security, the
mutual needs of nations have grown to the point where the reflexes

25

of nationalism can no longer be allowed to act as a restraint on
international management for the good of all. We must now find
a way of giving practical recognition and institutional expression
to the wider loyalty that our instinct of human solidarity dictates
and our technological progress has made both possible and necessary. We may not have as much time as our complacency implies.
Let me end, therefore, by urging that your Congress be neither
cramped nor craintive in responding to the challenge of its theme—
and by leaving with you a vignette of encouragement and hope.

Some months ago Nelson Mandela managed to smuggle a letter
out of the infamous prison on Robben Island where he had spent
more than seventeen years. The letter was in response to the
necessarily delayed news that he had been awarded the 1979
Jawaharlal Nehru Award for his commitment to the struggle for
human political rights, freedom and justice in South Africa. In its
tolerance and wisdom his message of acknowledgement contains
insights for us all. Mandela, in the name of the movement he
represents, expressed a determination to join with the people of
India, and with people all over the world, in striving towards a
new tomorow, towards making a reality for all mankind of the sort
of universe that Rabindranath Tagore dreamed of in 'Gitanjali'—
written, we do well to remember, as the world prepared for the
twentieth century: a place in time 'where the world has not been
broken into fragments by narrow domestic walls'. Mandela also
quoted in his letter from the prison memoirs of Nehru who, like
him, could not be contained by iron bars:—

'Walls [wrote Nehru] are dangerous companions. They may
occasionally protect from outside evil and keep out an unwelcome
intruder. But they also make you a prisoner and a slave, and
you purchase your so-called purity and immunity at the cost of
freedom. And the most terrible of walls are the walls that grow
up in the mind which prevent you from discarding an evil
tradition simply because it is old, and from accepting a new
thought because it is novel.'

Could it be that at the end of the day the real limits to
technological innovation are these walls that have grown up in
human minds; that they more than anything else will determine
whether the technological revolution will be harmonised to human
needs or be a factor for danger and distortion? If so, there is no
greater role in relation to it than the role of the universities—for
you have the unique vocation to help us to lay the intellectual and
moral foundations for an enlightened global future in which walls
are no longer our companions—in which technology need not be
a flawed god.

FIRST PLENARY SESSION

Monday, 15 August

Chairman: Sir ALEC MERRISON

Vice-Chancellor of the University of
Bristol and Chairman of the Association
of Commonwealth Universities

TECHNOLOGICAL INNOVATION:
UNIVERSITY ROLES
(Keynote Address)

Sir ADRIAN CADBURY (*Chancellor of the University of Aston in Birmingham and Chairman of Cadbury Schweppes plc*): It is a great privilege to have been asked to speak at this first session of the thirteenth Commonwealth Universities Congress. I was delighted to accept the invitation, because you are honouring my home city by holding the Congress here and because it came from Lord Hunter, with whom I always look forward to putting the world to rights on the train between Birmingham and London. I also consider it extremely broad-minded of you to invite a university chancellor to speak; our more accustomed role, like Victorian children, is to be seen and not heard.

It is entirely appropriate that a Congress with this theme should be held in Birmingham. The growth of this city and of this region was based on technological innovation and industrial enterprise. Those who provided the business drive were great respecters of education and our midland educational institutions are rooted in the life and work of the region. A mechanics' institute existed in the city from the 1830s and the Birmingham and Midland Institute opened in 1856, providing both academic courses and technical training for all who wanted to take advantage of them. Aston University earned its standing as a technological university by building on this experience of municipal technical education, while the University of Birmingham developed from the Science College founded by Sir Josiah Mason in 1875.

So the two parts of our theme—technological innovation and the roles of universities—are well met in Birmingham. I intend to look to the past not from nostalgia but to provide pointers to the way forward. Given my background I shall deal with industrial innovation, while recognising that agricultural innovation is at least as important and the innovatory process is common to both. The thread which runs through what I have to say is the contribution of the individual to innovation and the need to cherish the individual spark of enterprise.

When we approach themes with as broad a sweep as the one which will direct our discussions this week, we may seem to be dealing with impersonal forces, proceeding necessarily towards programmed goals. I do not believe on past evidence that technological innovation can be forced into such a deterministic framework. Individuals promote innovation and universities are involved with individuals. Much as I admire C. P. Snow's novels they are a caricature of university life, because his university has no students. I am sceptical about business generalisations (principles would be too grand a term)—they have the same predilection for ambiguity as the Greek oracles—but a sound operational maxim is that we should back people not projects. It is relevant that Birmingham's first historian, William Hutton, who came here in 1741 was struck most by the people:—

> 'I was surprised at the place, but more so at the people, they presented a vivacity I had never before beheld. I had been among dreamers, but now I saw men awake. Their very step along the streets showed alacrity. Every man seemed to know what he was about. The town was large and full of inhabitants and these inhabitants full of industry.'*

Of course many of those people had not come to Birmingham by chance. They were driven here in the 1660s by religious persecution, by the impositions of the Clarendon Code enacted to ensure that the Puritans and their like were never again returned to power. Because Birmingham was more than five miles from any city, town corporate or borough, it escaped the Code's restrictions. Birmingham, therefore, became a centre for non-conformists of all persuasions and its inhabitants not only had freedom of worship, but freedom to trade as well, without the burden of the guild restrictions which applied to corporate cities. Birmingham retained this independence from the established civic structure for many years, only becoming a parliamentary borough in 1838.

Looking back at the industrial revolution and at the growth of this region, what is striking is the part which the non-conformists and the Quakers in particular played in that whole process of change in Britain's economic structure. Abraham Darby of Coal-

---

*William Hutton, *History of Birmingham* (1782).

brookdale was the Quaker who founded the iron and steel industry and the history of his family's contribution to technological innovation can be seen at first hand at Ironbridge. The Quaker guiding hand is, however, there across the broad spread of British industry from iron and steel, railways, chemicals, and engineering to consumer goods of all kinds with a particular corner in tea, biscuits and chocolate. As a consequence of their involvement in industry and in agriculture, they developed the business of banking as well; both Lloyds and Barclays banks originated as Quaker enterprises.

The interesting question is why the Quakers in the eighteenth and nineteenth centuries should have played such a leading role in transforming the country's economy, a role out of all proportion to their numbers in the community.* I can only touch on some aspects of this question, if I am not to stray unacceptably far from our theme.

Everett Hagen in his *Theory of Social Change* looks at the industrial revolutions of Britain, Japan and Colombia and suggests that in each country there was a particular social group from which the majority of the innovators came. He identifies them as the nonconformists in England, the Samurai in Japan and the mining families in Colombia. The link between these groups is that they had no accepted role in the society of their time. They had lost their place in the existing structure and so were not inhibited from changing it. The emphasis of Hagen's explanation is not so much on the particular beliefs and attitudes of the innovatory group as on their position or lack of it in the community.

This is a useful general approach, even though I do not find the thesis entirely satisfactory in relation to Quaker innovators in Britain. It could well, however, provide some pointers as to the social groups within a developing country most likely to generate innovatory ideas. The reason why I find it incomplete in respect of the Quakers is that there is a clear relationship between their religious beliefs and the lead they gave to British industry and commerce. In the first place they lived their religion in their working lives; they saw no separation between the spiritual and the material. This meant that they were trusted as bankers, that they charged fair prices (at a time when bargains were usually struck by haggling) and that they treated those who worked for them as individuals of equal worth. These attributes were the outcome of their religious beliefs and were sound business precepts as well. They would go far to account for Quaker success in

*In comparison with their numbers in the population, Quakers have secured something like forty times their due proportion of Fellowships of the Royal Society during its long history.

29

industry and commerce, but not necessarily for the degree to which they were innovators.

There seem to me to be at least three reasons why we could expect Quakers to be innovators. One was that they were excluded from all positions of public office, from most professions, from the larger trade guilds and from English universities. They were driven, therefore, to find new types of business, in which they could employ their energies and their savings. Even within established trades their beliefs prevented them from taking advantage of some of the growth industries of the time, like the manufacture of cannon and shot. So the Quaker iron-masters developed a range of domestic iron goods, examples of which you can see at Ironbridge, for which the market grew rapidly.

Another reason is that the kind of people who broke with established religions were men and women who thought for themselves, who took responsibility for their lives and work and who were determined to prove their worth. They were innovatory in belief and therefore in action, since they saw life as a whole. Their innovation in action was assisted by their exclusion from established guilds and professions, with all the barnacles of past custom and practice which went with them.

The third reason concerns education and its links with innovation. The fact that the Quakers were excluded from the English universities until 1871, when the Corporation Act was repealed, was, as it happened, an advantage. Oxford and Cambridge in that period looked to the past and their view of education can be somewhat unfairly summed up by this quotation from the Reverend Thomas Gaisford, who, I hasten to add, was the Regius Professor of Greek in the University of Oxford: 'The advantages of a classical education are twofold. It enables us to look down with contempt on those who have not shared its advantages and also fits us for places of emolument, not only in this world but in that which is to come'. The Quakers were spared that deadening influence on their thinking, while maintaining a high regard for education. They encouraged continuing education for themselves and for those they worked with. Joseph Sturge, a Birmingham Quaker, started the first adult Sunday School here in 1845. The Quakers favoured the study of practical subjects like arithmetic, geography, natural history and what they referred to as the modern tongues. William Penn, on leaving England for America in 1682, set out his views on how his children should be educated:—

'For their learning be liberal . . . but let it be useful knowledge, such as is consistent with Truth and godliness . . . I recommend the useful parts of mathematics, as building houses or ships, measuring, surveying, dialing, navigation, but agriculture is especially in my eye; let my children be husbandmen and housewives, it is industrious, healthy, honest and of good example, like Abraham and the holy ancients, who pleased God and obtained a good report.'*

What practical guidance can we look for from this sketch of the role of the Quakers in commerce and industry? Not, I trust, that persecution is the way to stimulate innovation, since persecution is equally capable of driving innovatory talent elsewhere. A more humane deduction would be that a country is more likely to gain from receiving persecuted minorities than from expelling them. The positive message from the Quaker experience is the link between education and innovation. This suggests that it should be possible to create an intellectual climate favourable to innovation, through what is taught and how it is taught. It is to that point that I will return.

First, however, I would like to take one further example of the links between education and innovation from the history of this region. The Lunar Society of Birmingham was formally founded in 1776, but the remarkable group of men who made it up had been meeting for some time before then. They arranged their meetings to coincide with a full moon, so that they could 'have the benefit of its light in returning home'. The contacts between them were not limited to these pre-arranged meetings, since they lived in and around Birmingham and met or wrote to each other regularly. There were only 14 members of the Lunar Society over the years: Matthew Boulton, Erasmus Darwin, Thomas Day, Richard Lovell Edgeworth, Samuel Galton, Robert Augustus Johnson, James Keir, Joseph Priestley, William Small, Jonathan Stokes, James Watt, Josiah Wedgwood, John Whitehurst and William Withering. But it was said of them: 'There was not an individual, institution or industry with pretensions of contact with advancing technology throughout the land, but some member of the Lunar Society group had connexions with it'.†

Their interests were astonishingly varied and their discussions covered the whole field of human activity, but the special interest they had in common was science and the ways in which it could be applied to industry. Their network extended to America and Benjamin Franklin introduced William Small to Matthew Boulton, at the same time asking Boulton to let him know of anything new in magnetism or electricity, or any other branch of natural knowledge which had occurred to his fruitful genius, since last they had

*Arthur Raistrick, *Quakers in Science and Industry.*
†Clow & Clow, *The Chemical Revolution.*

31

met. The Lunar Society was therefore an outward-looking group, whose members pooled their astonishing range of knowledge and experience in the interests of the scientific advance of industry and much else besides. Dr. Joseph Priestley dedicated his book *Experiments on the Generation of Air from Water* to the Lunar Society.

'There are few things that I more regret in consequence of my removal from Birmingham than the loss of your society. It both encouraged and enlightened me; so that what I did there of a philosophical kind ought in justice to be attributed almost as much to you as myself. From our cheerful meetings I have never absented myself voluntarily and from my pleasing recollection they will never be absent'.

Four of the members ran their own businesses. Matthew Boulton made silverware and a wide range of metal goods at his Soho works in Birmingham. James Keir founded an alkali works at Tipton and the chemical industry with it. Josiah Wedgwood established his pottery business at Etruria in Staffordshire and Samuel Galton made guns in Birmingham to the considerable concern of his fellow Quakers. As a result a stream of practical problems were put before the members of the Society, who contributed advice, ideas and an unbounded enthusiasm for experimentation. Wedgwood made the first earthenware drain and water pipes, a notable contribution to public health, and was helped by Darwin and Watt to arrive at the right formula and process for producing them. Between them the members made considerable advances in metallurgy to assist Matthew Boulton and in geology in the cause of promoting canals. They took a great interest in transportation of all kinds and a scheme for a fiery chariot was a regular subject for discussion.

The versatility of the members is exemplified by Dr. Erasmus Darwin—Charles Darwin's grandfather. He was a highly respected physician, but his publications span natural history, the classification of flowers and vegetables, *A Plan for the Conduct of Female Education in Boarding Schools,* and poetry. His *Botanic Garden* can claim to be the only widely popular scientific poem ever published; one verse from it runs:-

'Soon shall thy arm, UNCONQUER'D STEAM, afar
Drag the slow barge or drive the rapid car;
Or on wide-waving wings expanded bear
The flying chariot through the fields of air'.*

All of which may have helped to inspire Matthew Boulton's interest in the development of the steam engine.

---

*Erasmus Darwin, *The Botanic Garden* (London, 1791).

What conclusions can we draw from the workings of the Lunar Society, which are relevant to our theme? One is the value of the flow of knowledge and ideas across the artificial boundaries of subjects, disciplines and professions. Not only were problems in one field solved by insights from another, but the pooling of all these skills and interests encouraged a process of intellectual fermentation, which generated new thoughts and approaches with great vitality. In seeking to stimulate technological innovation we should be looking for ways of breaching the compartments so impermeably constructed by specialists around their particular interest or function. In this regard it is worth keeping in mind George Bernard Shaw's comment: 'No man can be a pure specialist without being in the strict sense an idiot'—the qualifications in that phrase are important.

Another conclusion can be drawn from the interest of the Lunar Society members in education. Dr. Darwin's book on education for girls has already been referred to, but it was Richard Lovell Edgeworth who made the most notable contribution to educational theory, in addition to studying the higher reaches of mechanics and aerodynamics. In co-operation with his daughter, Maria, he published *Practical Education* in 1798. It drew on Dr. Priestley's ideas and no doubt on the Edgeworths' extensive experience of family life—Richard Edgeworth married four times and Maria was one of 22 children. The book had considerable influence in encouraging educators to develop the natural abilities of children, rather than setting them in an educational mould.

The examples of the Lunar Society and of Quakers in industry and commerce suggest that the free flow of ideas and an educational approach which recognises the world of work will encourage innovation. I do not, however, regard technological innovation as an inevitable process, whose timing is solely determined by the ebb and flow of economic forces. Kondratiev identified long waves in the level of economic activity in the developed countries of the West, with business cycles lasting roughly half a century from peak to trough. The upturn in each cycle was largely ascribed to a major technological innovation—steam power in the 1790s, railways in the 1840s and electricity plus the motor car at the turn of this century. One of the reasons why this explanation is not entirely convincing is that it is the putting of innovations to effective use which influences economic activity rather than the emergence of the innovation. The concept of steam power had been around long before 1790; Hero of Alexandria did after all describe the power of steam in the first century AD. The steam engine itself had gone through many stages of development before Matthew Boulton had the vision to see what this innovation was capable of and where the market for it lay. He told James Boswell in 1776: 'I sell here, Sir, what all the world desires to have—POWER'. He also said, of the Boulton and Watt engines: 'It would not be worth my while to make for three counties only, but I find it very well worth my while to make for all the world'.*

It is possible to date Boulton's perception of the potential market for power more precisely than the innovation of the steam engine, and it is that combination of the individual and of the market which promotes economic activity. The concept of business cycles fuelled by innovations can be misleading, if it suggests that the link between innovation and exploitation is a simple one and that a trough in activity will automatically generate a revival. If we are aiming to encourage effective technological innovation we have to begin by recognising the complexity of the process. There seem to me to be three elements involved in putting an innovation to work on a scale sufficient to effect a discernible shift in economic activity.

First there are the innovators themselves. While the role of great men and women in shaping history may have been exaggerated in the past, it would be equally unbalanced to regard them all just as products of their time. A more accurate criticism of the importance of the individual spark would be that many innovators were before their time and there has to be a potential market for an innovation if it is to be developed on any scale. Nevertheless individual innovators persisting obstinately in the face of rejection and indifference recur so frequently in the history of technological progress that their role must be accepted as literally vital.

It is however rare for innovators to have the other abilities which are required to market their innovations successfully. So the second element is the necessary marketing, financial and production back-up to turn individually brilliant ideas to commercial use. Watt needed Boulton's vision, drive and business sense just as much, admittedly, as Boulton needed Watt's steam engine to extricate himself from his financial difficulties. The commercial development of the steam engine also required considerable advances in such techniques as casting, machining and turning in order to make the engines efficient.

To put the point another way, Charles Babbage was a brilliant innovator, whose ideas were far in advance of his time and of the engineering capacity to put them into effect. He began work on his difference engine in 1823 and then moved on to his analytical engine, which was the forerunner of the computer. His difference engine was wholly mechanical and was fed by punched cards; even

*Robert E. Schofield, *The Lunar Society of Birmingham.*

34

to attempt to build it he had to devise a range of major engineering improvements, which included the die-casting of parts, the designing of a form of turret-lathe and the first research into tool-grinding. The back-up for Babbage of finance and of supporting technologies to put his extraordinarily advanced ideas into practice simply was not there.

Babbage also points up the third element in the process, which is that there must be a latent demand which the innovation can satisfy. There was no effective demand in the early nineteenth century for speed and accuracy in computing, which was what Babbage had to offer. The same was true of the punched card system which controlled his engine. Jacquard operated the first fully automatic draw-loom by punched cards in 1801. Babbage, interestingly enough, had a five-feet-square woven silk portrait of Jacquard, which had been made on a Jacquard loom; 24,000 punched cards, each capable of taking 1050 punch holes, were used in its manufacture. The astonishing potential of the punched card for the processing of information and for the control of machines was not realised until the demand for information and for automation in this century. Demand pull and innovatory push are both essential for the effective diffusion of technological advances, with market demand determining the timing of the advance.

The key point is that effective innovation is a complicated process involving individual innovators, a strong supporting cast with business and financial skills and above all an identifiable market. All three elements are essential to the process and this is why I am sceptical of the ability to direct innovation centrally. The attributes which technological innovation requires are not amenable to direction and are rarely available to governments or other central institutions. Those whom governments invite to sit around the table and discuss where and how innovation should be encouraged are those who already have a stake in the existing order. The innovators are uninvited, because no-one has yet heard of them and they are busy sawing through the legs of the table round which the established presences are sitting.

Technological progress in society is the outcome of a continual struggle between frustration with the existing state of affairs and the need for continuity and order. Governments understandably weigh the scales heavily in favour of order. Applying this analysis for a moment to the British economy, our fundamental problem as a country is that we suffer from structural arthritis. The institutions in our society, whether political, industrial, syndical or educational, have long histories and are extremely rigid; they can only be changed slowly and with difficulty, absorbing a great deal of energy in the process. If Britain is to achieve the growth it should be aiming for, and to provide the jobs that would go with it, we have to loosen up our institutions and lower the barriers to innovations of all kinds.

To return, however, to the main theme, where do universities fit in the innovatory picture? The first point to make is that the relationship between the worlds of work and of education is becoming closer, as economic activity becomes increasingly based on knowledge rather than on human or mechanical muscle. New England, as an old industrial area of the United States, was badly hit by the decline of its traditional trades. Its economy has now been regenerated and the local Board of Education, admittedly not a disinterested observer, puts this down to the critical mass of higher education in the state. There are 65 colleges and universities in the greater Boston area alone and that, says the Board, 'has enabled the region to adapt to shifting dynamics in the national and even international economy. In recent years these institutions, collectively, have given the region a competitive edge in technology-based industries and also helped to stimulate, as well as attract, entrepreneurial talent and to encourage new business start-ups'. These words should be reflected on by governments, whose response to the financial pressures arising from slow growth is to cut their investment in higher education.

Before leaving the United States it is worth turning to the Charpie report which was published in 1967. This report to the President identified some of the factors which led innovatory companies to cluster in particular locations. The factors included:—

● venture capital sources which are 'at home' with technologically-oriented innovators and able to appraise their prospects;

● technologically-oriented universities in which staff and students are encouraged to tackle technological projects and themselves generate new ventures;

● close, frequent consultations among technical people, entrepreneurs, universities, venture capital sources, and others essential to the innovation process.

The Report's conclusions refer directly to the role of universities in promoting technological progress and we should keep in mind that, although the references are to innovation in industry and commerce, they apply equally to agriculture in societies where that is the mainspring of the economy. In practice it may be necessary to push the case for studies connected with agriculture even harder than the case for those concerned with industrial technology, since they may fit less easily into the accepted tradition of university education; this is another example of the need to loosen up our institutional thinking.

To come nearer to home, Aston University is sited at the heart of a great industrial city and it has a specific mission to promote technological studies; Aston has four points of contact with the world which it exists to influence. In the first place the content of its courses and the range of its research activities reflect its technological purpose. They, in turn, are reinforced by attracting a considerable number of industry-based students, who combine working for their companies with studying at the University.

The second point of contact is through extension education, the facilities for which I hope you will see tomorrow evening at the Aston reception. This cuts the tie between the education which a university can offer and attendance in its courts; in itself this is an example of loosening an institution up. It also helps to ease another rigidity, which is that education should finish at school- or university-leaving age, when work begins. The idea that a single, even if prolonged, dose of education should inoculate us for the rest of our lives is curious and outmoded. Equally the separation of knowledge from experience and education from training is inefficient, to say the least, since they should reinforce each other.

The third point of contact is through the Aston Science Park, which is next door to the University and is promoted jointly by the University, the city of Birmingham and Lloyds Bank. The Science Park is a nursery for high technology companies, where they have ready access to university ideas and knowledge and to venture capital.

Fourthly the University has a company which provides technical and consultancy services to businesses and to public authorities. The aim is for this arm of the University to be developed as a research institute responding to local needs. Such an institute would be a valuable staging post between the University and business worlds, attracting staff from both spheres.

The common thread which runs through these four points of contact between the University and its constituents is that the flow of ideas should be in both directions. Universities have a role in influencing the outside world and the outside world has a role in influencing universities, particularly in helping them to determine the direction they intend to take. Maintaining the appropriate balance of influence in each direction is the task of all of us who are concerned with the future of universities and of the communities which they serve.

There is one lead in the Charpie report which I would wish to see followed up. I think that we should encourage the use of our urban universities as a meeting place for professional bodies and for trade union and employer associations. The universities represent a resource on which these bodies could draw with advantage, and they form a natural clearing house for the dissemination of ideas and the development of new lines of thought. A common meeting place would help to reduce the height of the partitions which professions and associations erect around themselves by way of protection. Again the influence would be two-way, to the mutual benefit of the universities and of those who widened their horizons by meeting on their campuses.

My last point is a reminder that technological innovation will have a profound impact on university teaching. The cost of microcomputer systems is falling rapidly and we have in them a tool for universal learning. Their versatility and ubiquity could with imagination transform teaching methods. They have a further advantage in that many who find paper and ink a barrier to learning take enthusiastically to computers and to dialogues with machines. Microcomputers offer the opportunity of de-institutionalising education and using common central resources in an entirely individual way.

I am sure that many useful initiatives will develop out of this week's discussions. It is all part of improving the flow of ideas across boundaries, natural and man-made, which was a feature of the great periods of technological innovation of the past. It also keeps the focus on education, which has played such a crucial role in maintaining technical progress through the centuries. But broad generalisations about both technology and education should not be allowed to obscure the importance of the individual innovator, who brings about change in the face of all the forces with an interest in resisting it. The greatest contribution which the universities can make is not so much by solving the problems of the working world within their walls, as by educating those who will go out and solve them on the spot. The role of the universities is not only to provide their students with the necessary knowledge to advance society's frontiers in a practical way, but also to inspire them to make the most of their individual abilities and to have the faith and tenacity to change the world for the better.

Group Discussions

TOPIC 1

THE SOCIAL CONSEQUENCES OF TECHNO-LOGICAL INNOVATION

Co-ordinating Chairman: Professor Sir BRUCE WILLIAMS
Director of the Technical Change Centre and former Vice-Chancellor of the
University of Sydney

For index to names, see p. 427

Sub-Topic 1(a)

Chairman: Dr. A. Z. PRESTON
Vice-Chancellor of the University of the West Indies
Rapporteur: Mr. J. D. BUTCHART,
Registrar of Monash University

Monday, 15 August

The Chairman opened the session by outlining the kind of questions arising from the subject to be considered, particularly in relation to developing countries. How are choices to be made between large- and small-scale production and between efficiency and employment? Should the technology adopted be modern or traditional? How is this technology acquired, and at what cost? What are the likely effects on people, and how should they be trained to cope? Such issues are an essential concern both of society in general and of universities, which are expected to provide knowledge to help find answers; and the answers themselves seem to change almost daily. Science and technology policy is not a discipline; it is a set of problems: problems which determine the material state of populations, the means by which production is maximised, and employment and unemployment, in both developed and developing countries today.

THE IMPACT OF TECHNOLOGICAL CHANGE ON WORLD POPULATION, WEALTH AND EMPLOYMENT

Professor Sir BRUCE WILLIAMS (*Director of the Technical Change Centre and former Vice-Chancellor of the University of Sydney*): In the last 200 years technical changes in the production of goods and services have transformed the productivity of workers, types of employment, the range of consumer goods and styles of living.

41

In the 130 years after 1820, production per head of population in the industrialised countries increased by a factor of 5, and then in the 30 years after 1950 by a factor of $2\frac{1}{2}$. Employment in agriculture has fallen from 60% to less than 10% of the workforce, and has been balanced by an almost opposite movement in services. Rural depopulation and urbanization have been a common feature, the proportion of lifetime spent at work has fallen by one-third, and the proportion of workers in the same occupation as their parents has fallen even further.

Technical change is not new. The familiar distinction between the stone age, bronze age and iron age is based on technical change. Museums in China provide ample evidence of a great range of inventions in ancient China. The screw for raising water which is still widely used in Egypt for irrigation was invented by Archimedes over 2,000 years ago. There was a major technical change in warfare in the fourteenth century when gunpowder was adopted. The invention of movable type and type metal in the fifteenth century was another major technical change. But it was not until the eighteenth century that technical change became cumulative and self-sustaining.

Cumulative Change

In the eighteenth century Britain led the world into industrialisation. The first revolution was in agriculture, where improved methods in cultivation and animal husbandry and the introduction of new crops brought a great increase in the quantity and quality of food. This made possible an increase in population by 40% between 1750 and 1800, and by a further 55% between 1800 and 1830. But such was the increase in productivity that the proportion of labour needed to produce food fell. The surplus agricultural labour was readily absorbed in industry. The industrial revolution, based on mechanical inventions in cotton textiles, Watt's steam engine and innovations in smelting, was firmly established by the end of the eighteenth century.

The differences between economic conditions in Britain in 1700 and in the Roman Empire at the outset of the Christian era were not very great, but the agrarian and industrial revolutions changed that. Despite the great increase in population, production per head of population in Britian grew by 50% between 1770 and 1820.

Further experiments and improvements in the making and machining of metals made possible the production of machines by machines and opened the way for mass production. The increase in the efficiency of steam engines made possible the railway age which reduced costs of transport, extended markets and brought a more productive division of labour. Production per head of population in Britain increased by almost 120% between 1820 and 1870—at twice the annual rate achieved in the previous 50 years.

A. N. Whitehead once wrote that the greatest invention of the nineteenth century was the invention of the art of invention. A third wave of growth, starting in the last quarter of the nineteenth century, grew much more directly from formal research activities than the first two waves. From advances in physical and chemical theory came the electrical industry, a great transformation of the chemical industry, and the growth of industrial research laboratories. The opportunities for growth centred around innovations in the electrical, chemical and automobile industries were handled much better by the USA and Germany than by Britain. Their growth rates between 1870 and 1913 exceeded British growth rates between 1820 and 1870, while the British growth rate declined by one-third. In the industrialised countries as a group the compound annual rate of growth in production rose from 2.2% to 2.5%, and in production per head of population from 1% to 1.4%.

Growth rates were much lower in the interwar period, and the great depression of the 1930s generated fears of chronic technological unemployment and gloom about future growth. Yet unemployment and growth did revive. 1950 to 1973 was a period of sustained high growth, based on innovations in plant and animal breeding, and in the chemical, pharmaceutical, aircraft and electronic industries. The rapid growth in applied research and development during and after the second world war, the increase in the supply of scientists, engineers and technicians, heavy investment in new plant and equipment, full employment policies, aid to underdeveloped countries and measures to increase international trade, all contributed to an annual growth rate in output per head of population at $2\frac{1}{2}$ times that achieved between 1870 and 1913. By 1979 production per head of population in the industrialised countries was 13 times greater than in 1820, and $2\frac{1}{2}$ times greater than in 1950.

Since 1973 unemployment has risen to serious levels, and growth rates have been halved though they are still very much higher than in the thirties. There was a depression from about 1870 to 1885 following the second wave of growth, a depression from about 1925 to 1937 following the third wave, and now a depression from 1973 following the fourth and strongest wave of growth. This has encouraged speculation that there will be a fifth strong wave of growth (perhaps led by information technology) from the late eighties or early nineties. I would not be surprised if there were, though understanding of the reasons for fluctuations in growth rates and the bunching of major innovations is not sufficient to validate prediction.

Consequences

Life expectancy has increased as a consequence of improvements in diet, housing and clothing, advances in medical knowledge, the invention of new drugs and preventive immunization. In Western Europe, years of life expectancy at birth have risen from 35 to 72 since 1770. Since 1950 life expectancy at birth has increased from 65 to 72 in the industrialised countries, from 36 to 46 in Africa and from 43 to 55 in Asia. Current forecasts for the end of the century are 73 for the industrialised countries, 57 for Africa and 64 for Asia.

Population has grown substantially as a consequence of this increase. Between the beginning of the Christian era and 1750, world population did not increase by more than 5% every 100 years. But in the 100 years after 1750 it increased by 60% and in the next 100 years by 130%. Then in the 30 years after 1950 it increased by 80%. This very rapid increase after 1950 was mainly due to the rapid diffusion of health technologies from the industrialised to the less developed countries.

In the industrialised countries the reduction in death rates was followed by reductions in birth rates. In Western Europe, Canada and the US, Australia, New Zealand and Japan, crude birth rates now average under 15 per 1000 women. In the less developed countries however the rates are much higher—28 in China, 37 in India, 45 in Pakistan and almost 50 in Bangladesh and Nigeria. Economic development programmes, and family planning measures to speed increases in material standards of living, will bring these rates down. There are already signs of such a decline and some demographers expect world population to stabilize by 2100 at about twice its present level, assuming of course an adequate increase in the capability to produce the food and the materials required for growth in the developing countries. Given the potential for further productive R&D on these problems, there is, I think, reason for a qualified optimism.

One of the consequences of a slow spread of industrialisation throughout the world, and of the greater ease in diffusing technologies such as health that are not capital-intensive, is that the distribution of population has changed substantially and will change further. In 1800 the population of Western Europe was 20% of the total; it is now 8.5% and will probably fall to 5% by 2100.

The population of Europe (and Russia) is now about 12% (18%) of the total, and may fall to 7.5% (12%). The population of Western Europe, North America, Australia and New Zealand, which is now 15% of the total, may fall below 10%. The proportion of the population of China and Japan, now just over 25%, is likely to fall to 22% or 23%, while that of Africa and Latin America, now 10% and 8% of the total, seems likely to rise to about 14% and 10% respectively. Both politically and culturally these population movements will make the world a very different place.

Income per head increased in the industrialised countries even while their populations were increasing rapidly, but even more after their birth rates declined. There were substantial differences in incomes per head before industrialisation, but the uneven incidence of industrialisation greatly increased the differences. In 1975 production per head in North America, Western Europe, Australia, New Zealand and Japan averaged US$5,400, which was twice that of Russia and Eastern Europe, five times that of Mexico, 15 times that of Nigeria, 16 times that of China, and well over 20 times that of India and Pakistan. The greater diffusion of advanced technologies would reduce those differences. Relative levels of income are not static. In 1700 the Netherlands led the world in production per head and exceeded the British level by 50%, but by 1800 lagged 10% behind Britain. In 1820 Britain's production per head was a third greater than the American but is now a third less. In 1820 the German output per head was only 60% of Britain's and is now 25% more. In 1870 Australia led the world but now lags 25% behind America. Since 1870 Japan's output per head has risen from one-third of the American to more than two-thirds, as a consequence of massive investment in new technologies and education.

Hours worked per year are strongly influenced by technical change. In the industrialised countries hours have fallen by about 40% since 1870. The average age of entry to the labour force has also risen and the age of retirement fallen, as a consequence of a rise in family incomes and, following increases in taxable capacity, greater government expenditure on education and pensions.

The work environment has been improved by this reduction in hours and by the mechanization (increasingly automation) of heavy and dangerous work, but not by fluctuations in employment that technical change has generated. The nature of work has been changed by the effects of invention and increases in incomes on patterns of demand. In Britain before the agrarian and industrial revolution, 60% of workers were in agriculture, 15% in industry and 25% in services. By 1870 these percentages had shifted to 23,

42 and 35, and they are now 3, 38 and 59. In other industrialised and industrialising countries there have been similar shifts in sectoral employment in response to increases in output per head and incomes.

There have been persistent fears, ever since Marx forecast a progressive alienation of workers as a consequence of growing mechanization in the factory system, that technical change would be *de-skilling*. In countries made rich by the creation and adoption of new technology, the labour force is much more highly educated than in poor countries. A more highly educated labour force is needed to create and use the more advanced technologies, and the more advanced technologies make it possible to finance expensive programmes of education and research.

But industrial de-skilling has proved to be a transitional problem. To the extent that labour became 'a mere appendage of the machine' the tasks became ripe for automation. Such displacement of labour, however, creates fears of technological unemployment. Technical change both creates *technological unemployment* and (by creating new products) *technological employment*. Apart from the very large job-creating effects of population increase, the net effect of technical change has been to reduce the demand for labour. But labour mobility, retraining and the adjustment of hours have so far prevented any long-term increase in technological unemployment. However, fluctuations of employment have continued, and this major cost of technical change is not borne evenly by the community. Despite the high hopes created by the long post-war boom, governments have not yet found the way to maintain a steady flow of innovations and full employment.

Industrialisation has had profound *environmental effects*. Technical innovations in communications and buildings that made possible the growth of large cities brought very mixed blessings. The extent of the pollution of the land, water and air is now a major problem. The pollution of the air from the burning of fossil fuels, the radioactive water from atomic power stations, the adverse effects on the environment and health due to the widespread use of chemicals, will all become more serious problems as modern technologies are further diffused throughout the world. Some of the bad environmental effects were not foreseen; some were known but thought not to be serious because the cumulative effects were ignored. Much can be done to repair damage (as the state of the Thames and the atmosphere in Britain's industrial cities indicate), and doubtless much could be done through R&D to reduce the currently heavy costs of reducing pollution to tolerable levels. Our capacity to sustain further growth in population and production will soon depend on our will to deal with problems of pollution.

The greatest threat to the environment comes from technical innovations in weapons of war. *War technology* has now reached the stage where it is capable of wiping out all the good effects of technical change, and the people as well, in a few hours.

Those who know the Old Testament will recall that passage in Genesis—

'And the Lord God commanded the man, saying, Of every tree of the garden thou mayest freely eat:

But of the tree of knowledge of good and evil, thou shall not eat of it: for in the day that thou eatest thereof thou shalt surely die'

—and remember God's curse on Adam, that on being cast out of the Garden of Eden he would be required to sweat for his daily bread. The 'curse of Adam' has been progressively diluted by the growth of knowledge, but it is by no means clear that we are learning to manage the human problems of greater leisure.

To find solutions to the grave problems of pollution, war and leisure is a very great challenge to homo sapiens and to his universities.

THE CULTURAL IMPACT OF INDUSTRIALISATION AND TECHNOLOGICAL INNOVATION

Professor T. H. B. SYMONS (*Vanier Professor, Trent University, and Honorary Treasurer of the Association of Commonwealth Universities*): In his thoughtful paper Sir Bruce Williams has pointed to some of the remarkable gains made by mankind as the result of industrialisation and technological change. In particular, he has reviewed the impact of such change on population, wealth and employment.

In cultural terms, too, the impact of industrialisation and technology has been immense, bringing enormous advantages to the quality of life of huge numbers of people, including an enhancement of educational opportunities, a quickening of intellectual life, and an enrichment of the arts and letters. Such developments have been made possible by, for example, improvements in transportation and communication, the development of systems of schools, universities, colleges, libraries, research institutes, archives, galleries, museums, theatres—and the many other public institutions and arrangements that support our current mode of cultural life.

The two or two-and-a-half centuries since the industrial revolution is commonly thought to have begun have clearly brought the benefits of progress to our social and cultural lives on a fantastic scale. One has to look no further than the city in which we are meeting to perceive something of the net gains to society resulting from technological change and the many good things it makes possible. Yet I feel some hesitations—in fact, a profound unease— about adopting too readily a view of the social consequences of industrialisation and technology as essentially benign and progressive, provided only that we can remedy this or that difficulty that they bring in their train. Nor do I share in any conscious, or unconscious, belief that industrialisation and technology have the solutions to mankind's social ills, or even that they can do much to satisfy our deepest social needs. On the contrary, there is a risk that our concern with the material questions that are at the core of industrialisation and technology will turn our attention away from the larger questions: what is happening to man, himself? And what is happening to the values of civilisation?

It may be useful, first, to take a critical look at the very concept of the industrial revolution and the era of technological change it undoubtedly ushered in. G. N. Clark, in a splendid piece entitled *The Idea of the Industrial Revolution*, put at least a question mark behind the notion that this so-called revolution began at a more or less identifiable time, often placed about 1750. Partly for fun and partly in earnest, he explored the literature of history to see what alternative dates were claimed for this supposedly modern event. He found, of course, George Unwin's argument for an industrial revolution in the late seventeenth century, and then Mrs. J. R. Green's fifteenth century industrial revolution, while in the Netherlands they claim an industrial revolution in the textile towns in the eleventh century. However the record for temporal remoteness appears to be held by Professor Gordon Childe, with his 'industrial revolution of the late bronze age' in prehistoric Britain.

At the other end of the time scale, Sir George found that, even if the industrial revolution began about 1750, it took three or four generations, nearly 100 years, before people identified it, realized what was occurring, and gave to it a name. Although the industrial revolution may have begun in Britain, it was a French economist, Jérôme Adolphe Blanqui, who first so named it, in 1827; and the term was used in England in 1848, in a rather tentative manner, by John Stuart Mill in his *Principles of Political Economy*.

The fact that the industrial revolution was identified as such only so long after it was far advanced, and affecting profoundly most aspects of British life, should encourage us to look carefully at what is happening in our own time that we may not perceive, but that may be so clear to students in future generations. When will its nature and direction be recognized, and by whom? If it took us 100 years to recognize that the industrial revolution was going on, and to give to it a name, it should not be surprising that, another 100 years after that, we are still only just identifying many of its consequences, and trying to assess their significance.

Current generations hold the confident view that the industrial revolution is an unending process—a tide irresistable— that has taken on a life of its own becoming cumulative, self-sustaining and accelerating. Behind this view there lie the assumptions that it will continue, inevitably, and that it will be, on balance, a force for good. But perhaps such assumptions may be wrong, or only partly right, and so do a social disservice. At any rate they need critical examination. The depression from about 1870 to 1885, the great depression of the 1930s, and the current depression since the mid-1970s, for example, must be reconciled to such assumptions. One of the social consequences of the assumption that industrial and technological change and progress are cumulative and self-sustaining is that the public develops certain expectations, and the difficulties of coping with depressions, and other socio-economic failures, are rendered all the greater when these expectations are not fulfilled.

At any rate I hope that we will not subscribe to the simplistic view of history as a story of unending progress, onward and upwards to a better life—with industry and technology as the motor. It may be salutary to recall that, even in the history of technology, not all is progress. Libya, which was once the breadbasket of the Roman Empire is, today, Colonel Gaddafi's desert. British plumbing is said, by scholars of such matters, not to have attained again the high standard enjoyed by Roman Britons in the fourth century, until the eighteenth century. And I must confess that I occasionally have doubts about even that. Or, to take a shorter and more recent historical perspective, we are still dealing, towards the end of the twentieth century, with the same three basic questions about industrialisation and technology that concerned John Ruskin and the great socio-cultural thinkers of the middle of the nineteenth century:

(1) the preservation of nature, and of ecological balance, in the face of man's rapacity;

(2) the exploitation of man, by man;

(3) and, internationally, the exploitation of the less developed parts of the world by the more developed parts of the world.

Yet in the arena of public policy industrialisation and technological change have brought strong response, and vast socio-cultural changes. The difficulty in this arena is that the resulting changes have been numerous and often in direct conflict with each other. Thus it may be argued that, conceptually, industrialisation and technology have been the fathers of capitalism and of the early modern laissez-faire state. However it can just as well be suggested, at the other end of the political spectrum, that industrialisation and technology are the fathers of communism or, at least, of Marxism. You will recall that both Marx and Engels dwelt in their writings upon the evil social and economic consequences of the industrial revolution, and went on from there to urge their communist approach to the improvement of man's lot.

But it may also be said that industry and technology have fathered the concept of socialism, or social democracy in its varying forms, with the concept that the state should use its powers to mitigate the harsher effects of private conduct and private enterprise, and to ameliorate the lot of its citizens.

In these and other ways the conceptual impact of industrialisation and technology on political thought has been immense, and diverse. Perhaps the only common ground in the three rival political ideologies of which I have spoken, each of which claims some causal relationship to the industrial revolution, is the concern they all purport to share about conditions in the workplace, and the lot of the working man.

It seems to be generally accepted that 'the work environment has been improved' as a result of, or at least following on, the industrial revolution and technological change. This is true in many cases, and perhaps true overall. But there may also be situations in which it is not true, situations in which the work environment has not improved, and may even have deteriorated as the result of technological change. On the one hand are all the advantages of mechanisation, computerisation, and many labour-saving devices. But on the other there is the increasing alienation that comes with boredom and repetition and clock-work functions. Check-out clerks at grocery stores become machines themselves when they have to process a precise average of 25 items per minute, while being monitored by machines to see that they do so. It will not be surprising if there is increased tension and conflict in the workplace as a result of this snooping and invasion of privacy by machines on behalf of the employer. Indeed the possibilities for exploitation of the worker are hugely increased by the marvels of electronics. In this and other ways new technology is raising new moral questions that deserve more thought than they are getting.

Today's high-tech world may possibly have provided the tools for a golden era of human activity. But basic questions remain unanswered, including who gets the gold. Will it be true, as some argue, that new technology will bring massive unemployment, create unrewarding unskilled jobs, and result in a two-class, have and have-not society? Is a new gulf opening between the prosperous information-rich and the poverty-stricken information-poor? There does seem to be some evidence now that the people whose jobs are made more creative, more interesting and more satisfying by the application of more technology are often design engineers, corporate planners and others who need quick access to large amounts of information; and that many of the jobs actually created by advanced technology are of a low-skilled, low-paying and menial nature, requiring little education. Management goals are, by and large, and understandably, to make workers more productive and to better monitor and control their work to this end; or, better still, to eliminate their jobs altogether. Technology can be the one-sided ally of management in pursuit of these goals, unless such technological change is accompanied by an appropriate moral code and a sense of social responsibility.

It has long been assumed that industrialisation and technological change have played a key role in the emancipation of women and in the change in their place in society. This has clearly been the case, but many thoughtful people are re-examining precisely what the changes have been and what their value is. It is true, for example, that the long hours of heavy work that tied women to the home have been reduced by the results of technology, including vacuum cleaners, cheap carpets, washing machines, new fabrics, dishwashers, microwave ovens, refrigerators, and so on, so that a high proportion of married women now seek paid employment outside the home. But is technology improving life by this? Instead of working for herself or for her family, most of these women now work for someone else, in the vast majority of cases performing menial tasks. There is a long way to go before the industrial revolution or technology can be said to have brought about a real change in the status of women. Studies in all our countries show that in every field of activity, at every level, women are paid on

51

average a great deal less than men for doing the same or comparable work.

There is, in fact, a good deal of evidence that technological change has helped to keep things this way—slotting women into minor technological roles in offices, in factories and in certain vocations. Even in these minor roles new technology threatens their security. A recent study by the Equal Opportunities Commission of the United Kingdom examines the impact of the microchip on women's jobs and concludes that women's jobs are particularly vulnerable to the new machines and much more likely to be affected than those of men.

The impact of industrialisation and technology on the family unit has also been enormous. The weakening of family and kinship bonds continues to be one of the principal social costs of industrialisation. This results, for example, from the extensive mobility required by industrialisation, involving the physical and social separation of kinsmen. Industrialisation has also contributed to the social separation of the generations, and—whether for good or ill—a minimization of parental control, earlier independence of children, a great increase in marital conflict, and changes in the scope and nature of delinquency. One of the great problems engendered by industrialisation is, thus, the rise of 'family disorganisation', in many forms.

At the community level similar problems of disorganisation also arise, with a loss of identity and of emotional security, in particular in situations of over-urbanization, when population in the cities exceeds employment opportunities.

In religion, too, the large effect of industrialisation has been to erode faith and habit, and to promote secularization. I express no judgement on this development, simply observing that it is a significant consequence of the industrial revolution and of technological change.

In all these fundamental areas of society and culture—the family, the community, and faith or religion—what is occurring is the atomization of the community of belief. Things which kept people together socially and culturally, at an intimate level and in continuing ways, have been lost or replaced by short-term intimacies and by crowd activities without much true social interaction.

Perhaps this would be less a picture of things of social value lost if one could point at the same time to the part played by industrialisation and technological change in the easing or elimination of class barriers and hereditary social differences. To some extent this has certainly happened. But it is increasingly evident that industrialisation inevitably provides a new set of social positions and a new form of class structures. Industry and technology in fact multiply the ranks in society and render its stratification more elaborate and complex. It is perhaps worth noting that these inequalities of income and power arising from industrialisation appear to be at least as great in socialist as in capitalist economies.

Technology and industrialisation have made possible profound changes and some vast improvements in education. This is not only the result of the wealth they have generated, much of which has found its way to support teaching and research. It is the result also of the improvement in scientific techniques and instruments, and the creation of knowledge itself by the trial, error and cumulative experience of industrial activity. The demands of industry, science and technology have pushed out the frontiers of human knowledge at an astounding rate in recent decades. But the resulting knowledge has often been of a factual, rather than of a reflective nature, extending our inventory of things known but not necessarily of things understood.

This industry and technology route to knowledge has placed a premium on specialization, upon a form of vocationalism in higher education—whether as an aeronautical engineer, a biophysicist or a specialist in enzymes. It has not kept up a commensurate pressure for the development of capacities to synthesize knowledge, to assess and evaluate it, and to relate properly one part of it to another. Yet it is the very fact of the knowledge explosion, that owes so much to science and technology, that is making the generalist of increasing importance at the higher levels of education and intellectual activity in our society. It is still true and will, I trust, always be so that the last judgement must always be a value judgement.

Industrialisation and technology have had some curious effects on the curriculum, as well as many good ones. There has been, for example, a pressure on history to become as a discipline nothing more than the history of demographics, the history of no history. In this new kind of history, nothing is judged, only counted.

Industrialisation and technology are, in themselves, creating new fields of knowledge for teaching and research. These include, for example, the emerging field of industrial archaeology and the study of the relationship of the arts and of ideas to the changing material world that is being produced by industrialisation and technological change.

The experience of industrialisation has had, and is having, fundamental effects on the ideas people hold about their position in society, their relations to each other, and their individual natures and identities. Sometimes this experience has led to tunnel vision. There was, for example, Sir Titus Salt, in his time an enlightened employer who sat in the British House of Commons as a Liberal. But he did not speak there, or very much anywhere else. When asked what his subjects of possible conversation were, he replied 'alpaca wool'. You may agree that such specialization can be inhibiting, even in a brilliant man.

In addition to many capable industrial leaders, a new breed of intellectuals emerged in response to the industrial era; tough, aggressive, managerial, and concerned with the social problems of production, promotion and distribution. The other side of the coin was the emergence of a more thoughtful reform Toryism, concerned with social conditions and with the organic unity of society. This reform Toryism had its strongest roots here in the Midlands and in the north of England. But it has been paralleled by the emergence of a similar tradition in other parts of the industrialised world, including the radical or red Tory tradition in Canada.

Let me note quickly a few other areas in which industrialisation and technological change raise some difficult questions: these include problems about the invasion of privacy and about other aspects of civil liberties; about quality in the content of what is being communicated as opposed to quality in the means of communication; about industry as the motor of modern imperialism, and about the destruction or distortion of indigenous cultural and social systems by external forces; and about the ways in which, for good or ill, industrialisation and technology can reinforce the problems of regionalism and nationalism.

However the two most conspicuous difficulties arising from the achievements of industrialisation and technology are the threat of war and the threat to the environment. In the case of war, it is clear that mankind faces the possibility of a most appalling calamity, something that has been made possible by the achievements of science, technology and industry. But perhaps less recognized is the impact of this situation upon us now, even without the occurrence of a full-scale war. The fact is that the reality that we now must live with, that such a total calamity has been made possible, is already profoundly affecting our lives day by day. The consequences of this situation include not only the huge economic costs and the burdens of taxation, and the vast diversion of energy, labour and much of our best mind-power, but also the psychological burden that has been placed on the human spirit and the whole effect of this burden on our state of mind and way of life.

In regard to the environment, I know that you must all be familiar with the concerns arising from the industrial pollutions affecting water, land and air. Many of these concerns have been examined with exemplary care in, for example, the nine reports to date of the United Kingdom Royal Commission on Environmental Pollution of which the most recent, on the increasing dangers of lead in the environment, appeared in April of this year. Rather than presuming to review with you the range of these environmental problems, may I simply point to the need for balance, and for much more knowledge and research. For example, impact studies should precede major industrial and technological undertakings. Such studies should include an examination of social and cultural consequences, as well as of economic and market questions. But this is frequently not the case. We in Canada have in fact made rather a specialty of damming rivers, blasting mountains and building lakes without much prior examination of the conse-quences. Perhaps our greatest coup along these lines came in the 1970s, when we flooded areas as large as many of the countries of Europe without first conducting the research studies needed to tell us what the consequences would be for the ecology, or for the surrounding areas, or, indeed, without even finding out what minerals were under the ground that was to be flooded. As a final feather in our cap, we made thousands of Indians and hundreds of Eskimo families homeless by this activity.

In terms of their social and cultural impact, industrialisation and technological change thus confront us with some serious challenges, challenges that range from some loss of identity and loss of community to questions about family life, human rights and civil liberties, to new needs in education and research, to threats to the environment, and even to the possibility of a catastrophic destruction by war. From this litany you might under-standably conclude that I am a Luddite—wanting to destroy machinery and technology, for fear of its consequences. But such is not the case. On the contrary, I agree with the view that the prospects for living better with technology are reasonably good, provided that we take action *now* to reduce technological damage.

What I am endeavouring to suggest in these remarks is simply that all that comes in the train of technology is not sweetness and light. There is no immutable law that says progress is forever, or that technological change is the only key to it, or even that it is the most important key to it. More specifically, I want to suggest that the cultural impact of industrialisation and technology is more pervasive and significant than is sometimes recognized, and that it has become a matter of urgency that the consequences of this cultural impact receive greater attention.

DISCUSSION

After Sir Bruce Williams had presented his paper the discussion was opened by Lord Flowers (Imperial College of Science and Technology). He wondered why it was not until the eighteenth century that technical change became cumulative and self-sustaining. After all, Leonardo da Vinci had invented the art of invention some time before. Although it is clear that in countries enriched by high technology the labour force is more highly educated, it is impossible to know whether education is the horse and technology the cart, or *vice versa*. He thought it important to know whether technological developments do occur in waves, as Sir Bruce had suggested, because if so the fifth wave may already be with us. He suggested that only major new technologies have major effects on society, for example information technology, an 'enabling' technology which has an enormous number of immediate applications. However, to suggest that innovations occur in waves does not explain how the new technology miraculously becomes available just when required. Lord Flowers also questioned whether Sir Bruce's description of the technological development of the Western world is relevant elsewhere, or whether it is unique. Technological advance requires a positive cultural response on the part of the modernising society, and is not determined by purely economic forces, nor is it merely a question of phasing. Cultural differences and attitudes to work and leisure are equally important. The global situation is dynamic, and a change in the positions of countries in the 'league table' of technological sophistication can be expected in the future. The question of the applicability of the Western pattern of technological development to newly-industrialising countries was taken up by subsequent speakers.

Several speakers commented on the difficulty of extrapolating from history and of applying new technology to the developing countries. Dr. D. Mordell (Commonwealth Engineers' Council) commented that the increased productivity per head in the developed countries had been achieved by the availability of abundant resources of energy and capital investment. He doubted whether the developing countries would be prepared to take 200 years to gather the fruits of a higher standard of living, and thought that they would need to follow a very different pattern of development to achieve the progression from pastoral economy through cottage industry to full industrialisation in much less time without the abundant energy, raw materials and capital which had fuelled the Western industrial revolution.

Professor M. A. Raqib (Rajshahi) said that in Bangladesh, where 80% of the population live in rural areas and most are illiterate, there are special problems in applying new technology as it becomes available. Difficulties are experienced not only in using the new technology but also in maintaining it, because people sent overseas for training are frequently lost to the community as they fail to return. Developing countries are frightened of technological domination, which is often the result of the transfer of unmodified technologies. The existing system needs to be adapted, and much greater provision made for education and training.

56

Furthermore, the search for an increased standard of living is causing sociological changes, including the breakdown of family relationships, especially the extended family.

Dr. C. R. Mitra (Birla Institute of Technology and Science) questioned whether extrapolation from the Western experience was universally valid. He also commented on the need to be sure that the terms used in discussion had the same connotation in different socio-economic systems: for example, the word 'unemployment' has a rather different meaning in industrialised countries and in peasant communities. He said that there is a national, as well as an international, 'brain drain', i.e. a tendency for qualified personnel to move to cities from rural areas where they are most acutely needed.

Professor Raqib, in opening the discussion after Professor Symons had read his paper, re-emphasised the remarks he had made in relation to Sir Bruce Williams' paper. Technological innovation has led to an improvement in the quality of life but the massive drift to the cities has had far-reaching social consequences. Aspirations and class barriers are changing, and many of these changes lead to a feeling of alienation.

Other speakers referred to the need for balanced development, and to the role of universities in creating and maintaining that balance. There was further discussion of Professor Symons' comments about the adverse effects of technological change, which are often overlooked when considering increases in productivity. Professor I. H. Umar (Bayero) pointed out that some, like nuclear technology applied to war, and genetic engineering, are avoidable, but others are not. It should be recognised that the environment is in a state of constant change which cannot be arrested, but that some technological changes have an especially adverse effect on the environment.

Haji Sulaiman Abdullah (Malaya) was saddened by the Western attitude to work, which is seen as an evil to be overcome rather than as a necessary value in life. Unfortunately new technology is based on this assumption. This attitude to work accompanying new technology has spread to Malaysia, where trade unions have been addressing the almost inexplicable rejection by factory workers of safety equipment such as helmets: in fact, employees have been prepared to take any risk which might take them away from the factory on paid leave. The response of the Malaysian government to these attitudes has been to reject the Western philosophy and 'look east' to the Japanese. People will be trained to view technology in the correct perspective, although the response of the universities has been ambivalent.

In response to the lively discussion, Sir Bruce Williams said that he hoped the audience would regard his paper as dealing with only a part of the problem, and Professor Symons' paper as an essential complement to it.

Sir Bruce saw no reason to believe that the time taken for development now should be as long as that taken in the past by the West. On the question of undesirable effects of technology in India, he admitted that undoubtedly some aid programmes had been fundamentally ill-conceived.

Some very modern technologies which were appropriate to the factor prices in developed countries were introduced into developing countries inappropriately.

He emphasised the importance of providing suitable forms of education and training to facilitate the diffusion of appropriate, and as far as possible indigenous, technology. Without doubt, if the will is there, education and training programmes can be provided very quickly, in spite of the brain drain, and illiteracy solved within ten years. Problems have been incurred in the replacement of under-employment by employment in rural economies largely because the time needed to establish the necessary attitudes and infrastructure was underestimated.

On the issue of the undermining of traditional and religious values and ways of life, Sir Bruce said that industrialisation is the dominant culture, and that if developing countries want the benefits of greater wealth they will have to sacrifice those traditions which cannot survive in modern communities. It is clear from the post-war period that all countries are willing the modernisation of their societies, and will continue to do so. The development of new attitudes and forms of social organisation appropriate to the material goals desired as the benefit of that modernisation is not only a problem, but also one of today's great challenges.

Sub-Topic 1 (b)

MUST PATTERNS OF CHANGE IN DEVELOPING COUNTRIES FOLLOW THE WEST?
WHAT OTHER POSSIBLE PATTERNS?

Chairman: Professor R. F. WHELAN
Vice-Chancellor of the University of Liverpool

Rapporteur: Miss J. A. BRYAN-BROWN
Personal Assistant/Research Assistant to the Director, Technical
Change Centre

Tuesday, 16 August

The Chairman opened the session by emphasising the need to match the available technologies with the development needs of each country. In the past development was largely carried out by expatriates, and this created the danger of becoming locked into the Western pattern of change. Although we are to some extent prisoners of history, he questioned whether that Western pattern was inevitable, and stressed the need for fresh thinking.

Royal Professor Ungku A. AZIZ (*Vice-Chancellor of the University of Malaya*): By way of introduction, I should note that our topic is no idle medieval disputation between disinterested schoolmen inside an ivory tower. Vice-chancellors in developing countries have not only to make decisions (or to try desperately to influence the ultimate decision-makers) regarding the allocation of scarce resources that have alternative uses for the realization of given objectives, but occasionally also to try to assist in the revision of the very ends themselves.

For this paper, I shall assume that, apart from the older Commonwealth countries such as the United Kingdom, Canada, Australia and New Zealand, the rest may be classified as developing countries. Although some may be 'more developing than others', I shall not offer any sub-division of categories or rank orders. We

59

thus obtain a simple dichotomy of advanced or mature countries and developing or 'newly-emerging' countries.

We now come to a more difficult term 'the West'. As a political category, 'the West' now seems to include the countries of non-socialist Europe such as the Federal Republic of Germany, France, the Scandinavian and Benelux states, as well as Italy, Spain and Greece. It also includes the USA and Canada and occasionally, because of its OECD membership, Japan.

The confusion begins with the exclusion of even the more industrialised but recently near-bankrupt larger states of Latin America. For certain philosophical or historical reasons the term 'West' seems to exclude Yugoslavia, because it is socialist and therefore 'Eastern', as well as Turkey, because of nuances that stretch back to the days of the Sublime Porte. For other reasons Israel and South Africa are also excluded. The Brandt Commission has popularised a 'North-South' dichotomy, which is rather popular in Japan because it finds itself included in the North.

To help the discussants and readers of this paper, I will arbitrarily state that I shall use the term 'West' to include the United Kingdom, Canada, Australia and New Zealand in the Commonwealth and the USA, France, Federal Republic of Germany and Scandinavia, as well as the Benelux countries, in Europe. This should provide us with an adequate base to identify the 'patterns of change', if any common patterns may so easily be identified.

I am afraid that some attention needs to be given to the term 'patterns of change', both in the academic as well as in the trendy jargon sense. I would venture to suggest that 'patterns of change' vary from country to country. Even if the basic patterns are fairly consistent (as some development economists would have us believe) the tempo of change may vary according to the history of the different countries. What I am suggesting is that patterns of change in societies, nations or states do not have the same objectives. Nor do they possess those quantifiable characteristics typical of naturally-occurring mechanical, biological and chemical changes which facilitate the study of those changes.

Let us consider a rather simple analogy, such as the growth in the weight, volume and cell numbers of the human brain, especially in relation to other anthropometric observations. These parameters do not vary as much between individuals in one country as between individuals of different countries. Thus we can attempt to theorise about ratios of physical growth, the consequences of poverty and malnutrition, etc. However we cannot make similar generalisations with equal confidence about changes in the pattern of human behaviour and human institutions. The problem is of a different order rather than a different magnitude, simply because we are dealing with the human mind and not human physical states.

To take another illustration, let us try to examine the impact of the introduction of the bicycle in a rural area in a country such as Malaysia. In due course we find that not only does it become possible for a large proportion of rural teenaged girls to attend secondary schools, but also the widening of their social horizons may have radical consequences in the patterns of change in their family life, eating habits, employment, etc. One such change, which I am currently studying, is the willingness of such girls to leave home and work in the electronics industry, assembling integrated circuits. We could ask the question: will their children become juvenile delinquents swarming through the slums populated by the new industrial proletariat, or will they grow up into a world of better health and wider educational opportunities? All that might have been the result of the introduction of cheap bicycles into the rural areas. What then would be the effects of introducing cheap motor-cycles? And so on.

Even if we limit ourselves to the social consequences of techno-logical innovation — that is, we are able to itemize specific types of technology and identify the societies that we are going to look at — we still face one great barrier that pervades what may be considered rational thought.

Different societies have different value systems. For example, let us select an issue like secularism. In the development of universities in the West the majority of the citizens accepts a kind of binary system which differentiates between that which is rendered 'unto Caesar', or the state, and that which is rendered unto their respective churches. Throughout the eighteenth and nineteenth centuries the industrial revolution was accompanied by movements for secularism and opposition to the political and social domination of the Christian church in Europe. The idea of the individual being free to make his choice of God and morality dominated social and political thinking. This influenced the pattern of the development of universities, both Oxbridge and redbrick, through to the present. Tolerance became a watchword. I have seen a professor on British television apologising for believing in God.

However in a country, such as Pakistan or Malaysia, that recognizes Islam as the state religion, we have a totally different situation. Although other religions are tolerated in Malaysia and people are free to practise their particular creeds, for the Muslims and for the state there are rules and values as set out in the Quran and in the Sunnah which must be abided by without let or quibble. In such a situation, even if we had perfect technological changes, social patterns are bound to be rather different from those in Western secular societies.

Models in Passage

If a three-dimensional model is presented it can be copied, given the necessary raw materials and some knowledge of how to assemble or process the various pieces. If, however, the model is in a dynamic state of change, it becomes necessary first to create something that can match one phase of the model and then to follow serially the steps of the model or even grow in contemporaneous tempo.

In our context the best we can hope for is that country X or university Y be modelled on country P or university Q as it was at some stage in its evolution, and then try to copy its progress. The model builders must be able to identify, describe and analyse both the elements and the causal relations of what they are currently observing, as well as the model in its various stages of growth.

Today the physical features of a university or an electronics factory can be constructed almost anywhere. Some 'manware' can be provided by offering sufficient material attractions for living and for the carrying out of research, and by providing for the other occasional needs of the internationally mobile set of academics or technocrats. Nevertheless, the 'chariots of fire' may run differently when they are transported thousands of miles away from the waters and the ivy of the universities in the West.

This is well summed up in the literature of the current popular international topic, 'The Transfer of Technology'. Let me hasten to say that I do believe it is a feasible practice, but it needs to be done with attention to particular details, some of which will be apparent in this paper and some of which will, I hope, emerge in the discussions. The appropriate question is 'how?' rather than 'what?' Before going on to answer the question 'how?' I feel that the historical record of this five-yearly gathering, which is almost familial, behoves me to clear the record a little. What I have to say is more related to the past than the present. However, if we are sincerely to try to answer the question of our topic, we must be realistic in our appreciation.

For this paper we can recognize three kinds of states. First, there are metropolitan powers having colonial territories which both provide them with much wealth through the supply of relatively cheap raw materials and markets for their industrial products, and also act as a venue for transfer payments that generate affluence in the metropolitan country and relative poverty in the colony. The social and psychological distortions created in the colonies will later (after independence) leave draconian impediments to the adoption of industrial technology, but that is another matter.

Historically, the second world war not only led to political independence for most of the colonial territories but also finally dissolved part of the affluence of some of the metropolitan powers. Indeed, the vanquished Germany and Japan seem to have emerged from the wars in relatively better economic shape than some of their conquerors.

What has this to do with modelling? Well, even if we do not accept the thesis of Oswald Spengler whose *Decline of the West* was first published in 1926, we should ponder on the current situation where the United Kingdom has had to raise university fees to such an extent that the substantial flow of students from Malaysia and other parts of the Commonwealth has declined. If it were not for the loss of affluence, surely Britain would not have had to squeeze its universities by raising fees and cutting budgets.

Malaysia has no colonies. Having tasted the sweet fruits of independence she desires to base her growth on her own resources. To that extent the metropolitan model is not applicable. If we can develop our structure of higher education by assisting states like the Maldives, Brunei or some countries in the South Pacific, then we shall do so, by providing our own donations, by finance from the receiving country and possibly also by the provision of third parties through international aid authorities. I hope that our activities are guided by a large measure of altruism. Hence our model cannot be a Western one.

The point has now been reached where I shall deal with the essential question, which is: what patterns of change should developing countries seek to achieve? In answering this I shall move dialectically between the Western and non-Western models. First we must answer three questions:—

(1) Why are we seeking to change? In other words, what are our basic objectives?

(2) How shall we construct or guide the changes so that they lead towards the realization of our basic objectives?

(3) What resources and institutions (software and hardware) are likely to be available to us in the organization of the processes of change?

It should be noted that we are limiting the discussion to the field of technology and I shall narrow it down to exclude, directly but not necessarily indirectly, the humanities, law, medicine, etc. In 'technology' I have included engineering, architecture, agriculture, etc.

Why are we seeking change? I assume that developing countries desire change for the qualitative and quantitative benefits of economic growth, i.e. to reduce poverty. It is hoped that an increasing proportion of the population will have more nourishing food, better accommodation and improved health, educational and transportation services and will therefore be 'better off' and psychologically happier. In the Muslim states we hope they will be able to fulfil their roles as good Muslims better if they are materially better off and the recipients of improved services. It becomes the duty of the state and the faithful to identify changes that would promote both a better material as well as a better spiritual world. Teleologically, we are not seeking change for the sake of change but rather for material and spiritual betterment. If these two objectives conflict then we must seek to alter the patterns of change so that the contradiction is obviated. This may be difficult and may slow down our tempo, but it is the mandate given to our leaders, who are the democratically-elected representatives of the people.

In the specific case of Malaysia, our basic national objectives include not only the eradication of poverty for all races but also the restructuring of patterns of work and of the ownership of some forms of wealth in such a way as to substantially reduce the close identification of any ethnic group with particular sectors of the economy.

Education, particularly secondary education, is a vital cog in the model. Be it in the North, South, East or West, development implies the extension of education facilities. However, because the colonial system in Malaysia distorted secondary education by concentrating secondary schools in the large urban areas where 60% of the Chinese but only 10% of the Malays lived, a rather lopsided system was inherited. During the last twelve years the government has gradually extended secondary education to the rural areas so that tens of thousands of the sons and daughters of peasants can aspire to higher education. If these are the kinds of changes that are to be recommended, then exactly which Western model — British (Labour or Conservative), French, German or American — is to be chosen? We are actually giving some thought to this. Recently the Malaysian prime minister, Datuk Seri Dr. Mahathir Mohamad, has recommended the nation to 'look East' for its economic development, especially for improvements in areas such as work motivation.

Add to this the widespread desire for education and the extensive use of the Malaysian language as an attempt to unite all races into one nation loyal to one state, and we have one rather large problem that does not have many models to go by. In addition we have to bend the old (colonially tinged) system away from its 'Baboo' orientation towards the arts and some social sciences into the direction of technology and applied sciences, so that our graduates prefer the hard hat, blue collar and dirty hands to the necktie, attaché case and air-conditioned office.

The Nature of Technological Change

While there may be some very limited scope for discussing the desirability of 'technological change' *per se,* the main thrust of the discussion should be concerned with the direction and pace to be taken in its pursuit. This is really what the second part of the sub-topic — 'What other possible patterns?' — is all about.

A country has to pass through six stages of technological evolution before it can reach the ultimate stage of 'innovation'.

Stage I consists of learning operational skills such as driving trucks, tapping and processing rubber, and performing simple line-process tasks such as assembling integrated circuits. High skills, including supervision and management, are provided by migrant workers. Semi-processed materials and parts for assembly are imported. Education is provided at primary and secondary levels; if it exists at all at the tertiary level, more emphasis is given to the arts and social sciences than to technology, medicine and natural science.

Stage II involves learning maintenance and servicing skills progressively, up to the maintenance of heavy equipment and plant as well as equipment involving higher technologies such as electronics. To obtain specific skills trainees are sent abroad to special institutions or to firms' own training programmes. During this stage universities and higher secondary institutes provide courses in engineering, technology and science, taught mainly by foreigners.

During *Stage III,* the skills needed for repair and replacement of imported technology are learned. At this stage more and more parts for the assembly-cum-manufacturing processes will be fabricated locally. Universities and technical institutes provide various grades of technologists and managers who constitute local manpower for the assembly processes up to increasingly sophisticated technological production processes. Research institutes are established and local personnel trained overseas and in local universities.

Stage IV entails learning the adaptation of imported designs to local conditions, paying particular attention to the unique conditions of climate, raw materials and labour and to the practical needs of the local or regional market. At this stage close links need to be forged between relevant departments in the universities and private industry so that the teleology of research is pragmatic. Universities begin to report registration of patents as well as lists of technical publications in their annual reports. Opportunities for local staff to travel and observe foreign industry as well as to collaborate with international colleagues should be adequately supported.

In *Stage V,* the skills required for the manufacture of whole products and the local construction of plants to meet local needs are developed. Regional markets are expanded in order to obtain a scale of operation sufficient to lower unit costs of production as well as to provide an adequately large base for technical training facilities and research and development. At this stage the links between the public and private sectors and university teaching and research institutes should be close and mutually supportive. Some facilities may be offered to train technologists from other third world countries.

Stage VI consists of learning to make machines that produce machines; learning to innovate on a par, but probably on a much reduced scale, with the developed industrialised nations; being ready to approach the frontiers of modern technology in such fields as computers, robotics and biotechnology; using the jungle and the ocean as sources of energy and raw materials without causing irreparable damage to the environment; and becoming an exporter of high technology products.

Each of these stages has as a prerequisite: the successful realisation of the preceding stage. There is no magic way of jumping straight into the higher stages and bypassing the earlier preparatory stages.

The political management of national resources and national budgets can determine the pace at which a nation can pass through one stage into the next. Education is a major instrument for completing this passage. As a nation passes through the several stages there will be synergistic reactions between industry, the public sector and the education system, especially the universities. In the early stages a few local intellectuals will have to struggle to enlarge their community. To some extent the places where they have obtained their education overseas will determine their ideas about suitable models. In a colonial situation, many of the bureaucratic and feudal élites will send their children to the metropolitan country for higher education. In some Western countries which have been dominant colonial powers, it is not surprising that the majority of the pre-war and immediate post-war leadership consisted of students in law, medicine and economics who obtained their education in the better universities in the UK, Holland and France.

In those days few students from Malaysia had a chance to go to the USA, Germany or Japan for higher education.

As countries pass through the fourth stage it is desirable for them to broaden their intellectual horizons internationally so that they can develop a more balanced view of the global patterns of modern technology.

Just as local academics and intellectuals who achieve power through nationalism are replaced by national bureaucracies after the achievement of independence, so too do the administrative élites have to yield to the new professionals consisting of accountants, bankers, managers, architects and lawyers who achieve power through the manipulation of wealth. Our experience in Malaysia is that at this stage the democratically-elected members of parliament come to consist of a significantly higher proportion of graduates of local universities, compared with the earlier vintages of politicians who were grass-roots nationalists or ex-civil servants.

It is worth noting in passing that in countries where the professional group has not been successful, and because the appropriate technological stage has not been achieved, for various reasons, military coups tend to occur. This has been the experience of many countries in Africa, Latin America and parts of South East Asia. Whether the same thing can happen if the professionals fail to satisfy the conditions needed for the eradication of rural poverty, because they are individualistically concerned with material gain and political power, remains to be seen. After all, technology is only one prerequisite for progress in developing countries; the other is the abolition of rural poverty.

Technological innovation can only provide a partial solution to the whole problem. I am deliberately omitting the other areas from this paper. Nevertheless, they can become equally critical factors, which can if neglected wreck the crystal structure of the six stages of development.

I would like to conclude with a further caveat. All technological change is some form of modernisation and involves industrialisation. This is so whether we take models from Japan, China, Korea, the USA or the UK. There are many by-products or side effects that seem to have sprung up within the ambit of this technological modernity. If the price of technological sophistication is junk food, drug culture, rock music, rising juvenile crime, and increasing environmental pollution, then many third-world intellectuals think that price too high. It seems unduly high in the context of the religious revivals taking place in some third-world societies. While in some instances these religious revivals may appear 'fundamentalist' and contradictory to the Western

eighteenth- and nineteenth-century liberalistic philosophies, there
are many third-world leaders and intellectuals who seek to reconcile
the need for technological advance with a renaissance of spiritual
life, which could provide an inner peace of mind that seems to be
commonly lacking in the so-called Western world today.

Professor A. K. DE (*Director, Indian Institute of Technology, Bombay*):
The division of the world into two distinct economic groups, *i.e.*
the rich and the poor nations, came into existence nearly one and
a half centuries ago. The coming of this division was accompanied
by the industrial revolution, which initiated a period of rapid
growth in the Western countries, based on the continued accretion
of technological innovation. Following the West, third-world
countries have been relying on science and technology to help
them solve their problems, such as poverty, ignorance, malnutrition, disease and educational backwardness. But should they copy
the West indiscriminately? Is the Western way the only correct
way to attain the desirable standards or are there other alternatives?

Developing countries have their own distinctive cultures and
their own historical and political backgrounds, which cannot simply
be ignored. These countries are characterised by the availability
of almost unlimited unskilled labour, scarcity of capital, and low
capital accumulation rates and production levels. However the
long-range aim of development of all developing countries is to
increase the living standards of their people.

It must be observed that during the first phase of their industrialisation programme the developing countries had to start in many
respects from a more difficult situation and from a lower level of
attainment than those experienced by the developed countries at the
corresponding period of their industrialisation. These difficulties
typically include high energy costs, lack of abundant raw materials,
and population pressure. Industrialisation, in its proper sense,
started in the developing countries of Africa and Asia only after
the attainment of their independence in the middle of the twentieth
century.

One therefore has no other alternative but to start from where
one stands, from the traditional sector with its skills, techniques
and organisation. Many developing countries employ at least 80%
of their labour forces in agricultural and traditional industries.

The modern sector may employ no more than 10% of the labour force, and the remaining 10% remains either under-employed or unemployed. With the population growing at the rate of about $2\frac{1}{2}$% per annum in most developing countries, even if the modern sector's need for workers grew at 20% per annum this sector would not be able to employ the entire annual increase in the labour force. It is, therefore, obvious that the traditional sector will have to absorb the currently employed labour force as well as part of the increase.

There is a natural tendency for developing countries to use the technology established in developed countries for their industrial growth. However this is not an easy task because, after the industrialisation process starts and attains a certain level, a certain logic comes into operation. The later this industrialisation process starts, the longer is the preparatory stage and the greater becomes the difference in development levels. Modern technology is much more capital-intensive (per worker) than the old technology, and its application therefore requires greater skills, special qualifications and technical training. Not only are qualified personnel in short supply, but also the capital and skills needed for education and training.

The crucial problem before the third world is how to promote the viable growth of the traditional sector and organically link the modern sector's growth with the traditional sector in a manner that supplements and reinforces the growth and development of the latter. In terms of technology choice there are two issues: first, up-grading traditional technology, and secondly, adapting and improving modern technology, keeping in mind the development objectives, institutional structures and natural resources.

However it should be realised that the widespread application of labour-intensive technology cannot become the general method of industrialisation in developing countries. The problem must be examined separately in each case. There is a number of industries, for example metallurgy and many branches of chemical engineering, in which there is no alternative but to opt for the latest technology. Developing countries should not hesitate to adopt modern technologies if their use is warranted by their growth logic. Examples of appropriate technologies include the application of remote sensing techniques for surveying and locating natural resources, better medical technology, and the fixing of tyres and ball bearings to bullock carts to improve transportation in remote areas. Third-world countries have hard choices to make and cannot just blindly copy the Western pattern in their industrialisation programmes.

DISCUSSION

Royal Professor Ungku A. Aziz highlighted the main points in his paper and made a number of additional observations on the problems created by inappropriate terminology and lack of clarity in specifying problems; the need for care in interpreting a 'snapshot' of development which might be part of a slow or fast, a continual or interrupted, pattern of development; the effects of context on the consequences of introducing particular technologies; the need to use dynamic, not static, models; the difficulty of understanding just what is in the minds of people in a particular society at any one time, let alone over time; the failure of some direct transplants of Western-style culture to the developing world — as, for example, the importation of the Oxbridge model of universities to Malaysia; the need for developing countries to define their objectives and make their own models for problem-solving, for example in education where in Malaysia 90% live in rural areas, but the teaching of Ordinary and Advanced levels had been concentrated in the cities; the need to re-orientate Malaysian education towards technology and science; the need for more than five universities in Malaysia, which has had 18,000 students in the UK for many years and is now sending students to the USA, Germany, France and Japan as well; and, finally, the requirement that developing countries proceed sequentially through all the six stages referred to in his paper.

After Professor A. K. De had made his opening remarks (see above), Dr. D. Mordell (Commonwealth Engineers' Council) elaborated on three points from Professor Aziz' paper: (i) the shortage of indigenous opportunities for education, which costs developing countries a great deal of foreign exchange in sending students abroad; (ii) the need for each country to find and follow its own appropriate path of development, rather than copying models used in other places and circumstances; and (iii) the diversity of modern technology.

Professor I. H. Umar (Bayero) was pleased to hear Professor Aziz talking about patterns of change, but was still uncomfortable about the phrase. He wondered what it was in the Western pattern that developing countries are trying to avoid. It is not the time lag, because advances in communications which have occurred since the Western industrial revolution will mean that countries developing now will take much less than 200 years to advance. He reminded the audience that one of the uses of history is to learn from it; therefore developing countries should look to the West, pick out what is good, and modify it to fit their circumstances. He called for progressive thinking so that socio-economic systems such as the extended family are not perpetuated for their own sake when they have outlived their social purpose.

Professor T. K. N. Unnithan (Rajasthan) referred to the desirable aspects of technology such as more social mobility, the increasing accept-ance of egalitarian values and a growing sense of equality, and greatly increased agricultural production. He added, however, that although the Marxist and capitalist systems were well-known the Gandhian strategy had not been tried, and suggested that universities should play a positive role in finding the optimum use of technology without upsetting traditional values. Although education can be an effective instrument of social change, it can also have the effect of maintaining the status quo. The answer, he thought, lies only in proper educational planning. He also emphasised the need for research programmes on the social consequences of displacing large numbers of people from rural areas to the cities.

Professor W. U. Malik (Kashmir) stated that India has already covered the six stages of development described by Professor Aziz. He contended that, in the main, Indians learn by doing rather than from organised expenditure on science and technology. He cited India's atomic energy establishments and space research as evidence of the level of advancement that has been achieved through the acquisition of highly sophisticated foreign technology. But he added that many Indians feel that through technological sophistication man has become a servant of technology and has lost his appreciation of the values of religion and morality. Professor Malik supported Professor Unnithan's opinion that the answer lies in appropriate or intermediate technology, that is, technology which is labour- rather than capital-intensive, simple and understandable rather than complicated and intimidating, and small- rather than large-scale. Developing countries need institutions, such as India already has, where such appropriate technology can be developed.

Professor Malik thought that the key roles of universities were to contribute to the solution of development problems an intellectual approach to technology; to assess the consequences of scientific developments for the common man; to stress the constructive and beneficial effects of science while remaining aware of its potential dangers; to emphasise intermediate technology in their research programmes; and to provide extension services for the promotion of low-level industry.

Dr. G. P. Sinha (Patna) referred to the great increase in agricultural productivity in India made possible by better water resources, fertilizers, insecticides and herbicides, but added that this has not raised living standards very much because other forms of technology — particularly public health measures such as water supplies, sanitation, and medicines — have led to rapid population growth and accentuated shortages of housing and clothing.

Professor Sir John Crawford (Australian National) adopted a more optimistic role when he outlined the effects of co-operation between Australia and developing countries in agricultural research. The Australian Centre for International Agricultural Research (ACIAR) enables Australian knowledge and experience — particularly in tropical crops, livestock production in semi-arid areas, and the use of legumes — to benefit developing countries. An Australian with special expertise in legumes, for example, works with scientists in, say, East Africa, and in this way Australian financial resources back a programme that is developed and executed in the recipient country by its own scientists. The scheme has in every case been extremely well received, not only in developing countries but also in Australian universities.

Professor A. Wandira (Makerere) urged further attention to three areas: (i) problems incurred by borrowing other countries' technology, especially if it is not adapted (for example, an urgent medical cure), and the implications of this for the role of universities; (ii) contingency planning for the unexpected; and (iii) problems of the selection, choice and integration of borrowed technology. He called for emphasis in university education on teaching to equip students for this selection process.

Professor G. D. Sims (Sheffield) agreed with Professor Wandira that technological borrowing is a problem for curricula. In his opinion, however, adaptation of Western technology is often unnecessary and the problem is that of selling both high-technology industry and appropriate technology to customers who may not want it.

Dr. Fong-Ching Chen (Chinese U. of Hong Kong) suggested that technological advance is a self-sustaining process and that it may not be possible to modernise half-way. Once the process has started it is difficult to control it and eliminate undesirable side-effects, especially the erosion of traditional and religious values. It might, he thought, be a contradiction in terms if each country wanted to modernise in its own way. The role of universities should be to seek a leading edge in competition rather than trying to restrain it within the existing mould.

Professor D. W. George (Newcastle, Australia) quoted an instance of technology transfer and research in an educational context. At the Asian Institute of Technology, near Bangkok, students from over 20 Asian countries undertake postgraduate study. He thought this Institute exemplary for two reasons: (i) students gain from the experience of learning in a high-level institution undertaking the whole range of low- to high-technology studies (the solution of low-technology problems needs minds equally as agile as does that of high-technology ones); and (ii) studies of alumni show that over 94% are working back in their own countries.

Dr. L. F. Kristjanson (Saskatchewan) thought that the effective role of universities depends on greater emphasis on research institutes in developing countries.

Professor F. H. Hinsley (Cambridge) pointed out that there are subjects to study other than science and technology. He believed that too great a concentration on science and technology at the expense of arts and humanities in university curricula in developing countries would make it more rather than less difficult to preserve the balance between good and bad in modernisation.

Haji Sulaiman Abdullah (Malaya) commented that many of the comments made in the discussion seemed to be based on the philosophy of seeking the adaptation of technology to achieve economic growth for its own sake, even though economic progress *per se* does not ensure security and happiness. He quoted Gandhi's observation that it took the plunder of India to get one England; so how many universes would India have to plunder? Adaptation, therefore, might not be possible in the way that the now-industrialised countries had managed. He considered it important to teach in universities the effects of technological advance.

SUB-TOPIC 1 (B): PATTERNS OF CHANGE

Dr. H. Kay (Exeter) disagreed with Dr. Chen's view that there is an inexorable and accepted pattern of development — *inter alia* the timescale has shortened in this century. There is a large gap between the level of man's understanding of his physical environment and of himself, and he hoped that universities would strive to restore and maintain the balance.

In response to the discussion on his paper Professor Aziz welcomed Professor Hinsley's contribution and said that study of the history and philosophy of science is compulsory in the University of Malaya. On the point made by Dr. Chen, he referred to the effects of the differences between the predominant religions of the Chinese and Malays on attitudes, and hence the greater ease of the Chinese in adopting the pursuit of wealth as a key objective. Professor Aziz also drew attention to a problem incurred in the kind of practical technology transfer achieved by ACIAR but not mentioned by Sir John Crawford. Technologists from developed countries are seldom concerned with the impact of new technologies on the distribution of income and power. The Green Revolution in South-East Asia, based on the introduction of 'miracle' rice, has led to dominance by those who supply the necessary fertilizers, seed and energy. Although hybrid rice gives very high yields, the seed is infertile and farmers have to buy new seeds for every sowing; therefore most of the farmers have remained very poor and have sunk further into debt. 'Whoever has the technology or the commodity on which that technology depends always becomes dominant.'

Sub-Topic 1(c)

CHANGING TECHNOLOGY: THE CHALLENGE FOR UNIVERSITY RESEARCH

Chairman: Professor I. H. UMAR
Vice-Chancellor of Bayero University

Rapporteur: Mr. W. HANSEN
Registrar of the University of Canterbury

Tuesday, 16 August

Professor L. M. BIRT (*Vice-Chancellor and Principal, University of New South Wales*): The challenge to university research which arises from recent rapid changes in technology is to be seen as the modern expression of mankind's continuing efforts to harness its technical knowledge and skills for the betterment of society. It has been sharpened in this century by marked increases in the pace of technological development and in the scope of man's capacities for technological manipulation, which now embrace the exploitation of both animate and inanimate matter. Our ability to understand and regulate individual and social behaviour, on the other hand, is much less well developed.

Technological development poses a dual challenge for university research activities, which embrace all areas of human knowledge: first, to provide the knowledge and information necessary for promoting technological change itself, and to do so in a way which is suitably responsive to the needs of society; and secondly to assist society to make the political, social and economic adjustments necessary to cope with the ensuing technological developments. Six aspects of this dual challenge are examined.

The first aspect of this challenge is to ensure that research enables society to exploit resources, both renewable and non-renewable, in an effective and economic fashion. Of particular importance are ways of conserving scarce resources, and the identification and characterisation of new useful materials. The universities will, therefore, be asked to maintain wide-ranging

74

programmes of basic research, to make wise choices for concentration of effort in these programmes, to select appropriate areas for effective applied research, and to justify the value of the entire research effort to the community at large. These requirements will be met only if universities are able to develop effective working partnerships between themselves, and with government and private organisations engaged in research, development and demonstration. These partnerships must promote and maintain effective interaction between the universities' research workers, and scientists and technologists in industrial and government research groups. Effective interaction would be greatly assisted by arrangements which permit and encourage research staff to move across sectorial boundaries, with university workers spending time in industry or government laboratories, and conversely. The value of such movements is not only in assisting the flow of research findings into effective technological development and commercialisation, but also in promoting a better understanding, within each sphere of research activity, about the scientific and technical environment within which the collaborating research workers must operate.

The second aspect is to make an adequate response to the needs of society for highly trained, and re-trained, manpower. In particular, it will be necessary to relate university research effectively to postgraduate programmes producing the highly trained scientists and others required to contribute to the advancement of knowledge, and to assist society in the application and management of technological change. University research must, therefore, be related to training programmes for creative scientists who will work at both basic and applied research at the highest level, highly trained research technologists who will contribute to development and demonstration activities in government and private organisations, and for all scientists and technologists who require re-training or continuing education programmes to enhance their understanding of current scientific thought. These requirements should be met by a range of postgraduate programmes offered by the universities, to meet the needs of those who will serve as scientific managers and highly trained research staff in industry and government, through relatively short-term training programmes; of those who will direct or manage large private or government research enterprises, requiring a more extensive postgraduate programme (perhaps at doctoral level); and finally of those who will work as scholars and scientists in educational and research institutions, requiring training in research methods and techniques and the conduct of individual research projects. It will probably be necessary for the universities to diminish their emphasis on purely academic and scholarly values in postgraduate training programmes.

The third aspect is to ensure that universities align at least some part of their research effort with national needs and requirements. The basis on which this is done will necessarily vary from one country to another, because the relationships between government and the universities which determine the indentification of, and response to, national research needs are greatly influenced by cultural and social factors. Nevertheless, each national university system must find some way of ensuring that it is adequately responsive to its own society's interest in, and demand for, appropriate applied research leading to technological development; and that a proper balance is maintained with the university's other commitment to basic research. Moreover, universities must preserve appropriate balance between the independence necessary for each individual university in its choice of, and support for, particular research projects, and the surrender of independence necessary to permit effective co-operation and collaboration in research between different universities. Finally, universities will be challenged to organise their research activities so that they can accommodate to changing demands for intensive effort, by phasing out less productive work and introducing and building up new programmes. This may require greater university direction of the research efforts of its staff, and a re-organisation of the academic structures within which teaching and research are conducted. It may also be necessary to adopt structures which permit the separate conduct of teaching and research activities, and which increase the flexibility for the deployment and redeployment of staff resources to meet changing research demands. All of these requirements underline the need to establish and maintain effective co-operative interactions between the universities and government, government agencies and private organisations.

The fourth aspect is to make the best possible use of the new information technologies in the conduct of university research. These technologies offer enormous potential advantages to research workers, but also pose difficulties because of the sheer volume of information that is now readily accessible. The challenge will be to identify and make use of the information which is in fact relevant to any particular inquiry, an exercise of judgment which will require considerable scholarly skill and precision. It is desirable, therefore, for universities to ensure that, wherever possible, research teams are assembled under the leadership of outstandingly gifted research workers with the requisite scholarly skills. These considerations reinforce the financial arguments for the more widespread establishment of research groups within universities.

The fifth aspect is for university research to contribute more effectively to the development of an adequate understanding of the nature and complexity of the social, industrial, economic and political adjustments which are required, of individuals and communities, by technological advance. This advance is such that societies will need much more knowledge to guide individual and social adjustment to changing technology. Universities will be challenged to provide, through research, balanced and comprehensive assessments of the costs and benefits of proposed introductions of new technology. This points up the need for intensive research effort into human behaviour, individual and social; and universities should play a leading part in this endeavour. Meanwhile, and until new concepts arising from research have been thoroughly tested, universities must not appear to claim certainty about topics about which there is little firmly established knowledge.

Finally, as institutions with an especial commitment to basic research and the pursuit and application of knowledge, wherever it leads, universities will be strongly challenged by changing public attitudes to the morality and acceptability of certain kinds of research endeavour. This is apparent from the public interest in such fields as genetic engineering and nuclear technology. It can no longer be assumed that community and government support will be forthcoming for all that can be done in science and technology. Strong arguments are being mounted for the acceptance of voluntary abstention from certain kinds of research work. The response (whether positive or negative) to these arguments will come most appropriately from universities as institutions, rather than from individual scholars. The university should attempt to provide, for public scrutiny and debate, the best possible assessments of the 'balance of debit and credit' for proposed scientific and technological developments. The universities themselves should accept the responsibility for offering these assessments, which frequently will need to draw on the insights of the entire 'community of scholars'. The universities will also be asked to accept the legitimacy of the claims of society to query, be informed about, and perhaps request delays in or the cessation of, particular types of research. In taking up this challenge the universities may find that their own intellectual life is strengthened, as the internal discussion necessary to provide responses will require scholars in many different disciplines to consult with and aid each other, as they attempt to formulate a comprehensive view of the issues in question. This challenge may, therefore, help us to find new ways of re-awakening within our universities a productive sense of scholarly community.

77

DISCUSSION

In presenting his paper Professor Birt outlined briefly the six challenges discussed, and these were addressed by most of the delegates who commented upon particular aspects of his paper. Discussion was opened by Dr. T. A. Brzustowski (Waterloo) and the following delegates addressed the session group: Dr. L. I. Barber (Regina); The Hon. Mr Justice R. E. McGarvie (La Trobe); Professor M. G. Taylor (Sydney); Professor G. Igboeli (Federal U of Technology, Makurdi); Dr. D. Harrison (Keele); Professor R. S. F. Campbell (James Cook U of North Queensland); Professor D. R. Stranks (Adelaide); Dr. Fong-Ching Chen (Chinese U of Hong Kong); Dr. R. O. H. Irvine (Otago); Professor W. U. Malik (Kashmir); Professor H. G. Gelber (Tasmania); Professor Sir Bruce Williams (Technical Change Centre); Dr. R. Hill (Bristol); Dr. J. H. Burnett (Edinburgh); Dr. P. P. M. Meincke (Prince Edward Island).

A theme evident from the various comments and questions was the sound of social conscience. As in the area of ecology and resource management, where we are ever being reminded of the social impact of change, so too in the roles and activities of universities are we being reminded of a social obligation—to weigh carefully the consequences of innovation and invention. This theme has been evident in other topics discussed; if given full weight it could provide a restraint or even be a millstone about the neck of 'progress'.

It was interesting to note a general acceptance of Professor Birt's six challenges as being the most significant: nobody asserted a wider compass of challenge. The voice of pragmatism was heard. What are we going to *do* about facing such challenges? Enough of talk—let us see some action! Those who recommend the formation of committees to seek solutions may not be very optimistic about practical advance. It is quite clear that the technological changes that the universities have helped to spawn are causing unease to our sleep now and may soon return to haunt us. It may be that universities have no great concern about the social consequences of research, invention or innovation. To illustrate: Alan Blumheim, who died in 1943 at the age of 38, had filed no less than 128 patents (an average of one every six weeks of his working life) on a range of electronic ideas of great originality and novelty. His patent on stereo BP394323 is still a bible for audio engineers; he cut two channels within a single groove of a disc record in 1933 and 1934. This is an unrepresentative description of a person described in the following terms: 'There was not a single subject to which he turned his mind that he did not enrich extensively'. This is an extreme example, but it does highlight whether researches should be proscribed by social mores or restraints. Better that society can benefit—or reject the fruits of such labour. Is it really the job of the university to try to determine what adjustments should be made and to anticipate their effects? Universities are no better equipped in this than is any other institution. What we need is the wisdom of Solomon; that was given but once.

One can feel a measure of optimism that somehow and in some way the challenges outlined will be met; the most intractable would seem to be the need to cope with complex social, economic, political and personal issues, and with changes that will be precipitated by technological change. Economic and social pressures (notwithstanding the cry to preserve old traditions) will lead to the full application and exploitation of new technology. There is nothing from the past to suggest that the unemployed suddenly became artists or poets, artisans or actors. Present indications would suggest that by taking 'man' from manual labour we have not necessarily improved the 'quality of life'.

Who is responsible for a concern about and resolution of social pressures? Does it lead to central direction which strikes at the heart of 'western' democratic capitalism? It may be unduly pessimistic to suggest that there are no ready solutions at this time to the challenges outlined by Professor Birt. Certainly universities have made their contribution to technological change; at present none of us appears to have the capacity to recognise—let alone control—the full impact of technological change. Nevertheless one can hope that, from the immense intellectual capacity of *homo sapiens* and the resilience of the human spirit, progress can be made. As Terence told us 2,000 years ago, nothing is so difficult that it cannot be found out by research.

The advent of the computer and the silicon chip in its various forms identifies a reservoir of knowledge. The human brain, a computer pre-eminent, still has an edge in its identification of *relevant* knowledge.

In the end one returns to the philosophers, or at least to one philosopher who had a profound effect on the development of the modern university in New Zealand. In a series of important publications Sir Karl Popper has totally demolished the view that science deals in inexorable and human truths—the sort of ideas machines could produce if they were given the facts. Science, Popper emphasises, is a human activity, dependent upon human imagination to produce its hypothesis. And, despite the alarm and the gloom, that will remain the case for as long as can be foreseen.

Sub-Topic 1(d)

CHANGING TECHNOLOGY: IMPLICATIONS FOR UNIVERSITY CURRICULA

Chairman: Dr. D. HARRISON
Vice-Chancellor of the University of Keele

Rapporteur: Miss IRENE HINDMARSH
Pro-Vice-Chancellor, and Principal of St. Aidan's
College, University of Durham

Thursday, 18 August

Dr. C. R. MITRA (*Director, Birla Institute of Technology and Science*):

The Nature of Technology

There are two ways to approach an understanding of how technology will affect the future. One is to predict the most likely technological developments along with their most likely social effects. The other is to identify respects in which technology entails changes and to suggest the kind of patterns of change that it will force on other entities. This paper adopts the second attitude and confines itself to the limited domain of university curricula.

Technology has an inherent capacity to force change and also an ability to make available new possibilities. These together keep on altering the spectrum of options available to a society. This flux in the hierarchy of social choices opens up the question of values.

However the change that technology induces is rarely reversible and is not merely additive. Actually the change comes continuously through a dynamic process in which innovation is the dominant factor. Since this paper is restricted to the implication of these changes for university curricula, we turn to the epistemological problem of technology. Technology deals with a mission and task which are always multi-disciplinary. Through technological innovation we see the manifestation of theory in practice and practice amending the theory. Through this dialectic process the

80

entire stock of knowledge undergoes continuous change. In this case the word 'knowledge' also includes the word 'skill'. The whole technological order is involved in this change.

The Nature of the University

A university is the one institution which deals primarily with knowledge in all its aspects. However its traditional approach is discipline-orientated and not mission-orientated. Further, its basic attempt to transmit values makes it inherently less change-prone and hardly innovative. Curricula are therefore normally composed of the tested stock of knowledge, and some current skills, divided into traditional disciplines. Nevertheless universities cannot escape the continual need to update curricula, because the practice of knowledge in all its aspects alters the conditions through which the teaching of knowledge and skills is continued. These are the internal impulses through which normal curricular changes take place in universities. Such changes have not been insignificant. New disciplines have been introduced; interdisciplinary areas of studies have been started; new tools of analysis and skill formation have taken place. But even the necessity of these changes has not been felt by the university to alter very radically its method of operation or its institutional structure.

The changes induced by technology in the stock of knowledge have recently been so rapid and overwhelming that their impact on university curricula has created a new problem for the university system. It has already been mentioned that through internal impulses universities have accommodated the need to change curricula in the past. But external impulses originating from technological innovations have substantially complicated the problem. These internal and external impulses sometimes oppose each other, and sometimes augment each other, to such an extent that the university system finds it difficult to cope with the problem of scale.

The education system is characterised by the fact that its response to innovation is slow compared to other areas such as health, defence, transport and industrial production. The reason for this slowness lies in two characteristics: first, the education system attempts to transmit existing values and therefore often views innovation as an implied disfunction; and second, the organisational approach of the education system is to seek a satisfying solution rather than the optimum one. It operates on a genetically compatible solution rather than on the optimum solution.

81

To overcome this inherent and institutional duress of the education system all proposed innovations have to be examined in the light of the following variables:

(i) the relative advantage of the innovation: how far it appears to be an improvement on the ideas and solutions it supersedes;

(ii) its compatibility: the degree to which it is consistent with the existing values of the prospective users;

(iii) its divisibility: whether it can be tried on a limited basis and its utility demonstrated before general adoption;

(iv) its complexity: how difficult it is to understand and use;

(v) its communicability: the extent to which its results can be administered to all concerned and the knowledge of it passed from one member of the system to another;

(vi) the type of decision-making processes on which the rejection or acceptance of the innovation depends.

The Need for Innovation

It will be apparent that changes forced by technological innovations cannot be incorporated merely through curricular changes, however imaginative and far-reaching. The need for fundamental changes in the structure of curricula as well as in the mode of teaching, together with the acquisition of new skills, must now be accepted. But these changes will never be effected if the university as a system remains static. In short, the university will have to innovate and alter itself to remain congruent with changes in technology. Thus the traditional mission of the university must be broadened so that it can readily respond to and deal with innovation. In the past the university has been the principal repository of knowledge. It is to be hoped that in the future the university system will become also the primary institutional source of innovations.

Dr. Mitra was unable to present the paper reproduced above, and asked Professor Sir Bruce Williams (Co-ordinating Chairman of Topic 1) to introduce the sub-topic. A summary of Sir Bruce's introduction follows.

The 'knowledge explosion' of the last 50 years is due to great improvement in scientific instruments and the increase in research made possible by the growth in wealth. The consequences for curricula are the continuing tendencies to overload and—following the increase in the number and specialisation of staff—to fragment.

Universities have responded to the growth of knowledge by creating more specialised first degree courses—though not only in sciences and technologies—and, more creatively, by providing a growing range of postgraduate and refresher courses. There are within universities both the conservative forces stressed by Dr. Mitra and the dynamic forces stressed by Sir Eric Ashby at the Sydney Congress (1968) when he spoke of the role of disciplined dissent in scholarship. There is, however, growing public concern about the extent of specialisation in many undergraduate courses. Although it is difficult to find an optimal balance between range and depth of study, developments in information technology (IT) could help towards a solution. Developments in IT will also change the balance between formal and informal processes of education. There are now greater opportunities than before for self-education, and universities should now give more explicit attention during first degree studies to ensuring that students have an analytic capacity and a desire for continuing self-education. Unless universities succeed in this, the pressures to de-institutionalise higher education may become uncomfortably strong. Universities would be wise to ask whether they have decentralised policy too far and allowed too many of the decisions on the nature of undergraduate education to be taken by staff in departments absorbed in highly specialised research activities.

In his final section Dr. Mitra expresses the hope that universities will cease to concentrate on teaching and research and will regard it as part of their mission to put new knowledge to work by engineering process and product innovations. We could all produce a list of the dangers to scholarship and education involved in such an extension. During the student revolt there was much criticism of the links between the universities and 'the military industrial complex', and we should not allow the rhetoric to obscure a point of substance. The detachment of applied research and development from the production and marketing of the product impedes innovation, but few, if any, universities are equipped to run successful business enterprises, and would become very different and less desirable places if they became so.

The rural and medical faculties are in the best position to bridge gaps between research and innovation because experimental farms and teaching hospitals do not clash with the culture of universities. Through 'teaching companies' and consultancies, some members of science and engineering faculties can help to bridge gaps between research and applications, though in a more limited way. There are some fields—for example bio-engineering, drugs and programming—in which the links between university research and industrial applications are now quite close, or thought to be close, and the pressures on staff in those fields to get involved in industrial applications may increase. Recent experience, particularly in the USA, indicates the need for a clearer definition of roles, and for more institutional inventions to cope with mixed roles and complex activities.

There may be another very different effect of changing technology on curricula. The decline in the number of unskilled jobs, and the increase in average age of entry to the labour market, are likely to bring stronger pressures on universities to improve the lot of 'the disadvantaged'. To deal with that great social problem, at least some universities may need to provide a greater variety of courses and methods of instruction.

DISCUSSION

Professor P. H. Karmel (Australian National) introduced the discussion. Sir Bruce had already covered several important points he had wished to make, but he wanted to stress the importance of Dr. Mitra's point about the internal tensions in universities—between the discipline orientation of undergraduate courses and the multi-disciplinary approach to research, and between the scholarly and entrepreneurial approaches to life. The main business of universities is the conservation, transmission and extension of knowledge, not the production of goods and services, at which universities are amateurish. It is dangerous for academics to think that they can solve industry's problems. Change is easier in times of expansion, when 'new blood' is being appointed, than in times of stasis or contraction, when the lesser willingness and ability of older staff to adapt leads to problems of adjustment.

Yet there have been major changes since the mid-1960s. Totally new disciplines, such as computer and environmental sciences and industrial archaeology, have emerged. In old-established subjects, such as economics, new questions and issues are being raised and new solutions found. There is a willingness to update curricula, but the proliferation of undergraduate courses is not very productive, nor does it lead to the best use of resources. Because of the tendency of staff to wish to 'do their own thing' without reference to the totality of courses as experienced by undergraduates, the number of courses offered is often alarmingly closely correlated with the number of teaching staff in the faculty.

Universities should be aware of the need to update knowledge continually, beyond the provision of postgraduate courses. Perhaps they should take responsibility for creating 'packages' of retraining and providing

these in collaboration with the professions to ensure that their requirements are met?

Responding to changes in student preferences often requires major
shifts in curricula, but in current conditions institutions cannot change
or add to their existing staff. This is an argument for not appointing
new staff on long-term contracts.

Professor Karmel suggested that in times of relatively full employment
both the general public and students tend to favour general rather than
vocational courses, but in times of rapid social and technological change
and higher unemployment there are dangers of over-producing specialists,
leading to skilled unemployment. Initial stages ought to be more broadly
based so that the student may have greater flexibility of job choice.
Medicine is in a different category, but law and engineering need not
be. Because people will have shorter working lives and greater job
mobility, leisure before university education and after retirement is
becoming increasingly important. He agreed with the Leverhulme report's
recommendation for a general approach followed by specialistion, but
not with its proposal for two-year undergraduate courses.

During discussion earlier in the week, emphasis had been placed on
the widening inequalities between North and South. He was struck during
his visit to Ironbridge by the realisation that the industrial revolution
was just as disruptive as the technological revolution in today's society,
the major difference being that it produced unskilled jobs. Now the
opposite is true: there is an increasing number of social failures, a fact
not previously mentioned in the discussion sessions. The bottom 20% of
a class a generation ago found unskilled jobs during the high employment
of the 1960s. They may not do so now because the massive change in
the occupational structure ensures that they cannot be employed at the
socially acceptable minimum wage. The answer can only be either
subsidised employment or increased productivity. Should such general
problems of society be the concern of universities? Since relations between
schools, colleges and universities are close, consideration of university
curricula must be related to the other segments of the education system,
right down to the primary level.

Professor G. D. Sims (Sheffield) asked whether we are engaged in
planning the ideal university when we have to live in the real world. A
curriculum should be coherent and well-planned and leave the student
able to think at the end of the course. In science it is possible to have a
specialised curriculum: project work gives opportunities for a multi-
disciplinary approach, giving both breadth and depth, but in practice
such courses are rare. We owe it to our paymasters not to disregard
entrepreneurial activity: much depends on how we do it, but we cannot
ignore it. We would be wise to give more attention to our links with the
outside world.

Professor M. G. Taylor (Sydney) said that universities are good at
some things but not at others. They ought to be good at scholarship,
and he hoped that in our eagerness to satisfy society we would not be
impeded in our responsibility to choose and promote scholars. Nor should

we feel guilty if we do not produce innovations which are immediately marketable. Investment in scholarship is a good investment, even if governments have to wait for returns.

Dr. D. Mordell (Commonwealth Engineers' Council) reminded the session group of the implications of changing technology for pre-industrial societies, such as those in Southern Africa. Relevance is essential in curricula: he cited an instance in which Zimbabwean engineering students were given as a practical exercise the design of a central heating rather than a ventilation system. Universities in developing countries must consider their future industrial societies when planning courses. He touched on Dr. Mitra's point about universities' structural arthritis and said that although young staff may be highly radical, in fundamental university problems they are the most conservative.

Dr. W. Taylor (Institute of Education, London) emphasised the lack of homogeneity in the institutions of higher education. Universities in different parts of the world vary greatly in the proportion of the population going to them, in size, and in their proximity to other local institutions of higher education. Therefore the implications of changing technology for curricula also differ extensively.

Haji Sulaiman Abdullah (Malaya) spoke of universities as centres of scholarship and regretted the lack of emphasis on history and philosophy for all students. New technology and the greater complexity of modern society has made the mastery of basic principles and language even more essential. Certain specialisms within disciplines, such as environmental and resource law, can no longer be regarded as optional extras.

Professor I. H. Umar (Bayero) referred to the difficult problems of choosing curricula in developing countries. It is impossible to avoid including courses in atomic physics, electronics and energy studies in a physics first degree, but this is hard in three years, and a student may have to select, even among essentials. He would prefer a four-year course, but that is an unrealistic hope. Broadly-based courses have advantages, but the lack of depth may handicap those students who will go on to take higher degrees abroad and who must be prepared so that they can fit in. Often it is easier or necessary to teach from a foreign textbook, even though the examples may be inappropriate; there is a pressing need for dedicated people who can adapt such books for local use.

Professor E. Thumboo (National U of Singapore) pointed to the problems that arise when innovating departments do not keep each other and the central university administration informed. Thus when engineers design low-cost public housing, social scientists in sociology, psychology and social medicine ought to be involved but frequently are not. Unless universities learn to manage changes in curricula better than this, changes may be foreced upon them.

Dr. A. E. Sloman (Essex) contrasted the UK, where it is the responsibility of the individual university to make decisions on change, with many other countries, particularly in Europe, in which universities do not have this autonomy. On balance he was optimistic about the evolution of both graduate and undergraduate courses and of continuing education.

SUB-TOPIC 1 (D): IMPLICATIONS FOR CURRICULA

There would be unanimity of view that UK universities had been more responsive to change than many European institutions, and he hoped that responsiveness would continue.

Dr. J. H. Burnett (Edinburgh) pointed to the low levels of graduate unemployment, and the high levels of unemployment among early leavers who are often illiterate and innumerate. There may be two million innumerate or illiterate in the UK, and the cause is often the way in which learning is presented to them at an early age. Schools often complain about the indirect effect which universities have on school curricula through young academics acting as public examiners. Universities could help to bring a controlled revolution right through the school system by increasing research into teaching and learning and transferring the results into the school system. It is possible to affect the climate of society and bring many from the unskilled into the skilled category. But the worry that the faster pace of technological innovation may increase skilled unemployment remains.

Professor P. A. Reynolds (Lancaster) asked why we should advocate change if we are not clear about our objectives, which differ between fields. There is an important difference between the two key objectives in university education. The first is to teach students to grasp the highest level of existing skills, for which scholars are needed; the second is to achieve the conceptual, imaginative and practical approach which equips students to tackle future problems and situations. Distinction in scholarship need not be expected of all university teachers. The normal pattern in the UK of undergraduate study followed immediately by postgraduate work results in the unjustified assumption that the practical approach evolves out of the scholastic, in both teaching and learning. He advocated a break between first and higher degrees for two reasons: first, those students re-entering higher education would be those identified by the professions as the most useful and creative; and second, this would stimulate more sponsorship of postgraduate study, so releasing government funds for other purposes.

Professor L. R. Webb (Melbourne) said that the IT revolution has been presented as a problem for universities to consider and as a possibility for self-education and de-institutionalisation. As an economist he felt that it is not such a pressing problem and that universities ought not to concern themselves with bringing within their orbit all social problems. He asked Sir Bruce to explain how the universities might help the bottom 20% referred to by Professor Karmel.

In his summing up, Sir Bruce drew attention to the diversity of approach from delegates and wondered to what extent their contributions could have been predicted from their subjects and nationalities. There will continue to be very big differences in the applicability of subjects, but it was clear that this did not explain the variety of opinion evident from the discussion. Both Geoffrey Sims, an electrical engineer, and Michael Taylor, a medic, are in fields in which research can lead directly to application, but their views on the roles of universities and the autonomy of scholars are poles apart.

Although some big industrial companies have a distinguished record in basic research, he thought it vital that the distinctive culture of universities, which is so important for the generation of new knowledge, is not lost in universities' attempts to emulate the very different culture of industry and commerce.

He emphasised Dr. (W.) Taylor's and Dr. Mordell's points that appropriate curricular changes should be related to particular circumstances. Such intra- and international differences arise not only because of different interests and problems, but also because of differences in institutional structures.

In reply to the question of how to help the bottom 20%, Sir Bruce said that the answer had been given by Dr. Burnett when he explained how university research into teaching and learning could transform the school performance of these pupils. This could be a very important example of that innovatory action for which Dr. Mitra had pleaded.

Sub-Topic 1(e)

POLICY IMPLICATIONS: UNIVERSITIES, GOVERNMENT AND INDUSTRY

Chairman: Professor Sir JOHN CRAWFORD
Chancellor of the Australian National University
Rapporteur: Mr. F. S. HAMBLY
Secretary of the Australian Vice-Chancellors' Committee

Thursday, 18 August

Dr. H. I. MACDONALD (*President, York University, Canada*): In narrowing my topic I shall focus upon Canada, from which general illustrations can be drawn, and a new crown corporation of which I am Chairman, IDEA Corporation, because it provides a good example of ways in which certain opportunities can be exploited.

From my work in university and government, I have first-hand experience of the gaps between universities, governments and industry. I would suggest, however, that IDEA Corporation of the Province of Ontario represents an attempt to bridge such chasms— and that it is technological change itself that has provided both the need and the catalyst for such an initiative. In addition to wearing my hat as President of York University, therefore, I shall be wearing my other hat as Chairman of IDEA to present a case study of the issues for this panel through an account of the role and objectives of IDEA Corporation, and its relationship with universities and industry.

The acronym IDEA stands for innovation development for employment advancement: our mission is to provide significant leadership in advancing technological innovation and, as a result, employment opportunities. There is, of course, the potential conflict between technological advancement and job displacement, but in my view the former must yield sufficient advancement in economic growth and increase in productivity to more than compensate for the latter. With adequate planning and appropriate public policy, the application of technology can be controlled, the direction of the economy influenced, and adjustments by individuals to the impact of technology can be made.

First of all, I think it important to be mindful of the way in which we view technology—it is not a threatening storm, nor is it a villain to be feared. Technology will advance only as far as we allow it to advance, and a prime function of the universities will be to encourage ethical and moral decisions about technology and our control of it—decisions which artificial intelligence can never make.

This truth should be self-evident, but, given the degree of resistance to and suspicion of technology, we can assume that it is not. Indeed, while we read much about the impending doom of job displacement by technology, we find on the other hand very little about the challenge and excitement that many will find in adapting to change in the workplace. Our universities can play a major role from the perspective of attitude by educating our students to a willingness to retrain and relearn in order to cope with change.

If we are to assume a commitment to technology, then, there are two consequences that must be recognized:

(1) a higher level of growth requires a major effort over a long period of time;

(2) displacement of jobs requires a major commitment to retraining, rehabilitation, and readaptation of people.

Therefore technology and education are partners in progress, and in order to maintain a balance between them education should become a growth industry on a scale never before imagined. Governments must become convinced of this in every part of the world.

In the universities, meanwhile, certain commercial opportunities arising from fundamental research should be taken advantage of. Similarly, universities and industry could form new partnerships and exchanges through which research in the universities could be commercialised on the industrial side, with economic growth the result. I believe, contrary to many studies of the limits to growth, that there is sufficient capacity for economic growth for some decades to come, and that the quality of that growth is determined by our own social values and attitudes. A new long-term perspective for economic growth involves three factors:

(1) a basic reliance on our human resources and their adaptability to change, requiring renewed and enlarged investment in education at all levels;

(2) an unprecedented commitment to technological innovation and adaptation (which we have already assumed in perceiving technological change as a touchstone from which new beginnings will be made);

(3) the restructuring of domestic economies appropriate to fuller participation in the emerging world.

Of the three requirements, the most important of all is to enhance our human resource capacity by investing more in education. In the new opportunities that technology offers for the storage and dissemination of information and knowledge we have, in the universities, an even greater accessibility that advances what has been, historically, a gradual democratization of our institutions of higher learning. Universities need not fear for their future in this process; instead, they must adapt and interpret social change itself so that we can all make sense of our very lives.

On the restructuring of our economies, we should not be looking backward and forming strategies for a great age that is now at or near its close. We should instead be looking forward and forming strategies for sunrise industries based on the new technology. That leads me to the third objective—a higher level of technological innovation and adaptation, and IDEA Corporation. The role of IDEA is to confront major impediments to development in technology and to assist in breaking them down. IDEA acts as a catalyst in converting good ideas into commercially viable products by searching out and evaluating new technology that might otherwise lie dormant and unknown in universities, government laboratories, and in business. It helps to fill the resource gap by providing funds to the private sector, for developing new ideas, in exchange for a share of future royalties. At the same time that it facilitates access to research, it seeks out the skills required for conveying projects from the conceptual stage to the process of commercial application. In so doing IDEA is developing a clear overall and systematic conception of innovative research in Ontario.

In turn, universities can form partnerships and exchanges with other universities throughout the world, and may initiate the transfer of technology to developing nations. But perhaps the most specialized role that universities must play is in acting as the conscience of civilization as we all face decisions and changes essential to the human condition.

DISCUSSION

Dr. J. H. Burnett (Edinburgh) said that there was an optimism in Dr. Macdonald's presentation which, based on experience in the United Kingdom, he could not accept without qualification. Dr. Macdonald's underlying thesis was that technological change is the catalyst that leads to the need for new knowledge. It is too optimistic, however, to expect that money will be provided to fund the new knowledge. Moreover, knowledge and availability are not enough. Knowledge without wisdom is very dangerous.

Dr. Burnett could not accept the propositions that a high level of technological innovation will lead to long-term growth and that it is not necessary to worry about the short-term consequences. He also had some doubts about the role of the universities in the technological revolution which would depend, at least in part, on vice-chancellors taking management decisions on what the universities might or might not do. He said that it is well accepted that universities, industry and government must work together to facilitate the transfer of technological innovation. In this the universities have a special role to play, because they have the right environment in which to promote co-operation in that they do not suffer to the same degree from 'human selfishness': industry is for profit, governments are for prestige, whereas universities can be more objective. Universities can bid for both public and private funds, they can decide which kind of research—pure or applied—to support, and there is opportunity for rational discussion within universities on these issues. In reaching decisions universities may be influenced in part by the financial rewards which might be available to them through operating at the interface between universities and industry.

Dr. Burnett pointed out that there are a number of policy considerations for the universities. First, it is often contended that universities are conservative and must follow their traditional ways of operating. But it must be realised that present traditions are only about ten years old, and the widely-held view that universities are not leading is incorrect. No country has solved the problem of the transfer of research to application. This problem must be tackled, and can be solved in part by the exchange of personnel between universities and industry. The universities must look at why this interchange has been notably unsuccessful in the United Kingdom. Many of the impediments might be financial, such as superannuation difficulties, and it is important to determine if these and other problems can be overcome.

Second, it is important to look at how universities mould their students' attitudes to life. It is here that the universities are in a position to do the most but probably do the least. Most of the people who move into research and development are trained in the universities, and this is the way in which universities can do most to further relations between universities, industry and government. Universities have a special opportunity to train attitudes of mind—people trained in other environments do not bring the same understanding to problems. Universities must recognise that the kind of education which they offer inculcates attitudes and that these will ultimately determine the policies to be followed elsewhere.

The Hon. Mr. Justice R. E. McGarvie (La Trobe) doubted if technology does operate for good and for economic growth. In Australia structural unemployment has resulted and, while some have claimed that it will disappear, it has in fact remained. As a result many educated people have not obtained jobs and some are losing confidence in themselves despite their willingness to retrain. Those present at this Congress have been successful, but there are many other people and groups in society which have not been so successful, and there is little evidence to suggest that this position will change. As a result universities should not assume, in developing their policies, that there will be a change in the state of the economy. They should recognise that many people, including graduates, will spend a considerable time out of employment. Therefore, in their training programmes, universities should be teaching the humanities as widely as possible and teaching how to cope with enforced leisure. Mr. Justice McGarvie described this as a 'what if not?' contribution. While other speakers were more optimistic about the future, he stressed that there is no evidence at the moment to suggest that things will improve.

Professor R. S. F. Campbell (James Cook U of North Queensland) pointed out that Dr. Burnett spoke of industry as manufacturing industry. He stressed that in global terms the important issues are in agricultural production rather than in manufacturing industry. He said that in India, for example, there is a close relationship between universities, industry and government, and a commitment to a planned relationship between them in the development of agriculture in that country. Thre is a lesson to be learned from this in that other countries, including those from the developing world, can show the West the way forward.

The Chairman warned against generating too much gloom about the future which could easily happen in developed countries. He supported Professor Campbell and said that India and some other countries have managed to make progress in agricultural research without altering the structure of their agricultural industries. Pessimism is nurtured in some countries because of unemployment, but he has seen the Green Revolution at work in India. Close co-operation between universities, industry and government in the development of technology does work, and there is scope for optimism. He pointed to the need for universities to consider what initiatives are open to them to help industry and government.

Dr. E. Margaret Fulton (Mount Saint Vincent) pointed to the need to examine both the present structure of the workforce and the possible need to restructure it. She said that economic growth is thought of in terms of the output of goods, but in the future we must possibly think more about the output of services. In this regard consideration must be given to redefining the concept of work to include other than paid work. Much of it—probably two-thirds of the world's work—is unpaid: the amount of paid work is limited and will become increasingly more limited. Unless we redefine the concept of work it will not be possible to recognise all the work that is being undertaken.

Professor A. K. De (Indian Institute of Technology, Bombay) commented on Dr. Burnett's point about the universities moulding the attitudes of young men and women. He asked how the universities can tell them what to do after graduation, and stressed that it is necessary to develop attitudes while students are undergraduates because this will not be possible after they leave university. He also pointed to the need to train entrepreneurs. Besides being technologists or engineers, it is necessary to teach people to take risks if the benefits of technology are to be fully realised.

Dr. W. Taylor (Insitute of Education, London) commented that the relationships between universities, industry and government in research will depend on the magnitude of the research and development (R & D) budgets to which universities have access.

Professor H. G. Gelber (Tasmania) said that he was more optimistic than other speakers, doubted if there has been an overall reduction in the number of jobs, and suggested that the problem might be the way in which technologies have been exploited. He suggested that it is easier to make predictions about the loss of jobs because of new technology than to predict the number of new jobs which might result. History shows that new jobs are created and that those countries which have suffered the least loss of jobs, or have made good the loss most effectively, are those which have been able to make the best use of the new technologies. While there might be changes in patterns of employment and demands for different kinds of skills, this does not necessarily mean that there has to be an overall loss of jobs. He agreed that there is a moral component in the issues involved, but suggested that the universities were not united in their views on either what the moral problems are or what the answers should be.

Dr. P. P. M. Meincke (Prince Edward Island) said that the key issue is not the number of jobs which will be available, but rather the kind of employment which will be available in the future and its distribution within the world. He suggested that new technology should enable people to live where they want to work, otherwise they will be asking what we want our technology for.

Dr. H. Kay (Exeter) said that there were few instances where the social consequences of technological change had been foreseen. Although technology does solve some problems, it invariably creates others. On the question of how universities influence the attitudes of students, he commented that it is not what is said to students but what academic staff think of their subject and how they teach it which leaves lasting impressions and develops attitudes. Dr. Burnett interjected that when he had introduced the idea of 'attitudes' he had meant attitudes to research and what it would be used for. He said that he had been misunderstood in the discussion.

Dr. H. W. French (Loughborough U of Technology) spoke of his experiences at Loughborough University and made four points relating to the close relationship between his institution and industry: (i) because many of the academic staff have been recruited from industry and are not career academics they tend to engage in research which relates to the requirements of industry; (ii) because much of the education and training is through sandwich courses many of the students, while continuing to work in industry, are nevertheless under the influence of academic staff and this inculcates proper questioning attitudes; at the same time academic staff cannot be ivory tower teachers because they are teaching people from industry; (iii) links with industry are actively pursued, which means that much industrial research is carried out in the university and this, in turn, attracts government research funds for work on projects which are relevant to industry; and (iv) through the organisation Loughborough Consultants Ltd. it has been possible to attract R & D contracts from industry. Dr. French acknowledged that other universities have similar arrangements with industry.

In his summing up Dr. Macdonald stressed that he would prefer to adopt an attitude of optimism to the social consequences of technological change rather than one of pessimism. Economic growth and change will proceed anyway. The important issues are what we do with new technology and how we adapt to it. The long-term consequences and opportunities are the matters to which universities, in particular, should be directing their attention. Politicians and others are concerned about the short-term consequences. We should not be concerned about losing jobs but about creating new ones and about retraining people to undertake these jobs. Above all, we must be positive in our attitudes. Society must rethink and possibly redefine what it means by work; universities must be reassuring about what constitutes a life relevant to society; and universities must encourage students to be aware of the social consequences of technological change.

TOPIC 1

THE SOCIAL CONSEQUENCES OF TECHNOLOGICAL INNOVATION

Co-ordinating Chairman's Commentary

on the Group's Discussions

Final Plenary Session
Friday, 19 August

Professor Sir BRUCE WILLIAMS (*Director of the Technical Change Centre and former Vice-Chancellor of the University of Sydney*): In the many countries of the Commonwealth the extent and consequences of technological innovation vary greatly. This variety was reflected in the range of our discussions and it added considerably to the quality and educational value of our five sessions.

We started with an outline of the major social consequences of past changes. These changes have transformed our capacity to produce food and to sustain a world population many times larger than Malthus thought possible, and have made possible even greater increases in the material wealth, and the range of consumer goods, in industrialised countries. Other features of industrialisation are urbanisation, and increases in health, leisure and education, and the extent and efficiency of scientific research. But the costs and benefits of technical change have been unevenly spread, and industrialisation has increased pollution, the destructive powers of weapons of war, and fluctuations in employment. At the present time there are great fears for the future of employment, for the stability of industrial (and 'post-industrial') societies, and a lurking suspicion that somehow new technologies evolve almost autonomously and force us to adapt to them.

Views such as those expressed by Heidegger, that technological forces have moved beyond man's will, did not surface in our discussions, but concern about the future of work and the possible need to change the very concept of work certainly did. Current fears that new technologies will abolish many more jobs than they will create are not new. Knowledge that new technologies provided the basis for recovery from the great depression of the 1880s and the still greater depression of the 1930s provided an antidote to a deep depression of expectations, but although we did not conduct a head count I suspect that a majority were inclined to doubt whether in this respect history would repeat itself.

Research is certainly a more extensive and intensive activity than in the thirties. The number of researchers in universities has grown greatly since world war two; improvements in scientific instruments have increased the productivity of research; and the increase in the proportion of 'science-based' forms of production, both military and civil, has encouraged greater public and industrial support for research. However we do not yet know whether this will bring more dramatic changes in employment than hitherto.

In the light of past and prospective changes in technology, we considered the implications for teaching and research. Two of the major problems for the design of degree courses are 'the knowledge explosion' and the increase of specialisation in teaching and research (which is in part a consequence of the growth of knowledge, and in part a consequence of the marked increase in the average size of staff in departments and the desire of staff to lecture on their special fields of knowledge). You will be disappointed but not greatly surprised to learn that we did not find an agreed solution. Some of us treated recent trends as a sensible response to a new situation where attempts to be jacks of all knowledge would end in being masters of none. Others took the view that a broad-based undergraduate education was still an important objective, and that we should look to postgraduate and post-employment courses for the creation of the masters. I noted with interest that differences of opinion cut right across differences of the subjects and countries of participants.

As a consequence of the current recession, and recent developments in electronics and biotechnology which appear to be bringing research and industrial innovation closer together, universities in industrialised countries are more frequently advised to come out of their ivory towers and make their research 'more relevant'. It seemed to me this has brought the views of delegates from the developed and developing countries on the role of university research much closer together than they had been at the Sydney and Edinburgh Congresses. The Australian Professor Birt in his paper did not go as far as the Indian Dr. Mitra in advocating more explicit social and economic relevance in research, but he went far enough to shock some Australian (and African, British, Indian and North American) participants, who asserted the continuing primacy of the purely private judgments of first-rate scholars on the choice of research projects.

97

In three of our five sessions there were lively discussions of the issues involved in calls for universities to develop more explicit research policies. How judge what to select and what to reject? Who should judge? What balance between internally- and externally-generated research? What moral and ethical considerations? Many doubts were expressed, but there was a general recognition that there will be an increasing societal interest in university research on grounds both moral and commercial, and that universities would be well advised to respond now to the challenge.

Dr. Mitra's proposal that universities should regard it as part of their mission to apply their research encouraged a very lively discussion. In response to a tendency to treat his proposal as dangerous, it was noted that through their experimental farms and teaching hospitals the rural and medical faculties had been both active and successful in applying their research. It was noted also that some faculties of science and engineering, in the more difficult field of industrial innovation, had (for example, in teaching companies) developed ways of helping to bridge the gap between research and applications without undermining fundamental research.

We ended, I think, with a fair measure of agreement that there would be increased pressures on universities to take a greater interest in doing (what powerful groups decided to be) relevant research and in the applications of results; with agreement also that more interest in applications could be of mutual benefit to higher education and the community, so long as there continued to be financial and institutional inventions and procedures which provided buffers between universities and business (as the University Grants Committee in Britain used to provide buffers between universities and governments). An important safeguard would be a variety of institutions (for example, universities, universities of technology, and institutes of technology) with recognised differences in values and roles.

The group also realised that funds for research into many social problems, created or intensified by that technical change which created the opportunities for more education and research, were more likely to be available if universities were recognised as having a capacity both to contribute to economic growth and to organise the multi-disciplinary research teams required for research into many of those major social problems.

In the second part of our first session on the cultural impact of industrialisation (introduced by Tom Symons), in the second session on patterns of development (Ungku Aziz) and in the final session on universities, government and industry (Ian Macdonald), the continuing criticisms of industrialism were outlined and the key question of objectives discussed.

Several participants from developing countries, while supporting innovations that reduce poverty and create opportunities to extend education and the social services, were also uneasy about the possible corrosive effects of industrialism on religion, the family and cohesive social traditions. There was reference also to the strong influence of religious revivals in some predominantly Muslim third-world societies in spreading doubts about the wisdom of adopting Western-style industrialism. It was, however, recognised that the leaders of such societies have not yet found a way to reconcile their desire to eat apples from the tree of technological knowledge and ensure a renaissance of spiritual life that would give more inner peace of mind than exists in Western industrialised societies. Perhaps people of all religions, their saints apart, see better things and approve them, yet follow the worse. Certainly views on the virtues and dangers of industrialism cut across the boundaries of societies and subject specialisms, and participants, whether from East or West, North or South, were agreed on the need to develop a sufficient understanding of technical change to increase the benefits and reduce the costs.

Why do governments allow so much pollution? Why is there not more research to establish a firm basis for environmental policy? Why is there a continuing tendency to excessive materialism? Why do nations risk the future of mankind by piling up nuclear weapons? I suppose that most of us in the group would give confident answers to those questions, though when faced with the further question—what then should be done?—we would be less confident. But we would agree again that universities would not be fulfilling their mission if their graduates did not work hard at finding some answers.

Group Discussions

TOPIC 2

THE CONTRIBUTION OF UNIVERSITIES TO INTEGRATED RURAL DEVELOPMENT

Co-ordinating Chairman: Professor R. W. STEEL
Former Principal of the University College of Swansea, and
Member of Council of the National University of Lesotho

Chief Rapporteur: Mr. V. J. CARNEY
Registrar of the University College of Swansea

For index to names, see p. 427

Sub-Topic 2(a)

ECONOMIC DEVELOPMENT AND ITS
SOCIAL CONSEQUENCES

Chairman: Professor R. W. STEEL
Former Principal of the University College of Swansea,
and Member of Council of the National University of Lesotho

Rapporteur: Mr. I. D. THOMAS
Senior Lecturer, School of Development Studies,
University of East Anglia

Monday, 15 August

Sir PETER SCOTT (*Chancellor, University of Birmingham*):

CONSERVATION AND DEVELOPMENT

Professor Steel has most kindly given me a fairly free hand in
what I talk about this afternoon. 'Economic development and its
social consequences' is our specific main topic, but I am no expert
in economics, nor yet in sociology. So in this talk I want to set
the scene in a more general sense for the whole week's discussions
and to give you some overlying principles to keep in mind when
we are considering the question of rural development. And I also
want to suggest the kind of contribution that can be made by
universities to the solution of one of two horrendous dilemmas
facing humanity.

The problems that confront us are, first, how to avoid blowing
ourselves up, and second, of equal urgency, how not to destroy
the life-support systems of our planet. Human welfare, quite
possibly even survival, has been and is being put at risk through
massive misuse of natural resources. This is so great and so
widespread that it is frustrating the efforts of many of the world's
poorer countries to achieve any lasting social and economic progress
at all; and often entirely offsetting the material benefits of progress

103

in the privileged nations as well, such as those in Europe. It is this second dilemma that I want to describe to you in greater detail.

It is a problem both of conservation—in the sense of the care and wise use of natural resources, and of development—in the sense, for example, of providing more goods for people, more food, more energy, clean water, and adequate housing. I am aware that both this statement of the problem and this definition of conservation are very much 'man-centred'. I personally believe that all other species of flora and fauna have as much right to their place on earth as does *Homo sapiens*. I do not believe that the only reasons for conserving nature are economic or scientific or aesthetic, in other words for the benefit of mankind, because I think there's a moral issue as well. So I do not believe we must assume that the only reason for the existence of other species is for our benefit, or that we should necessarily be free to use them for our purposes, and often use them up.

That being said, I have to acknowledge that pointing out the economic advantages of practising conservation—pointing out that no economic development will last more than a very few years if it is not based on a sustainable use of natural resources—does have the great advantage that it gives governments and business-men what they will consider rational, sensible reasons for conser-vation.

Conservation is not only about the prevention of extinction of species—important though that is. It also has a crucially important role to play in the solving of such key issues as threats to human health, threats to food and fuel supplies, and long-term threats to the biosphere and its life-support systems.

It becomes increasingly apparent that the huge quantities of chemicals used by our industrial civilisation produce significant hazards to human health. Some of these are well known and well documented. The 'Minamata' disease in Japan was only one dramatic illustration. Some risks have not yet been fully evaluated, although a great deal of evidence, much of it disconcerting, has been produced in recent years. The risks to whole communities in the United States and Europe from accumulations of toxic waste have produced a new wave of concern in industrialised countries. And, of course, people in developing countries are also being affected, some even more severely, by widespread use of agricul-tural chemicals. The average rural worker in central America carries about eleven times as much DDT in his tissues as the average citizen of the USA. Developing countries are becoming a dumping ground for many toxic chemical products which are banned or limited in their use in the industrialised countries which export them. Not much morality in that. Then there is the devastating effect of acid rain and the danger of an increased mutation rate in human beings arising from chemicals and radiation.

But by far the greatest immediate source of misery, disease and death is lack of fresh drinking water and adequate sanitation for millions of people in the developing world. This is the issue which should, I believe, hang most heavily on our consciences. The disease and misery it causes is not in the dim, distant future; it is happening *now*. And we can't plead lack of knowledge—we have the knowledge and the techniques to prevent it. Indeed it has been estimated that to provide clean water and adequate sanitation for all the people of the third world within the next decade would require some £15 million a day in increased development assistance, which is 10% of the amount spent each day on cigarettes, and less than 2% of what is spent on armaments. There could scarcely be a more cogent indictment of our generation and how it sets its priorities.

In addition to the acute and immediate misery which millions in the developing world suffer from water-borne diseases, there is the growing spectre of starvation through the undermining and destruction of the ecosystems which the people rely on for their food. Yet literally millions of hectares of productive land are now being destroyed by desertification, soil erosion and salination. At the same time growing populations, and the need to increase per capita consumption, will increase the pressures on food supplies for the foreseeable future. Current food surpluses in some of the principal food exporting countries should not allow us to be lulled into complacency. First of all there is no assurance that such surpluses will continue indefinitely: indeed there is now evidence that, for example, the productive capacity of the great plains of North America is being jeopardized by ecologically unsound utilisation. And in any event it is *not* feasible for developing countries to rely on the availability of surpluses from exporting countries to meet the basic food needs of their people.

I would like to mention the dangers arising from destruction of species of plants and animals with the consequent loss of genetic stock. Many of them are important elements or potential elements in maintaining food production.

Developing countries are also suffering widespread destruction of forests through unsound timber harvesting practices, clearing for farming and settlement and the continuing need to reach ever farther for their supplies of fuel wood for cooking and heating.

Closely related to the issue of food supply is the basic need of the majority of people in the developing world to rely on fuel wood as their principal energy supply. Although for the industrialised countries awareness of an impending energy crisis has receded into the background, its full implications for the developing world are only now beginning to be appreciated. While considerable progress is being made to increase reforestation and create tree plantations that can be operated on a sustained yield basis, this still comes nowhere near meeting projected fuel wood needs and the prospect is for mounting pressures on diminishing resources.

And now for the long-term threats to the biosphere. This category of issues is in many ways the most difficult to deal with. First of all, the risks to which they give rise are farther from us, both in space and in time. It is harder to obtain precise information on causes and effects. And the trade-offs involve immediate costs which fall unequally on some, to avoid risks which are likely to arise, if at all, only in the more distant future. However, these too are risks which by their nature could be decisive for the future of the human race on this planet, and for the ability of the biosphere to sustain life as we know it. And in many cases by the time we have all the evidence we need to be *sure* of what is happening to us, it may already be too late.

I am speaking of such issues as threats to the ozone layer in the atmosphere and the increase in the carbon dioxide content of the atmosphere, the filter which determines the heat balance at the earth's surface on which climate depends. Also pollution of the waters of our planet—the oceans, lakes, river systems, estuaries and ground water—is quietly but relentlessly encroaching on our basic life-support systems. These systems have a high degree of resilience. but as Maurice Strong has pointed out, we must realise that the margins within which human life can be sustained are also very narrow. Indeed, as our own knowledge penetrates further into the universe, there is still no evidence that the conditions we have on planet earth exist anywhere else, although on the basis of cosmic mathematics we may speculate that they may. And we know that even on our own planet conditions conducive to human life have only existed for a relatively short period of our geological history. So we must realise that life on earth is a very rare and precious thing. And if we don't yet know all that we need to know about what we are doing to the earth's life-support systems, we do know that our own activities are impinging on the vital margins of these systems in ways that can alter them decisively.

The role of conservation in helping to address these threats is set out in detail in the *World Conservation Strategy*. I expect and hope that some of you will be familiar with this important document, but maybe not all of you will be. It was published three years ago by the International Union for Conservation of Nature and Natural Resources (IUCN), with the help of the World Wildlife Fund (WWF), and the United Nations Environment Programme (UNEP), and it explains the importance of natural resource conservation in the development process. The only development that is sound and sustainable is that which preserves the *integrity of the ecological systems* on which the health and the food and the fuel supplies of people depend.

As I see it, the role of conservation in development is to intervene in the development process in a positive way. It is not to stop development, but to facilitate the kind of development which will ultimately produce the most benefits to the people concerned on a basis that is *sustainable*. Development is a complex process in which the interaction of economic, technical, social, cultural and political factors produce results which are often different from those intended—or at least intended by any one of those who are pursuing a single purpose. In our own programme we have learned that to preserve a species of wild animal or plant we have to take account of what is happening in the habitat in which it lives, the pressures on that habitat from the people who depend on it for their livelihood or recreation, the motivations of these people, and the alternatives available to them. We must direct our efforts to supporting those people in their choice of the alternatives that will produce the soundest results in terms of development and conservation objectives.

The *World Conservation Strategy* represents a change in attitude. The confident assertion of the 1950s and 1960s that man would find solutions to *all* his problems has been supplanted by a new humility, born of the realisation that even man's most astonishing achievements cannot offset the disastrous devastation we have wrought upon so much of the earth and upon so many of its plants and animals. What the *Strategy* says quite clearly is that only by working *with* nature can man survive; conservation is in the mainstream of human progress. We must recognise that we are a part of nature and must resolve that all our actions take this into account. Only on that basis can the fragile life-support systems of our planet be safeguarded, only thus can the development of our own species go forward.

All these considerations put you, as educators of the future leaders and decision-makers of the world, in an absolutely crucial role. I have never been a pessimist, but maintaining an optimistic frame of mind depends on the assumption that the next generation will be able to tackle all these problems which we of this generation have bequeathed to them. The future of our world will depend upon their initiative, resourcefulness, and far-sightedness. It is up to their educators to give them the tools with which to display these qualities.

Virtually all university faculties are involved. These issues must be brought before natural scientists, social and political scientists, lawyers, economists, doctors, linguists and geographers, and all these curricula may need revising to take the issues I have been talking about into account. Our goal should be for every educated citizen throughout the world to be aware of the fundamental importance of natural resource conservation to the development process.

Dr. D. M. E. Curtis (*Lecturer, Institute of Local Government Studies, University of Birmingham*), and

Professor K. J. Davey (*Professor of Development Administration and Associate Director, Institute of Local Government Studies, University of Birmingham*):

The Record

Over the past three decades economic development policies in rural areas have largely concentrated upon increasing agricultural output and productivity. Output has risen by 2–3% per annum world-wide, but keeping pace overall with the appetites of the growing population[1]. Rural economies have developed in less recorded ways as well—in construction, processing, infrastructure, commerce, transportation and miscellaneous services. But, except in the oil-producing states, growth in non-farm output has been closely related to and dependent upon increases in agricultural production.

Global figures conceal considerable differences in rural fortunes. In the 1970s agricultural production grew 50% faster in middle income countries than in low income countries. Within countries the benefits were distributed variably between areas and income groups. Increases in output have been due far more to rising productivity than to expansion of cultivation. The main ingredients have been the use of improved varieties of seed, irrigation or

---

[1]Statistical data, unless otherwise stated, is drawn from the 1981 and 1982 World Development Reports.

ground water and fertilisers. By and large the wealthier and more influential farmers have had disproportionate access to these opportunities. Moreover the greater profitability of farming has encouraged owners to use land they have previously rented or share-cropped, and to acquire or lease additional land where possible, leading frequently to the concentration of effective land use in fewer hands.

In high income countries, increasing farm size combined with mechanisation and use of herbicides have led to drastic reduction in the numbers employed on the land; the agricultural share of the labour force is only one-third of its 1960s level. Such an absolute decline has not yet occurred significantly in third-world countries, but agricultural employment has not kept pace with the growth of rural population. Increased population pressure has also been associated in the low income countries with environmental deterioration, illustrated by growing salinity, soil erosion, loss of soil fertility, shortages of grazing, firewood or building materials.

Another distinction between the economic fortunes of the rural population in rich and poorer countries is the impact of the terms of trade. Most primary producers in third-world countries have suffered from declining international terms of trade. A Mali farmer has to sell five times as much cotton to buy a bicycle as in 1976. In many countries this is exacerbated by internal policies such as artificial rates of exchange, tariffs forcing up consumer-good prices, taxation of agricultural exports.

And so rising rural production—both on and off the farm—has not eradicated a large core of intense rural poverty. The World Bank estimates that those crudely defined as 'absolutely poor' number one billion, and that 90% of them are in rural areas.

The Public Response

During the last ten to fifteen years public policies and programmes have shown far greater awareness of the social consequences of development, and have sought to address rural poverty directly. The poverty focus of public investment has had four characteristics—

(1) An emphasis on meeting 'basic needs' in social infrastructure—a widespread diffusion of elementary education, primary health care, potable water supplies, for example—emphasising minimal service to the many rather than high quality provision to the few.

(2) The development of production packages of credit, seeds, water supplies, extension, etc., specifically targeted at the poorest

rural families; these may well cover not merely the conventional export of cereal crops, but horticultural or small livestock husbandry accessible to those with little or no land.

(3) Integrated development programmes seeking to attack the broad range of constraints—agricultural, tenurial, educational, medical and infrastructural—curbing the opportunities of the rural poor.

(4) Use of broader measures than simple gross domestic product to gauge progress, particularly social statistics relating to illiteracy, malnutrition and the paucity of basic household goods.

The experience of basic needs programmes has often been relatively successful. Adult literacy in third-world countries has increased overall from 30% to 50% in three decades; the average life expectancy in low income countries has risen by 15 years over the same period. But the experience of large-scale rural development or poverty-focused production programmes has been far less encouraging.

There are several reasons. The first is the misplaced assumption that the technology which produced spectacular growth in the Green Revolutions of the 1960s has only to be repackaged with new delivery systems to reach the target population. Experience shows that the needs and production resources of the rural poor often require new approaches. Then there is the bureaucratic complexity of multi-sectoral approaches—the difficulty of getting different disciplines and departments to harmonise their allocations of time and money and pursue common objectives at specific places and times. Another reason is the lack of political and bureaucratic commitment to real discrimination in favour of the poor when programmes reach field level, the continual diversion of economic benefits to other income groups.

Again there is the difficulty of maintaining momentum in programmes inevitably requiring a long gestation period. At national level much of the investment has been debt-financed; servicing these loans without much direct cost recovery, together with the maintenance burden of basic needs services, has considerably added to the budgetary strain experienced by many third-world countries during the current recession.

Most daunting perhaps is the apparent intractability of rural poverty, the difficulty of breaking through the cycle of deprivation, analysed by Robert Chambers as the mutual reinforcement of physical weakness, vulnerability, geographical and political isolation, lack of productive assets and absence of bargaining power.

The consequence of these relative disappointments has been some retreat by public agencies from these fields of investment.

110

Fewer large-scale foreign aid programmes are now being planned in the general rural development field. Governments are placing greater emphasis on pricing incentives, as opposed to more direct assistance to farmers. Insofar as public assistance—credit, tube-wells, seeds, fertilisers and pesticides, etc.—remain on offer, there is less direct field delivery by government. It is up to farmers to organise their own access and delivery, or to private firms or co-operatives to act as distributors. This is not a total abnegation of a poverty focus, nor a total return to the growth obsessions of the 1950s and 1960s, more a change in emphasis and degree.

Within this broad scene the role of the non-governmental organisation—international, national and local—has assumed increasing importance. Such agencies are often more attuned to the demands of micro-level schemes. Small organisations are better able, as a whole, to adopt multi-sectoral approaches, being less compartmentalised internally. Non-governmental organisations (NGOs) are not necessarily dependent totally on private funds. They can be useful vehicles for public money. They can also act as intermediaries, mobilising groups of the rural poor to bid for the resources available through government programmes. Which brings us to the role of universities as organisations on the boundaries of the public and private sectors.

The University Contribution

The move from the 1970s to the 1980s has been one to an era of tighter resources and more selective investment. The ready money of the aid process over the last couple of decades will not be so apparent over the next few years at least.

In the last three decades the world has learned many of the answers to increasing rural production in gross terms, though more so in 'wet' than 'dry' land and in respect of cereals than of other crops. It has also learned that the benefits of such development are most unevenly distributed, that a hard core of rural poverty is scarcely affected, and that many can be positively worse off. Solutions to these problems have not been established with any degree of confidence or universality. This leaves an enormous field of research and development for universities to till.

Two dimensions critical to the social impact of rural development are changes in rural technology and in the nature of the institutional framework for development. Technology can be selected or developed specifically for its social impact. For example, a technology which demands an increasing supply of nitrogenous fertilisers inevitably relies upon credit and therefore credit-worthiness; one

111

which exploits nitrogen fixation is more widely accessible, if not yet as productive. Ground water may be preferable to irrigation in that the benefits of investment can be more widely diffused territorially, and poorer farmers may be less vulnerable to the arbitrary control over water flows exercised by remote officials or the richer farmers 'up stream'.

Secondly, institutions at all levels are vital to the success of rural development projects. Many of the shortcomings of rural development projects in the 'ready money' era can be traced back to the poor development of institutions through which target groups could gain and control access to the resources being channelled towards the rural areas. Particular trouble spots have included the institutionalisation of credit and arrangements for the maintenance of all kinds of plant and equipment, from irrigation canals to village domestic water supplies. At grass-roots levels there is evidence of the weakness of farmer or artisan organisations; at higher levels of area management, a lack of adequate attention to the requirements of financing a recurrent budget. An exploration of institutional alternatives is sorely needed as a counter-balance to economic analysis.

These then are two dimensions of development to which universities should be devoting attention. Universities cannot tackle them within the confines of a single discipline. The technical feasibility of a plant trial has to be supported by the economic appraisal of the effects of innovation upon a farm budget, or the sociological understanding of its impact upon the pattern of family labour. Current concern with silviculture as a means of combating shortages of fuel wood, building material and animal fodder requires the development of new institutional arrangements for owning and controlling village wood lots. An academic concern for rural poverty means that technological experiment needs to focus upon exploiting resources available to the poor (solar energy, for example), to seek substitutes for other resources such as wood fuel of which they are increasingly deprived, and to improve the less productive dry land crops and farming techniques upon which they largely depend.

The university contribution to rural development calls for an integration not only of disciplinary understandings, but also of activity—of research, teaching and advice.

For a start, universities are now addressing themselves to a wider audience, becoming increasingly involved in in-service training, adult education and post-experience teaching. Continuing education means addressing practitioners as well as pre-career students. This makes its own demands on supporting research. It reinforces the need for multi-disciplinary approaches, for the conscientious practitioner cannot limit his attention to one facet of the situation with which he has to deal. It emphasises the significance of institutions, which condition his professional responses. It makes secondary research equally as necessary and respectable as primary research. It means that teaching and its research support have to be action-oriented. Rural development requires the type of applied and experimental research-cum-consultancy which is becoming a growing feature of university activities generally. This means extending its field work from the laboratory and the research station to the farm and the village. It means working with particular rural communities, just as science and engineering faculties are now working with manufacturers in 'science parks'.

These are not entirely new forms of behaviour for universities. Nevertheless, several of the types of involvement in research, development, dissemination and training, which we have outlined, will present a considerable challenge to universities as conventionally established:

(1) multi-disciplinary work requires inter-departmental structures if it is to be kept within the ambit of existing faculties and not to disappear into new institutes;

(2) a substantial field presence needs a new approach to staffing departments and to the incorporation of research experience into undergraduate degree work;

(3) practical field collaboration with government and NGOs may need new sets of relationships;

(4) new patterns of departmental work may require more flexible types of financing and financial management.

The challenge to universities is to overcome their own institutional constraints, to bridge the disciplinary gap between natural and social scientists, to follow experimentation through to the farm level, to bring the practitioner—the government veterinarian, the agri-businessman and the farmer himself or herself—into the academic dialogue. All these purposes and, above all, the traditional social conscience of the university can be served by a direct involvement with rural communities, by exploiting the enormous potential role of the NGO in rural development.

113

*Professor B. L. PANDITHARATNE (*Vice-Chancellor, University of Peradeniya, Sri Lanka*):

NEGOMBO FISHERMEN:
A Study of the Impact of Mechanisation of Craft, Rural Change and Development

In the South Asian realm fisheries resources have been under-utilized because of several social, cultural and religious constraints. In the past three decades, however, several developmental measures have been undertaken to augment fish production as a means to supplement the nutritional levels and to improve the living standards of the fishing community. Some of these measures were mechanisation of craft, adoption of nylon nets, improved artefacts and gear and methods and techniques of fishing and several institutional changes in the marketing, transportation, curing and storing of fish.

Studies of Firth (1966), Alexander (1975, 1976), De Silva (1977) and Stirret (1980) have emphasised a type of polarization and economic differentiation within the fishing community. The Food and Agriculture Organisation (FAO) has provided certain insights to the problems and trends of small-scale fishermen (Bay of Bengal programme reports).

Negombo is one of the important fishing centres along the west coast of Sri Lanka (just 20 miles north of Colombo). This study of the Negombo fishermen (based on 3742 fishermen in the surrounding 10 villages) attempts to indicate the impact of mechanisation of craft, improved methods and techniques and institutional innovations, and their consequent effects on the quality of life of the fishermen.

Part II of the study describes the fishing industry and technology around the 1950s—the craft (mainly the outrigger canoe), methods and techniques, artefacts and gear used, and the nature of specialization among the villages.

The traditional fishing industry depended entirely on the elements which limited the number of fishing days, and the seasons. The Roman Catholic church exercised a significant influence on all aspects of the fishermen's life pattern, particularly in respect of the organisation of the sales of fish through the auction system (*rende*) at the auction places (*lellams*). At the auctions the church collected the *tithes* (a voluntary contribution of 10% of the auction value). These funds also supported the maintenance of the church,

*Although Professor Panditharatne was unable to attend the Congress copies of his paper, of which a summary is given here, were available to those participating in this Group Discussion.

the parish priest, the ceremonies and several other welfare measures.

The women also played a very active role in helping the men as regards transportation of fish, as vendors, in the repair of nets, in decision-making as the keeper of the purse and in the general upkeep of their homes.

The state's modernisation programme since 1960 showed phases of hope and success, failure and despair, and it had to recheck and readjust the programmes to ensure their success. Some of the direct results of the state's policies were: (*a*) the gradual decline of the influence of the church on the fishing industry; (*b*) the prolife-ration of several state-sponsored industries in the supply of motor engines, boat-building and boat repairs, financing of craft and artefacts, marketing, insurance and welfare measures; and (*c*) the growth of several private enterprises.

Although the production of fish was highly variable, Negombo produced approximately 10% of Sri Lanka's production of marine fish. In the 1950s the entire fishing operations were carried out by the outrigger. In the 1980s more than 90% of the entire production was carried out by the $3\frac{1}{2}$-ton mechanised craft and fibreglass outboard craft, and only about 10% by the traditional outrigger. Further, the villages showed some degree of specialisation—as, for example, Pitipana and Grand Street in the use of the $3\frac{1}{2}$-ton mechanised craft; Sea Street in the use of fibreglass outboard craft; and the large outrigger was used in Grand Street and Munnakkare, and the small boats in lagoon fisheries in the villages fronting the Negombo lagoon.

The price of fish at the auctions at the *lellamas* depended on certain variables: (*a*) the size, type and condition of fish; (*b*) frequency pattern and the flow of fish; and (*c*) competition among bidders and buyers. The bid raising at the auctions was a potent factor in the determination of prices. In the auction system, however, the *malu mudalaly* or his agent held a virtual monopoly, and the state, though in principle operating the *Prathamicas* on co-operative lines none the less seemed not to be bothered about the monopolistic trends because of their long practice and acceptance by the fishermen, the auctioneer and the buyers.

Have the modernisation policies affected the Negombo fisher-men? Levels of education, age structure, housing, quality of life, social status, attitudes and values, and communication and mobility pattern have changed quite considerably during the period 1960–1980. Contrary to the popular notion of 'illiterate fishermen', a sample survey in 1980 indicated that approximately 60% had formal education up to standard 5, 39% to standard 10, and 1%

115

had passed the General Certificate of Education (Ordinary level). With education they have become increasingly receptive to innovations in the mechanisation of craft and methods of fishing and have improved their knowledge and skills in respect of the behaviour and migration in the physical and biological environment in which they fished. They were also more responsive to institutional policies and procedures. It was also evident that a proliferating class of the educated children of fishermen was establishing closer contacts with the children of the traditional land-owning non-fishing middle class, a trend which indicated towards greater social integration in the villages.

In age structure, one third belonged to the group between 17 and 30 years. They accepted fishing because of better incomes and improved living conditions and with the desire of looking after their parents. The group 31–44 years—the largest group (44%)—gave the industry stability and continuity; and the group 40–60 years constituted 21%—the experienced able men who propped up the morale of the younger groups, especially in periods of distress, and kept the age-old traditions alive.

Conspicuous changes were noticed in housing and improved living standards. Land values spiralled upwards and land sales increased which gave rise to the house-owning class of fishermen which emerged side by side with the traditional land- and house-owners. The state also improved the infrastructure of these housing areas, providing electricity, pipe-borne water, water-seal lavatories which improved the sanitary conditions and prevented the incidents of gastro-intestinal disease. Based on varying levels of status, power affluence and effects owned and found in the household, a three-fold classification was suggested:

(*a*) an élite class of *malu mudalalys* and their agents (12 to 15%) had well-furnished, solidly constructed houses, owned vehicles, and their women-folk and children wore gold jewellery;

(*b*) the bulk of the fishermen (60–70%) had two-room cottage-type houses with separate kitchens and with limited furniture and personal effects;

(*c*) 10–15% lived in hutments made out of cadjan with very few household effects.

Education, mechanised craft, higher incomes, have changed their attitudes and values, especially in respect of their relationships with the church, state and society. They no longer felt obliged as a matter of sacred duty to pay the *tithes* to the church, though as a measure of goodwill and maintenance of tradition they continued to contribute 1%. The parish priest was now looked upon as a person to perform the religious rites and ceremonies. His former authoritarian role had declined. They patronized the state institutions as they were beneficial but criticised the bureaucratic procedures and were cunning enough to defraud the state its dues and even absconded from meeting their obligations.

The fishermen have also become more mobile. Nearly half of the craft of Sea Street and Duwa fishermen migrated to fishing locations according to the sequence of weather and climate pattern. Most of them travelled to purchase boat equipment and materials, made pilgrimages and frequented the cinema for recreation. The accepted role of arranged marriages for children by the parents has changed for marriages by choice. Family planning was practised but not talked about. In general, women and children were better dressed than men.

Unlike other occupations it was difficult to assess the income of fishermen as the catches varied widely from day to day, season to season, year to year, according to the different craft, methods and techniques used, and the conditions of a fluctuable market. However, based on the different types of craft, methods and techniques used, data on income and expenses of a specific fishing day have been presented to show the range of variations and the uncertainties of incomes.

This study, as its conclusion, sought the opinions of the fishermen as regards issues and problems, and what they suggested as possible solutions:

(*a*) Increasing cost of fuel, engines, spare parts, gear and artefacts and repair costs. They felt that the high cost of inputs despite the increase in the price of fish has reduced their incomes, and, taking into account the uncertainties of fish catches, rendered them bankrupt. They expected the state to subsidise the extra costs, to introduce and train the fishermen in a craft with which it was possible to economise on fuel (a combination of motor and sail craft).

(*b*) Extension of pelagic species owing to over-fishing in limited areas by $3\frac{1}{2}$-ton mechanised craft was another problem. They expressed the hope that, if they could venture out to deeper waters and extend the fishing areas, this may be solved. But this meant more powerful craft capable of longer stays and combined operations at greater depths (16 to 60 fathoms), which necessitated a different type of trained fishermen and heavy capital investment which only the state could sponsor.

(*c*) Fish marketing. They preferred the existing system of auctions with fluctuable prices than a fixed price system based on weight of fish. They considered the *malu mudalaly* acceptable and benevolent as he raised the prices at the auctions.

117

(*d*) Closely tied up with the expansion of fishing, ancillary industries and activities have proliferated and in certain cases the non-fishermen entrepreneurs have made rich incomes. The fishermen expressed an open view and did not mind others getting rich ('live and let live attitude').

(*e*) The fishermen, while appreciative of the state's sponsorship of developmental activities, resented the bureaucratic procedures and hoped for a less formal approach at the grass-roots level.

(*f*) The younger educated fishermen wished for 'status' (as in traditional society their status was relatively low). They wished the state to sponsor a scheme of 'gentlemen-fishermen' (similar to gentlemen-farmers) in deep-sea fishing in more powerful craft involved in advanced methods of fishing at greater depths, and expected a salary to ensure a sense of security, continuity and status.

This study affirms the success of the state's modernisation programme for the small-scale fishermen of Negombo. Consequently, the morphology of these villages has changed quite considerably in social, economic, cultural and political aspects and in upgrading the quality of life.

DISCUSSION

A. Sir Peter Scott identified two global problems: (1) how to avoid blowing ourselves up, and (2) how not to destroy the life support systems of the planet. He concentrated on the latter. His concern was with both (1) conservation—how to husband natural resources, and (2) development—how to provide goods for people.

With reference to the United Nations Conference on Human Environments (Stockholm) he examined the extinction of species, threats to human health from chemical sources and from the failure to provide and safeguard water supplies, threats to food and fuel supplies, and long-term threats to the biosphere such as interference with the ozone layer and pollution of the oceans. The *World Conservation Strategy*, published three years ago, emphasised the need to maintain the integrity of ecological systems, and Sir Peter saw conservation as part of the process of development on a sustainable basis. The universities train those who will have to tackle the environmental problems we bequeath them and who will have to establish sustainable systems.

SUB-TOPIC 2 (A): ECONOMIC DEVELOPMENT

QUESTIONS AND COMMENTS related to—

(1) The key factor in resource depletion is consumption levels (Dr. B. D. Sharma (North-Eastern Hill)).

(2) The universities are now training those who will need to tackle the problems of the next 30 or 40 years (Dr. S. Mookerjee (Kalyani)).

(3) Attention must be given to the absorptive capacity of resource use systems; in some areas despite very intensive resource use the rapidly increasing demands threaten to disrupt the system—as in the irrigated lands of the Punjab (Mr. H. Dickinson (Edinburgh) and Dr. S. S. Johl (Punjabi)).

(4) Population growth is rapid and, whereas we welcome development that increases the expectation of life at birth, in countries such as India and elsewhere population growth should be controlled because it is one of the principal causes of the dilemma (Dr. R. C. Shukla (Bhopal) and Sir Peter Scott).

B. Dr. Curtis and Professor Davey provided an overview of the major socio-economic issues in rural development and posed current challenges to the universities.

Although agricultural output and productivity has increased dramatically in recent decades there remains a large core of intense rural poverty. Population has increased rapidly, the international terms of trade have been unfavourable for many primary producers and what economic development has occurred has often intensified income inequalities. Attempts have been made to tackle rural poverty directly with public investment. However breaking the 'cycle of deprivation' has not proved easy, and public agencies (national governments and the World Bank) have withdrawn somewhat from direct intervention in rural areas.

The universities have a role to play in research and development designed to improve the quality of rural development projects and to find solutions for complex problems. This requires an increased emphasis on: (1) multi-disciplinary work; (2) greater participation in the field; (3) closer collaboration with government and non-governmental organisations; (4) more flexible funding arrangements for university work. All of these demand new structures and institutional arrangements by the universities to foster more direct involvement with rural communities.

QUESTIONS AND COMMENTS related to—

(1) The universities should concentrate on (a) training extension personnel and encouraging international co-operatoin in research—e.g. in agriculture (Professor R. B. Shukla (Gujarat Agricultural)); (b) primary research—at least this should not be neglected in the course of encouraging multi-disciplinary research (Professor Sir James Stewart (Lincoln College)); (c) training the critical faculties of students who will then work effectively, in whatever capacity/institution they are employed (Professor John Ashton (Newcastle upon Tyne)).

(2) Examples were given of university participation in village development in Bangladesh (Professor A. M. Patwari (Bangladesh U. of Engineering and Technology)), India (Dr. M. Aram (Gandhigram Rural Institute)) and Lesotho (Mr. A. M. Setšabi (National U. of Lesotho)).

(3) Also university staff were members of state planning commissions (*e.g.* Dr. M. Aram (Gandhigram Rural Institute)—Tamil Nadu) or served time as ministers concerned with rural development (Bangladesh).

(4) Micro-level planning (district, block, village) remains as an area for research and development by comparison with macro-level planning (in India, Dr. M. Aram (Gandhigram Rural Institute)).

(5) The apparent inertia of some rural communities and the transfer of resources from rural to urban communities are sustained by powerful social and political forces which need to be more fully researched (Dr. B. D. Sharma (North-Eastern Hill)). Intervention sometimes creates disorganisation (Dr. Sharma).

(6) The universities must be fearless in speaking out on public issues such as toxic wastes (Professor R. B. Shukla (Gujarat Agricultural)); disarmament (Dr. M. Aram (Gandhigram Rural Insititute)); the costs and benefits of schemes (Sir James Stewart (Lincoln College)); and rapid population growth (Dr. R. C. Shukla (Bhopal) and Sir Peter Scott).

Sub-Topic 2(b)

CHANGE AND DEVELOPMENT OF
THE RURAL SPACE

Chairman: Professor K. B. DICKSON
Vice-Chancellor of the University of Cape Coast

Rapporteur: Mr. E. K. KIGOZI
Executive Secretary, Inter-University Council
for East Africa

Tuesday, 16 August

Professor M. D. I. CHISHOLM (*Head of Department of Geography, University of Cambridge*): Universities are generally identified with the urban sector of national economies: they are, almost invariably, located in cities; and the values and attitudes embodied in universities are essentially urban. This fact probably does not matter too much in a highly urbanised nation such as Britain, where many of the pressures on the countryside arise from the very success of the town-based economy, and where there are well-established agencies whose functions are to cope with the problems of agricultural innovation, recreational pressures, etc. Similarly, in countries such as Canada, Australia and New Zealand, where agriculture remains a major source of employment and space is plentiful, but also possessing a well-developed urban structure, the urban qualities of universities is not a matter of major concern. The problems of rural development may differ from those in Britain, but call for rather similar responses from universities.

The position is quite different in my third group of countries, in the Indian sub-continent, Malaysia and most nations in Africa. These are essentially rural societies, albeit with some or many substantial cities, and assumptions about the role of universities valid for the first two categories of nation do not necessarily hold. The key to better standards of living must lie in improvements in the agricultural sector. Therefore agriculture, on the one hand, and the whole range of rural issues, on the other, ought to be proportionately more important in the universities than need be

121

the case in Britain, western Europe and the USA. At the same time, the way universities are structured may need to be different, and their role in society is likely to be somewhat different also.

Clearly there is need for basic scientific research akin to that conducted elsewhere, as exemplified by the post-war development of hybrid wheat and rice, leading to the so-called 'green revolution'. Furthermore the requisite scale of this research effort, and the associated teaching, must be large, given the magnitude of the problems faced, the range of environments and the diversity of crops and livestock.

Post-war experience suggests that, however important rice, wheat and cattle may be as food sources, and also cotton, vegetable oils, etc. as cash crops, serious attention ought to be given to the less fashionable products, such as yams, sweet potatoes, cassava, millet and Guinea corn, and local varieties of livestock. For example, it is only recently that a sustained effort has been made to see whether indigenous herbivores might be better sources of meat in the regions of savanna grassland than cattle of European origin. If non-fashionable crops and livestock are to be experimented with, the urban-based universities must not cut off their rural roots. At the very least university staff will have to maintain their sources of traditional knowledge and their first-hand experience of 'field' conditions. An object lesson for me was watching a woman in New Guinea harvesting sweet potatoes with a digging stick. My first reaction was of amazement at the laborious and inefficient method. My second was of wonder at the ecological sanity. By locating each tuber individually she was able to obtain her harvest while leaving intact the trailing foliage that entirely covered the ground, protecting it against erosion. Subsequently, near Kundiawa in the Highlands, I had some inkling why a one-thousand-foot slope approaching 45° could be cultivated from top to bottom without any terracing and without overt signs of serious soil loss. Entirely to understand this feat of cultivation would require intimate knowledge of the whole farming ecology and associated social systems. Thus if cognisance is to be taken of the lessons available from indigenous practices staff and students must maintain close links with the 'real' world outside the universities' purlieus.

There is plenty of evidence to show that in the poorer countries the dissemination of new practices may be slow, may be a task as hard or even harder than discovering/inventing the practice itself. In Britain the necessity for universities actively to engage in agricultural extension work has declined, to be replaced by attempts to foster closer links between universities and industrial firms. In the 'third world' the priority is almost certainly the other way round, with an urgent need for universities to be involved in actively promoting the diffusion of knowledge through the rural areas.

Actively to facilitate the diffusion of new practices requires a deep understanding of the societies that comprise that population. There are many reports of social taboos relating to seemingly curious things, such as the colour of a pig. Much more important, it is necessary to recognise that changes in farm practice often imply quite radical changes in social structure and/or the criteria of social esteem. One of the traditional marks of a good husband-man is his store of seed grain. If hybrid varieties do not breed true, seed-grain must be purchased annually and this particular symbol of esteem is removed.

In short, while good science is essential it seems abundantly clear that it must be tailored to the objective needs of the populace on the one hand, and to what they can reasonably be expected to accept and use. In the present-day ugly jargon, 'appropriate technology' is needed. This is not a particularly glamorous road to follow. In order to follow it, the links with the rural sector must be fostered, not broken.

Universities face a quite general problem, that they are institutions providing for upward mobility of the populace. In the United Kingdom context this is viewed in class occupational terms, as young people seek to move from the blue-collar occupations of their fathers into the white-collar professions. When I was in Nigeria in the mid-1960s the same aspirations were virtually synonymous with escaping from 'the bush' into urban occupations. I believe that these perfectly understandable motives still prevail, not only in Nigeria but in many other countries.

This suggests that the task facing universities in my third group of countries, in so far as it relates to change and development of rural space, is in fact much more challenging and difficult than is the case in the first and second groups. In this context we may note the problem of disciplinary boundaries. The pressures of academic sociology and career structure make for a very conservative view of disciplinary demarcations. The prevailing views originated in the universities of western Europe. Even within this domain there is chronic dissatisfaction. Occasionally dissatisfaction becomes acute. One such phase, when it was possible in part to re-draw the academic map, was the post-Robbins era of expansion. Several of the new universities broke away from the traditional departmental form of organisation and established schools of biological science, environmental studies, etc. Observing these experiments one

123

is forced to conclude that, while their achievements have been impressive, the success has not been unqualified. However the lesson which I want to extract is the following. If it is felt necessary to experiment with the academic map within a nation such as Britain, then by the same token it is likely that the academic configuration as between nations ought to vary. In the context of my third group of countries, I am led to question the division between physical science and social science—more specifically, between agricultural science and rural sociology. If rural change and development is to be intelligently fostered, it seems to me that there must be a strong cadre of graduates who have a sensibility for *both* of these major aspects of rural development.

A practical way of implementing this approach would be to establish a university field station, not necessarily in an area that could be regarded as a show-case for successful development, but where both success and failure can be studied under circumstances that represent the way a sizeable segment of the rural population actually lives. I have in mind an analogy with the field stations that some universities maintain for the study of natural phenomena. Such a field station, in the present context, would be different from a university farm or an agricultural experimental station. It would be located in a normal farming area and allow staff and students to mount programmes to monitor agricultural practices and the progress of changes, programmes to investigate the social dynamics, and other related matters, including the deliberate introduction of innovations. The research conducted at such a field station, and the field experience of students, would be an integral part of the work done on campus and would provide one practical means for combating the urban bias of universities.

In a brief paper such as this, which is intended to provide the basis for discussion, it would be inappropriate to try to end with a single conclusion. However the central theme of the paper is the proposition that in this diverse world there is no single model of how universities should be structured. To the extent that the needs of society do vary from one nation to another, so ought the scale and nature of academic endeavour in the various fields vary. All that I have attempted is to review some issues where the taken-for-granted assumptions need to be questioned. This review does lead to a practical suggestion.

The Association of Commonwealth Universities could play an active role in fostering rural development by providing a mechanism for collecting and disseminating examples of universities' 'best practice' in the way they are organised internally and relate to the external world. Vice-chancellors and heads of departments are busy people and do not always have the time to work from first principles to build appropriate structures and modes of operation. If the Association would collect and distribute examples of 'best practice', the Commonwealth universities could learn from each other and, individually, consider whether to adapt their structures in the light of experience elsewhere.

Professor A. ABDULLAHI (*Vice-Chancellor, Ahmadu Bello University*): The Commonwealth includes many countries with very diverse historical, political, social and economic backgrounds. But they have many common goals which they strive to achieve in order to improve the welfare of their citizens. Professor Chisholm's valuable paper looked in a realistic way at the different categories of states within the Commonwealth. This is the only way in which there can be meaningful discussion on rural development in Commonwealth countries.

A number of the key words and phrases call for careful definition, such as 'development', 'rural area' and 'integration'. There is a great deal of difference between, for example, a rural area in Britain in terms of the level of its infrastructural development compared with urban centres and rural areas in countries such as India or Nigeria. The term 'integrated' as a concept means a package of components necessary to achieve maximum benefit for the development of the people living in areas affected by such programmes. Rural development is not confined to agricultural considerations but it embraces every aspect of the community and affects a whole range of the government officials working in such an area.

The Nigerian experience is of particular relevance to consideration of the prospects of rural development programmes. Notwithstanding the importance of oil in the economy of Nigeria, Nigeria remains very much a developing country with 80% of its population of perhaps 80 million people living in rural areas. As a result Nigeria, like many other developing countries, is very poor notwithstanding the natural resources with which it has been endowed. As with other developing countries in the Commonwealth, Nigeria lacks the capacity to harness and take full advantage of its natural resources. It is the recognition of the need for effective manpower as a prerequisite for development that has led to Nigeria making an enormous investment in education. Ahmadu Bello University is one of the older universities in the country but all of them are young, and many of them have been established only very recently.

All Nigerian universities are highly regarded by the community and are accepted and appreciated for their fundamental role in both teaching and research. They are intended to extend the frontiers of knowledge by fundamental research as well as to serve the societies in which they are placed. It is essential that they disseminate information about themselves and make themselves well known in order to justify the heavy expenditure that is necessary to provide them with the facilities and opportunities that they need.

Alongside the universities there have been many other educational developments, and education must long remain a major user of such resources as are available from government and other sources. Research is absolutely vital for the wellbeing of universities in Nigeria, as elsewhere in the world. Unfortunately and regrettably the fact is that, whereas in developed countries funds are usually available for research on a considerable scale, this is very rarely the case in developing countries. Governments and the people expect the universities to provide solutions to many of the problems that face rural societies but a far greater provision of research funds is essential if the universities are to play their proper role in this area.

Better methods of agriculture hold the key to the improvement of the welfare of a high proportion of the population of Nigeria, and agricultural faculties and programmes for rural development are bound to call for considerable expenditure in the coming years. A multi-disciplinary approach is essential, bringing in all the subjects with contributions to make to the tackling of these major problems. Increased food production is just as important as an increase in the output of cash crops. Universities have a great opportunity to work in close collaboration with both the federal and the state governments in order to overcome the technological, sociological, environmental, institutional and manpower constraints that affect the progress of integrated rural development programmes in many parts of the country.

Universities, I believe, always reflect the society in which they are situated and which they seek to serve. In this respect there are many common features between the universities in the developed and the developing countries of the Commonwealth; but the challenge of integrated rural development is particularly great in countries such as Nigeria, and the universities have, I believe, a great opportunity to make major contributions in this important area of development and of service to the community.

126

Dr. G. BENNEH (*Associate Professor and Head of Department of Geography, University of Ghana*):

PLANNING AND IMPLEMENTATION OF RURAL DEVELOPMENT PROJECTS IN THE UPPER EAST REGION OF GHANA

Using the Upper East Region of Ghana as a case study, an attempt is made to review the different interventions made in the rural setting by national and international bodies aimed at improving the levels of living of the people in the region (Fig. 1, below). The three rural development projects reviewed are:

(1) the Land Planning, Soil and Water Conservation Programme, which was launched by the colonial administration;

(2) the Onchocerciasis Control Programme;

(3) the Upper Region Integrated Agricultural Programme.

Land Planning, Soil and Water Conservation Programme

By the late thirties the high population densities in the upland areas of the region had resulted in soil erosion and a decline in yields of crops. Studies by agricultural officers in the region served to underline the seriousness of land degradation. The North Mamprusi Forestry Conference (1947) recommended that the catchment areas and watersheds be constituted into Planning Areas and that comprehensive measures to counteract soil erosion and to conserve water should be taken. As a result, the following Land Planning Areas were constituted: Dedoro-Tankara (12·6 sq. miles), Bumbugu (15 sq. miles), Tamne (20 sq. miles), Frafra (52 sq. miles) and Wiaga (6 sq. miles).

Conservation and productive methods in Land Planning Areas. The conservation measures taken consisted of watershed protective forest reserves, the contouring of arable land to control run-off from sloping land, the construction of dams to regulate the movement of water and control gullies near the watershed, and the demarcation of fencing of grazing areas. Productive measures consisted of the planting of fuelwood plantations, the introduction of improved farming methods and of fish farming, building of clay-cored dams to supply water for irrigation and stock, and the sinking of wells. But to a large extent the success of the Land Planning Programme was to be judged by the improvements of farming methods based on the introduction of bullock ploughing, coupled with the use of

127

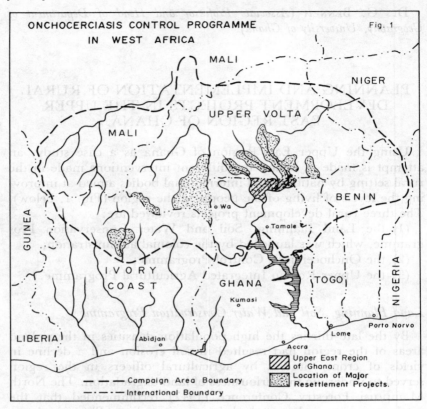

ONCHOCERCIASIS CONTROL PROGRAMME IN WEST AFRICA — Fig. 1

Upper East Region of Ghana.
Location of Major Resettlement Projects.
— · — · — · Campaign Area Boundary
·········· International Boundary

farmyard manure and fertilizers on blocks of contiguous land of adequate size.

By the end of the financial year 1961–62, 135 dams had been constructed in the Land Planning Areas in the Upper East Region, 1115·29 miles of narrow base contour bunds had been constructed and 7768 acres of land not suitable for arable purposes had been fenced and partially reseeded as grazing camps. Under irrigation, completely controlled or partially so, were 946 acres of bunded rice fields, and there were 335 acres of organised dry season gardens. There was spectacular progress in the introduction of mixed farming. From one plough farmer in Bawku in 1938 the number had increased to 60 in 1946 in the Bawku district. By 1950 this had increased to 299 in the district, as compared with 592 for the whole of the Upper East Region. So successful was the Land Planning Programme that by 1960 there were 2645 bullock plough farmers in the Bawku district and 3599 in the Region.

128

In spite of the improvement in the living standards of the people as a result of the activities of the Land Planning Organisation, the implementation of the Programme encountered many difficulties, not least of which was the non-availability of experienced professional specialists necessary to draw up plans and to train technicians for the follow-up work.

Based on the recommendations of a Working Party appointed in 1959, the government of Ghana applied in 1960 for United Nations Special Fund for the purpose of preparing plans for the development of the land and water resources of the Upper and Northern Regions of Ghana. The request was approved in 1961; the Food and Agriculture Organisation (FAO) was appointed as the executing agency for the project; the field work started in 1962 and was completed in 1966.

While the FAO survey was under way the Ghana government launched a new agricultural policy in 1962 which shifted emphasis from small-holder agriculture to large-scale mechanised farming. The new socialized agricultural policy had the effect of dismantling the Land Planning Organisation. Personnel and machinery were withdrawn to the Vea irrigation dam near Bolgatanga where large-scale farming was to be practised. The United Ghana Farmers Co-operatives Council was made responsible for agricultural extension. Farmers in Manga Dawku in the Bumbugu Land Planning Area complained to the author in 1969 that since 1962 the visits of extension officers had been most irregular. This was confirmed by the poor condition of the contour bunds in the village at the time of the author's survey. Not only had parts been washed away due to poor maintenance but some farmers had started growing crops on them.

The small dams or dug-outs which were constructed to conserve water for use in the dry season and also for use by livestock and for crop irrigation were not maintained. A survey in 1974 enumerated 68 dams, reservoirs or dug-outs of various sizes within the Bawku district. Most of them had either silted up from eroded top soils within their catchment areas or dried up because of high evaporation. Furthermore, as they became sources of water-borne diseases their use became less attractive and the lack of treatment facilities and the incidence of river blindness forced many to move away from them.

The rehabilitation of the dams was to be entrusted to the Upper Region Integrated Agricultural Development Project (URADEP) which was launched in 1976. However, since 1974, the water supply situation has changed considerably in the Region. This is due to the water supply for the Upper Region, which has been

129

implemented by the Ghana Water and Sewerage Corporation with the assistance of the Canadian International Development Agency (CIDA).

The Onchocerciasis Control Programme (OCP)

Earlier investigations in the Upper East Region had shown that resettlement of the virtually empty river valleys could not be possible without river blindness being controlled. It was not, however, until 1970 that the World Health Organisation—at the request of the seven countries in the Volta River Basin (Benin, Ghana, Ivory Coast, Mali, Niger, Togo and Upper Volta)— decided to combat the disease in the river basin (Fig. 1, above.) The Programme commenced in 1974. The first phase is for 20 years and Ouagadougou, the capital of Upper Volta, is the headquarters of the Programme.

To administer the Programme in Ghana the government has established an advisory body, the National Onchocerciasis Committee, and a National Onchocerciasis Secretariat which is the implementing wing of the Committee. The membership of the Committee is multi-disciplinary, involving specialists from government departments as well as research institutions.

The main objective of the Programme is the economic development of the river valleys infested with river blindness. This would, however, follow the control of onchocerciasis in the region. While this approach may be justifiable for project funding, it is nonetheless based on the erroneous notion that onchocerciasis is the chief obstacle in the development of the onchocerciasis-ridden areas and that, once controlled, development would automatically follow. This is not, of course, the case. Apart from other health problems such as human and animal trypanosomiasis, there are several other limiting factors to development such as heavy soils in the river valleys, unreliable rainfall and an inadequate infrastructure.

River blindness has, however, serious implications for the economic development of the region. Not only is there a reduction in the productive capacity of those afflicted by the disease but the blind and the near-blind become a burden on society. On the other hand, vector control would create new development opportunities. Human misery would be reduced, people would be healthier and hence have the potential to work harder and better. Furthermore, cultivable land would be made more accessible for productive use.

Control of onchocerciasis. The OCP has concentrated its efforts on an insecticidal attack on the larvae of *Simulium damnosum*. The breeding areas of the fly are sprayed with insecticides. The techniques used are sophisticated and very expensive. The annual budget of the Programme is about $25 million. To operate on a large scale the use of aircraft and helicopters has become necessary.

These methods have resulted in a fairly spectacular control of the vector. Field work carried out by the author in the Nangodi, Zebilla and Tili areas in 1978 showed that the previously abandoned river valleys were being cultivated. Local inhabitants confirmed to the author that the nuisance factor arising from the many bites from the black fly had been considerably reduced. Again there has been the development of mechanised large-scale rice cultivation in some of the valleys, notably the Fumbisi valley in the Navrongo district. But whereas a tolerable level of the incidence of the disease may have been reached in the area, the disease will not disappear before 15 or 20 years due to the longevity of the vector. Furthermore, an ancho-freed area could be reinvaded by the black fly.

It is in the light of this, and the possible long-term effects on the flora and fauna in the area arising from massive insecticide spraying, that a case can be made for increase in funds for research in fields other than spraying. Furthermore, neither Ghana nor any other of the seven states connected with the Programme, has the funds, materials, human and technological resources to continue the fight after the end of the Programme. The need to find more cost-effective ways of disease control cannot therefore be over-emphasized.

While the control of the disease is being done on a regional basis and financed from a central (trust) fund contributed by the donor countries of the Programme, the economic development of the freed areas is a matter for each of the governments of the seven countries. Six development areas have been identified in the OCP area in Ghana. One of these—the Fumbisi/Yagaba/Soo area—although located mostly in the Northern Region has a spillover into the Upper East Region. Lying 70 km south-west of Navrongo, near the confluence of the Sissili and Kulpawn rivers with the White Volta, this area has potential for investment in settlements and in agricultural production, principally rice. The spillover area in the Upper East Region has been an agricultural frontier attracting large-scale rice farmers from other parts of Ghana since the late seventies. The area is sparsely populated with hardly any infrastructure.

The Fumbisi/Yagaba/Soo area is being given top priority for development. A two-year project has been proposed which aims, among other things, to carry out new surveys and pre-feasibility studies to produce basic data not yet available but required for its development. The Upper Region Agricultural project (URADEP) was expected to prepare plans for the development of all the areas freed from onchocerciasis in the region.

The *Upper Region Agricultural Development Programme* (*URADEP*) was inaugurated in 1976, about two years after the OCP was launched.

The project's main objectives were to increase and sustain farm production and family incomes of the Region's 125,000 families. These twin objectives were to be achieved through: (*a*) the development of about 90 service centres that would provide improved extension and management services to the Region's farmers; (*b*) the improvement of production of some 108,000 hectares of land under cultivation through the supply of inputs and farm loans; (*c*) developing seven applied research and demonstration units and ensuring proper seed multiplication. In addition the project was to construct 120 new dams and rehabilitate 100 existing dams to provide water for livestock, dry season (irrigation) farming and for general water conservation purposes. It was envisaged that through new soil conservation measures a minimum of 160,000 hectares, including the catchment area of dams, would be protected. URADEP was also to prepare plans for the future development of onchocerciasis-eradicated areas in the Region.

As conceived, the project was expected to increase the output of the basic crops grown in the Region. The annual incremental production by 1981 was expected to be of the order of 4000 tons of millet, 12,000 tons of sorghum, 5000 tons of maize, 30,000 tons of rice, 11,000 tons of groundnuts, 15,000 tons of yams, 7000 tons of cowpeas, 18,000 tons of seed cotton, 6000 tons of tomatoes and 3000 tons of meat. It was hoped that if the project targets were achieved family incomes from improved crop production could be increased by 32%. This would have increased the *per capita* income from ¢41 at the start of the project to ¢54 per annum, representing an income growth of about 6% per annum.

Implementation of the project. The first phase was to cover a five-year period 1976–77 to 1980–81. It was hoped that the project's design would not unduly disrupt existing government services. But from the discussions the author had with officials on the project during his field survey in 1978, a number of problems surfaced soon after the project was launched.

The first major problem was the conflict between the Programme management and the 2500 employees of the ministry of agriculture which the project absorbed. The status of the personnel of the ministry of agriculture was not well defined by the project document. Although they were supposed to be a part of the project

132

they enjoyed inferior conditions of service compared to those employed directly by the project. Indeed, the status of the project itself was left ambiguous as to whether it was part of the civil service organization, a para-statal or a corporation. This administrative confusion was to lead to tensions and strikes organised by the General Agricultural Workers Union. The Ghana government had to set up a committee of inquiry in 1980 to probe the causes of unrest in URADEP.

The implementation of some aspects of the project appears also to have suffered from the late arrival of equipment ordered from overseas. Procurement under some of the loans at times took about two years. Thus, the rehabilitation and construction of dams, for example, had not begun at the time of the author's survey. The delay was largely due to the cumbersome procedures laid down for the utilization of some of the foreign loans.

The project has also had its problems with recruitment of senior qualified staff. Apart from the long time it took to fill important posts, not all those recruited proved suitable. There have also been problems associated with the early distribution and sales of insufficient inputs.

On the whole, at the end of the first phase—the end of the 1980–81 financial year—most of the objectives for the first phase had not been achieved.

Towards a New Paradigm of Rural Development Planning

So far this paper has thrown up some elements which are common to the three development projects reviewed. There has been very little if any involvement of the target populations in the identification of their problems and in the implementation of the projects once they had been formulated and launched. Admittedly, in the case of the Land Planning Programme, there was local representation on the project committees for each of the Land Planning Areas but, as Billes observed:

'The local people have on the whole welcomed these operations and there has been no case of opposition. They appreciate very much the improvement of water supplies and the opportunity of earning wages, but do not always take advantage of all that is done for them, such as irrigation schemes, and they have little conception of the purpose of the operations. It is probably along broad lines of general community development that economic development will make the most rapid progress'.

It is therefore not surprising that, once the government withdrew its personnel and equipment from the Programme in the early sixties, the development process became aborted.

If the main goal of rural development is to enhance the capacity of rural people and individuals to cope with the changing circumstances of their lives on a sustained basis, then there is something wrong with a planning methodology which ignores the contribution of those who stand to benefit from the plans. Although the progress of the implementation of development projects funded by international agencies is monitored by visiting monitoring or supervision missions, these do not include local people who live with the problems and who could make valuable contributions to the success of the project.

Another common element of the three projects is the extent to which their implementation has depended on imported technology and inputs. The implementation of two of them has suffered from late arrival of equipment or inputs, or their non-availability. Since most third-world countries have balance of payments problems, dependence on imported technology and inputs is bound to be a major constraint in the successful implementation of rural development projects. At any rate, it would be difficult for any third-world country to continue an expensive development project after the withdrawal of foreign support, because of the demands which such big projects would make on its resources.

There is clearly a need for new kinds of rural development projects which will use, as much as possible, available resources within the developing countries and which will be based essentially on the principles of increased participation of the rural population, decentralisation of decision-making processes rather than of government structures alone, flexible planning and a trial-and-error learning process. An acceptance of this view may have far-reaching implications for both donor and developing countries. It would mean developing a new methodology for project design, implementation and evaluation. There is no doubt that some of the present problems are related to the planning methods used by donor agencies and their local intermediaries.

The task ahead for universities with an interest in integrated rural development is the development of this methodology which, while meeting the needs and aspirations of the rural people, takes care of the concerns and demands of both donor countries and local bureaucracies. It is a task which cannot be accomplished by specialists from only one discipline. This would argue for interdisciplinary approach to rural development planning and research.

SUB-TOPIC 2 (B): THE RURAL SPACE

DISCUSSION

Professor Chisholm, in talking to his paper, pointed out that, although universities were apt to take an essentially urban view of change and development of rural areas, the dichotomy of their role was not a major difficulty. However, because there was a diversity of rural problems as well as of views on ways of solving them, it was necessary to visualise three general categories of society: (a) highly urbanised, e.g. the United Kingdom; (b) urbanised, but with agriculture still a major occupation and/or plenty of wide open space, e.g. Canada and Australia; (c) essentially rural societies despite sizeable cities, e.g. India and most African states. He raised the following questions:—

(a) What are the problems posed by rural change and development?

(b) What is the appropriate nature of the response by universities? Hence—

(c) What kind and scale of teaching and research should they foster?

Over the years, in any given country, the role of the university had been changing just as the problems themselves had been changing. The United Kingdom was cited as an example. In Britain, where there was a well-developed pattern of research institutes, the balance of new scientific discovery had tended to shift away from universities to specialised institutions. For the benefit of future farmers and farm owners subjects such as agricultural sciences should be offered generally by universities, although it was acknowledged that the role of universities in agricultural extension work had to a large extent been taken over by other agencies. The speaker pointed out that universities ought to examine the serious adverse ecological consequences of intensive, science-based farming; that universities in Britain had a role to play in conducting research into non-traditional rural employment opportunities in order to provide a solution to the problems created by the depopulation of the countryside; that the universities of Edinburgh, East Anglia and Exeter, as well as Wye College, were researching into the relationship between farmers, foresters, conservationists and leisure services; and that there was work in Birmingham on changes in land use in the uplands.

In the second category—countries such as Australia and Canada—the nature of the rural development problems was similar to that described under the first category, with similar implications for the role of universities. One of the striking features of Australia and Canada was the existence of vast and fragile areas coupled with different farming activities. Universities were well equipped to investigate technical problems which tend to threaten the ecological balance in those countries.

The third category, which included the developing countries, experienced problems of development for which university structures based on the model of the first category might not be appropriate. Universities were geared to upward mobility of people, that is to say, people went to universities in order to escape from the rural areas. Consequently rural areas lost the manpower required for development. Dissemination of information was still a major problem in the developing countries. Universities in, say, India, must create not only knowledge but also the means of disseminating it. The inter-disciplinary approach seemed to provide the best solutions. Universities had to respond appropriately to the needs of the societies in which they operated.

Professor Chisholm warned against the danger of wasting time on platitudes. Vice-chancellors and registrars had no time to 're-invent the wheel'! He therefore suggested that the ACU secretariat should explore the possibility of compiling a compendium that could be used by university administrators throughout the Commonwealth.

Professor Abdullahi, after stressing the need to define such key words or phrases as 'development', 'rural area' and 'integration', discussed in his paper the Nigerian experience, pointing out that, in spite of the oil, Nigeria in many ways fitted the definition of a developing country. 80% of its approximately 80 million people lived in rural areas; it remained poor, lacking the capacity to harness and take full advantage of its natural resources; and realising that effective manpower was a pre-requisite for development, Nigeria had made an enormous investment in education.

Universities in Nigeria were highly respected and accepted for their primary role of teaching and research. Universities were intended to create new knowledge as well as to render service to the societies in which they were located. However, not always well understood, universities had to disseminate information and make themselves well known in order to justify the heavy expenditure they incurred. Professor Abdullahi regretted the fact that, whereas in developed countries funds were available for research, this was not the case in developing countries where research was expected to provide solutions to the many problems that faced the rural societies. In an essentially agricultural country characterised by inequalities, such as Nigeria, better methods of agriculture held the key to the improvement of the welfare of the citizens. Agricultural research and development required a multi-disciplinary approach, and universities should work in collaboration with governments to overcome technological, sociological, environmental, institutional and manpower constraints.

Dr. Benneh spoke to his paper, which used the Upper East Region of Ghana as a case study to examine the problems of unequal development in a 'less developed country'. The paper also reviewed the different interventions made in the rural setting by national and international bodies with a view to improving the living standards of the people in the region.

The region experienced periodic droughts about once in every five years and the rain falls in a single season. The soils were classified as upland soils and river valley soils. The upland soils had been subjected to intensive cultivation for many years, resulting in soil degradation and decline in crop yields. Pressure of population was such that little or no land was available for animal grazing, and food production had not kept pace with population growth. Areas adjacent to the rivers had very low densities of population and in many parts were virtually empty. There was a big migration loss in the region, which had considerable health problems.

Dr. Benneh described three development projects/programmes that were carried out in an effort to improve the situation. The study revealed that there was very little involvement of the communities concerned. Since the main objective of rural development was to enhance the capacity of the rural people to cope with the changing situation on a sustained basis, it was unwise to plan a scheme that ignored the contribution of those it was intended to benefit. Another element of the three projects was their dependence on imported technology and inputs. Such expensive projects were bound to be difficult for third world countries to sustain after the foreign support came to an end.

In the discussion following, it was suggested that the Nigerian experience indicated that universities tended to be centres of urbanisation; that over-specialisation of universities created problems; and that it was essential for universities to carry out integrated formulation of policies. It was vital to win political will in order to ensure success of development projects. Ideas must be relevant to facilitate the application of appropriate technology.

Dr. A. T. Porter (Sierra Leone) urged that, since as much as 90% of the population of the majority of the third world were rural, then rural development in those countries coincided with their national development. Universities had a big role to play by getting their agricultural faculties involved in extension work and in monitoring project results. He, too, emphasised the importance of the political dimension.

Dr. D. Kimble (Malawi) informed the group of the university intervention in what was the Gold Coast more than 25 years ago in an effort to make clean water available to the rural areas. The local people were informed of the project and were involved in the exercise to ensure that they themselves would maintain the wells for their own good. He suggested that universities ought to be centres of information for both local and worldwide use. He thought the concept of a 'third world' was not useful as numerous variations existed within the category.

Dr. S. Mookerjee (Kalyani) held that there was no universally accepted definition of the term 'development' and that countries regarded as 'developed' could sustain more population in terms of land/man ratio. He pointed out that while universities were not expected to replace national governments in the task of alleviating miseries of the rural masses, they had a responsibility to discharge to their hinterlands and their inhabitants on whose support they depended. Universities ought to re-organise their faculties, re-define their objectives, and re-design their research interests in order to improve the welfare of their immediate neighbourhood. He urged universities to adopt an interdisciplinary and integrated approach to the numerous problems of society.

Professor J. K. Maitha (Kenyatta University College) urged universities to encourage integrated courses to help graduates face the many complex problems facing their societies. He pointed out that lack of political support quite often resulted from the tendency of universities to ignore governments.

THE DESIGN AND PROMOTION OF APPROPRIATE TECHNOLOGY

Chairman: Professor J. D. FAGE
Pro-Vice-Chancellor and Vice-Principal of the
University of Birmingham

Rapporteur: Mr. C. N. DEVAS
Lecturer, Institute of Local Government Studies,
University of Birmingham

Tuesday, 16 August

Mr. H. DICKINSON (*Senior Lecturer, School of Engineering, University of Edinburgh*):

TECHNOLOGIES FOR SOCIAL AND ECONOMIC DEVELOPMENT

Despite wide agreement on the aims of rural development, and the willingness of institutions to be associated with such aims, there have always been difficulties in obtaining the necessary allocation of scarce resources to the conflicting demands of urban industrialisation and rural improvement. This issue has been resolved, in one way or another, in all countries which have become 'developed'.

The industrialisation picture that emerges is less than optimistic and the time necessary for the industrial transformation of any society is bound to be long. The final burden to be borne by those new to industrialisation is the realisation that the costs of industrialisation are always increasing. This is true if for no other reason than that the old industrial nations, which changed from agricultural dependence over a century ago, were able to take their initial steps in an age when there was little competitive demand for the materials needed for the growth of industry. In addition the extraction of many natural raw materials, especially energy-rich materials, is now increasingly costly as the high-grade sources of many such materials are approaching exhaustion. New sources are, in general, less convenient and of ever increasing marginal cost.

The possible university responses to the problem of rural areas of developing countries have been summarised in a report of an Inter-University Council working party (*Rural Development Overseas: First Thoughts on the Co-operative Role of British Universities and Polytechnics,* 1976), from which the following quotations have been extracted:

'. . . . effective development in the rural sector may be difficult to achieve. The difficulties encountered in promoting rural development are often due to unexpected complexities in situations which may at first sight appear to be simple and straightforward. Some of these complexities are social, educational, legal or economic in nature; others are more closely linked with applied science, medicine, public health, engineering, agriculture in its many aspects, and related technologies. Many disciplines have to come together to investigate these complexities if they are to be resolved and workable and mutually compatible solutions found to the component problems as these are identified.' (Section 4.1).

It is not only the engineering or applied science departments which are able to play a part in the practical aspects of development. All universities, in all but the wealthiest of countries, are unique aggregations of professional and analytical skills able to serve the economies in which they exist.

Universities can aid, or lead, social and economic development in three main ways:— (*a*) development policy considerations; (*b*) research and development (R & D) programmes; and (*c*) advisory services.

The central problem of finding 'appropriate technologies' (or better 'socially appropriate technologies') lies in making scientific and technical knowledge available to those in the less-developed countries. No one doubts that the laws of science are universal but access to the benefits of science depends on the quantity, quality and cultural orientation of the available scientists and technologists. Until responsible scientists and technologists with adequate funds are available to enable poor countries to obtain freedom of technical choice there is little likelihood of the mass of the world's population escaping from poverty. Should suitable technologies become available, the choice to use them or not will still depend on the wisdom of political leaders—new technologies can only offer new opportunities, they cannot guarantee results.

The proponents of socially appropriate technologies believe that they have made and demonstrated their case. The next move is to convince the governments of the developing countries that only through such technologies will they attain full advantage of technological choice. It is, after all, the only way that many of them can afford to go—and it is only the universities which can lead them. 'Political economy, as it gradually emerges from its semi-scientific stage, tends more and more to become a science devoted to the study of the needs of man and of the means of satisfying them with the least possible waste of energy—that is, a sort of physiology of society.' (Kropotkin.)

Dr. M. ARAM (*Vice-Chancellor, Gandhigram Rural Institute*):

GANDHIAN PERSPECTIVE ON INTEGRATED RURAL DEVELOPMENT

Today there is a new-found interest in Gandhi and non-violence around the world, thanks to Sir Richard Attenborough and his epoch-making film.

I. Gandhi's Vision of Sarvodaya

To understand the Gandhian conception of integrated rural development we may have to go back to the year 1908 when Gandhi wrote his little book *Hind Swaraj* (*Indian Home Rule*) in South Africa. In this unusual work Gandhi characterised modern civilisation as a 'disease'. He advocated non-violence as a superior ideology.

In South Africa Gandhi was introduced to the British writer John Ruskin and his book *Unto This Last*. This book cast a 'magic spell' on Gandhi who decided immediately to transform his life and conduct in accordance with its principles: (i) the individual good is contained in the social good; (ii) all occupations have equal value; (iii) the life of labour is really worth living. Gandhi translated the English title, a biblical phrase, into *Sarvodaya* (*Welfare of All*). This Indian word has, in course of time, come to connote the ideal social order of Gandhi's conception—non-violent, decentralised, egalitarian.

The constructive programme. After Gandhi returned from South Africa he made a close study of the rural realities in India. Then he developed a new programme of service activities called the constructive programme. They included Khadi (hand-spinning and hand-weaving), village industries, village sanitation, removal of untouchability, prohibition, basic education, adult education, women's uplift, tribal welfare, and others. Gandhi dreamt of a village-based social structure—'Gram Rajya' (village rule), as he called it. He also called it 'Ram Rajya' which meant the kingdom of God.

II. Concept of Integrated Rural Development

Mahatma Gandhi set up several all-India organisations in order to promote specific programmes of rural development. When he saw that these organisations were working in isolation, without a total perspective, he called for 'Samagra Seva' (integrated service). This was the beginning of the concept of *integration* in the history of rural development in India.

Bhoodan movement. In 1951 Vinoba Bhave, Gandhi's spiritual heir, started a new movement called Bhoodan (land gift). He walked on foot from state to state. Thousands of acres poured in as free gifts. The Bhoodan movement attracted international attention. Top socialist leaders like Jayaprakash Narayan joined the movement. Altogether 4·5 million acres were received all over India—no mean achievement. Soon a new dimension developed. Whole villages opted for Bhoodan. It was called 'Gramdan' (village gift). As many as 36,436 villages accepted Gramdan. Now the village community could redistribute the land and start a new programme of co-operative living.

Community development. The government of India initiated the community development programme in the year 1951. It included agriculture, animal husbandry, rural health, rural industry, rural housing, education, communications, etc. It was a comprehensive approach to rural development. Pandit Jawaharlal Nehru took personal interest in the programme. He suggested that each village should have three basic institutions, namely, school, co-operative and Panchayat (local government).

When there was a decline in the tempo of the community development movement it was proposed that there should be 'democratic decentralisation' to encourage greater involvement of the people. This was called 'Panchayati Raj' and it was inaugurated in 1959.

Green revolution. In 1960–61 the government started another major programme called Intensive Agricultural Development Programme (IADP). This was intended to increase food production substantially in selected districts in India. It turned out to be a great success and was popularly called the Green Revolution.

While the Green Revolution augmented food production, it also augmented intra-rural disparities. So the government developed new programmes like the Small Farmers Development Agency (SFDA) to help small and marginal farmers. Special development plans were designed for backward and tribal areas. Such schemes followed the 'target groups' approach.

In 1976 the Union Minister for Planning, Shri C. Subramaniam, made a major policy statement in parliament and announced a national programme for 'integrated rural development' (IRDP). This programme aimed at the integration of the natural resources in the area, human resources available there, and science and technology. In 1977 the emphasis was on block level planning. The thrust was to develop block plans for 2000 blocks in India. In 1980 Prime Minister Indira Gandhi announced a 20-point programme which included many items of rural development, particularly for the welfare of the weaker sections. The IRDP has come to stay. Today all the 5011 blocks in India are under IRDP.

Over a period of 36 years, from 1947 till today, efforts have been made both by the government and voluntary organisations to tackle the problem of rural poverty. Much progress has been achieved no doubt. But the problem is not solved as yet. Rural industrialisation on a massive scale is perhaps the answer. Here comes the critical question of the nature and level of technology for rural industrialisation.

III. *The Concept of Appropriate Technology*

In the year 1965 the late Dr. E. F. Schumacher, well-known British economist, visited India at the invitation of the Planning Commission. In a seminar at Hyderabad he spoke on the need to create 'millions of work-places' in rural India. Mahatma Gandhi said: 'Not mass production but production by the masses'. Dr. Schumacher's ideas are in harmony with the ideas of Gandhiji. In his famous book *Small is Beautiful* Schumacher quotes Gandhi approvingly. Dr. Schumacher suggested that India should go in for intermediate technology. He suggested four criteria: (i) small, (ii) simple, (iii) capital-cheap and (iv) non-violent.

142

'Intermediate technology' had certain connotations which meant inferior or second-rate, so the expression 'appropriate technology' was suggested. Appropriate technology is location-specific. It is characterised by three features: (i) employment for the local people; (ii) use of local resources; and (iii) production for local markets.

Small-scale technology causes less pollution and less ecological imbalance. The Western world is faced with a grim possibility of complete annihilation by nuclear war which may start either by design or accident. Thus appropriate technology has a message to the West as well. If the developing countries are to abolish poverty within a certain time frame, and to provide employment to everybody, they will have to take recourse to appropriate technology. Here are three examples:—

Khadi and village industries. Gandhi gave Khadi (hand-spun and hand-woven cloth) an important place in his constructive programme. The government of India set up a Khadi and Village Industries Commission, a high-level autonomous body. There has been phenomenal growth of Khadi and village industries which together produced in 1980 goods worth Rs.4350 million, and 2·7 million people were given employment.

Biogas plants. Another outstanding example of appropriate technology in India is the biogas plant. By July 1980, 80,000 biogas plants were in operation in India. Government has launched a big programme of expansion. Experimentation in biogas technology is going on. In Gandhigram we have a Regional Research Centre where the relative merits and demerits of different models, including the Chinese model, are under study. Large-size community gas plants have been set up.

Bullock carts without bullocks. A third example is the improved bullock cart. In India there are about 15 million animal-drawn vehicles and about 20 million people are involved in the bullock cart business. A most interesting development is to design a carriage without bullocks, but still use their bio-energy to power the carriage. It is stored in electrical batteries, and with the use of a small motor the wheels of the carriage could be driven.

IV. The Role of Universities

In India the University Education Commission, constituted in 1949 soon after independence, proposed the setting up of rural universities. The idea of rural universities was accepted by the government of India and in 1956 10 rural higher institutes were started. The Gandhigram Rural Institute was one such, and after

20 years of successful experimentation attained the status of a university in 1976.

Service area. One distinctive feature of the Gandhigram programme has been its service area for extension work. This area today consists of 26 villages in which intensive extension work takes place. Ours is a comprehensive and integrated approach to rural development.

Courses of study. All the courses offered in Gandhigram pertain to integrated rural development. Every student in the degree course takes up a specific rural problem for study. Gandhigram also offers postgraduate courses such as: (i) MA in rural development; (ii) MA in rural economics and extension education; (iii) MA in rural sociology and Panchayati Raj; and (iv) MA in co-operative management. The proposed new courses include a diploma course in biogas technology and alternative energy sources, an MPhil course in micro-level planning and an MSc course in applied science for rural development.

Seminars, studies, training. Our university has organised recently special seminars and symposia on current problems relating to integrated rural development. The Research and Extension Centre for the university has taken up studies in social forestry in collaboration with the state government. Besides study, training is also provided.

Thus Gandhigram is acting as a major centre for promoting the movement for integrated rural development in India. Governments, business and industry and voluntary organisations are taking keen interest in rural development. All working together, it should be possible to transform the rural scene into a happy and satisfying environment.

DISCUSSION

In the first paper Mr. Dickinson outlined some of the particular problems of rural development: while there may be agreement on the aims, there are often unexpected complexities in achieving them; the need for an integrated and multi-disciplinary approach; competition for scarce resources, particularly with the urban/industrial sector; and the fact that the technology available is often inappropriate. He advocated the development of technologies which were appropriate to the social and economic conditions in the countries concerned, as well as to the production needs. In the search for, and dissemination of, these technologies, universities could play an important role through development policy consideration, research and development programmes and advisory services. He recommended the establishment of technology consultancy centres attached to universities, such as the one at Kumasi University of Science and Technology in Ghana, and identified three particular areas for future work: energy policy, protein policy and materials policy.

Mr J. Matthews (Trent) raised the problem of cultural and language barriers in understanding what was appropriate, and asked whether the speaker considered that the Bata Shoe Company, operating in 93 countries, could be regarded as 'appropriate'. Mr. Dickinson replied that, in many cases, production by a company like Bata would be less appropriate than by local craftsmen, but Bata products have the appeal of 'modernity'. He suggested that there was a need for a United Nations agency which could give independent advice to less developed countries on proposals put forward by multi-national companies and aid agencies; this is a function which universities could fulfil.

Dr. B. D. Sharma (North-Eastern Hill) suggested, first, that there is a need to ask the right questions about the problems and needs of the rural poor and, secondly, that one of the main difficulties in dealing with the problems of the rural poor is that such activities are not always regarded as being 'academically acceptable' but as being 'second best'. In reply Mr. Dickinson stressed the need for thorough analysis of public responses to proposals, of reasons for failures as well as successes, and of the processes of change which take place.

Professor J. Ashton (Newcastle upon Tyne) reminded participants that the output of universities was students, and that universities would be judged by the quality of, and effect on society of, those students, rather than by any consultancy work. In reply Mr. Dickinson pointed out that the role of universities was changing rapidly, that there was a need to think 20 years ahead, and also that universities have a responsibility to provide the services that the community, which is paying, wants.

In his paper Dr. Aram outlined Gandhi's vision of *Sarvodaya* (welfare of all), and of his pioneering ideas and programmes of integrated rural development, village construction, community development and land redistribution. He also described Schumacher's development of the concept of appropriate technology and mentioned three applications: Khadi and village industries; biogas; and bio-energy for carts. He outlined the role in this of universities like Gandhigram Rural Institute, with its service area of 26 villages and its applied training programmes.

Professor S. V. Chittibabu (Annamalai) stressed that development means growth plus change, and that universities must serve the community rather than being 'ivory towers'. Rural farmers often distrust bureaucrats, while universities could provide people who can get to the heart of the community, providing that they are willing to be proud of 'getting their hands dirty'. He described the wide range of action-oriented programmes, involving all faculties, which his University had been able to establish over the past two years.

Professor W. F. Musgrave (New England) raised, first, the problem of how in practice an interdisciplinary approach to economic and rural development could be achieved within universities and asked, secondly, what was the objective of Dr. Aram's form of development, and whether this matched the perceptions of others in the group.

Professor T. Ratho (Manipur) asked how, with so many advanced universities in India, Gandhigram managed to attract its students. Professor G.-B. Martin (Laval) asked about the qualifications of staff at Gandhigram. Professor A. M. Patwari (Bangladesh U. of Engineering and Technology) asked which of the various models of operation was likely to be the most effective, and mentioned that at his University such activities had been institutionalised through two specific institutes. In reply Dr. Aram described the organisation of Gandhigram through the Rural Industries Centre, for production and training, and the Rural Health and Sanitation Centre, a unique centre in India, attracting people from all over the world. He described the decentralised nature of Gandhigram, with the co-ordinating role of the Centre for Research, Extension and Integrated Rural Development. Gandhigram had been able to attract well-qualified staff, with PhDs and good records of teaching.

Dr. M. N. Viswanathaiah (Bangalore) mentioned that many 'urban' students are required to do work in the villages and they do it well. He also pointed out that in Indian villages people depend on agriculture and are generally poor and exploited: economic improvement, through better marketing and higher prices for produce, is the key, whereas improvements in technology, even if modest, generally increase costs and thus are not affordable.

Dr. A. K. Dhan (Ranchi) drew attention to the fact that India's educational system, with its colonial origins, was urban-biased and too little related to the real needs of the country. The predominance of agriculture and the poverty of the rural population meant that integrated rural development was essential, and universities must get involved in such issues if they were to survive.

In conclusion Mr. Dickinson stressed that rural development is a complex issue which cannot be treated in isolation from industrialisation; the universities, if they are to be involved, need to have an understanding of both sides.

Dr. Aram concluded that the aim of universities such as his was to synthesise the best of urban and rural life, in order to help stem the flow of people from rural to urban areas, and to facilitate the evolution of an intermediate, 'rurban', pattern of life.

Sub-Topic 2(d)

RURAL DEVELOPMENT AND THE
COMMUNITY

Chairman: Professor K. J. C. BACK
Vice-Chancellor of James Cook University of North Queensland

Rapporteur: Dr. D. M. E. CURTIS
Lecturer, Institute of Local Government Studies, University of
Birmingham

Thursday, 18 August

Professor Sir JAMES STEWART (*Principal, Lincoln College, New Zealand*): I intend to relate two experiences in two parts of the world which may not be referred to elsewhere in these symposia. I hope they contribute to our objectives. The experiences are in the South Pacific and in the People's Republic of China. The South Pacific experience has a direct university connotation, the Chinese one only indirectly.

New Zealand has historic, geographic and political ties with the small island states of the region, which accounts for it being the focus of our aid programme. Within the vast, diverse and extreme archipelagic physical environment of the region three organisational forms of agriculture are recognised:—

● integral subsistence systems
● mixed subsistence/cash cropping systems
● the plantation mode.

The subsistence systems are traditional and equivalent to those existing before European contact. They include inter-dependent sub-systems of field agriculture, tree crops, animal husbandry, fishing, hunting and gathering. Throughout the region these systems have been substantially changed in the direction of becoming more commercial, or they have become extinct.

Mixed subsistence/cash cropping is now widespread. This is based on small-holder systems, usually with some specialisation in particular cash crops, often for export. Sometimes commercialised livestock production or fishing is integrated with these units.

147

The plantation mode is characterised by foreign capital and often ownership, expatriate managers, alienation of land, employment on wages, and export.

There are opposing views on the most desirable policy objectives in regard to the structure of agriculture, but there is agreement on one matter: that rural communities and economies are in decline. It would not be possible in this paper to review the regional situation—there is wide variation between different countries. The agriculture of Western Samoa, as an example, is worse than static. While in recent years substantial development expenditure has gone into the rural sector there has been very little response in production. Copra production has not expanded in 20 years, cocoa production has fallen by half in the same period, and banana production is 5% of its peak level. Consequently food imports have expanded by about 20% per annum over the last decade. The outlook which is widespread in the region is increasing urbanization, continued out-migration, further production declines and increasing dependence on imported foodstuffs, in short, increasingly dependent economies.

It was in this context that last year I was invited by the University of the South Pacific to lead a group to report on the University's school of agriculture at the Alafua campus in Western Samoa. Previously Alafua had been the South Pacific College of Tropical Agriculture. Under an agreement between the University and the Western Samoan government, from 1977 the College became an integral part of the University, as a second campus approximately 950 km from the central campus at Laucala Bay in Fiji.

The daunting task faced by the University in developing a school of agriculture, in the face of the physical, geographic, economic and ethnic diversity of the region it has to serve, the logistical problems for which there was no other model, and with its own immense difficulties of resources acquisition and staffing, may now be apparent. Nevertheless, recognising in its *Calendar* that 'Agriculture is both the foundation and the key to economic development in the South Pacific region', and that the 'most important constraint is the shortage of trained high-level man-power', the University has had to confront these problems.

Some of the conclusions that arose from our review were as follows.

The teaching and research aspirations of any such institution in developing countries should relate to the discerned technical, social and economic needs as they are at the time, and in that place. What one observed was a tendency for emphasis on teaching methods, texts, etc, more appropriate to developed countries with more sophisticated commercial agriculture. An essential base for the success of such a programme was well-farmed land, demonstrating current husbandry and technology at a level acceptable and credible to the students and to the industry, and to politicians and others providing finance.

There appeared to be a very deep-seated desire of students that their courses fit them for urban-based jobs, for which they saw themselves competing with graduates returning from universities in more developed countries. Many of them were urban in their outlook and in their aspirations. They said that they were discomfited in the presence of farmers and villagers. So, it seemed, were some of their lecturers, especially expatriates on whom the University of the South Pacific has had to depend very heavily. Consequently there was a propensity to confine the teaching, which should be heavily field-based, to the lecture room, and to traditional, often Western, texts and examples.

Teaching methods can be developed which are appropriate, which do expose the students at first hand to the people they must serve, in one way or another, as extension and change agents, as administrators, as researchers, or as community leaders. We came to the conclusion that if the school of agriculture was to make the essential contribution to arresting the decline of Western Samoa's agriculture, and of rural communities in the region, it would require:—

(*a*) a major upgrading of its farming activities on which to base its teaching and extension, and technical leadership;

(*b*) a strong orientation in the teaching programme towards field, technical, and community-based programmes.

The most important manpower requirement for rural community development in the region is for 'change agents' and these need to be people who can do things as well as explain, who have an empathy with rural people, and whose familiarity with agricultural systems is based on observation and analysis of those systems in the field. To be effective in producing this kind of graduate and diplomate the University itself needs to have its feet in the soil, as well as its eyes on the stars.

China

The agricultural statistics for the People's Republic of China are mind-boggling, but there are two that are relevant to my experiences there. These are that only 11% of the land area is cultivated, and that over 80% of the population of 1100 million

149

live in rural communities. There are vast areas of unutilized, underutilized, or unutilizable hill and mountain lands. Much of it is severely eroded as a result of uncontrolled, itinerant grazing, denudation of tree and grass cover for cooking fuel, and regular burning to provide fresh grazing.

The communities living amongst the hills naturally are sparser than on the intensely cultivated plains and the great river valleys, and in general they are poorer, because their agriculture is poorer. There are possibilities for intensification of land use on these hill lands on the basis of subdivision, oversowing, topdressing, and grazing management. Following our identification of areas suitable for the application of New Zealand technology in two regions we are establishing 'model farms' which are to serve as a focus for teaching, demonstration and extension for communities which have control over massive areas of this land.

Technical parameters are complex—extreme climate range, soil deficiencies, erodability, absence of suitable pasture species, live-stock species which have evolved for purposes other than utilization of improved pastures. The logistics are a challenge to ingenuity and resilience, and the stratification of decision-making a challenge to patience. But the key to the success of the co-operation between us will be whether the community education and development aspects of the projects are successful. The project has been a technical success. But the real test of success is still to come, and it seems to me that this is the test which is central to our theme here. What kind of legacy for community development do we leave behind? There are so many well-intentioned agricultural development projects in advanced stages of reversion around the world, through the failure to provide such a legacy.

With the co-operation, indeed the insistence of our Chinese colleagues, we have had working on the project up to 30 graduates of agricultural colleges or universities. They have been required to participate in the actual physical development, working long hard days on fencing, cultivation, construction, tractor driving, stock work. They have also had regular technical demonstration classes and formal lectures on topics related to their current and seasonal work. Similarly staff from the state farm, of which our unit is a part, have participated in the project. In this way we have aimed to build up a group of motivated people, confident in their ability to go out and actually do the practical things that the new technology requires, as well as act as 'change agents' in their own communities.

The cultural and technical change, while it may appear simple, is in fact quite major. The historic system of land use has been

150

spasmodic and itinerant grazing with traditional rights of access has been associated with spatial overgrazing, regular cutting of grass and denudation of shrubs and trees for cooking fuel, and annual burning. The appearance of fences, gates and stiles requires a whole new human discipline to be imposed or self-imposed.

The community effects are still evolving. We have been able to provide paid employment. We have been able to provide superior grazing for village cattle. We have been able to assist villagers with problems of animal health. We have trained officials and technicians both at the project and also in New Zealand. But nevertheless the stability and persistency of the legacy will remain a niggling concern.

Professor J. RAMACHANDRAN (*Vice-Chancellor, Madurai-Kamaraj University*):

UNIVERSITIES AND RURAL DEVELOPMENT: A SUGGESTED APPROACH

'In the course of world history, seldom has the greatness of a nation long survived the disintegration of its rural life. For untold ages man by nature has been a villager and has not long survived in any other environment . . . . . So long as a nation's rural life is vigorous it possesses reserves of life and power. When for a long time cities draw the cream of life and culture from the villages returning almost nothing, as has been the case in India during the last two centuries, the current village resources of culture and energy become depleted and the strength of the nation is reduced'[1].

Gandhiji was quite concerned about this and wrote: 'If the village perishes, India will perish too'[2]. Several schemes have been tried in many parts of the world to bring about a renaissance among our rural population, increase their standard of living and make rural settlements beautiful, healthy, and attractive from the point of view of both employment and healthy living. These efforts in fact have not been really successful in producing the desired results.

[1]*Report* of the University Education Commission, Vol.1, p.388, second reprint 1983.
[2]*Harijan*, 29.8.1936, p.226.

The socio-economic goals that have been aimed at need to be transformed into realities. This can be done only by making the people conscious of their role in bringing about this transformation. The deterrent for the implementation and realisation of the goals has been the inertia of the machinery used for this purpose, the apathy of the people, not to speak of the weakness in administrative structure, the absence of a central decision-making body, the lack of power to deal with the out-moded land tenure laws, the mortgage system, legislation, absentee-landlordism and lack of micro-level survey of available resources. These are all factors which can delay progress by years. In fact these diverse factors could even negate the reforms brought about by legislation. The attitude of people is also very important.

Rural development may be viewed as a process of socio-economic change directed primarily towards:—

(*a*) satisfying basic needs (food, shelter, clothing, health, education, transport, communication)—starting from the needs of the rural poor;

(*b*) creating self-reliance.

The provision of the goods and services corresponding to basic needs cannot be a matter of charity which is neither economically sustainable nor consistent with the dignity of the recipients. Employment opportunities should therefore be created, so that the target population could earn the purchasing power to secure their basic needs.

Can the universities do something? Our society expects our universities to be ivory towers, frontier posts and service stations all at the same time. While direct involvement in rural reconstruction may be desirable and feasible in the case of technological universities and institutes, it cannot be applied as a general rule. For the affiliation-type universities with a large number of colleges—liberal arts colleges—it is often not possible to get directly involved. Even without getting directly involved, universities can play a significant role. For example, with the availability of diverse expertise it is possible for the universities to assess the potential for development in our rural settlements; survey the resources of men and material available and plan for their rational utilization; explore the possibilities of establishing new industries or introduction of new plants and animals to increase the agricultural production.

In rural development activities we have to help the rural settlers to help themselves. Any direct involvement like cleaning or building roads, although it inculcates in the young minds that there is nothing 'infra dig' about manual labour, has hardly had the desired impact on the rural dweller. The university could get involved in rural development in a more meaningful way by assessing the available natural resources and suggesting methods for their rational utilization. By studying carefully the 'inputs' and 'outputs' it is possible to suggest ways and means of increasing the output.

The first task would be to create a mechanism by which a survey of the natural resources, available manpower, available technology, a health survey, nutritional survey, economic and development potential survey, could be taken up. Because of the availability of manpower in the university—the students—it is possible for the university to undertake these surveys. Further, a large and varied expertise is available to guide in these surveys and make useful deductions. For example, the botany and zoology departments could be involved in a survey of local flora and fauna availability and distribution with an eye on those capable of utilization. The geology department can survey the geological formation, types and kinds of rock and available minerals. The chemistry department could make a soil survey and prepare soil maps; the physics department could prepare weather maps and also study local weather conditions. The geography department could help in preparing accurate maps. The mathematics and statistics department could assess the available potential wealth and prepare models for field testing. The agricultural as well as botany and zoology departments could be involved in the introduction of new crops and plants. The economics department may make an economic survey and the sociology department could study the social structure, manners and customs. The history department can look at the rural settlement in its historical perspective and the political science department can look at village government. The language departments have a significant role to play in the development of communication skills.

Nutritional status of the community is as important as health. It is generally believed that most of the rural poor suffer from malnutrition. Vitamin A deficiency is fairly high among children in rural areas. Severe cases of vitamin A deficiency leading to blindness have been reported. Further, nutrition is believed to play a dominant role in brain development. As pointed out by Dr. Swaminathan[1]: 'the human brain reaches 80–90% of its full weight by the age of four and . . . if children do not get adequate protein during this critical period the brain never develops properly. Comparative studies on intelligence of different ethnic groups will have to be viewed hereafter from this point of view'.

[1]Swaminathan, M.S. (1967), Parliament review.

Similarly, ecological survey of the rural settlement is a very important aspect of rural development. We need complete details of all factors which are of ecological significance like land, soil, water, climatic conditions and natural biological resources. Detailed studies on microclimates, evapotranspiration and moisture cycle could be undertaken by the biology students. These are interesting areas of work and would help us to assess the potential of the rural settlement, and may also help us to reduce environmental degradation. Ecological survey also includes an inventory of biological resources. We require data on: number of trees and their type; number and type of shrubs, weeds; animals (wild) sighted; animals (domestic); common parasites; common predators; crops grown; cropping pattern; common plant diseases.

A continuous monitoring of health is necessary. Most of us do not work to our maximum capacity because of ill health. Studies on capacity to work have not been made. Recent studies on porters who carry heavy loads have shown that most of them do not have the minimum calorific input necessary. Somehow they are able to work. This is another area where precise measurements could be made by students of physiology. How much energy does a manual labourer use when he carries heavy weights, ploughs a field, takes water, drives a bullock cart or is engaged in stone-quarrying? These are valuable data that would help us to plan the overall strategy.

Once the surveys are completed and ready, we can take an overall look at each urban settlement, assess its 'plus' and 'minus' points and plan the strategy for its development without environmental degradation. This will also help in planning for a rational utilization of the available resources.

The promotion of *scientific and technological information centres* is essential in order to create an appreciation of the role of science and technology in development and the choice of technology appropriate to the local needs. These centres, to be set up by the universities/colleges, must use audio-visual aids to create an awareness among the rural settlers about science and technology. The centres could also serve in technology transfer and help select the technology appropriate to local needs.

A study of the available skills and traditional technologies is necessary. Not all traditional technologies are necessarily bad. Slight improvements to an existing technology often lead to considerable output. A ball-bearing fixed to a potter's wheel has led to an increase in the output by several folds.

Universities, if properly geared, can play a key role in the transfer of technology to rural areas. This would mean setting up demonstration units and actually operating them to show that it is feasible. This would also mean that we should be able to develop communication skills, *i.e.* develop the idiom to communicate with the shrewd villagers. Considerable emphasis will have to be laid on this aspect, which is one of the neglected areas of work in most universities. The communication skills need to be developed using all available media—spoken and written word, audio-visual aids, mass media, media of entertainment like cinema, television and so on. In the area of rural development, the universities can serve as a 'think tank' and planning body.

Once the surveys are completed we can set up a series of models. Once we have an assessment of the 'inputs' and 'outputs' we can theoretically calculate the 'output' if the 'inputs' are increased— by a factor of 10, 100 and so on. The entire rural settlement should be studied as a 'system'. Thus, knowledge about flows of energy, materials, people and information, would be invaluable in our rural development activities. A systematic approach is needed. We must not lose sight of the fact that in many policy decisions related to human settlements conflicts may arise between the desire to obtain short-term benefits and the need to minimise long-term adverse consequences.

Functional literacy of adults is another area where universities can play a significant role. In many developing countries literacy levels are low, especially in rural areas. Many adult education campaigns have been mounted. The neo-literate becomes an illiterate as soon as he learns the alphabet since there are few literatures for neo-literates. We must devise a new strategy, a programme in which it is desirable to aim at functional literacy; production of a number of simple books using the most common words used in that particular trade or vocation. Start with the word—simple ones first. In this way an adult learner would be able to associate the word with the object and slowly learn to spell. In this way he will not be driven away from the classes by boredom, which is normally the case when adult learners have to learn the letters of the alphabet slowly. Using the words in every-day use in their trade and vocations would make it interesting and would prompt them to learn. . This would be particularly useful in functional literacy programmes for farmers. There is also a need to produce a large number of reading materials especially for neo-literates.

The universities can also play a role in bridging the communication gap between the rural and urban settlers, between the educated and illiterate persons. Mass media could be used effectively. Radio has played a significant part in the Green Revolution in India. Cinema is the most important medium which has a tremendous hold on the people, and so also the television. We have to use these effectively to get across messages on family planning, nutrition, hygiene, health, and use it to transform the rural settlements into heavens of prosperity and good living. These most effective media are being used now mostly for entertainment. Universities should plan to have cells for developing an effective communication system, including the use of mass media like wall newspapers, radio, cinema, stage plays and so on.

In any rural development activity the key person is the villager himself. Unless we create an awareness among the rural population, expose them to the possibilities for raising the standard of living and make them participate willingly and effectively, all schemes for rural development may fail. The universities could play a part in developing the necessary communication skill to bring about the change of attitude by creating this awareness.

*Mr D. G. R. Belshaw and Mr I. D. Thomas (respectively *Reader* and *Senior Lecturer, School of Development Studies, University of East Anglia*):

THE RURAL DEVELOPMENT CHALLENGE TO THE UNIVERSITIES: SAFETY IN THEORY OR DANGER IN PRACTICE?

The universities often may seem remote from rural communities but they continue to draw a proportion of their students from the villages and small towns and, increasingly, a concern for the welfare of the rural inhabitants informs and directs the teaching, applied research, and theoretical debates of many university faculty. This paper seeks to explore some of the ways in which these interests have developed in recent years, and looks forward to the further strengthening of these links to the mutual benefit of the universities and the rural communities. It is concerned principally with the welfare of rural communities in third-world countries, and particularly those of the tropics. A basic distinction is made between those rural development studies with a prime interest in

*Mr. Belshaw was unable to attend the Congress but the paper was presented by Mr. Thomas.

explaining the process of rural change, and those with a commitment to the specification of strategies of change. It is the old dichotomy of those seeking to understand and those seeking to change the world they observe.

Four points are made. The universities have a responsibility, and never more so than in the developing countries, to direct a proportion of their research and operational activities towards the needs of the poor, particularly the rural poor. This may be seen as a deviation from the traditional role of the academic. Secondly, because of the character of the problems which rural communities face, there is a special need for interdisciplinary research. A commitment to interdisciplinarity or at least a willingness to work in multi-disciplinary teams may be seen also as a new emphasis for university staff. A third requirement is participation in activities— research, training, executive work—which may seem at an inappropriate level or in an undesirable location by comparison with university-based work. Finally, if a substantial number of the members of a university are to devote significant proportions of their time to rural-focused and rural-based research and operational work, new institutional arrangements are required within the universities.

Of course none of these things is entirely new. There have always been some faculty who have undertaken fieldwork in, and devoted their energies to the understanding of, rural communities and who have sought to improve the lot of the inhabitants of rural areas. There are cogent grounds, however, for examining the case for an increase in the scale of this participation, and for a review of the nature of the links between universities and rural communities.

This paper does not consider the recruitment and training of students from rural areas alongside others from cities and towns, but focuses on three other ways in which individuals or institutional groups of researchers in universities may affect the development of the rural communities: the development of theory, research in and for rural communities, and training of rural community workers.

When directed towards the analysis of rural development processes, the traditional academic concern with the pursuit of understanding through theory and model construction and testing often leads ultimately to new governmental policies and programmes, or to new directions for the efforts of international agencies. National agricultural programmes emphasising hybrid plants and farm mechanisation, for example, have as one explanation of their origin theories about the most effective and rapid method of stimulating national economic growth or income redistribution, as well as the more obvious explanation noting the years of laboratory or workshop research and field trials with plants, animals and machinery. Again, economic, social and political theories have been generated rapidly to explain the apparent continuing failure of efforts to develop agriculture and industry, to stem rural-urban migration or the rate of national population growth, to improve the balance of trade, or to enhance the performance of the various forms of organisation found in the public and private sectors. New theories have often led to changes in development objectives or the means chosen to achieve them.

A dilemma exists in that the recognition given to much university work in the social sciences is related to the speed with which new insights about processes and strategies are identified and old theories are toppled to make way for the new. This form of academic progress is built on critical analysis of the weaknesses of former theory and practice. The faster (and, by implication, the more successful) the pace of this intellectual development, the faster the overthrow of each theory or set of supposedly key factors and forces. By contrast, it may be argued that resolute commitment to a basic strategy for development and its long-continued application with a well-defined, preferably single, objective is the surest way to achieve an impact in rural areas. This interpretation is itself debatable, however, and is the subject of controversy in the field of rural development theory and planning.

A review of the evolution of development theory contrasts sectoral and project approaches to rural improvement with those based on integrated rural development or comprehensive community schemes; it also traces the evolution from top-down to bottom-up styles of intervention in terms of public sector organisation and behaviour. Concurrently with these changes in theoretical perspective there has been a growing awareness of the necessity for adopting both multi- and inter-disciplinary approaches to the understanding of the development process as, for instance, in the investigation of the distribution and causation of rural poverty, and in the use of models derived from general systems theory or from political economy. This has meant adjustment in styles of thinking, re-tooling, and new working environments for many academic staff. A basic choice facing universities has been whether or not they will encourage, and provide the institutional resources to support, individuals who wish to commit themselves to 'engaged problem solving', compared with the more traditional activity of 'disengaged analysis' and, if they do, with what degree of priority.

The other two sets of university activities with an impact on rural areas have a more immediate effect either in specific rural communities or more widely across the rural sector as a whole. The first case arises directly from problem-solving work in the rural areas. The second follows from a variety of forms of training which may take place at the university or elsewhere, but is for people who have rural development as their prime concern.

University faculty work in rural communities for many purposes. These range from the short-term visit for case studies or field trials to sustained involvement in pilot projects for educational, agricultural or industrial schemes, to wholesale adoption of communities as field laboratories for agricultural development (*e.g.* the 'land grant university' model), community medicine, and other schemes with an improvement component, or to involvement with local planning at one level or another (village, ward, district, etc.) over periods of several years.

Some of the more important applied research areas, briefly described, where university-based researchers are playing significant roles are in developing: monitoring of rural-urban balance at the macro-economic level; continuous planning; decentralized planning for rural regions; equity-oriented planning; rapid rural appraisal; integrated natural resource assessment; environmental impact assessment; village resource-use and -access planning; appropriate technology research and development; farming systems research; micro-project screening and evaluation; social impact analysis; and management information systems for rural development.

Some key issues in this type of work with rural communities are: the degree of commitment of the researchers to the real interests of the community members as opposed to the research findings and their effects within academic circles; the extent to which the community becomes dependent on the outsider for initiatives and support; and the replicability of the work as a model for use more widely throughout a nation and the willingness of local or national governments to adopt the model and to adapt it to different environments.

An in-service training role is simply an extension of the function of universities as producers of a national stock of high-level manpower. and represents a capitalisation of their skill as teachers or as producers of programmes and texts for learning. Training may be given within the university for central or local government staff concerned with rural development, or directly to members of rural communities. Programmes may vary in duration from a few days to a year or more. Alternatively training may be offered on an extra-mural basis in the rural community. This might involve faculty in local travel for courses of short duration, or substantial spells away from the university in the case of community-located training programmes. The dilemma here is twofold: should university personnel devote time and energy to this form of activity or are they better engaged in other work? And how suitable are normal university teaching methods for the type of instruction which is most effective for in-service training? It is the contention of this paper that unless university staff play their part in elaborating, testing and evaluating the mutually supporting methodologies which are emerging as useful components of effective intervention and participation in the direction of rural change and in explicating these methods in training texts and courses, the quality and timely availability of improved procedures and trained manpower will suffer.

The university sector, individual universities, and departments and faculty members each have a possible range of responses to the issues raised, and these will reflect the degree of commitment to the needs of rural communities. The resources devoted to rural-focused university work and the location and growth paths determined for rural-located institutions is one sign of this degree of commitment. The relative status afforded applied and operational units, including research centres and training institutes, within each university is often more an indicator of a preconceived attitude to the value of these activities than a reflection of their intrinsic potential value to society or their actual performance over time. The adjustments to terms of service and the significance afforded operational, training and applied work in matters of promotion and representation are further evidence of the degree of support, or lack of it, among the community of scholars and administrators. Ultimately the willingness of academics to concern themselves with rural problems and to produce work of scholarly worth as well as practical value is a key factor, but the structural and contractual circumstances may favour, or discourage, these endeavours.

This paper argues that rural development problems are sufficiently important, and the complexity of the issues presents such an intellectual challenge, that the case is a compelling one for continued and enhanced involvement by universities in both the study of the processes of rural change and the design of more socially beneficial modes of intervention in that process. The challenge from the rural areas is clear: it remains to be seen whether the universities have the will to utilize the capacity which they undoubtedly possess not only to develop and test theories but to deploy directly their rigorous and systematic approach in problem-solving and in training to assist the processes of rural development.

SUB-TOPIC 2 (D): IN THE COMMUNITY

DISCUSSION

Professor Sir James Stewart discussed current experiences of his College in projects in the South Pacific and the People's Republic of China. These are areas of great geographical and cultural diversity in which institutions have to operate their development role.

The first project mentioned was a consultancy report on the school of agriculture in Western Samoa, a constituent college of the University of the South Pacific, whose main campus is in Fiji about 950 km away. The role of that institution in supporting agriculture as the foundation and key to development could be furthered if courses could be made more relevant to the time and the place and if staff were more appropriately oriented to rural life and contact with farmers. More practical work should feature in the curriculum and farm units of the college needed to be upgraded to make this possible.

In the People's Republic of China his College, along with private consultants, had become involved in work with the Department of Agriculture in a project to upgrade vast tracts of hill areas that were suitable for grazing development. These areas are currently overworked and suffering denudation. Here the lesson was that a high degree of participation by 30 or 40 Chinese agricultural students in practical as well as theoretical development work would ensure that fencing, fertilizer application and anti-erosion work would be seen as a practical as well as theoretical matter and so have some chance of becoming established in normal practice.

In general Sir James argued for a high degree of personalised teaching with manual as well as theoretical work as a means of involving universities in rural development while continuing their teaching function.

Professor Ramachandran, in his paper, argued that the involvement of students in manual work in the rural areas was less useful than their involvement in various kinds of surveys to be used in development planning work. Virtually every department in the university could play its role in using specialised knowledge to design surveys and collect, process, or disseminate information. Professor Ramachandran also discussed the experience of his University in introducing undergraduate courses in rural development. While these proved popular, the experience had been disappointing in that these students saw the degree as a means of escape from rural life rather than as an opportunity to play leadership roles in rural areas.

Professor W. F. Musgrave (New England) drew the attention of the meeting back to the two questions he felt were left unanswered. The first concerned the nature of integrated rural development where, he felt, there was a 'trade-off' between equity and efficiency. The second concern was the interdisciplinary and practical work, where there might equally be trade-offs between practical involvement and the maintenance of excellence in scholarship and research.

Sir James Stewart acknowledged that there was a knife-edge balance to be maintained, particularly in institutions of the land grant model like his own, committed to extension as well as teaching and research, but argued strongly that this balance can be maintained with excellence on both sides.

Professor J. M. Mungai (Nairobi) cited the great diversity of rural peoples and asked whether universities understood the small-scale farmer or pastoralist. He cited his recent continuing education work with primary school drop-outs where there had been a disappointing percentage of 'non-learners'. This led to some discussion of comparative experience elsewhere.

Mr. Thomas preceded his summary of the Belshaw/Thomas paper with a list of issues which he had identified during the week and in subsequent discussion added another. Overall there is the question of whether universities should engage in rural development at all. Then there are the questions—

● who should fund work done in rural areas?
● what are the terms and conditions under which university people should work on these projects?
● is interdisciplinary work really possible?
● is there value in some universities being local institutions rather than national?

The paper emphasised the responsibility which rests with academics if they choose 'engaged' development work in the field as against 'disengaged' theoretical work in their institutions of learning, and took an engaged position associated with a gradualist as against a revolutionary view of change and development. The paper discussed some 14 means of involvement of universities, and recognised and outlined a number of problems in the new roles that these require. These problems include: the need to develop new kinds of rewards for academics; the need to avoid creating dependency of local communities upon academic personnel; a requirement that activities be replicable; the need to get local people involved in modifying new ideas to their own cultural situation. The paper also discussed alternative institutional arrangements for the involvement of university staff in 'engaged' work and the funding and personnel problems that may be encountered.

Professor M. Chisholm (Cambridge) favoured university involvement in development as well as teaching and research. However generalisation was difficult when circumstances in the different countries of the Commonwealth were so diverse. In some countries there was only one university which must have diverse functions. In some, such as Malaysia, there were few universities and each specialised in, say, science or technology or agriculture. In other countries again, such as India or Nigeria, there were many universities and some internal differentiation was possible. But was the fact that in India there were ten agricultural universities to be applauded as recognition of the importance of agriculture or regretted as a failure of other universities to become more involved?

Dr. (Mrs.) Jyoti H. Trivedi (S.N.D. Thackersey Women's) felt that universities should be left to experiment with diverse ways of becoming involved with their own environments. Extension work was now a fundamental role in Indian universities where most institutions should no longer be viewed as apex bodies but as places with strong local commitments. Curricular development for training of officials and of villages themselves using new telecommunication facilities should now play an important part for universities.

Dr. R. D. Baeta (U. of Ghana) felt that universities in Africa had an unfortunate hold on primary and secondary school curricula because of their recruitment policies. This enhanced the urban academic orientation of schooling and encouraged youth migration from the rural areas. He also noted that universities served local as well as national communities and felt that Africa should move, along the route taken by India, towards American-style local universities.

Dr. S. S. Johl (Punjabi) argued that in India the pros and cons of involvement were argued out long ago. The poorer countries now could not afford a university system which was disengaged. Universities had long been involved in the dissemination as well as development of knowledge. What was needed now was more care for the recipient system: 'we are pouring food on closed mouths'.

Professor A. M. Patwari (Bangladesh U. of Engineering and Technology) outlined the different position of Bangladeshi universities in comparison with those in India and discussed the research role which was possible in Bangladesh in relation to the work of the Department of Rural Development.

Dr. W. C. Found (York, Canada) felt that the remaining barrier to engaged work was the classical education traditional of western Europe. However the American land grant colleges had marked a major shift away from this tradition which was happily being followed elsewhere. Action research and interdisciplinary research now presented no problems. However field involvement could never be managed by a university alone. Aid agencies, local universities, consulting companies and banks provided vital knowledge and skills. A further problem for universities occurred when there was a confidentiality requirement in consultancy work.

Mr. G. B. K. Hooja (Gurukula Kangri) discussed his experience in agricultural as well as conventional university setting with involvement in community development and other activities. Universities, encouraged by the Planning Commission, were now being systematically linked with major developments in the Gangetic plain, the Himalayas and elsewhere.

Dr. A. T. Porter (Sierra Leone) entered into debate with Sir James Stewart on his views about the role of universities in the training of change agents.

163

Sub-Topic 2(e)

THE DEVELOPMENT OF PEOPLE: EDUCATION AND TRAINING

Chairman: Dr. D. KIMBLE

Vice-Chancellor of the University of Malawi

Rapporteur: Mr. D. ANDERSON-EVANS

Senior Administrative Officer, Committee of Vice-Chancellors and Principals of the Universities of the United Kingdom

Thursday, 18 August

Mr. N. A. KUHANGA (*Vice-Chancellor, University of Dar es Salaam*): For some time now the debate in developing countries of Africa has been focusing on the relevance of education and training to national needs and problems. Both the Economic Commission for Africa (ECA) and the Organization of African Unity (OAU) have joined in the debate urging African universities to re-examine their role in national development programmes, and since in virtually all countries the economy is agriculturally based (except perhaps in Nigeria, Sudan and the Arab countries in the north) the urge has been directed toward orientating university curricula to rural development. Indeed Unesco, too, has joined forces with ECA and OAU in urging African universities to re-examine their role in rural development. In 1980 it convened in Dakar, Senegal, a meeting of nine experts from African universities to discuss how best universities could be involved in rural development activities. Again, in 1983, Unesco convened another meeting of 15 experts at the University of Yaoundé, Cameroon, to discuss the question of reorientating and re-structuring university teaching and research in order to meet developmental needs of the countries they serve.

At the national level politicians and government leaders have been questioning the justification of investing heavily in university education at the expense of other equally important sectors like agriculture, communication and health, etc. In Tanzania, for example, President Julius K. Nyerere (who is also Chancellor of the University of Dar es Salaam), while acknowledging the

164

contribution made so far by the University to manpower development, has challenged the University to show whether it could not
have done better in terms of producing experts whose attitude
toward working in rural areas was positive enough actually to
make them work in rural areas.

The response of universities to the call for curriculum orientation
toward relevance in order to reflect national realities has varied
from university to university. Some universities have received it
with some scepticism, seeing it as an interference in academic
freedom; others have tried genuinely to respond positively with a
remarkable degree of success. In this short paper I shall try to
share with the participants the experiences of the University of
Dar es Salaam in its efforts to contribute towards training of
manpower for rural development.

Tanzania, like most other developing countries, has a population
which is basically rural. About 85% of the people live in rural
areas, where the main pre-occupation is agriculture, and for the
most part subsistence agriculture. Because of this the government
has made a deliberate decision to increase investment in rural
development under the conviction that an effective attack on
poverty '. . . can only be made by going directly to the rural areas
and dealing with the problems there . . .'

Indeed it has now become the pattern to plan for integrated
regional development. What this means is that a whole administrative region is studied comprehensively, and its economic potentials
identified, in order to exploit such potentials, and to determine
the kind of infrastructure which would be needed in order to effect
meaningful development. For rural development '. . . must be a
description of the whole strategy of growth—the approach to
development, and the prism through which all policies are seen,
judged, and given priority . . .'

It has now become the practice to encourage donor countries to
finance integrated regional development programmes. As a result
mainland Tanzania has now been divided into 'spheres of influence'. For example, the Federal Republic of Germany, Japan,
Norway and the World Bank have each selected a region in
which to carry out integrated development programmes. Such
programmes normally include agriculture, education, health, transport network, etc.

Involvement of the University

The University of Dar es Salaam has been involved at two
levels, namely, at the level of research and feasibility studies, and
at the level of training.

Research. Through the Institute of Resource Assessment (IRA—formerly known as the Bureau of Resource Assessment and Land Use Planning (BRALUP)), the University has been involved in planning for integrated rural development in four regions—Rukwa, Iringa, Mbeya and Ruvuma. In Rukwa the study had two stages. The first stage was to map out economic zones of the whole region, showing arable land, grazing land, areas for afforestation and water catchment areas, etc. This stage has been completed; a map has been produced which shows all the economic zones in the region. The study has now entered the second stage. This stage entails orienting leaders of the region—party and government leaders alike—on how to make use of the information supplied on the map. At the same time a planning team has already been set up to plan concrete projects for a systematic exploitation of the economic zones identified during the study.

In the other three regions the study has been a part of the regional comprehensive study. It has been concerned with drawing up water master plans aimed at proper utilization of available water sources in the respective regions for economic use as well as domestic consumption. The idea is that as far as possible rural water supply should not involve the use of pumps which run on diesel or petrol, in order to avoid the problem of maintenance and constant repairs. Thus shallow wells which use hand-pumps should be preferred to deep wells. In fact, if the target of providing water for every village within 400 metres is to be reached in the near future then there is no alternative to choosing the cheapest approach to doing so.

The master plans for the three regions are now ready and study has entered into the second phase—one of implementation. A few villages have been selected for a pilot project. In the selected villages, villagers are fully involved in all aspects of project implementation. They are involved in the selection of sites for the shallow wells, or in the location of domestic points of pipe water. They in fact determine the number of families to be served by a well or domestic point so as to avoid congestion, etc. Villagers are also involved in the actual construction of wells or in the laying of pipes, as the case may be. Total participation by villagers has two advantages. The first is the reduction in costs in providing water to a village. The second advantage which is even more important is that villagers accept the project as their own and feel accountable for its success or failure. So far the pilot project is progressing well. It is hoped that the experience gained from it will be useful in the rest of the regions.

In agriculture the department of crop science, in conjunction with the division of forestry, has been carrying out demonstrations on the use of compost and animal manure and intercropping of maize with leguminous plants. The initial results have been so successful that the government decided to bring all regional and district functionaries from mainland Tanzania (20 regions and 86 districts) together with decision-makers for a two-week seminar on how to prepare and use compost manure. The objective is that small farmers should be encouraged to use compost and animal manure instead of chemical fertilizers which are both expensive and difficult to obtain. Farmers from villages around the faculty of agriculture, forestry and veterinary science were invited to come and learn from the demonstrations throughout the demonstration period. It is now intended to move the demonstration to some of the neighbouring villages where the staff and students will work with villagers on selected plots. At the national level, regional and district agricultural officers together with their respective authorities are expected to identify villages which can start putting into practice what has been learned from the demonstration farms of the University.

Training. Right from its inception the University of Dar es Salaam has been involved in training manpower for rural development. Up to 1975 it was involved, through the Institute of Adult Education, in both long and short training programmes for adult educators who came from the co-operative movement, the community development field, agriculture, health, education, etc. The primary objective of the training was to equip trainees with skills and techniques of helping the people they were working with to plan projects which were based on their own needs. Thus the training included skills in identifying problems and their causes; working out possible solutions; identifying resources available locally both human and financial/material; and, finally, working out strategies for solving the problem so identified.

Running parallel to the programme of adult educators was a radio study group programme patterned on the Swedish study circles system. This programme was aimed at helping village leaders to acquire skills similar to those imparted to adult educators but at a less sophisticated level. The approach used was to provide the groups with study materials and study guides prepared specifically for that purpose, and discussion leaders who could guide discussions in the group. The groups met twice a week to listen to radio broadcasts on a given topic and at the end of each broadcast they held lengthy discussions, all the time relating the subject matter of the broadcast to local situations. The idea was that at the end of each unit of study villagers would come with concrete action plans. Topics covered included agriculture, education, health, etc.

The overall aim of the programme was to enable rural people to control their own activities within the framework of their village communities. They must 'participate not just in the physical labour involved in economic development but also in the planning of it and the determination of priorities'. Indeed the general aim was achieved, for in most villages the programme resulted in action of one type or another. For instance some villages decided to build pit latrines, others decided to construct dispensaries or classrooms for their children, etc. After the reorganization of rural life into better planned villages with legal village governments, self-determination has become a permanent feature for all villages.

Unfortunately the Institute of Adult Education is no longer an organ of the University. It has been made an independent institution since 1975. However it has maintained most of the activities it used to carry out under the University, although not with the same intensity.

In the regular academic curriculum the University has introduced a fourth term of eight weeks during which students are afforded the opportunity to acquire practical experience in the field. In professions which will involve our graduates in work in rural areas—for instance agriculture, veterinary science and medicine—students must spend some time in rural areas. Agricultural students spend a minimum of one term in the neighbouring villages where they participate in farm activities with villagers. Medical students spend one full term in a field station where they learn how to run rural health services, sometimes under primitive conditions. This is an important component in their training programme because most of them will be called upon to run rural health centres as satellites of their district hospitals.

Finally, the University has decided to introduce an agricultural extension and education programme. The primary objective of this programme is to help students who study agriculture, forestry and veterinary science to acquire skills of communicating knowledge to the user, that is, the farmer. Experience has shown that much of the new knowledge derived from research and experimentation never reaches the farmer at all owing to lack of communication between the researchers/policy-makers and those who are expected to use it to improve production. In order to rectify this situation the faculty of agriculture, forestry and veterinary science, in conjunction with the Ministry of Agriculture and the Ministry of Livestock Development, has instituted an in-service training programme for field workers intended to help them to acquire skills in and techniques of communication and disseminating information. It is hoped that when they go back to their posts they will be able to establish permanent channels of communication between the centre and the farmers, which will enable information to flow both ways.

Conclusion

In this short account the aim has been to give a few examples of the ways in which the University of Dar es Salaam is trying to contribute to the training of manpower for rural development. It has been indicated that some of the training is done indirectly through the involvement of villagers in programmes which are intended to provide services to rural populations, such as the provision of water. But most of it is through deliberate training programmes designed to help experts to function effectively in rural setting.

However, it must be emphasized here that this is not a success story of the role played by the University in integrated rural development, for to be able to tell such a story objectively one would have to give empirical data to quantify the amount of success achieved. This has not been done in this account, nor was it the intention to do so. It is hoped, however, that the examples given in this short paper are sufficient to stimulate a useful discussion.

Mr. A. M. SETŠABI (*Vice-Chancellor, National University of Lesotho*):

THE VIEW FROM THE NATIONAL UNIVERSITY OF LESOTHO

The National University of Lesotho is making its contribution to integrated rural development mainly through its Institute of Extra-Mural Studies (IEMS). The basic philosophy of the institute is one of: *people helping themselves* through education. Its courses are based on the practical philosophy of: meeting the specific learning needs of those who are engaged in tasks that are related to the building of communities, community organisation and the nation.

169

The accomplishments of the institute include the establishment of the following development organisations: the government's Department of Community Development, later upgraded to the level of the Ministry of Co-operatives and Rural Development; the Lesotho Credit Union Movement; Lesotho Credit Union Scheme for Agriculture (LECUSA); businessmen training centre; eight wholesale co-operatives; co-operative housing projects; part-time university study opportunities; women's development organisations; regional educational centres; workers' training programmes; a Labour Documentation and Research Centre for Southern Africa; also the establishment of the Lesotho Society for Development and Peace (SODEPAX), and promotion of adult education programmes in neighbouring countries.

Once established these organisations become autonomous of IEMS. University staff remain catalysts, educators and consultants.

But This is Not Enough

It is important that the University go beyond this. The goals and programmes of IEMS should not be separated from the nature and goals of the University as a whole. It is important that the entire University community come face to face with the needs of the people and their communities. Leaving extension education to an institute is not sufficient. Lesotho can maintain the vitality of a liberal university which is also a community-oriented institution. Our country needs the action research, the consultation, the advising, the tutoring and the teaching of the entire University community. Poverty, inappropriate technology, inappropriate consumer practices, inappropriate business procedures, environmental degradation, inappropriate agricultural techniques, and uninformed decision-making are only a few of the areas in which the University's best resources could be employed.

University continuing education must not stop with the establishment of an institute of extra-mural studies or whatever it might be called at any one of our universities. The entire university should be extension and continuing education oriented.

Scenario Formulation

Allow me to formulate a scenario for a more effective contribution of universities to integrated rural development.

Education should be concurrent with the conduct of the responsibilities of adulthood. Enrollees should span the generations. Classes should be held in community centres in public schools, in people's homes, in factories, on farms, etc. Education should be viewed as a continuing (never-ending) process throughout life. Groups who have been traditionally submerged by the tides of history should be on their way to awareness and power. The university should in some way provide access to all citizens when they have the need to learn.

The university should act on the teachable moment, *i.e.* it should reach out to individuals wherever they are at the time that they need to learn something special. It should *not* practise age or occupational discrimination. It should realize that workers of every type and age need opportunities to renew their enthusiasm, strike out in a new direction and improve their skills as much as any professor on sabbatical leave does. The university should not practise credential discrimination either. It should find ways of reaching out to those adults who did not have an opportunity to complete secondary school. Nor should it discriminate against those with heavy family and work responsibilities. It should find ways to provide informal and practical instruction that is geared to family and work schedules and those who have achieved competence in their profession, their industry, their trade, their organisation and their community. In so doing the university will not have lowered standards. Rather, it will have established many standards. It will have various standards for various groups.

The focal point should be the needs and interests of individual learners and community. The university should change with new conditions, demands and circumstances. It should not be trapped by tradition. But it should not forsake tradition for the sake of innovation. It should go beyond reacting to people and community needs and interests. It should forecast the shape of society to come and lead it to an understanding of impending change.

But it should not aim at providing all educational opportunities. Rather, using its ability to research, programme and co-ordinate, it should link various community organisations together in the provision of horizontally and vertically articulated learning opportunities.

It should also find ways to aid those who are in need of better housing, health, employment, and a more full citizenship. It should directly address specific problems, *e.g.* drought, erosion, urbanization, over-population, declining farm production. It should make a significant contribution to the growth and stabilisation of local economies, to holding living costs in check, to a wiser use of local resources and to a regaining or maintenance of local control over basic needs and life-support systems.

By taking on such responsibilities the university need not abandon its important role of generating knowledge. There need not be an inconsistency here. Naturally the university will not be able to solve all of the ills of society. But it is the best institution qualified to research, identify, analyse, carefully define and see the inter-relationship of societal problems. It is the best institution qualified to design well-thought-out problem-solving approaches to societal problems. It should be a catalyst and counsellor to those organisations and agencies which *can* take necessary problem-solving action.

The university should be plugged into society. There should be citizen advisory and assistance bodies working closely with each of its faculties, institutes and projects. Its new and enthusiastic constituencies will be demanding, will be enriching, will be challenging, will shake us up, and will be supportive. But the university will be better supported than ever before. Its new and community-wide constituency will make it far less susceptible to the whims of narrow interest groups.

And finally the university should be flexible. Each of our universities exists in a different cultural milieu. Each must respond to differing national and individual aspirations and expectations. But the point is, we must respond to something other than a closed institutional interest.

In these ways the universities will be contributing more effectively to integrated rural development.

Dr. B. D. SHARMA (*Vice-Chancellor, North-Eastern Hill University*): The role of universities in rural development can be appreciated in the context of the position which rural areas have come to occupy in the global and national economies after the industrial revolution, and the historical development of the universities themselves in the changing context. A process of polarisation between the Western countries and their dependencies started soon after the industrial revolution, in which the former specialised in the secondary sectors of economic activity while the latter were obliged to continue as predominantly primary-sector economies. The dependencies supplied raw materials to the colonial powers and also provided markets for their machine-made goods. This polarisation is now taking place within the developing economies themselves as between the urban and the rural economies.

The benefits of new advances in science and technology are now becoming available to all nations in ever-increasing measure. The economy of the world is getting integrated. However, in view of the fact that national boundaries are now, more or less, inviolable, in the ultimate analysis the optimum level of development in a country will be determined by the matrix of its population and natural resources. The sectoral structure of a national economy will no doubt determine its level of development but any differences on account of skills and technological inputs should eventually level up unless they are sustained artificially. To that extent such differences are transient.

The countries of the world, from the point of view of rural development, can be broadly divided into three groups:—

(1) Countries with low land-man ratio with predominant urban population and also a predominantly secondary-tertiary sector economy — UK and other West European countries

(2) Countries with high land-man ratio—

(*a*) having a large urban population but a substantial primary sector economy — Canada, US, USSR, Australia

(*b*) primarily rural with a predominant primary-sector economy — African and Latin American countries

(3) Countries with low land-man ratio with a predominant rural population and a predominant primary-sector economy — India, China and South-East Asian countries

The countries in category 2 (*b*), even though predominantly rural, can adopt the models of the urbanized countries in category 2 (*a*). The countries in category 3, however, will have to develop their own models of development in which the rural sector will continue to be predominant in the foreseeable future.

The need for distinctive models of development for many countries which account for a major part of the world's population raises some basic issues about viable production levels and consumption patterns. These issues are relevant even to the advanced countries because of the ecological limits and the rising per capita consumption levels which are already excessive notwithstanding their smaller population size. If we take the present technological parameters as given, since they are not likely to change significantly within a short period, the maximum ecologically sustainable production potential of the world can be worked out. Let it be E and the total world population be N, then the maximum per capita sustainable consumption limit will be defined by E/N. If establishment of an egalitarian social order in the world community is

173

accepted as the desired goal, consumption level for all members of the human society will have to be broadly comparable within certain acceptable tolerance limits. If the consumption level of a section of population is above E/N, either the egalitarian principle will continue to be violated or at some stage the ecological viability norm will be transgressed. Therefore any consumption above the ecologically sustainable per capita consumption level is destructive. The current levels of consumption in the advanced countries, taking the world economy as whole, have already crossed the destruction limits. The same analysis can be applied to the national economies, treating them as closed systems with the national resources and population configuration as given parameters. The consumption patterns of the urban population in these countries, which tend to follow the advanced countries, are destructive and non-sustainable.

The entire question of rural development, therefore, has to be considered within this broad frame both in the global and national contexts. If we turn our attention to the role of the universities in the modern world, they have three important roles. *First,* they are responsible for preparing an increasing proportion of people in all countries for a large variety of tasks in the complex socio-economic systems. *Secondly,* they contribute significantly to the new fund of knowledge in different disciplines, which is the bedrock of all modern developments. *Thirdly,* the universities exercise great influence in the building up of the general social milieu, which, in its turn, determines the structure of the economy.

The universities in the advanced countries have successfully adopted the role of meeting the growing skill requirements of those economies. Education is now a life-long process. In the developing countries, however, the universities have not been able to come out of their traditional frame which has lost much of its significance. Moreover university graduates in these countries, irrespective of their background and attainment, expect good positions in the modern sector. Even the agricultural graduates are keen to have a place in research organisations, extension agencies or other institutions and would prefer to participate in agricultural development as researchers or advisers rather than go to the village and engage personally in agriculture. Consequently there is tremendous overcrowding of the universities.

The role of universities in India in relation to providing skills to the people in the rural sector has been rather limited. However in the past few years restructuring of the undergraduate courses has been initiated under the guidance of the University Grants Commission, which aims at bringing about consonance between the national economy and the university education. A new experiment has been launched in North-Eastern Hill University with the same objective, keeping in view the rich natural resources available in the region. Under this programme study of subjects like agriculture, horticulture, pisciculture, animal production, has been introduced as a part of the arts stream. A student can offer for his BA one of these 'non-traditional' courses besides two traditional academic courses. These courses are quite distinct from formal technical courses with similar nomenclatures. They aim at providing certain skills to the students hailing from rural areas which can be used by them, should they decide to work on their own in their village homes taking advantage of the rich natural resources. Moreover the agricultural universities in India have made significant contribution to the growth of rural economies.

So far as the second role of the universities is concerned, the universities in the advanced countries have largely directed their research effort to solving the problems of their economies. Research in some disciplines like mathematics and physical sciences is universal in character and is not country-specific. However research in applied sciences like agriculture and social sciences must have a national frame, even though the scholars must be quick to capitalise on the advances elsewhere. Research in agriculture in India has now acquired a national character and the economy is getting rich dividends. In other fields, however, where the link between higher studies and their application to specific national issues is not visible, there is a tendency to follow the models developed in the advanced countries, which may not be applicable to the national economy. This tendency is reinforced by the lure of possible international recognition which ironically may also fetch rich rewards even within the country. The tasks of advanced research in familiar areas which require development of new tools, new frames and consequently also the best brains, are relegated to lower priorities. Even within the national economy the modern sector, which has the advantage of having ready-made tools and models, may attract better talent. The preoccupation of the university system in the developing countries with areas of knowledge relevant to the advanced countries and the modern sector within their own economies, which could do with considerable borrowing of research findings in the advanced countries with suitable adaptation, has resulted in considerable redundancy in the national academic pursuits.

The third role of universities is crucial in the developing countries since it provides the frame for their first two roles as well. In the first instance, it is necessary for the universities to understand the

175

real nature of the dualism both in the world economy as between the developed and the developing and in the national economy as between the urban and the rural. Unless the basic equations which are heavily loaded against the rural areas are corrected and the tremendous invisible transfer of resources which is taking place from the rural areas is checked, these areas will continue to lag. The universities have a serious handicap in this role. Traditionally they belong to the high and the urban and have served their needs well in a variety of ways. The universities in developing countries have an added handicap in so far as they tend to borrow the conceptual frame for various disciplines from their peers in the advanced countries. Those frames are unable to accommodate the phenomenon of poverty in general and the conditions of the rural areas in particular in these countries.

The most important task of the university system in the developing countries is to inculcate those values which will help in laying the foundations of an egalitarian system in which the rural and the urban, the organised and the unorganised, the high and the low, all blend harmoniously. This is one of the weaker spots in the Indian university system. A genuinely rural Indian perspective on many an issue facing the economy in areas of technology, of organisational forms, of distributive justice, of consumption patterns, of educational policies, of investment priorities, etc., remains to be developed. There are occasional lone voices but the general milieu continues to be influenced by perspectives developed in the advanced countries and for the modern sector.

The world university system itself has to rise to the occasion. Even in the higher academic circle ethnocentricism tends to prevail. The purely national interests may be posed in the form of concern for the humanity and the inequitable propositions may be painted in the most attractive colours. Here lies the great challenge to the university system all over the world: to provide the right leadership in the realm of ideas so that education can become a positive force for moving towards a social order imbued with the great ideals of equality, fraternity and liberty.

DISCUSSION

Mr. Kuhanga explained that his purpose was to illustrate the experiences of the University of Dar es Salaam in its participation in rural development. The impetus had come both from government wishing the curricula to be oriented towards such developments and from studies established in 1980 and 1983 by Unesco. The University's contribution had been at two levels: research and feasibility studies; and manpower training. The first had entailed mapping out economic zones in selected regions and identifying what could be economically exploited. The consequent implementation involved the full participation of the local inhabitants.

The manpower training for rural development had taken the form of short- and long-term training of adult educators from many subject areas, the objective being to equip trainees in skills and techniques to assist those with whom they worked to identify problems and their causes and to create projects for their solution. Additionally, the University conducted a fourth term during which students acquired practical field experience in rural areas. An agricultural extension and education programme had also been established.

Mr. Setšabi explained that the National University of Lesotho made its contribution to what the United Nations had called 'integrated rural development' mainly, though not solely, through its Institute of Extra-Mural Studies. The basic philosophy underlying its work was of people helping themselves through education. Essentially, its courses were organised for the purpose of helping people to become better at what they are doing. Future plans included university extension centres throughout Lesotho. These should not, it was believed, be separate from the nature and goals of the University as a whole. The entire University community should come face to face with the needs of the people and their communities. Above all, the University should provide access to all citizens who should move in and out of it throughout their lives. Also it should address itself to specific problems such as drought, erosion, urbanisation, overpopulation and declining farm production.

Dr. Sharma first outlined the particular handicap of rural areas in developing countries in contrast with those in industrially advanced countries. Whereas the urban economy tended to imitate the ways of advanced countries, the rural economies formed a languishing sub-strata. Thus development in developing countries could be said to be synonymous with rural development. This entailed careful consideration being given to the issue of equitable distribution and conscious choices about appropriate technologies for different sectors and sub-sectors.

Dr. Sharma then outlined the different classification that could be given to developing countries in respect of land:man ratio, and its consequences for rural development. In respect of the roles for the universities in the economic development of a country, these could be characterised as: (i) preparing an increasing proportion of people for a large variety of positions in the socio-economic system; (ii) contributing to the fund of knowledge in different disciplines; and (iii) influencing the social climate. In respect of the first greater efforts should be made to provide consonance between traditional academic subjects and those related to manpower requirements. Research should be encouraged in areas other than those more usually associated with advanced countries and related to the empirical experience of the students. The distortions in the national economy should be corrected if rural development is to succeed. Universities must rise above the limitations of belonging to and being centred in an urban and organised environment.

Dr. Sharma concluded by describing a variety of ways in which Indian universities and related research institutions were involved in rural development.

SUMMARY OF ENSUING DISCUSSIONS

● To succeed in this pursuit universities needed to work in close collaboration with government ministers and not solely with civil servants (Professor S. M. Guma (Swaziland)).

● Universities tended in this area to assume they had the correct approach but had no strategy to influence. They should educate voluntary organisations about their particular role which, for some traditional universities, might be difficult to play at all (Mr. J. Bikangaga (Makerere)).

● People with skills should put them at the service of the community best suited to those skills (Mr. G. K. Caston (UK Vice-Chancellors' Committee)).

● Evaluation and documentation of work in development programmes should be encouraged to assist subsequent researchers.

● Relationships between universities and governments, who after all were the funding agencies, required careful cultivation (Mr. E. K. Kigozi (Inter-University Council for East Africa)).

The following general principles seemed to have common agreement:—

(i) Encouragement of interdisciplinary studies.

(ii) The need for community-based work in the field.

(iii) The desirability of involving the local community in projects.

(iv) The need for socially appropriate technology.

(v) The importance of evaluation and case studies of successes and failures.

(vi) The value of staff and student exchanges between universities (Mr. J. Matthews (Trent)).

Clearly great ignorance of what was going on in universities in different countries suggested a need for more inter-institution visits followed by case studies. Above all efforts should be made to break the dichotomy between 'developed,' 'developing' and 'underdeveloped' countries (Dr. D. Kimble (Malawi)).

Topic 2

THE CONTRIBUTION OF UNIVERSITIES TO INTEGRATED RURAL DEVELOPMENT

Co-ordinating Chairman's Commentary on the Group's Discussions

Final Plenary Session
Friday, 19 August

Professor R. W. STEEL (*former Principal, University College of Swansea, and Member of Council, National University of Lesotho*): We had a series of very helpful papers which gave rise to lively discussion, much of which had to be truncated because of lack of time. On the very first afternoon we lacked one speaker, Professor B. L. Panditharatne, the Vice-Chancellor of the University of Peradeniya in Sri Lanka, who was prevented from coming to Birmingham though he had already sent in a long and very interesting paper on the Negombo fishermen of Sri Lanka.

The Chancellor of the University of Birmingham, Sir Peter Scott, who spoke to us on *Conservation and Development,* not only read an outstanding paper but enlivened it with numerous asides and participated fully in our discussion throughout the afternoon. He identified two global problems—how to avoid blowing ourselves up, and how not to destroy the life-support system of the planet. Concentrating on the latter problem, his concern was with survival (how to husband natural resources) and with development (how to provide goods for people). His paper gave us a background to all our later discussions because there was no point in thinking about rural development if in fact the environment in which it takes place had been destroyed.

A great deal emerged from our five crowded sessions, where we had a considerable range of expertise and experience, especially from universities with a marked rural component and well-established development programmes, but we had no time to discuss the format of my report, and mine is, therefore, a personal statement though I hope that I shall take most, if not all, of the group with me in what I say.

179

We looked at economic development and its social consequences; change and development of the rural space; appropriate technology; rural development in the community; and the development of people through education and training. We did not spend too much time on definitions. As I had said at the outset of our discussions, integrated rural development so often means what you want it to mean. But the participants in the group were so involved and so understanding that they all recognised that rural development implied much more than agricultural improvement or increased productivity. Development in rural areas must be planned and comprehensive, and in our universities its study must clearly range over many different departments and disciplines.

Some members were at pains to remind us—and this was particularly true of the agricultural economists—that teaching, scholarship and research, with academic excellence in all these aspects, were vital to any university, and they were concerned lest these were being diluted by concern with rural development. But most of the group, while not dissenting from these views about the nature and purpose of universities, also saw the need to apply our studies, and to adapt some at least of the training of our students, and the research of our colleagues, to practical problems. There is, as one very experienced participant put it, a knife-edge between scholarly excellence and activity in the agencies of social change. Another member of the group, in a joint paper entitled *The Rural Development Challenge to the Universities: Safety in Theory or Danger in Practice?*, said:

'Rural development problems are sufficiently important, and the complexity of the issues presents such an intellectual challenge, that the case is a compelling one for continued and enhanced involvement by universities in both the study of the process of rural change, and the design of more socially beneficial modes of intervention in that process. Rather than accept the implied conflict between theory and practice implied by the subtitle of this paper, it will be clear from the preceding discussion that the greater involvement of universities in rural development will provide enhanced opportunities for theory development and testing. Furthermore, the rigorous and systematic approach to knowledge and training which the universities possess needs to be deployed if the complex problems of rural development are to be resolved effectively in practice. The challenge from the rural areas is clear: it remains to be seen whether the universities have the will to utilize the capacity which they undoubtedly possess.'

It was clear on many occasions that we were dealing with many different kinds of university with a wide diversity of problems and opportunities, and that any blueprint applicable to one would not necessarily be useful to another, even in the same continent. But what was very apparent was the need everywhere for an interdisciplinary approach to the problems of rural development. Too often lip service is paid to such activity, and we were all familiar with failures, even disasters, in these cross-disciplinary enterprises; but this should not deter us from striving to approach these problems from the widest possible and most varied points of view. Moreover in such work universities need, as a New Zealand speaker put it, to have their feet in the soil as well as their eyes on the stars, and it may well be necessary for such problems to be tackled with the determination and single-mindedness of a task force or, as one participant put it, 'an activity agency'.

The seminar recognised that many, indeed most, universities in the Commonwealth are urban-based. The chances are that our students, even those from rural areas, will seek work, and find it, in the towns. Somehow we have to fire some at least of our students with a sense of vocation and mission so that more of them will see their careers as lying in the rural sector among the farmers and others who live and work in the countryside. We learned, for example, how the University of Dar es Salaam is contributing to the training of manpower for rural development through the involvement of villages in programmes which are intended to provide services to rural populations such as the provision of water; and most of the training is, therefore, by programmes deliberately designed 'to help express the development function effectively in a rural setting'.

The rural development group is particularly anxious that I should report on a proposal that we should ask the Council of the ACU to look at as understandingly as possible. We believe that a compendium or directory of organisations and of programmes relating to rural development throughout the Commonwealth would be of great value. It would encourage discussion between interested parties; it would assist India to talk to Africa and the Caribbean islands with the Pacific islands; and small countries could learn from large countries, while economically prosperous countries could share experiences with those that are economically less developed. We know that the existing staff in John Foster House, already over-stretched and heavily committed, could not undertake such work but we have reason to believe that one or more of the appropriate trusts might look sympathetically and generously at any proposal put forward by the ACU on our behalf.

Time does not permit me to refer to many other points that

emerged from our discussions—including the danger to the environment through the use of some toxic substances produced in developed countries such as our own and then sold to developing countries; the need to ensure that the ecological balance of the environment is not disturbed by programmes of rural development; the necessity to create wealth before it can be redistributed by systems of taxation or any other means; the importance of understanding and co-operation between universities and government departments—and non-governmental and international agencies too—in programmes of rural development; and the inadequacy of many of our definitions such as 'the third world', and even 'the North' and 'the South' of the Brandt report. But I trust that I have succeeded in conveying something of the enthusiasm of the group and of their hopes for positive action as a result of our discussions.

The observant among you may have noticed, as we went through Kidderminster last Wednesday on our way to Ironbridge, the name of the well-known West Midlands estate agents, Dolittle and Dalley. That name would seem to be a suitable motto for many international, Commonwealth and even national gatherings. What we have talked about in Birmingham will be enshrined for ever in the report to be published in a year that George Orwell has already made memorable, 1984. But our group hopes that there will be more than that report, valuable though that will be. 'Dolittle and Dalley' must not be true of the wonderful Congress provided by the ACU and the University of Birmingham during the past few days. We hope to see something specific emerging from the Congress and, far from being 'Dolittle and Dalley', we trust that the Council will be prepared to undertake a great deal, for the sake of us all, and to do it quickly.

In discussing integrated rural development we felt that what we were thinking about was every bit as important as—and in some countries far more significant than—the other topics that we shall hear about during the course of the afternoon. There are countries represented here—Tanzania, for example—where 85% of the people live in rural areas and the main occupation nearly everywhere is agriculture; hence the Tanzanian government's deliberate decision has been to increase very considerably investment in rural development since this is the only effective way to make an attack on the poverty of the masses.

Rural development we see as a great challenge. The theme of the Congress, *Technological Innovation: University Roles,* means for many of us the encouragement of development in the rural sector, whereby we ensure that societies living in the countryside receive at least as much attention as those resident in urban areas. As you, Mr. Chairman, put it in your welcome to us on page 3 of the Congress *Handbook:* 'The prime duty of a university is to scholarship, but that is not to say that the universities can be isolated from society; and we who are privileged to work in them are acutely aware of the effect that our efforts will have on our societies'. Those who contributed to our group discussions subscribe entirely to what you say, and we hope that through this Congress the problems and the potentialities of integrated rural development will be better appreciated and understood than they have been in the past.

The world's needs in this field are considerable, and as Sir Peter Scott reminded us, 'the future begins tomorrow'. So there is no time to lose.

Topic 2

OTHER CONTRIBUTIONS

Among the other papers brought to or circulated at the Congress were those mentioned below, which related to this Topic.

Professor R. B. SHUKLA (*Vice-Chancellor, Gujarat Agricultural University*), in a paper on the 'Contribution of Gujarat Agricultural University to Integrated Rural Development', described his university's contributions in the areas of—

● vocational education
● research
● publications in the local language
● training programmes for extension personnel and rural people
● integration of teaching, research and extension.

Mr. K. KOTESWARA RAO (*Member of Syndicate, Andhra University*), in a paper on the 'Role of Agricultural Universities in the Socio-Economic Development of India', discussed the development and functions of the agricultural institutes and universities—their purpose, their distinctive features, their achievements so far, and what they still have to accomplish.

Dr. (Mrs.) JYOTI H. TRIVEDI (*Vice-Chancellor, S.N.D.T. Women's University*) contributed a three-part paper* of which the final part dealt with 'The Contribution of Universities to Integrated Rural Development', and also a report on the first four years of a rural development programme, mainly for women, that had been set up by her own University. In the former, Dr. Trivedi examined the problem of rural development in India, the steps taken by the government of India, the importance of participation by the local community, voluntary organisations and young people, and the part to be played by education. The 'Report of the activities at Udwada (1979–1983)' describes the setting up of the University's rural development project there, the socio-economic context within which it operates and the various activities involved.

See also end of section on Topic 5.

Group Discussions

TOPIC 3

UNIVERSITY/INDUSTRY PARTNERSHIPS

Co-ordinating Chairman: Sir HENRY CHILVER
Vice-Chancellor of Cranfield Institute of Technology

For index to names, see p.427

Sub-Topic 3(a)

DEVELOPMENT OF UNIVERSITY/ INDUSTRY PARTNERSHIPS IN BRITAIN

Chairman: Dr. G. WALCOTT

Acting Vice-Chancellor of the University of Guyana

Rapporteur: Dr. Y. W. LAM

Dean, Faculty of Science, Chinese University of Hong Kong

Monday, 15 August

Dr. S. L. BRAGG (*Regional Broker, Eastern Region, Science and Engineering Research Council*): The British system of support of higher education consists basically of an annual grant to each institution, which is very roughly proportional to the student population, weighted for laboratory subjects: this grant is expected to cover all normal running costs, salaries and basic equipment. Although the money comes from the Department of Education and Science it is filtered in a way which makes earmarking for specific purposes difficult and each institution is autonomous. By the same token the institutions are generally free to set their own objectives, and (unusual in today's climate of modern management) have little information on the criteria (other than purely financial ones) by which they will be judged.

The Research Councils, and in particular the Science and Engineering Research Council (SERC—until 1981 the Science Research Council, SRC), have the role of supporting research of timeliness and promise and of supporting postgraduate students. Unlike the general block grant their support is distributed in a very discriminating way. However until recently the SRC tended to play a passive role. Academics put up proposals for research programmes and applied for finance for postdoctoral research assistants, technicians, equipment, supplies and so on. The proposals were sorted by discipline—chemistry, physics, electrical engineering, etc.—and judged by committees of their academic peers. Those considered most worthy were funded in full, others in part or not at all. Alternatively a head of department put in a

187

bid for research or master's course studentships. His peers in committee allocated a quota to the department, and SRC provided living expenses, laboratory and tuition fees for the PhD or MSc students chosen by the department to fill the quota.

Although much of the work supported by SRC had relevance to industrial problems the system was haphazard and no attempt was made to steer researchers into particular areas. In particular, the PhD, with its emphasis on individual work, often in a narrow specialist field, was seen by many employers as a 'training in unemployability'. The first real attempt to change this situation was the introduction of the scheme now known as CASE—Co-operative Awards in Science and Engineering. Under this scheme the project for a PhD is chosen by an industrial company, in collaboration with an academic department. The project is approved by the relevant SERC committee (basically on the grounds of providing proper training in research) and the student chosen by the department and company together. The company is asked to give house room to the student for at least three months and to pay his laboratory fee (about £500 per year) and his expenses in connection with visits to the firm. The SERC pays the student's fee and gives him an award for living expenses—the company may add up to £1400 a year to the student's award. Similar schemes are available, though less popular, for research or design projects taking less than three years (*e.g.* an MSc or MPhil).

After a rather slow start this scheme has proved very popular. About one third of the 2000 new awards to students for PhDs are now CASE. They are ideal for investigating problems which a company can deal with empirically for the time being, and which it cannot spare a man to work on immediately, but which it feels could become important in the long term. Some large companies keep a 'portfolio' of CASE projects, using them as their method of recruiting PhDs. There are spin-off benefits in promoting regular contacts between an academic department and the company. A key to success is undoubtably keen interest by a member of the company's staff in the project. Problems are now being found in financing students for the increasing number of good projects coming forward: at least 1000 could probably have been started this year. However an increase at the expense of quota awards (of which there are still only one per academic every seven years *on average,* though the distribution is of course very skewed) would undoubtably be seen by the academic fraternity as an unjustifiable attack on 'pure' research.

At the same time, incidentally, the SERC's awards to students on taught master's courses have been limited to courses where it can be demonstrated that a minimum number of those graduating go out into industry afterwards. This is a pretty direct criterion of relevance. Another scheme is the total technology studentships where postgraduate training of a group of students is undertaken as a joint responsibility between an academic department and a company. About 30 of these are awarded each year.

A second major development has been the introduction of co-operative research grants (CRGs) for projects put up jointly by a company and an academic. The criteria for approval are that:

(a) the academic institution will benefit from the work by developing techniques or deriving new knowledge and understanding (otherwise funds could not come from the Department of Education);

(b) the company expects to exploit the results;

(c) collaboration is genuine to the extent of the company being prepared to put up a fair proportion of the resources required. The company's input can be in kind—salaries of people directly involved, equipment, etc.—as well as cash but must be at least one quarter of the total and is usually about one half: SERC funds the rest;

(d) the work is technically advanced.

The final criterion introduces a genuine problem in that the company will usually be interested in a specific application whereas academics tend to equate 'good science' with generalisation. All rights of exploitation belong to the collaborative company but a royalty may be due to the British Technology Group. There are the same problems of confidentiality as in any industry/academic partnership—in general they are solved by the company applying the results before they have been proved to the academic's satisfaction and getting into production before the academic has published. But there are certainly sensitive areas like pharmaceuticals where only rather fundamental investigations can be sponsored since applied work is very sensitive commercially and secrecy is never possible in an academic environment.

This scheme too has been successful in that well over 150 such projects have now been approved—indeed in some areas such as robotics virtually all university research sponsored by SERC has an industrial partner.

Both CASE and CRG schemes are still essentially passive in that proposals come from the university for approval by the SERC. A new departure was made by the setting up in 1976 of the Polymer Engineering Directorate. This arose out of a report on the state of the plastics industry, whose domination by chemists seemed to have led to neglect of research on production machinery—extruders, dies, etc.—and of use—design and repair of plastic products. The SRC not only earmarked a sizeable sum—latterly about £1m. per year—but set up a small group of technically qualified officers to promote work in particular fields of polymer technology, to co-ordinate what was being done, and to publish its results to the industry.

A similar directorate for marine technology was set up soon afterwards to be followed more recently by units for biotechnology and information engineering. One important result of this co-ordinated approach is the concentration of work in particular centres—with all the advantages of cost effectiveness and the disadvantage of possibly excluding work that does not appeal to the established experts. A complication of such arrangements in a system of constant size (and the number of well-qualified people one can afford to keep out of productive industry is limited even if the total funds available for research were not) is provision for eventual disbandment. If the cost of the directorates is not taken over by other agencies eventually, there would be no money left for new initiatives. One can however imagine that once work has been started by government funded initiative, and laboratories and centres established, they can be continued best as research associations or institutes supported mainly by the relevant industry or special department of government (*e.g.* energy).

On a lesser scale, but in the same league, are SERC's specially promoted programmes. These cover areas of research such as instrumentation, energy flows in buildings, grinding or robotics in which SERC wants specially to encourage research. No-one can direct academics to do particular work. But the knowledge that funds are available for support in these areas (and, by inference, more difficult to obtain in others) acts as a powerful incentive. The programmes are co-ordinated nationally by experts, usually seconded from or recently retired from industry, working on a part-time basis.

Another directorate runs the teaching company scheme. This was originally intended as a rather special training scheme, combining academic teaching in production engineering with work on an actual production project in a company. The name was suggested by analogy with the teaching hospital where doctors are trained. A company wishing to make major changes in its factory—for example, by introducing computer-aided design and manufacture—was given the services of an academic expert (part-time) plus two or more associates, who were usually graduates of about three or four years' standing who were to be trained. In effect the group acted as a sort of organisation and methods unit,

190

with the enormous advantage to the firm that no permanent commitment was entered into—although in fact associates often ended up as employees. The scheme, which is jointly funded with the Department of Industry, has been so popular that over one hundred projects have been funded already. A possible extension from manufacturing (or process) industry to design is being considered. This might help civil engineering in particular, which suffers in Britain from the separation of the design side (the consultants) from the production side (the contractors).

All the schemes devised to improve contacts between university and industry are hindered by fundamental differences of objectives, attitudes and time scales. The academic's aim is to generalise and explain a class of natural phenomena in a way which can be defended in argument with his peers: the industrialist needs a solution to a particular problem and does not think it sinful to employ a phenomenon he does not understand. Perfection is essential to the academics, speed to the industrialist. I am not convinced that nature produces career academics and career industrialists—a person's attitudes and sympathies are developed by his environment. It is vitally important that academics have some understanding of, and some sympathy for, the attitudes of those outside academe, and do not prevent their students—99% of whom are destined for the world outside—from developing such sympathy.

The next scheme, administered jointly by SERC and the Royal Society, aims to provide opportunities for generating such sympathy by facilitating secondment of an academic to a firm, or a company employee to an academic institution, by paying his salary while he is away for any period between 6 and 24 months. About a dozen such arrangements in each direction have been made over the last three years—the smaller number is more a result of the difficulty of finding exact matches which do not produce insuperable domestic difficulties for the man seconded: all those completed to date, however, have been rated fully successful by the participants.

Another possible reason for the slow take-up of new schemes is ineffective publicity. Large firms whose scientists and engineers are often involved in the SERC committee network are usually well informed. But the very large number of smaller firms, often occupying a special technological niche and with few academic contacts, if any, do not usually know the schemes that exist, nor where information is available.

Improvement is needed on several fronts. First, academic researchers must accept that it is their duty to publish their results

in a form comprehensible to generalists, in widely read papers—
Electronic Times or *Construction News,* for example—as well as in
academically prestigious journals. They must be convinced that it
is *their* fault (and a fault to be rectified) if their ideas are not taken
up or are misunderstood by busy industrialists. Departments must
make readily available simple data sheets, listing the expertise they
could offer industry and the special equipment they could make
available: such sheets must also give the name of the person who
will accept and progress enquiries. There is room, too, for more
effort on scholarship—the putting into context of what is already
known, from work overseas as well as at home—as compared with
the generation of new knowledge.

Finally I must mention the appointment, for a trial period, of
four regional brokers, of whom I am one. Our duty is to visit
companies, particularly smaller ones, in a region, assess their
interests, and put them in touch with academics who might assist
them using one of the schemes outlined above. Similar schemes
are run by the Design Council (which organises fifteen days' free
consultancy) and by the Small Business Section of the Department
of Industry. The scene is set for the development of a national
system of 'technology brokers' who can direct firms towards sources
of the expertise they need, perhaps based on a federation of local
academic institutions, and using a national computer data base of
information on current programmes and available expertise.

That, however, is for the future. Nor have we had time yet to
assess the real potential of science parks or of laboratories set up
in universities but funded by industrial consortia. There is enormous scope, too, for more widespread use of joint appointments
and for producing closer links between industry-based research
organisations and particular universities. It is even possible that
there may develop a national strategy for technological research—
indeed a far cry from the fragmented collection of individual
initiatives that seemed to exist in times past.

I have perhaps concentrated in this paper on government, and
particularly on Research Council, initiatives, but this is where
change seems to have been greatest in the last decade. Direct
contracts by industry, consultancies, honorary or associate appointments, etc., are still developing and we may discuss these in our
sessions, but they are not novel. Industrial units have been set up
in various universities, primed by money from, for example, the
Wolfson Foundation, and are a way of providing floating capacity
so that industrial problems can be taken on and tackled immediately: but this is merely another form of consultancy service. It is
the interplay between government, academe and industry which

is perhaps special to the British scene and it is that development which I have tried to describe.

DISCUSSION

After the presentation of the paper by Dr. S. L. Bragg the participants divided into three groups, chaired respectively by Dr. G. Walcott (Guyana), Dr. D. T. Wright (Waterloo) and Sir Frederick Dainton (Sheffield). A few of the case studies presented are reported in the following paragraphs.

In one case study Professor M. B. Waldron (Surrey) described the successful co-operation between the department of metallurgy and materials technology and a large building materials company, Redlands Ltd. The co-operation began in 1968 with the appointment of Professor J. E. Bailey of the University of Surrey as technical adviser of Redlands on a one day/week basis, which eventually developed to a situation where Professor Bailey was appointed Redlands Part-time Chairman in 1982.

A related study of one overlapping group research activity within the department of chemical engineering of the University of Surrey was also described, which led to wide-ranging industrial contacts including Redlands.

Another case study was described by Professor P. S. Mani Sundaram (Bharathidasan) where university/industry partnerships had included the introduction of special postgraduate courses to suit the needs of industry. A common feature of these courses was that the teachers were drawn to a large extent from industry and students were assigned projects of immediate practical interest to industry. The University, in its turn, sent its teaching staff to industry to acquaint themselves with the work of industry.

Dr. J. Attikiouzel (Western Australia) described a workshop which drew together people of six different backgrounds: engineering, marketing, accounting, management, industrial design and general; and was conducted over a period of four months. The main theme of the workshop was to develop people capable of managing new commercial operations based on invention and technical innovation. A number of inventions were selected and the final object was to develop business plans to put those inventions into marketable production through multi-disciplinary co-operation of people from education institutions, industry and government organisations.

Professor K. S. Dodgson (University College, Cardiff) described some difficulties that developed in what had initially been a successful university/industry partnership. The partnership was multi-disciplinary in

193

essence and involved an industrial concern, two College departments and a department of another institution of higher education. Initially successful and making excellent progress, the general direction tended to be in the hands of individuals and the enterprise was later bedevilled by personality problems.

In another case study Dr. A. M. Neville (Dundee) described the history of the development of a company, Drug Development (Scotland) Ltd. (DDS) with the University of Dundee, the Scottish Development Agency and Inveresk Research Foundation each holding 20% of the Company's shares, the remaining 40% being held by the University of Dundee Clinical Pharmacology Trust. The meeting was told that, apart from being a model interface between the pharmaceutical industry and university medical schools, one of the main objectives of this Company was to complement the research, clinical and teaching commitments of the University through profits gained from work carried out on drug development for the pharmaceutical industry.

On a similar line Mr. R. M. Mawditt (Bath) explained how through setting up a company called South West Industrial Research Ltd. (SWIRL) in 1970 wholly owned by the University, they were able to utilize fully the academic staff's talents and expertise and equipment to the benefit of the University in terms of generating funds for research and further stimulants for joint ventures with industry.

The discussions that followed Dr. Bragg's talk were mainly centred on two issues: division of benefits from the co-operation and incentives for academics' participation. The meeting was reminded that industry was undertaking a risk in supporting university research projects and in the process expenditures were incurred which must be accounted for. On the other hand opinions were expressed that if for all his ideas and efforts what an academic would get in return was merely the satisfaction of a successful partnership he might not be over-enthusiastic. In addition it was pointed out that academic promotions would depend to a large extent on scholarly publications, and industrial projects seldom led to such publications, which would further reduce the incentives of the academics. As a general reply to these comments it was said that flexibility of treatment to different situations should be a key to success in any venture of partnership. In regard to incentives for academics to participate it was suggested that due consideration should be given to the contributions to industry of the academic staff in the evaluation of their performance, or alternatively they might be permitted to share some of the profits in compensation for the sacrifice in their opportunities for promotion.

Various advantages in university/industry partnership were mentioned during case studies. These are summarized as follows.

To the university:-

   (i) generation of research projects and research funds;

   (ii) generation of research and technical staff support;

   (iii) ear to ground on new developments in industrial process;

   (iv) industrial training for students, particularly sandwich students, and employment opportunities for graduates.

194

SUB-TOPIC 3 (A): DEVELOPMENT IN BRITAIN

To industry:-
  (i) access to specialist research knowledge;
  (ii) access to scientific/technological manpower;
  (iii) access to university facilities;
  (iv) ear to ground on world scientific developments.

It was generally agreed that the partnership would improve understanding between universities and industry and the participation of industry in the development of university courses would ensure their relevance in modern industrial practice. Moreover, the co-operation should lead to full and economic utilization of university and industrial resources and brain power to the benefit of the whole community.

The question was raised as to whether it was possible to formulate some sort of resolution, but the consensus was against it as situations would vary from country to country and even from place to place within the same country. It was generally concurred that the great virtue of the meetings had been for delegates to exchange views and to learn from each other's successes as well as problems, mistakes and difficulties. In this respect the meetings have been immensely successful.

Sub-Topic 3(b)

THE CANADIAN EXPERIENCE IN UNIVERSITY/INDUSTRY PARTNERSHIPS

Chairman: Dr. CHAM TAO SOON
President of Nanyang Technological Institute
Rapporteur: Professor D. M. BOYD
Professor of Geophysics, University of Adelaide

Tuesday, 16 August

Dr. D. T. WRIGHT (*President and Vice-Chancellor, University of Waterloo*): As Sir Eric Ashby pointed out in his seminal essay, *Technology and the Academics:*

'The Industrial Revolution was accomplished by hard heads and clever fingers. Men like Arkwright . . . and the Darbys . . . had no systematic education in science or technology. Britain's industrial strength lay in its amateurs and self-made men . . . In the accomplishment of the scientific revolution . . . the British universities . . . played no part whatever.'

Ashby went on to try to identify why technology continued to be largely estranged from British universities even in modern times (his essay was published in 1958):

'. . . pure scientific research is akin to other kinds of scholarship . . . but teaching and research in technology are unashamedly tendentious and this has not been mellowed (as it has for medicine and law) by centuries of tradition. Technology . . . is under an obligation to deliver the goods. And so the . . . engineer, the technologist . . . are tolerated . . . but not assimilated . . . it is not yet taken for granted that . . . technology enriches a university intellectually as well as materially.'

Ashby acknowledged that, on the European continent, and in North America, somewhat different patterns had prevailed. France provided the model of the polytechnic university, dedicated to the training of manager-technologists. That model has come to pervade the continent and North America. Undergraduates in engineering

196

programmes in Canada and the USA see their study of technology as a means to an end. Surveys undertaken in Canada, at various times over the last half dozen decades, have shown a very consistent result; seven years after graduation with a baccalaureate degree in engineering, half the graduates are working primarily as managers.

The first industrial revolution brought machines to serve man. The second industrial revolution is now upon us. The driving force is not the steam engine but the semi-conductor, embodied, a quarter of a million at a time, on a tiny piece of silicon, a few millimetres square. Unlike many of the developments of the nineteenth century, these new advances are entirely based on science and technology. Without fundamental understanding no progress is possible. With such knowledge, amazing rapid progress is being made. An important part of the impact of the new technology is in the improvement of the capacity of machines to produce goods and to serve us in much more automatic, even intelligent, ways. But the more striking feature of the new technologies is that, in the limit, they are purely knowledge-based, and have as their main product information. In this new age knowledge is both the principal basis for the new technology, and its principal product. Knowledge may be said to be the most important commodity in the world today.

Knowledge is the business of universities. Notwithstanding the many well-staffed and well-supported industrial laboratories, universities still account for half or more of the ideas leading to technological breakthroughs. Even more importantly, perhaps, universities provide what is in our time virtually the only significant means by which young people can prepare themselves to use, and to contribute to the advancement of, science and technology, as knowledge workers.

Why is it then that universities have tended to run out of public favour in this same last decade, almost everywhere? Public concern and provision for universities reached a peak in the 1960s, some years before it was popularly perceived how vitally important science and technology were to our economic future. Just as that perception has increased, so has there been the diminution of public concern and support for universities. While many factors bear on this central concern, it is my conviction that the difficulties Ashby identified in the university accommodation with technology, some 25 years ago, remain. Technology is still ill-at-ease in many universities.

There are, of course, signs that as academics gain experience in dealing with industry, and vice versa, mutual trust and confidence becomes established, and it is being perceived that the relationship

197

can operate without prejudice for either side, and, in fact, can operate to joint benefit. But we have some way to go.

In Canada, as is widely appreciated, education, including higher education, is a matter of provincial responsibility, and policies and practices in the different provinces are by no means homogeneous. At the risk of oversimplification some general patterns can nevertheless be identified. All of Canada's older universities, and most of the newer ones, view themselves and their relationships with government and with industry and commerce in ways that would not be seen to be exceptional in, say, Britain or Australia. There is a long and well-honoured tradition of professional education in theology, law, medicine and engineering, and so forth, which inevitably involves close and usually healthy and harmonious relationships with the practitioners of those professions and with the professional societies involved. No one could reasonably describe these faculties as being in any sense isolated or alienated from the world around them.

Such professional and paraprofessional programmes probably represent over 60% of university enrolment in Canada. If the faculties of arts and science regard themselves as the heart of the 'traditional' core of the university, it is not because these faculties feel alienated from the external world, but rather that they are primarily concerned with general learning.

University research in Canada has traditionally been 'curiosity driven' with little if any external influence on strategic direction, except that provided through feedback from colleagues in the same discipline. Research has not had a high priority with Canadian industry until very recent times, and even today only a handful of industries in Canada are making major commitments to research and development. In the past twenty years, and particularly in the last five, attitudes in Canada have changed, in industry, in the federal and provincial governments, and in the universities. As a result new policies and programmes have been established, almost too numerous to catalogue. Most such efforts have been directed at the substance of university research programmes. The federal government and its agencies have made the greatest efforts, and have certainly provided the most significant financial support.

Until well within the past decade the federal research granting agencies provided support to individual university faculty members, in support of their research, on a peer-adjudicated basis, but focusing as much on the individual scholar or researcher as any eighteenth century patron. However, starting in 1977, and now operated by the Natural Sciences and Engineering Research Council, the federal government inaugurated a programme of strategic research grants. Governed by notions of strategic purpose, they tend to favour groups of researchers working as a team, and the adjudication process almost invariably involves review panels which include representatives from industry. Although these grants represent a truly radical departure from tradition, they have won high approval in the scientific community, with practically no significant criticism.

Other federal government departments and agencies have developed a quite long list of specialized programmes for research reports intended to provide means and incentives for relating university research to the needs of industry. There have been programmes and grants in aid, variously, of industrial research institutes, industry/laboratory projects, industrial research assistance, industrial innovation centres, centres of advanced technology, and microelectronic centres. Some of these programmes have been criticized for demonstrating more concern with politics, the need to have federal government assistance in evidence in different provinces and regions, than with any fundamental interest in the actual substance of the research and its prospects for impact on Canada's gross national product or employment. Such criticisms seem, in one sense, relatively insignificant; the amounts of money involved in these programmes have, in fact, been extremely modest when compared with the kinds of money really required to make an impact on the subject areas.

Provincial governments in Canada, except for Quebec, have only recently become interested in programmes for sponsoring research and development. As the new industrial order has impacted both resource and manufacturing industries in Canada in the past few years, provincial governments have become acutely concerned with the importance of technology. Most of them have initiated programmes to try to foster high technology industry and to cultivate applied research and development. The most significant initial efforts undoubtedly have been directed at encouraging small and medium-sized industry to adopt new technologies that could be incorporated into process and product, virtually on an 'off-the-shelf' basis. Such programmes leave some uncertainty as to prospects for the source of such technologies in the future. It is difficult to be competitive with second-hand technology.

While the total volume of activity by the federal government and the provinces certainly represents a major shift from the patterns that have prevailed a few months ago, total spending is still modest compared with investments in research and development in other countries and, as noted above, the programmes frequently demonstrate more the sensitive need to a high political profile than a well-developed sense of purpose about substantive objects.

For their part Canadian universities have also shown major shifts in attitude over the past years, as they acknowledge the interest of governments in fostering research aimed at subjects of strategic economic importance. There is, unsurprisingly, a mixed attitude, welcoming new monies, and resenting the insinuation that universities have been unresponsive to strategic needs.

Let me turn now, in my closing comments, to a few observations about my own University which was founded in 1957 with a commitment to co-operation with industry that was unprecedented in the history of higher education in Canada. That commitment took form, initially, in the organisation of studies at an undergraduate level. This is, of course, in direct contrast to the focus of most of the programmes described and acknowledged above which have a primary focus on research and development. The University of Waterloo introduced into Canada the notion of co-operative programmes which offered a new form of undergraduate study, in which students pursued alternate semesters of study and employment as they proceeded to a baccalaureate degree. Great emphasis is placed on continuity of employment, so that there are two streams of students, approximately equal in number. The University operates year-round, and jobs provided by industry may correspondingly be kept filled on a regular and continuing basis by successive co-op students.

Waterloo commenced with a faculty of engineering dedicated exclusively to the co-operative system. As the benefits of the system became evident enrolment increased rapidly until the school became the biggest in Canada. Today, all the faculties have co-operative programmes, and approximately 60% of Waterloo's 14,000 full-time undergraduates are in such programmes. With over 8000 students in co-op programmes, Waterloo now finds itself with the second largest co-operative programme in the world. Only Northeastern University, in Boston, with some 9000 co-op students, is larger.

While on their work terms students are paid a salary and are expected to be productive. Employers visit the University to interview students who apply for jobs, as is done ordinarily for graduate employment. The employment relationship is a direct one between company and student. Arrangements for all this are made by a special department of co-ordination and placement, dedicated to supporting the co-operative system. The professional staff who make up the department are called co-ordinators, and they provide advice to employers and to students regarding training programmes and so forth.

The popularity of the programme as measured by enrolment and acceptance by industry are attractive measures of success. Waterloo has also enjoyed qualitative success. Admission to the University of Waterloo now seems to be the most competitive of any university in Canada, and Waterloo's freshmen are on the average the most highly qualified in any Canadian university.

Instead of the common sequential mode in which some kind of training in industry follows the first degree and the first graduate employment, Waterloo has developed a form of concurrent cultivation of academic and work skills, hand-in-hand, as a young person matures. There are many benefits, not the least being that certain kinds of experience are best absorbed at a stage when expectations are modest, before a student has taken his first degree. There are financial benefits, of course, to all the parties involved. The University is able to use its facilities year-round. Students require less financial assistance because their earnings allow them to meet most costs of tuition, textbooks, maintenance and travel. Employers have able and ambitious young people engaged in productive work—and, perhaps most importantly, employers have an excellent basis from which to select graduates for permanent employment—and vice versa.

An important feature of the operation of the co-operative system is that academic programmes have been modified to take advantage of the kinds of experience students gain in industry, which often have to be simulated in more conventional programmes. This has in turn freed time for other kinds of academic experience, particularly an emphasis on computing, for which Waterloo has become well known. Starting in 1959, just two years after the founding of the University, general commitments were made to the teaching of mathematics, particularly finite mathematics and what has later come to be called computer science. One of the consequences of this was the development of a complete faculty of mathematics at Waterloo which now has a total enrolment of approximately 4000 students, which we believe to be the largest enrolment of mathematics specialists in the world. There is inevitably a great concentration of work in computer science and computing at Waterloo now pervades every faculty, and almost every subject from chemical engineering to English literature. We try to provide general campus-wide computer support services for computation, for text processing and, most recently, for graphics.

The principal significance of the co-operative programme as adapted and developed at Waterloo, and the academic developments that it has made possible, is, of course, the focus on a relationship to industry at the undergraduate level, involving the majority of our students, with very large numbers of employers— some 1400 at the latest count. Waterloo's relationship with industry is characterized by a daily working relationship involving literally thousands of people.

The co-operative system has been taken up in Canada by a number of other universities, in most cases with considerable success. At the present time there are about 8000 students in co-operative programmes at other universities in Canada. An organisation of universities and employers, the Canadian Association for Co-operative Education (CAFCE), has been established to assist in the development and maintenance of excellence in co-op programming, and to ensure harmonization of schedules, etc.

There was in the initial development at Waterloo, in common with many other new universities, a commitment to the need to develop graduate studies and research. As with most other university faculties, there was quite a bit of conventional specialist consulting by academics at that time, and opportunities for such activity were probably enhanced through the working relationships established in the operation of the co-operative undergraduate programme. Direct support for research from industry is primarily a phenomenon of the last decade. In recent years, as a taste for research and development in industry has increased, so have opportunities for co-operative research projects. Total funded research at Waterloo is now worth more than $24 million per annum, of which one-quarter is for work done under contract, primarily for industry. Although ordinary operating revenues at the University, in common with other universities, have tended to lag behind inflation in recent years, our research funding has increased by 30% or more per annum, compounded, in recent years, with the contract portion increasing even more rapidly.

Two particular examples of this work may be worth noting. The Waterloo Centre for Process Development was established in 1978 as an adjunct to the University's chemical engineering department. It develops chemical processes to the pilot-plant level, carrying academic research considerably further than had been traditionally possible. An Inventor's Assistance Programme was initiated by the University a few years ago, with federal government assistance. By 1981 this led to the establishment of the Canadian Industrial Innovation Centre/Waterloo. The Centre provides a kind of incubator for new enterprises, and as well serves to license new technology to existing companies. The Centre is now autonomous under its own board of directors, on which the University has representation.

Because of an early commitment to the use of computers for undergraduate student use, Waterloo experienced great difficulty some twenty years ago in handling the volume of student work on existing computers. To solve this problem the Waterloo fortran compiler (more widely known as WATFOR) was developed. With WATFOR we were able to offer our students greatly improved access to computer services. Since that time some 35 other pieces of software have been created at Waterloo to help meet the burgeoning needs of teaching programmes. As the utility of these systems became known they were taken up by other users, and today Waterloo is licensing more than 3000 user installations throughout the world. This, of course, constitutes a very significant and certainly unusual mode of co-operation between the University and the external world. The substantial fees generated by these licensing agreements are directed back to supporting more teaching and research in computer science.

Because of the volume of research in various specialities in computer science at Waterloo there has developed a number of research groups supported variously by combinations of government research grants, industrial contract research, and revenues generated from licensing their own products to other users. In 1982 these groups were brought together to form the Waterloo Institute for Computer Research, which is probably the most ambitious and comprehensive computer research organisation on any Canadian campus, and comparable otherwise only with computer research activities in the Massachusetts Institute of Technology and Stanford University in the USA. The formation of the Institute has permitted still more forms of University/industry co-operation to be developed. Undergraduate and graduate students find employment with the research groups on campus, and in the companies involved. The University assists industry in developing new products, and in turn benefits from subsequent license fees. In numbers of cases, forms of barter are arranged with the University receiving computer hardware or software in return for contributions to software development. An important feature of the new Institute for Computer Research is a facility for 'corporate partnerships' which provides co-operating industries with an opportunity to have a permanent presence on the University campus. In December 1982 we announced, jointly with the IBM Corporation, a major co-operative programme of research and development with a total value estimated to be in excess of $17 million. This will lead to the development of new software that will be of particular interest to IBM and will, it is expected, permit still more efficient use of IBM computers in universities and colleges generally. It will enhance substantially an already major concentration of computing power at Waterloo.

Although it is certainly too early to make final judgments it would appear to be reasonable to claim that the intellectual accommodation with technology that Ashby found to be so elusive can certainly be seen to be taking form in Canadian universities. For my own institution, which has been unambiguously committed to close co-operation with industry from the outset, I can fairly say that we never suffered the kinds of anguish noted by Ashby.

It must be asserted that it is myopic to regard universities as remote ivory towers. It is equally a trivialization of the potential of the university to regard it as standing in relationship to industry as a supplier to a client, producing graduates and research results, on order. The kinds of co-operation described reflect a much more subtle relationship in which the university utilizes its autonomy to try to take the longer, strategic view, in a genuine spirit of co-operation, in which, in fact, there is a distinct complementarity of roles. When this can be done Ashby's anxieties are indeed put to rest. Technology and its development are immensely important and exciting intellectual endeavours that demand the very best of human creative skills.

DISCUSSION

In presenting his paper Dr. Wright covered a number of broad issues on university/industry partnerships in Canada: he spoke mainly of the way in which relationships have developed between manufacturing industries and the faculties in the University of Waterloo and added, in the subsequent discussion, that the absence of reference to the developments in agricultural production, which are specially important examples of successful innovation during the twentieth century, was due to the wide scope of the subject. In the introduction he emphasised the overwhelming importance of the development of the human resources of a country, and then observed that there had been little direct connection between the science developed during the eighteenth century and the new technologies which were the main spring of the first industrial revolution. Although this continued to be so during the nineteenth century in Britain, the contribution of the various tertiary institutions in Europe and North America were more positively linked to the needs of industry.

SUB-TOPIC 3 (B): THE CANADIAN EXPERIENCE

However the revolutionary changes taking place in industry at the end of the twentieth century are due to new technologies which are founded on the basic sciences taught in the universities. Indeed, about half of the new ideas which lead to significant technological innovations originated in the universities. In spite of this many, though by no means all, universities are ill at ease with the problems raised by technology. This is serious, because it is through the universities that most young people receive the training that prepares them to respond to the changes which have come about through the effects of technology.

The importance of research in Canada has increased enormously during the last 25 years and more recently there has also been a change in the attitude to research: research has passed from an activity motivated by personally directed curiosity using funds from federal agencies which are awarded through a system of peer review, to goal-directed research which is funded by bodies such as the Natural Sciences and Engineering Council whose review panels include representatives from industry. Research support from these bodies is often given to teams rather than to individuals. Some of this funding has been less effective than it might have been because the decisions have been influenced by social and other considerations and in some cases the magnitude of the funding has not matched the ambitious goals set.

One of the aims in founding the University of Waterloo was to foster closer co-operation between the University and industry specifically in the field of undergraduate education. This has been achieved by organising a University teaching programme which runs through the whole year, is divided in such a way that a student can spend alternate terms with an employer throughout his course in the University and incorporates the student's work experience within the process of assessment. The division of the academic year into three terms which span the whole calendar year allows companies if they wish to employ a succession of students in the same position. This lets them schedule student labour more effectively than is possible with the conventional division of universities in which all students are available to take up employment during the same period of the year.

The arrangement of alternating terms of work experience and formal teaching is attractive to students and to faculty members on both financial and academic grounds. All universities in Canada which organise courses in this fashion co-operate to ensure uniformity in academic terms and similar matters. It was noted in the discussion which followed that the number of additional students who could be offered such courses is limited by the number of employers who are able to offer appropriate work experience.

The organised and purposeful flow of undergraduate students between the University and industry has had a number of important effects. The continuity of availability of students is considered to be a significant factor in the development of small-scale research projects which are relevant to industry. These projects which are at a level of complexity suitable for students seem to be about right for speeding the transference of the new technologies, and the continuing presence of a student or a succession of students in a continuing position within a company may also help. In the University, in turn, the fact that the students have this work experience allows some parts of the standard curriculum to be reduced and this makes room in the curriculum for greater emphasis on other subjects such as computing. This has had important consequences for many groups within the University.

Co-operative projects and contracts with industry which include groups of postgraduate students have grown rapidly in the last decade and funding has grown by about 30% per annum in recent years. Co-operation with industry which involves staff and research students allows departments to be involved in projects of a size and complexity which is not usually possible for a university. Within the mathematics faculty the computer groups have made numerous highly practical contributions to software which was developed to make more efficient use of the university's own computing equipment; from these developments they now derive a substantial income in royalties. The success of the computer groups led to the formation of the Waterloo Institute for Computer Research which has facilitated corporate partnerships and provides a range of employment for undergraduate and postgraduate students on the campus.

Dr. Wright concluded by saying that, while it was not possible to provide even an adequate summary of all the kinds of activities going on at present in Canada, it was clear that university/industry co-operation was varied, vigorous and successful in Canada.

In the discussion which followed many questions were asked about the organisation of the periods which the students spent with industry. The meeting was informed that the University arranged the initial contacts between students and employers but did not take part in the selection of students or in the salary arrangements. Students, however, are well briefed on the range of rates of pay and conditions of employment under which other students have been employed recently. At the end of each employment period students are required to write substantial reports on the work done by them and this report is seen and assessed by the employer, the faculty manager and by the supervisor. Students who do not perform satisfactorily on two occasions in this part of the course are not allowed to continue.

Comments were made about the advantages and drawbacks of the point in the course at which students worked, and what was the best length of work experience: the arrangement at the University of Waterloo where periods of four months' work alternate with four months' academic studies seemed to be regarded with general approval.

There were also remarks made on the problems and advantages of relating the work experience to the formal teaching parts of the course.

In the discussion of the major research projects it was clear that financial support was provided by industry with at times a very liberal attitude by the grantee regarding subsequent financial benefits which the University was able to derive from the project in the form of licences and royalties. It was also stated that government bodies providing funds to universities seem to understand that, if an institution which obtains grants from industry had its government support reduced in proportion to the external support, the support from industry would disappear.

Sub-Topic 3(c)

PARTNERSHIPS IN DEVELOPING
INDUSTRIAL COUNTRIES: INDIA

Chairman: Dr. M. Horowitz
President of the University of Alberta

Rapporteur: Dr. B. Segal
President of Ryerson Polytechnical Institute

Tuesday, 16 August

Dr. C. R. Mitra (*Director, Birla Institute of Technology and Science*):

I. *Definitions*

For the purpose of this paper certain oft-repeated terms are defined as below:—

University—an organisation that deals with diverse aspects of knowledge—transmission, codification, creation, application and preservation; historically even the same university has responded differently to this spectrum of functions.

Knowledge—not a collection of information but a tool to act intelligently upon the environment; it is the current synthesis of the dialectic outcome of theory and practice.

Engineering—the art and science of organised forcing of technological change.

Technology—represents a set of means by which man puts the forces and laws of nature to use with a view to improving his lot or modifying it as may be agreeable to him.

Technological order—a cultural milieu created by the total stock of technology and the technological acts.

Industry—an organised arrangement to produce goods and services at affordable prices for an increasingly larger number of consumers.

Innovation—a dynamic renewal process where the whole configuration of a system changes under the principle that a problem has a solution and the solution begets a new problem.

Development—a dynamic process of life which generates self-reliance and moves the entire society towards everwidening growth; it must, in its strategy, view man with his environment and in the context of his origin.

II. *Need for Co-operation*

(i) Product of university is used by industry. Therefore each has a stake in the training of the product and the manner in which the product is used.

(ii) Legitimacy of knowledge demands its understanding and working to ensure its dynamic unfolding. It is a dialectic interaction between theory and practice, where theory is manifested in practice and practice creates new knowledge, which must always replace outdated knowledge. Thus, this total stock of knowledge renews itself through intelligent application in a particular technological order. Since man is the subject, the process also continuously updates the stock of human capital.

(iii) The total culture or the technological order will change willy-nilly. Universities expand and diversify. Industries do likewise. Without going into the causality of the process, it is unthinkable that inexorable change should be an outcome of unguided chance. To influence decision, the two parties must co-operate.

III. *Social Goals to be Met*

Let us choose to focus attention on only two aspects of the above enunciation. These are:—

(i) the more effective training of an engineer or a professional during full-time study;

(ii) continuing education (updating, broadening, keeping up, etc.) as a life-long process for engineers who teach and engineers who practise.

Traditionally feeble attempts have been made for the above two objectives in isolated and alienated settings. Further, the discontinuity between full-time study and full-time work has also been an intractable problem.

Arising out of the above it is clear that the co-operation must become a reciprocal dependence, where both sides either rise together or fall together. The task is so gigantic that even in an imaginary situation where knowledge explosion does not take place a whole series of *ad hoc* actions within the conventional framework of attitude and organisation will fail to meet any objective. The urges and constraints of the two systems must be understood and new efforts must be made.

While it is gratifying that there is an increasing awareness of need of an action plan to achieve these objectives, there does not seem to be a systematic study of the various schemes in operation throughout the world. The suggested study will profit by understanding the nature of the interface between the university and industry. It is best described as a third state which though originated from the two systems has acquired a character of its own. Admittedly this interface is small in its dimension and symptoms are not always discernible. However illusive and difficult it is to grapple with this interface, out salvation lies only in recognizing, in understanding and in learning from it.

IV. The Case of India

(a) *Historical*. The university in the contemporary sense was fashioned in India after the British model and has generally catered to liberal arts and basic sciences. Professional education in subjects like engineering, medicine, architecture, mining, etc., either remained outside the purview of the university system or were only nominally connected to it. While it was recognised that professional education required that the graduating student must be exposed to the world of practice, no similar idea prevailed in determining the structure and the content of degrees in liberal arts and basic sciences. In the category of professional education, medical education required a period of service as an intern in a teaching hospital. But in other professional education nothing remotely similar to this was insisted upon. Further in professional education preponderance of diploma courses continued for a long time. These diploma courses were practice-oriented, unlike the degree courses.

After independence in 1947 a national government championed expansion of higher education, establishment of new industries and *inter alia* supported many schemes to initiate and enlarge various modes of partnership. Simultaneously, a chain of research and development (R & D) laboratories was also established. The outcome of these enterprises created the third largest R & D system in the world. India's position as an industrial nation rose to the sixth place in the world. However, under a democratic system with a free press diverse views maintain that the co-existence of high illiteracy, restricted opportunities and nationalised basic industries has created a lopsided development. Our task in this paper is to analyse the university-industry partnership in the wake of a very impressive growth in the country.

This partnership manifested itself in two forms, depending on whether the subject matter was research or simply training of the

210

undergraduate. In the case of research the system sponsored research and consultancy involving almost all universities and became a major source of funds to sustain PhD research in the universities. PhD research was also undertaken universally in the R & D laboratories. Funds for this sponsored research were channelled through central regulating organisations like the Council for Scientific and Industrial Research, the Indian Councils of Agricultural Research, of Medical Research and of Social Science Research, the University Grants Commission, etc. In the area of undergraduate teaching efforts were made to infuse with life the listless approach of a formal stay in industry by about-to-graduate students, or by fresh graduates, by means of such co-operative programmes as practice school, sandwich courses, etc. The same ideas prompted introduction of vocational components in the secondary school curricula. However, the traditional arts and basic sciences curricula remained untouched by these ideas.

(b) *Aims and outcome.* The university-industry relationship in India has not substantially gained in the meaning stated in this paper in spite of extravagence of objectives and handsome financial support. There is hardly any direct correlation between the growth of Indian industrial complex and the contribution of research emanating from the universities or R & D laboratories. The strategy of spending, regulation and exhortation adopted to introduce well-defined co-operative programmes for undergraduate education has simply not taken off. While more than a dozen universities introduced the sandwich programme for undergraduate engineering education, in most places the scheme has been given up. One observation is germane in this matter. There is no evidence to show that any of the schemes originated from the university system. On the contrary, they were invariably sponsored by an alert union government which certainly hoped that fund support would act as an agent for change. But even after accepting the schemes the universities concerned did not appear to have taken adaptive measures for the introduction of these alien ideas into universities subsumed with traditional attitudes.

(c) *The BITS experiment.* The most comprehensive institutionalised linkages between university and industry that any university in India has built up is the Birla Institute of Technology and Science (BITS), Pilani. In this task BITS attempted to innovate a new model. It was discovered that a mere transplantation of the UK sandwich programme or the co-operative and practice school programme of the USA served no purpose. On the other hand the analogue of a teaching hospital in the Indian setting was more relevant in designing a new co-operative programme for all undergraduates, namely engineering, basic sciences, liberal arts and social sciences. It was further discovered that none of the changes ever stick unless the structure and content of the education as a whole in the university are designed anew. It was also established that even though it was painful to innovate, the forward retention of custom was no less turbulent.

The specific channels through which university/industry partici-pation have been institutionalised at BITS are: (i) practice school programme; (ii) ME (collaborative) programmes; (iii) off-campus PhD programme; (iv) BITS consultants; and (v) Technology Inno-vation Centre. This spectrum of involvement evolved over a period of 15 years. The story began with one university's search to establish new educational programmes in partnership with indus-try. Today the compliment has been returned by industry when it invited BITS to assist in the continuing training of practising engineers through some of the new schemes which have been listed above.

(*d*) *Citation of sources*. Some institutions that are mentioned below would serve as important sources of information on the subject.

On India

(1) All India Council for Technical Education (Ministry of Education, government of India): various studies and recommen-dations in connection with scientific and technical manpower, starting of sandwich programme, practice school programme and other co-operative programmes, vocational education.

(2) Department of Science and Technology (government of India): different studies on relevant R & D, science and technology policy and suggested models for joint research between university and industry.

(3) Council for Scientific and Industrial Research (government of India): the various R & D programmes in operation.

(4) University Grants Commission: annual reports and various feasibility reports on educational reforms.

(5) Association of Indian Universities: massive data base on the Indian university system.

(6) Recommendations of Education Commission, 1964–1966.

(7) Planning Commission (government of India): various devel-opmental proposals.

On BITS, Pilani

BITS publications:

(1) Forward Plan (1970).

(2) Linking University Industry (June 1982).

(3) A case study of practice school as well as comments from industry, faculty and students (January 1983).

(4) A case study of ME collaborative programmes (April 1983).

(5) An Improbable Achievement (April 1983).

(6) BITS Consultants (April 1983).

(7) Technology Innovation Centre (April 1983).

(8) Education for Self-reliance (August 1983).

(9) Estimates Committee Report on Higher Technical Education— Lok Sabha Secretariat (January 1977).

(10) Tomorrow's Universities (A worldwide look at educational change), Westview special studies on education—Bolder, Colorado, USA (1982).

(11) Center for International Higher Education Documentation Newsletter, Northeastern University, Boston, USA, vol. 4 (April 1981).

(12) Worldwide inventory of non-traditional post-secondary educational institutions—UNESCO (1980).

(13) ACU Bulletin of Current Documentation (December 1980).

DISCUSSION

Dr. Mitra began by defining the rationale and need for co-operation between industry and universities. He considered there were social goals to be met through university/industry collaboration: these included the more effective training of engineers and continuing education as a life-long process for engineers in teaching and in practice. He argued for reciprocal dependence between universities and industry and suggested that constraints of the two systems must be understood by both participants.

After giving a brief history of the development of professional education in India Dr. Mitra proceeded to discuss the Birla Institute of Technology and Science (BITS) experiment and the five specific channels through which university/industry participation has been institutionalized at BITS. He described each programme, the essentials of which are that all 2000 undergraduate students spend 8 months out of the 4-year programme in 80 different industrial, governmental and community stations. During this period there is an unconventional off-campus curriculum in which assignments come from industry. Industry pays 25% of cash to students and professors to make the scheme operate.

The discussion dealt with clarification of curriculum issues (mainly the use of a foundation year for all students) and the operation of the

213

Technology Innovation Centre, which is designed to find ways for industry to absorb technology, manage change and solve technology problems.

The discussion also focused on the evaluation of the experiment. The BITS programme had been evaluated twice in 10 years with different interpretations of the results by the different constituencies, and this had resulted in some 'tensions'. The evaluation demonstrated that industry wants more opportunities for research and development, the students want more flexibility in station assignments and the faculty suffer from dislocation problems associated with being away from campus 2–3 years at a time. While the experiment appears to be successful, there is undoubtedly a price the university and its constituencies must pay.

Sub-Topic 3(d)

A CONTINENTAL EUROPEAN VIEW OF UNIVERSITY/INDUSTRY PARTNERSHIPS

Chairman: Dr. J. C. OLSON
President of the University of Missouri

Rapporteur: Dr. A. D. I. NICOL
Secretary General of the Faculties, University of Cambridge

Thursday, 18 August

Professor G. DENIÉLOU (*President, Université de Compiègne*): I have been asked to give a continental point of view on university/industry partnerships in Europe. Unfortunately, there can't be a continental view on this subject:

● university/industry relationship is a *worldwide problem* as we shall see further on;

● the situations in the various countries of Europe are too different to allow general affirmations.

Let us compare, for instance, Germany and France. In Germany the industrial and commercial development is older than in France; universities have been associated earlier with this development. In France there were not even universities during the nineteenth century: they had been suppressed by the French revolution. Nowadays the division between 'grandes écoles' and universities gives a distinct Gallic flavour to our problems . . .

I will thus speak using mainly the experience I could gain from the University of Compiègne, created ten years ago in order to strengthen the links between university and industry in France. It has apparently fulfilled its task. From this 'case study' it is possible to make more general remarks on the ways and means of improving communications between these two worlds, university and industry.

In the first part I intend to show you how we must avoid dealing with the problem on ethical grounds; how we must avoid any sense of *guilt* when we find difficulties in our relationships with industry. In a second part I wish to insist on the importance of complexity in university/industry links and to show that this *complexity* is a positive factor. In a third part we could meditate on the mediating role of the technical objects, between the world of knowledge and the world of action.

1. One could apply to university/industry relationships techniques used in ecumenicalism. Ask, for instance, a full professor in the university how he thinks that a vice-president of a company thinks about university professors: the answer will probably be as follows: 'he is a leftist; he doesn't work very much, they learn how to make Molotov cocktails in his laboratory; he has no idea about money; he doesn't care about delays and timetable'. Now ask a vice-president what is a professor's opinion about him: 'He has a top hat, he smokes cigars, he has no heart, he is interested only in making money; he is not cultured; he does not care about the future of mankind'. These caricatures, of course, have some kind of truth in them. But they can prevent any positive action to solve our problem. Besides, each side can begin feeling really guilty about it. And you will hear the vice-president think: 'I have no culture, I am not interested in mankind, etc.' You may yourself begin feeling that you know really nothing about money or that you do not work hard enough.

Let us show how all this feeling of guilt, all these mutual charges, are meaningless.

First of all, the world of knowledge has *always* been widely separated from the world of action. You can add up an infinite number of thoughts, it's not going to make a decision. You can pile up actions, this is not going to make a single thought. It has been pointed out that the role of science in the industrial development up to the last world war had been grossly exaggerated. Moreover, this opposition between knowledge and action is increasing with age, each member of one social group becoming less and less able to understand the other side. This gives rise to tribes with their own habits, their own way of living, their own language. We must think of these tribes as being as far from one another as Papoos from Eskimos. This must be our starting point. If we begin from this pessimistic view then we will be more prone to see how fast progress is made today.

And in fact this progress—and we can see it during such a Congress—comes not primarily out of our good will or out of governmental policy but out of sheer necessity. Yes, the world is undergoing a major transformation that we are sometimes inclined to underestimate. Perhaps we should go back as far as the neolithic revolution, when hunters and gatherers began to settle, invented cities, trade, kingdom, writing, mathematics, etc. The replacement of natural environment by man-made objects, the dramatic increase in world population, are clearly signs of some catastrophic event (using catastrophic, of course, in the rather technical meaning of discontinuity/continuity). The magnitude of the current revolution is certainly comparable to that of 5000 BC. No wonder then that we can see changes!

Universities are changing because science itself is changing! The scientific curiosity which was mainly directed towards nature, atmospheric phenomena, rainbow, thunderbolt, or tide or earth-quake, is now more and more directed towards cultural objects whether they be rockets, nuclear reactors (or trade unions). The development of mathematics, of calculus, of computer science, has allowed us to study complex phenomena which were completely outside the realm of hard science fifty years ago.

But industry itself is undergoing major changes—as the university is. People usually think first of robots but you can as well think of calculation. Fifty years ago very few objects were amenable to calculation. Knowhow, rule of thumb, were the most important factors in success and, of course, good management. Today almost everything can—and must—be calculated beforehand. You can see well-managed companies going bankrupt not for management reasons but because of the sudden appearance on the market of technological breakthroughs.

The internal structures of universities as well as those of industries are overturned. Sciences usually organised in disciplines see this sort of division as less and less relevant. Systems analysis, computer science, introduce interdisciplinary approaches. In industry professions have the same kind of trouble as disciplines. What is the name of the profession which is taking in charge the transmission of information through international networks? We do not know.

What we must clearly see is that the world technological revolution is promoted mainly by the fact that science has become socially relevant and politically important. Since world war II human knowledge is more and more important for human action. Science is more and more important for industry.

Is it not then easier to face the task of promoting partnerships between university and industry if we replace it within the framework of a world technological revolution? Can we then feel guilty facing such a formidable challenge? Can we render our partners guilty of not going fast enough? Is it not easier to be excited, to be exalted, by the magnitude and interest of the work we have to do together?

2. University—industry relationship is a complex business and you may hear many people complain about the number of govern-

mental agencies, the proliferation of *ad hoc* offices and commissions, of the variety (and of course scarcity) of financial support. More or less obscurely many people expect to find some trick or some knack to solve the problem, maybe one law, or one regulation, or one board of directors. Of course this makes no sense. Let us analyse—using for that the experience of the University of Compiègne—the links between one university and its industrial surroundings. We have identified 11 points:—

(*a*) Having industry people in our councils or scientific committees is the most straightforward and ancient link. One must be very careful about it: not doing it can prevent good relationships, but doing it is not necessarily very useful.

(*b*) Having industry people hired in universities (and vice-versa). This seems obvious though one must bear in mind that the industry people hired should be given the same positions and responsibilities as the regular faculty members. It is not enough to have some retired engineers come on the campus and narrate souvenirs of their brilliant careers for two or three hours per semester.

(*c*) Research contracts are clearly one of the most powerful means of contacts; although it is important to point out that these contracts must involve the university itself and not only such and such a faculty member.

(*d*) Periods in industry for undergraduate students have been found in Compiègne to be very effective. In fact relationships with big companies are usually rather easy because their research directors or the engineers responsible for projects are of the same type of culture as their university counterparts. This is not the case in small and medium-size companies. In this case the lower level of a student becomes an asset. One cannot be afraid of an undergraduate. The undergraduate becomes thus to technology what the mosquito is to malaria: a carrier. We have found that a minimum duration for such periods is five months. And that the student must be paid if you wish to be sure that he is really well taken care of.

(*e*) 'Taxes d'apprentissage'. French companies must distribute some money to teaching insitutions of their choice. This allows some kind of feedback from the customers—if I may say so—because the companies give more money to those schools and universities they are more pleased with.

(*f*) Alumni are of course a very good way of increasing university/industry relationship. Knowing well the old house (and from inside) they are especially able to detect the right professors or the right team to work with.

(*g*) Congresses. Organising congresses for industry even outside the direct field of interest of university is a very good scheme. First of all you use more efficiently the buildings and amphitheatres, etc . . . But, what is more important, you have visitors who can visit your laboratories, meet your research people and discover that they *have* to do something with you.

(*h*) Continued education is, of course, a privileged link either if it is done inside one company or proposed to many companies and done inside the university.

(*i*) Restaurant. We live in a kingdom of symbols and not only words are important for communication! The choice of a good restaurant in which to have researchers and engineers lunch together is of paramount importance. It must not be too expensive: this could frighten university puritanism (and anyway we cannot afford it). On the other hand food must be good enough. But the environment is even more important: it should be modest, calm, middle class . . .

Restaurant is not the only point. When we asked some of our old industrial customers why they had chosen our university instead of some more prestigious institutions, we expected them to say that they had been impressed by the youth and dedication of our outstanding scientists. In fact they answered us rather bluntly that it was because we were the only University where the toilets were reasonably clean . . . .

(*j*) Launching spin-off companies. We have found this was very important because it gave the University some inside experience of what a company was. Instead of reading it in books, the faculty hears daily from colleagues about turnover, cash flow, and month ends.

(*k*) Partnerships strictly speaking can have many legal forms. We have experimented with several of them. None seems to be the solution for all cases.

Bearing in mind the eleven forms of co-operation between university and industry and reminding us that many or several others do exist, the message I wish to convey is that *the combination of them all is more important than their simple addition*. If one has at the same time all these types of connection with one company, things become very simple. When one of our faculty people goes and visits such plant we can *at the same time* visit our undergraduate student, discuss a research contract, remind a director that he should increase his financial contribution to 'taxe d'apprentissage'. It often happens that following a period spent in industry by an undergraduate student one of his friends is hired by the company or that a research contract follows the report written at the end of the period. These are just some instances of interaction. But you will be able to find a thousand more.

But a fear can be felt when you face the number and complexity of the relationships described heretofore. Is not the university going to lose its spirit, to lose its academic freedom? Is there not some risk of confusion between the two worlds? Are not the Montagues of industry and the Capulets of university going to see many dramas occurring from their bringing together?

May I tell you a tale? In the French navy, some 70 years ago, there were still pigeons to carry messages. In Cherbourg they were taken care of by a petty officer whose IQ was not very high but who loved order and discipline. Noticing that the homers seemed to have a lot of fighting in their cages, that the bigger pigeons usually went over the smaller ones with much fluttering of wings and that the floor was littered with feathers, he decided to separate the big pigeons from the small ones. They were put into two cages and everything was clear instead of being confused. This was the end of pigeons in the French navy, no eggs having been laid thereafter.

This apologue shows that:

(*a*) we can improve order without increasing efficiency;

(*b*) we cannot have very strong relations without a minimum of confusion.

3. The tendency of university to escape from this base world is fairly well known. Of course the responsibility is often put on the lack of financial means. It is true that pencils and pens are less expensive than distillation columns and pilot plants. It is true also that many universities have a poor technician/researcher ratio. And that faculties are not so good at using screwdrivers and C-spanners. But there remains that all our culture favours people who do nothing with their hands. All our culture despises handworkers. Please, re-read Plato's *Republic*! There seems to be some natural trend in university to go in the direction of symbols, abstractions, and to set some scale of values which has mathematics and philosophy on the upper level and applied sciences on the ground floor. What is less known maybe is that such tendency does indeed exist in industry too. I was told by a German colleague that the board of some big company met after several mergers. Somebody asked: 'Where are our plants?' The answer was there was no longer any plant! There remained only financial interests, shares, participations, equities and so on. On the scale of industrial values, management customarily ranks high. Harvard has been the ultimate. A good lawyer often seems of more value than a good research manager. Many undergraduates take courses in finance

and economy but many of them forget good ol'drawing board. Indeed the kingdom of symbols and signs seems to be very attractive in industry and not only in the university. They go to finance as we go to mathematics.

But the technological revolution, the replacement of natural objects by man-made objects, forces us to go down towards the very nature of technological objects. May I recommend you to read Georges Simondon's master work *Du mode d'existence des objects techniques**? The man-made object can't be anything. It has its own internal necessity. You can't understand it just by the addition of physics and economy. Given Marx, Keynes, given Carnot and Galileo, I can't understand the automobile.

So, as soon as there can be meetings between industry and university in the physical presence of technical objects, then both sides, going down from the heaven of symbols to the earth of reality, can meet, can speak together, begin to understand each other. The mystery of the technical being acts as a mediator between them. This is the reason why the *technical installations of the university* are so important. If chemical engineering is only a matter of test tubes then you can bet that the relationship with industry will be very difficult. Of course, this has also its import-ance in the teaching business.

To conclude, may I suggest a rather paradoxical view. After all, as Kierkegaard used to say: 'Paradox is the passion of the mind. Woe to the mind without paradox!' What would happen if our universities were companies? Of course, not fabricating material objects to sell them on the market, but products in the service sector just like bankers, insurance companies, or 'le Club Méditerranée'? Is it not in a way already the case? Haven't we two major products, namely research and teaching, plus one new one—fast developing—continued education? Is there not compe-tition between our universities? Haven't we cash flow, turnover, customers, overheads? Why not agree on that? If we do so, instead of pretending to be more or less non-profit, cultural and leisure organisations, we will be much more readily understood by our industrial partners. We will be able to show our costs, our price list. This can in turn help us in our relations with the governmental bodies or agencies. Comparison of costs could help us in improving our own management techniques and eventually to take full advan-tage for ourselves of what we are accustomed to teach to other people.

*Paris, Aubier-Montaigne, 1958.

Be sure that when I have to produce this type of speech to industry people, I am in the habit of telling them that they had better consider themselves as a university because their capital is mainly made of people, and because in a world which is changing so fast, teaching and research are their only way to survival. And many seem to understand it.

DISCUSSION

The torrid climate of Birmingham was rendered bearable by the impeccable organisation and old fashioned friendliness of Congress and university staff, and, for Topic 3 devotees, the freshness of Professor Guy Deniélou's talk. This 'tour de force' had the qualities of a crisp summer salad rather than gun metal, but like all good salads some of the more memorable and titillating ingredients shall be savoured in the memory rather than recorded in the recipe. With a panache for which his countrymen are famous, Professor Deniélou honed the problems down to manageable proportions with breath taking ease and the assistance of occasional glimpses of previously unrecorded European and Colonial history.

Compiègne University had been established with an emphasis on exploring university/industry relationships on a basis different from the traditional French university. The industrialist and the academic had traditionally a view of the work and life of the other which induced in each a sense of guilt when facing the other. Professor Deniélou likened them to two tribes with totally different perceptions of life and this inhibited relationships between them. Industry with its tradition of doing and making, universities with a tradition for thought and disputation would seem superficially to be moving in divergent directions, but when younger staff on both sides were involved the inhibitions of tradition were less ingrained and the sense of guilt diminished. A substantial spur to finding common purpose was the technological revolution referred to above. This was inducing a greater awareness of the social implications arising from new interdependencies and changes of attitude. Profound changes were taking place in industry. In the past 'poor' industries foundered and 'good' ones prospered but now there was a new phenomenon. A 'good' industry could go to the wall finding itself technologically 'broke' as the result of the introduction of a new technology which it was not staffed to handle. Indeed the tightly drawn structure and sophistication of 'good' companies might make them more prone to this form of demise. Academic disciplines were similarly undergoing change, new skills, new technical applications were creating new needs and the boundaries of disciplines were changing. Under the impact of computers and solid state physics the two tribes were losing their original structures, industry becoming increasingly professional and universities more disciplined. These changes had created fertile ground for better university/industry relationships and the common cause was more clearly recognised.

Turning to the complexities of these relationships, Professor Deniélou drew upon the experience of Compiègne University and described eleven ways in which they had been fostered:—

(1) The University council was the ultimate authority and care was taken to ensure a strong industrial membership on that body. This of course is not an uncommon form of lay membership on university courts or councils in UK universities.

(2) There was a regular exchange of personnel between the university and industrial firms. Approximately one third of the staffing in the university at any time would be made up of industrial staff who would have the same responsibilities as their academic colleagues and be employed under similar contractual conditions. At the same time a similar proportion of academic staff would be working in industry and again they would be regarded as normal employees of the firm concerned. Of course there were difficulties to be overcome in individual cases but the general effect was to transfer knowledge and practice at first hand between the institutions.

(3) Industry placed a large number of research contracts with the university. The reasons for choosing Compiègne rather than more prestigious neighbouring universities were varied if not downright surprising!

(4) The undergraduate courses were conducted with a requirement that six months will be spent working in industry—a variation of the British 'thin sandwich' course.

(5) The University kept records of the progress of alumni in their careers, and in the American style sought donations from them or their companies to appeals for special university purposes.

(6) The University arranged conferences, seminars and congresses specifically designed to meet the needs of those working in industry or others concerned with industrial problems. These brought academics and industrialists together on topics of common interest and helped in the creation of longer-term contacts between individual members of the two tribes.

(7) The University pursued an active programme of continuing education and post-experience courses. It was no longer reasonable to assume that the contents of a degree course would provide a lasting source of intellectual capital for a whole career; or even a comprehensive framework into which as yet unknown techniques or technologies could be slotted. Continuing education would increase in importance in the future.

(8) A more careful study and practice of entertaining industrial visitors than was usual in older, more prestigious universities formed part of Compiègne's public relations policy. Industrialists entertained clients well, and the University ensured that industrial visitors were received and entertained in the style to which they were accustomed. This set the impression of high standards which visitors tended to use as a measure of the University's standards in general.

(9) Involvement in the industrial sector followed from the generation of 'spin-off' companies from the University's research work. This usually followed as a result of decisions by academic staff to set up their own companies to exploit the results of their research. As in many other countries computer and software developments were particularly prone to this kind of development.

(10) With help from capital investment the University encouraged joint industry/university ventures.

(11) Finally the University had learnt the wisdom of using its students as the carriers of news, views and ideas between the two sectors. They absorbed information readily and needed little encouragement to look with fresh eyes and no inhibitions at existing practices.

Turning finally to the obstacles he had encountered, Professor Deniélou explained how equipment costs were a considerable disincentive to involvement with both manufacture and manufacturing processes. This together with an ungenerous level of technical support produced a tendency for academics to move to theoretical problems. Similarly it was noticeable that progress up the industrial ladder was associated with an increasing concern and responsibility for non-technical matters. The best ground for collaboration between the academic and the industrialist, on the other hand, was in product-oriented problems; here contact and understanding were easier to establish.

At the end of the day, however, universities were themselves an industry, an industry of services, so why was it so difficult for both sides to talk in the same language?

During the short discussion which followed, Professor Deniélou said his graduates were not classified; they passed or failed, but their degree was supplemented with a full description of the credits gained in various courses. He thought this information was more useful to a potential employer than a base overall classification. Compiègne had been established with special objectives and though there were advantages in planning a new university and its academic programme from scratch this had been offset to some extent initially by their low position in the pecking order in the recruitment of students in competition with the other established universities. For the future he thought the country would have to seek a change in existing universities to meet the new demands of society rather than rely on further new establishments. He was questioned on the system of remuneration during periods of secondment and reminded the meeting that in France the academic staff were civil servants and in return for security of tenure they were content with salary levels which were some 25% lower than their industrial colleagues. It followed that secondment from industry was made feasible by rewarding such staff at a higher level than the academic staff. There was no friction over these arrangements. He was however anxious to increase the number of academics spending periods in industry. The present figure of 3–4% was too low.

Sub-Topic 3(e)

DEVELOPING UNIVERSITY/INDUSTRY PARTNERSHIPS IN THE SOUTH-WEST PACIFIC

Chairman: Dr. G. J. HILLS

Principal and Vice-Chancellor of the University of Strathclyde

Rapporteur: Mr. D. J. CLINCH

Secretary of the Open University (UK)

Thursday, 18 August

Professor B. G. WILSON *(Vice-Chancellor, University of Queensland):*

Introduction

The links between universities and industry are the focus of much study and interest in Britain today. Amongst the countries of the south-west Pacific there is growing concern that university/industry links should be stronger.

In the case of Australia, a major reason for the limited university/industry interaction lies in the small proportion of research and development expenditure which is directed to experimental development. Compared to other countries within the Organisation for Economic Co-operation and Development, two thirds, an unusually high percentage, of the gross expenditure on research and development in Australia is provided by the government sector, a relatively low fraction of which expenditure is devoted to experimental development. If the end result of experimental development work is the introduction of new technology into industry, it is clear that the funding of such work is at a relatively low level in Australia. The situation is similar in New Zealand. Whether or not there is such a direct relationship between development and innovation is difficult to establish. It is however possible to estimate a country's comparative performance by examining indicators such as the technological balance of payments and the number of patents filed

225

relative to gross domestic product, population or research effort. Results of such analyses indicate that Australia performs very poorly, while its comparatively poor performance in terms of ownership of overseas patents lends credence to the suggestion that the low level of experimental development work is having an adverse effect on the innovative capacity of Australian industry.

Another important aspect of research and development (R & D) performance relates to the degree of foreign ownership of industry in Australia. Nevertheless, it is not unreasonable to ask whether the relatively poor technological performance of Australia in the mid-1970s was due only to the lack of interest of industry in investing in experimental development, or whether it was, at least in part, due to the lack of interest within universities to become involved in this aspect of applied research. In 1976-77, for example, intramural expenditure in the natural sciences within universities included only 7% 'experimental development' as compared to 26% applied and 67% basic research. A great number of studies have been conducted on the technological development of Australia in recent years, and as a result of limited government initiatives and industrial and university self-interest, the strength of the university/industrial partnership has significantly increased. One measure of this is the level of non-governmental research support which, for Australian universities, increased from $17·4 million in 1976 to $46·2 million in 1981.

The Changing Face of University/Industry Partnership

Various techniques have been utilised to facilitate university/industrial interaction during the past 20 years. Virtually all universities in Australia and New Zealand have provided some encouragement for appropriate departments to provide testing services, particularly in engineering-related disciplines, and for individual staff to engage in (limited) consultative and other outside paid work activities.

However other developments have occurred during this period which may well have greater growth potential. Such developments include greater co-ordination and entrepreneurial interest by the institution as a whole through the development of 'consulting companies'; industrial co-operation to fund a research division or a centre for advanced technical education within a university; governmental support for the development of research specialities related to national goals within university departments; and governmental action to stimulate high technology industry in proximity to one or more institutions of higher education—'research parks'.

226

Mechanisms for Change

The formation of university consulting companies has been a feature of the Australasian scene of the past 20 years, both in universities and colleges of advanced education. The 'company' approach provides a mechanism to bring together multi-disciplinary teams with a profile of skills and a combined resource which can be tailored to the needs of particular projects or programmes. Particularly in the larger institutions, this is a strength that industries cannot match.

Academia has a major marketing advantage in that the base cost and resource of staff is provided from the parent body and, since the commitment to a project is a part-time one, the prime responsibilities of an academic continue, without hiring or firing, when an industrial contract starts or finishes. University consulting companies have, therefore, the flexibility of engaging those persons with the specific skills needed to meet the highly diversified demands of technology and society. Furthermore, academics have familiar access to an international network of knowledge. Inevitably, however, the success of a multi-disciplinary project team depends on strong project management.

The common interest of primary producers in improving productivity has led to the development of a variety of agencies which, either by levies on producers or by common interests of major companies, provide funds for research contracts. Many individual contracts have been let, for example, in the mining, sugar, cotton and meat producing areas, to university personnel. Ultimately this can lead to the setting up of a major facility for an industry either as an independent unit or within a university.

A similar investment may be made by government, through the establishment of a specialised centre with financial support for a number of years, by which time it is expected that the centre will have achieved commercial viability. Such an approach might be indicated where there is no immediate R & D capability in the industry and where specific expertise is seen to have national importance. Again, such a policy is most easily affected in a university environment where the researchers have expert skills and whose future career is not dependent on the success or failure of a particular project.

Research parks and innovation centres are other mechanisms for the stimulation of high technology development which provide, through geographical proximity, many of the advantages of the in-house consulting company with the entrepreneurial strengths of innovative commercial management. As yet these concepts are relatively new in the south-west Pacific.

The following examples of industrial activities in individual universities illustrate these different approaches; from the university as broad spectrum consultant on the one hand, to the university offering highly specialized services to a small segment of industry on the other.

A. *A Consulting Company: Unisearch*

In 1959 the Council of the University of New South Wales established Unisearch Limited, as a wholly-owned and controlled subsidiary of the University, to offer an organised technical service to industry and commerce. Through this mechanism the Council gave industry direct access to the special technological facilities of the University and took a further step in discharging that University's responsibility under its act of incorporation to 'aid by research and other suitable means the advancement, development and practical application of science to industry and commerce'. This responsibility derives from the origins of the University as an institute of technology. Unisearch was the first organisation of this kind in the (British) Commonwealth. It is a company limited by guarantee and has no shareholders. It is managed by a board of directors, elected by the members of the company who are themselves appointed by the Council of the University from among its own members. The members and directors of the company receive no payment for their services.

The work of Unisearch is carried out as a commercial operation. It actively seeks contracts from industry and commerce and charges fees for the services rendered. The operations are completely self-supporting in that all costs are charged to income received with the surplus providing funds for University purposes.

Unisearch undertakes research and development investigations for industry and commerce in Australia, irrespective of the size of the organisation. It offers a competent research service to assist in the solution of day-to-day and developmental problems and in the study of the application of specific areas of research to the particular operations of individual organisations. In its investigations for industry Unisearch makes use of the extensive laboratories, workshops, libraries, computers and other facilities of the University, with safeguards which make certain that the work carried out does not interfere with the primary tasks of the University in teaching and research.

Through the channel of Unisearch industry is able to draw on the vast bank of knowledge and experience which has been built up within the University, other universities and in the technical literature. As unprejudiced observers of a problem encountered by industry, members of the university staff are able more quickly to determine the exact nature of the problem and to bring to bear the scientific measures required for its solution. Experience over the past 20 years has shown clearly that there is a great and expanding need for the kind of services which Unisearch can provide. Unisearch undertakes substantial work in the engineering, metallurgical, construction, wool and textiles, electrical power generation, transport and mining fields, and for the cement, paint, plastics, rubber, chemical and food industries. It is engaged in the testing of many materials and processes and acts continuously for many companies in a consultative capacity.

On the other hand, the academic members of staff concerned obtain tangible benefits from their participation in this work, apart from payments received from Unisearch for their services. The application of their theoretical knowledge to practical problems is challenging and rewarding, often resulting in improved teaching for the benefit of their students and the addition of case histories to the store of research in their professional fields of expertise (while retaining confidentiality regarding the names of clients and results vital to their clients' purposes).

When Unisearch was established it was thought that a major part of its work would be to assist small industries with their problems. In practice the major industrial organisations, which have laboratories and laboratory staff of their own, have also used the facility.

A further important function of Unisearch is to develop and exploit inventions arising out of the work of the University of New South Wales. Eighty-two inventions are currently being administered.

The company has no laboratories of its own and makes use of all the University facilities. The University's policy is that where consulting or research services being provided by academic staff involve the use of University facilities, the work must be processed through Unisearch. Although consulting services, under University guidelines, can be provided by academic staff independently, many staff prefer to work through Unisearch to take advantage of the benefits the organisation can offer. Income for the year ended 31 March, 1982 amounted to $3·7 million, contributing to an operating surplus of $830,000.

Similar consulting companies in universities, though considerably smaller in scale of operation, include Anutech Pty. Ltd. at the Australian National University, the Applied Research Office of the University of Auckland, Durac Ltd. at Deakin University,

Tunra Ltd. at the University of Newcastle and UniQuest at the University of Queensland. Consulting companies have also been formed at certain colleges of advanced education in Australia, the largest operation being Wait Aid Ltd. at the Western Australian Institute of Technology.

A more unusual model has been adopted at Lae, in Papua New Guinea, in the establishment of the Appropriate Technology Development Institute. The Institute is related to the concept of a university 'consulting company', but is operated jointly with external agencies. It also has less of the remoteness associated with 'consultant' and is a strongly participative agency, not only in the development aspect but through the involvement of the community in its activities.

B. *A Research Institute funded by Industry: The Julius Kruttschnitt Mineral Research Centre (JKMRC)*

The Julius Kruttschnitt Mineral Research Centre (within the department of mining and metallurgical engineering at the University of Queensland) was established in 1970 as a specialist academic institute to carry out research and postgraduate training in mineral engineering. The terms of reference under which the Centre was established required that research projects should be worthy of study in the University in their own right, and likely to lead to substantial improvement in mineral engineering. As a result, the JKMRC maintains a very close relationship with the mining industry, with most of its research being conducted at the operations sites of sponsoring companies.

The Centre is located on a mine site about 5 km. from the main University campus. The operational funds are provided in the form of research grants from the mining industry made through the Australian Mineral Industries Research Association Limited. Research grants in 1982 totalled more than $900,000, covering more than 90% of the operating costs. In return the Centre has played its part in the dramatic evolution and development of scientific and engineering techniques that have taken place in the mining industry in the last 15 years.

As of June 1982, students of the Centre had been awarded a total of 17 PhDs, one DSc and 16 master's degrees; consequently the Centre provides a major component of the total postgraduate training programme in mineral engineering carried out in Australian universities.

The Centre's research philosophy is to concentrate on limited areas of interest in depth rather than to work on several diverse projects. Since its inception the Centre has been concerned with improving the efficiency of mining and mineral processing through the development and application of modelling techniques based on computers and microprocessors. The research procedure followed is to obtain data for mathematical models from a wide range of operations at various mining and mineral processing sites. The results of these studies are supplemented with special tests carried out in laboratories or pilot plants, often at the Centre. As a result researchers at the Centre are always familiar with the characteristics of different types of operating circuits, and machines currently in use in the industry. This practical knowledge is then applied to the formulation and application of models for future generations of equipment and circuits.

In addition to its own research work the Centre offers short specialist courses in specific areas of expertise. Engineers and other technical personnel from industry are encouraged to take advantage of these courses which can run from weeks to months. Visitors to the Centre for extended periods have included senior academic and research personnel from the UK, the USA, France, Germany, Poland, Norway, Japan and India. Short courses and specialist lectures have also been given in many universities and research institutes in overseas countries.

C. *An Advanced Engineering Study Centre financed by Industrial Donation: Warren Centre for Advanced Engineering*

The Warren Centre for Advanced Engineering has been established at the University of Sydney to promote excellence and innovation in engineering and greater co-operation between staff and industry. The Centre is being located in part of the existing engineering faculty buildings and will bring together for short periods, under distinguished visiting fellows, selected groups of experienced, practising engineers from industry, experts from Australia and overseas, and research and teaching engineers to consolidate existing know-how from industry, research and teaching, study advanced techniques, develop approaches to particular problems in engineering and technology and to disseminate findings through public seminars.

The Centre is quite separate from the usual work of the University and does not duplicate the service provided by any other organisation. It is intended to provide a unique forum for interchange and enhancement of skills and knowledge between those organisations both large and small concerned with the development and progress of Australia. The Centre is under the control of a

231

board of directors, representing industry and the University, with the majority from outside the University. The administration of the Centre will be handled in rotation by a part-time executive director from within the faculty of engineering.

An initial fund-raising drive of $2 million is under way to provide an annual base income of $200,000 to cover running costs and underwrite the establishment of each project group. At the time of the official opening of the Centre (May, 1983) three-quarters of the target had already been achieved.

D. *An R & D Laboratory initiated by Government: MITEC*

A Microwave Technology Development Centre (MITEC) was set up within the department of electrical engineering at the University of Queensland in 1980 to provide an R & D support facility for Australian firms working in the area of microwave technology. The establishment arose following discussions in 1979 with the then Department of Productivity, now Department of Science and Technology. The development of MITEC was seen as a possible model for R & D support centres in other areas of high technology. In such areas Australian manufacturers are usually dependent on overseas sources for components, and problems of supply can arise if overseas suppliers give low priority to the Australian market. Rapid changes in technology can render whole systems out of date within a short period of time and manufacturers must have the means of coping with such changes.

These problems can be countered by the establishment of R & D facilities in individual firms, which would provide the capability of design and development of the components required for manufacturing programmes. The experience in Australia, however, has shown that such R & D facilities are difficult to establish and to maintain. The University of Queensland facility provides R & D support for any Australian firm working, or intending to work, in the area of microwave technology. The Centre has been established with the support of the Federal Department for the development of designs and prototypes of microwave components and assemblies for industrial applications. Microwave technology forms the base of many modern telecommunication systems, including the proposed Australian domestic satellite system. It has other applications to navigation, defence, heating and sensor systems as well as medical care.

The aim of MITEC is to establish world-standard processes and state-of-the-art techniques in microwave engineering, and to provide industrial firms with access to high quality microwave systems. MITEC is responsive to industrial requirements and produces microwave designs and prototypes under contract to individual firms. The designs and technology are then available to industry for commercial development. The substantial costs of the establishment and operation of the microwave laboratory facilities required for such prototype development are thus shared among many firms, with access to advanced facilities becoming possible for small firms. Firms contracting with MITEC have the advantage of a continuing source of technical advice and the immediate availability of a NATA*-registered laboratory.

MITEC is an autonomous centre on a large university campus and is associated with a well-established department of electrical engineering which has outstanding research programmes in microwave engineering. It can thus monitor current world research work in microwaves as well as assist in the technology transfer required to translate the results of research into practical hardware. The work carried out in MITEC is under the control of a steering committee with representatives from the Department of Science and Technology, the University and industry.

After three years' operation it seems clear that MITEC has a continuing and important role to perform in assisting in the development and application of microwave technology in Australia.

E. *A Research Park as Government Initiative: Technology Park, Adelaide*

Technology Park, Adelaide—the first facility of its kind in Australia—represents a South Australian government initiative to rejuvenate and expand manufacturing industry and to encourage greater interaction between industry and academic institutions. The government is spending about $5 million in 1982–84 on the site development of 83 hectares of land adjacent to the South Australian Institute of Technology with the co-operation of the University of Adelaide, the Flinders University of South Australia, the South Australian Institute of Technology and the South Australian College of Advanced Education. Plans have been approved for a $3·4 million building development to accommodate small research and development organisations and to act as a 'flagship' for the project. The Park is currently available to clients in science-based industry. The type of science-based industries that the government is interested in attracting include those dealing in electronics, biotechnology, pharmaceuticals, telecommunications, digital electronics, software development and safety engineering.

*National Association of Testing Authorities

The initiative is based on the major development of high technology research parks during the past 20 years in the United States and later developments in Canada and Britain. Similar proposals are also under discussion in Western Australia, Queensland and Auckland.

Conclusion

The case studies in this paper provide examples of mechanisms of university-industrial co-operation which have been successful in practice. As noted earlier, much consultative work in universities in the south-west Pacific is still carried on by individual departments and staff, although the more specialised and co-operative activities are growing and will likely have a greater impact on technical innovation in industry. At a different level, work-study programmes (such as the electronics programme at the Chinese University of Hong Kong) and joint advisory committees play an increasing role in interchange of information about needs between the two sectors.

The great virtues of university participation in industrial research are the potential assemblage of otherwise unavailable talents for multi-disciplinary approaches to major problems and the immediate involvement of postgraduate students in 'real world' research which, on the one hand, brings relevance to the university curriculum and, on the other, imagination, energy and highly specialised skills to technological development in industry.

DISCUSSION

Professor Wilson introduced his paper by explaining the Australian context with which his paper was primarily concerned. Since 1964 all Australian universities have been federally funded, although only one was under federal control. Professor Wilson drew attention to some of the differences between Australia and other developed countries in the high level of government involvement in research and development and the conversely low level of industrial participation. The proportion of research and development expenditure on experimental developments was almost the lowest of any country within the Organisation for Economic Co-operation and Development. A number of reasons could be advanced for this situation, for example the historical importance of primary products in the Australian economy and the degree of foreign ownership of Australian industry. Significantly, only in agriculture and mining had

234

Australian universities made a major research and development input. The position was now changing, partly as a result of government initiatives and partly through the interest of the universities and industry. Professor Wilson went on to describe some of the institutional arrangements for facilitating greater university/industry co-operation. Professor Wilson acknowledged the continuing importance of the consultative work carried out by individual staff and departments of Australian universities and also of student project work, sponsored research students, staff exchanges and research contracts as other important means of university/industry collaboration. He concluded by drawing attention to the difficulty of motivating university staff to participate in industrial research and development work and the need for staff to be well-paid for their contribution.

In the discussion that followed the presentation of Professor Wilson's paper, three general issues emerged: the attitude of industry to universities providing commercial services; the relationship of industry's needs to student teaching and research programmes; and the matter of recognition for academic staff participating in industrial work. The general consensus was that in the Australian context there was not a problem about industry resenting or opposing the role of the universities in providing commercial services. The major reason advanced for this was that pricing was at commercial rates in order that costs should be fully covered. There was no suggestion of unfair competition.

There was not much support for the proposition that universities should attempt to design teaching programmes directly related to industry's needs. Needs changed quickly and were often quite specific. Universities had to provide programmes which recognised the process of change that would take place during the working life of the student. Professor Wilson did however observe an important difference in the preparation of engineers in North America and Australia. The engineer in North America was expected to become a manager within a few years and the training reflected this: in Australia training was for engineers who would be expected to remain engineers for much of their life.

Recognition of academic staff taking part in industrial work was discussed in the context of promotion criteria and financial rewards. A straw poll of participants indicated that relatively few institutions gave explicit recognition to industrial work in promotion reviews. Nevertheless a number of universities do recognise professional work, of which industrial work might form a part, when considering academic staff for promotion, and attention was drawn to the relevance of industrial work to the quality of teaching and research. For example, a well-developed case-study based on the industrial experience of a member of staff could be incorporated in undergraduate teaching programmes and assessed for promotion purposes. Financial rewards for industrial work (within the framework of institutional terms and conditions of service) were seen as necessary and appropriate: the fact that some staff had more marketable skills than others was generally understood and accepted by the academic community.

Topic 3

UNIVERSITY/INDUSTRY PARTNERSHIPS

Co-ordinating Chairman's Commentary on the Group's Discussions

Final Plenary Session
Friday, 19 August

Sir HENRY CHILVER *(Vice-Chancellor, Cranfield Institute of Technology):* Within the framework of the general theme, which Sir Adrian Cadbury presented so ably in his keynote address, partnerships between universities and other sectors of our society—such as industry—are vitally important. The theme of partnerships extends into the other Topic discussions in this year's Congress; partnerships play a role in the deeper understanding of the social consequences of technological innovation; the impact of universities on integrated rural development will depend on the relationships universities form with relevant bodies in that area; again, partnerships are an important agent in the transfer of technological ideas to many areas of society; the needs for continuing education are probably best determined through close links formed between universities and the world outside. Partnerships are, therefore, an important feature of all areas of our discussions in the past week.

In Topic 3 discussions were developed in two ways. The first parts of our discussion periods were devoted to talks—by leading authorities—on the general scene in partnerships in their own countries.

Dr. Wright described the vital role of partnerships in the modern Canadian scene. On a more general note, he reminded us of Lord Ashby's observation: that universities played little or no role in the industrial revolution in Britain. This is not unrelated to Sir Adrian Cadbury's equally important observations on the role—in the early days of industry in Birmingham—of small non-conforming groups. Dr. Wright went on to explain the diverse range of partnerships now developing in Canada. Particularly strong are partnerships in undergraduate teaching, which lead to a continuous flow of students between universities and industry.

Professor Wilson told us of the many new developments in partnerships in Australia and New Zealand, indicating again the growing interest and diversity of forms. Dr. Mitra described the importance of partnerships for India, and told us of the many difficulties that will need to be overcome to establish strong links; after a period in which it has proved difficult to develop links, the prospects now look better. Dr. Bragg showed us how the British scene has changed dramatically in the last decade, and how partnerships have become a feature of higher education policy.

To give ourselves some comparisons with countries beyond the Commonwealth, we invited Professor Deniélou to talk about the role of partnerships in France. He pointed out that 'partnerships' are a growing feature of the university scene world-wide, because universities, and the many different sectors of modern societies, have everything to gain from mutual understanding. He emphasised very strongly the need to see students themselves, and particularly undergraduate students, as playing a vital role in partnerships. Students—as well as carrying ideas into industry in their careers—frequently find it relatively easy to relate to those already working in industry.

In the second parts of our Topic discussion sessions we had the benefit of case-studies of partnerships from almost all countries of the Commonwealth. Around 40 case-studies were presented during the week. These showed first the growing numbers of partnerships—throughout the Commonwealth—and second the importance universities now attach to these.

As a result of the general talks on the one hand and the short case-studies on the other, our discussions were very wide ranging. Our sessions were highly participative, and everyone was able to contribute his ideas and views. We are very grateful not only to our main speakers but to all those who so readily presented case-studies on their own experiences.

What conclusions were we able to draw from this week of discussions?

The ideas exchanged have enabled us all to see the strengths of partnerships and their potential in the years ahead. A very considerable proportion of university education in the Commonwealth is professionally and vocationally oriented. Most university students pursue their later careers in the professions, industry and commerce. It is not surprising, therefore, to see the wide interest in partnerships.

Not only are they being developed extensively; at the same time they are very diverse in forms. Throughout the Commonwealth there are many styles of teaching partnerships. These have generally proved very successful and, if economic conditions allow, they will probably become more extensive in universities. Partnerships in research are very numerous and take many different forms, from industry-sponsored research to industrial proximity through science parks. Advisory and consultancy services are equally highly developed, and play an important role in relating universities to the real world around them.

The logic of these partnerships emerged from our numerous discussions. The role of universities is to develop—at the highest levels—centres of the generation of ideas. The generation of ideas is enhanced if it is conducted against the background of understanding of problems of the real world. University/industry partnerships have a vital role to play in helping to develop this understanding. Such partnerships are not pseudo 'commercial' ventures by universities—selling their 'surplus' services. Partnerships are, in fact, an essential element in relating universities to innovations—of all sorts—in the societies in which those universities operate.

A very important feature of the Topic discussions was the importance universities throughout the Commonwealth attach to partnerships. There are many different forms of partnerships, and, at the same time, these are evolving rapidly. In developed countries—as technological innovations permeate, increasingly, all areas of the society—'partnerships' take on increasingly diverse forms. In developing countries it is not as easy as transplanting the successful partnerships from more developed countries. Nevertheless, the development of successful partnerships is of world-wide interest. They are probably best initiated on the basis of undergraduate teaching programmes, in situations where research studies would prove more difficult to develop.

The Topic discussions focused on the attributes of 'successful' partnerships. They are most likely to succeed when the university is genuinely committed to the concept of partnerships. Their success depends critically on the ability of staff to identify areas in which the transfer of ideas can lead to genuinely useful exploitation of those ideas. In industry itself much innovation takes place in relatively small organisations. Forming partnerships with such small organisations is very challenging, and such partnerships must be achieved to strengthen university/industry links.

One of the most important roles of universities is to educate young people who will later transfer into industry and commerce. In this area 'partnerships' can help define and indeed finance new educational needs. Equally important is the transfer of staff, and here there is a need to increase the flexibility of employment of staff and to evolve reward systems to encourage their movement into industry, and particularly into forming new embryo organisations.

The critics of partnerships point to the importance of retaining a 'purist' role for universities in modern society; a role in which the university is to be seen as a centre of ideas generation which is remote from the problems of the real world. In developing university/industry partnerships, is there a danger—they ask—of undermining academic values? All those taking part in the discussions in Topic 3 agreed the need to retain academic values. At the same time they would argue that, for universities to fulfil a wider role in our society, they must develop stimulus from the world of 'real' problems and they must develop a deeper understanding of such problems. 'Partnerships' have a vital role to play in this. In this role they can indeed strengthen the academic values of both teaching and research in the universities.

Against this background the main conclusions that emerged from the wide-ranging discussions in Topic 3 were:—

(1) Partnerships—of appropriate sorts—are of considerable strength both to universities and to those sectors of society to which they relate.

(2) Partnerships do not mean the undermining of academic values. Indeed, they can be used to strengthen the pursuit of more clearly-identifiable basic studies.

(3) There is no single formula for successful partnerships; situations vary between countries and indeed within countries.

(4) Some of the characteristics of successful partnerships are:—

(i) they generally develop from the university side, but they depend on contacts on the industrial side who have an understanding of universities;

(ii) they have the general backing of the university;

(iii) they frequently originate from individuals who identify appropriate opportunities;

(iv) they gain from central support services, provided by the university;

(v) they are strengthened by flexible arrangements in staff appointments and appropriate reward systems; there was a general feeling that present staffing systems offered flexibility, although this was not always fully exploited by universities;

(vi) very successful partnerships can be developed through students and undergraduate courses.

The discussions in Topic 3 provided a very wide-ranging debate, greatly enriched by the diversity of contributions from all parts of the Commonwealth. All of us have learnt immensely from each other's experiences and views. All the participants in Topic 3 saw university/industry partnerships as playing a central and continuing role in universities in technological innovation.

Topic 3

OTHER CONTRIBUTIONS

Among the other papers brought to or circulated at the Congress were those mentioned below, which related to this Topic.

Professor P. S. MANI SUNDARAM (*Vice-Chancellor, Bharathidasan University*), in a paper on 'University-Industry Partnership', discussed the reasons for and the ways of achieving interaction between universities and industry. In conclusion he described three examples of successful partnership in which his own University and an affiliated engineering college participated, involving, respectively, curriculum development/continuing education, co-operative education and industry support of university. A rather more detailed account of the first and third of these examples was given in an accompanying 'Case-Study' paper.

Professor R. C. MEHROTRA (*Department of Chemistry, University of Rajasthan*) submitted a reprint from the *Journal of Higher Education* (University Grants Commission, New Delhi, vol. 8, no. 1, Monsoon 1982) of his article on 'Industry-University Interaction'—'an attempt . . . to present a bird's eye view of some illustrative directions of useful cooperation between universities and industry'. (Professor Mehrotra did not himself attend the Congress.)

Group Discussions

TOPIC 4

THE DEVELOPMENT AND TRANSFER OF TECHNOLOGY

Co-ordinating Chairman: Sir DENYS WILKINSON
Vice-Chancellor of the University of Sussex

For index to names, see p. 427

Sub-Topic 4(a)

RELATIONSHIP BETWEEN FUNDAMENTAL SCIENCE AND NEW TECHNOLOGY

Chairman: Sir DENYS WILKINSON
Vice-Chancellor of the University of Sussex

Rapporteur: Y. B. Datuk MUSA BIN MOHAMAD
Vice-Chancellor of the University of Science, Malaysia

Monday, 15 August

In his opening remarks the Chairman referred to the five Sub-Topics to be discussed under Topic 4 as having a common purpose though differentiated by name. In drawing the attention of the meeting to Sub-Topic 4(a) the Chairman requested the meeting to focus on the issue of whether new technology and innovation emerged from fundamental science.

Professor F. R. JEVONS *(Vice-Chancellor, Deakin University):*

A CASE OF DISPUTED MATERNITY

Motherhood in a New Context

In the period of great faith in science following the second world war, arguing for it seemed like arguing for motherhood. Science was accepted as the source of technological progress: science discovers, technology applies. But now doubts have arisen. Examples of applications arising from curiosity-oriented science are clouded by ambiguities. If science is the mother of invention, what impregnates it?

243

Of course there are other kinds of benefits. There are manpower benefits—the training of research workers, and the enlivening of teaching; but why can't we get them from applied rather than pure research? The cultural value of science is accepted but has changed in nature with the fairly wide recognition that scientific knowledge is not Truth with a capital T but subject to the scourge of relativism (Chalmers, 1976; Charlesworth, 1982). The internationalism of science is another benefit whose validity is not disputed but whose dollar value can be.

In addition public disillusion with the whole scientific and technological enterprise became marked in the 1960s. Old problems remained, despite massive expansion of science, and new ones—pollution, environment, non-renewable resources—had appeared.

So if arguing for science is still like arguing for motherhood, the context now is that there has been a population explosion and motherhood is something you can have too much of—especially when, as here, the mother is suspected to be flighty, the paternity is doubtful, and the children unruly. We need to make sure, therefore, that our arguments for science will not crumble under scrutiny. Against that background I will examine critically the generation of practical benefits via technology.

Is Science the Mother of Invention?

In the post-war euphoria about science it was widely believed that science had displaced necessity as the mother of invention. If so, the way to foster technological innovation is to foster science. The argument is still often put that because applications arise in unpredictable ways research should be supported without regard to any mission, even a long-term one. Many people remain sceptical, however, including politicians and public servants, as well as journalists to whom the topics listed in university research reports seem so esoteric that the temptation to have a bit of all too easy fun at their expense is irresistible.

In Australia the Australian Science and Technology Council (ASTEC) has sprung into battle and two reports have resulted (ASTEC 1979, 1981). They are bureaucratic defence manoeuvres. Pure research was lumped together with strategic to form the basic research which is their subject; this is a common modern practice, but the possible conceptual confusion for the casual reader is also convenient.

The 1979 report lists fourteen 'examples of basic research projects in universities which have produced social, economic or other benefits'. In half of them the strategic purpose is plain from the descriptions given. The conceptual difficulties that arise in the other half can be illustrated by two examples. A study of soil bacteria in a stone fruit nursery carried out in the plant pathology department at the Waite Agricultural Research Institute, University of Adelaide, is described as 'curiosity-motivated'. I would be surprised and sorry if the scientists were not curious, but I would be equally surprised and sorry if their curiosity was not shaped by a sense of strategic purpose. The discovery of a property of nitrogenase which was later made the basis of a sensitive assay method is described as 'a completely basic piece of work'. True, it is basic within the definition, but if 'completely' implies pure rather than strategic I find that difficult to swallow, nitrogenase being an enzyme responsible for biological nitrogen fixation.

Outside the 14 Australian examples there are similar ambiguities. Thus ASTEC (1981) says 'penicillin was discovered by pure research'. It is true that Sir Ernst Chain has been quoted (Ronayne, 1983) as saying that 'the only reason which motivated me to start the work on penicillin was scientific interest'; at the time penicillin seemed to be too unstable for therapeutic use. But I find it scarcely credible that work on a new agent that stops bacterial growth can be regarded as devoid of strategic significance. It is the nature of the research that counts, not the motivation of the researcher. A more convincing example is provided by nuclear energy: Rutherford, we are told, believed that the energy of the nucleus would never be released.

An important point made in the 1981 ASTEC report is that the relation between basic research and practical application is one of mutual support, not of one-way dependence. Microelectronics and recombinant DNA are given as examples, and both show convincingly the 'synergistic and reciprocating' relationship described by Evans (1983) in another context.

Is Necessity the Mother of Invention?

Mention of the reciprocal nature of the relationship leads me to look also at the 'reverse' effect. In the 1960s, the decade of disillusion with science, necessity was revived: the view came back into prominence that innovation is pulled by needs to be met rather than pushed by discoveries seeking uses (Gannicott, 1980; see also the critical discussion in chapter 2 of Ronayne, 1983). Of the spate of empirical studies of innovation in the late sixties and early seventies perhaps the most significant thing to say is that they did not show what they are often said to have shown. The best guide through the formidable conceptual and methodological difficulties is the critical review by Mowery and Rosenberg (1979), which concludes that the claimed primacy of market demand is not established.

For instance, one study often cited in favour of the primacy of demand is that by Myers and Marquis. This study of 567 innovations in five industries in the USA classed three-quarters of them as responses to recognition of demand. Obviously, however, both a need and the technical feasibility have to be there for successful innovation. Mowery and Rosenberg point out that the problem was not even being worked on in 27% of the cases until there was an input of scientific or technical information; in a further 56% the solutions were stimulated by such an input. Can one, they ask, accept the primacy of demand when 83% of the innovations were so heavily dependent on the stock of knowledge?

Similarly, the study of 84 Queen's Award-winning innovations (Langrish et al, 1972), carried out in what was then my department in Manchester, has often been cited for its conclusion that 'need pull' occurred twice as frequently as 'discovery push'. We used a simple taxonomy of two kinds of discovery (scientific and technological) and two kinds of need (customer and management); we rejected the linear model of innovation which gives it a single clear starting point and instead allowed two principal stimuli per case; and then, it is true, 'need' occurred twice as frequently as 'discovery'. The discoveries were technological rather than scientific in nearly every case. But these results came from looking at innovation from the point of view of the award-winning firm. The question we asked for this particular analysis was: what stimulated the firm into action? This would tend to downplay the role of discoveries, and especially of more basic discoveries which might have become embodied in technology or in techniques at an earlier stage.

It seems, then, that the two factors which must interact for successful innovation, the market and the knowledge base, are of comparable importance. Since the knowledge base is far from omnicompetent, a reasonable policy conclusion would be that governments, if they want to stimulate innovation, should stimulate knowledge production as well as the market: science policy should be policy for science as well as science in policy. The objection that knowledge is international and that the luxury of paying for its production can be left to other governments is countered by pointing out that active scientists at home are needed to dip into the international pool.

Nursemaid, not Mother?

What can I conclude on the question of maternity? I must at this stage refine my terms. Instead of talking loosely about invention I will refer to technological innovation, which is one or more inventions put to use. And when I refer to science, it will be science as distinct from technology.

Technological innovations, I feel tempted to suggest, bearing in mind the requirements of equal opportunity, are the children of symmetrical families. They result from dialectical interactions between two kinds of unisex parents—needs and technical possibilities. If this seems facetious there is a purpose in that, namely, to drive home the point that to seek one or even two clear-cut origins for an innovation is not particularly fruitful. A technological innovation is an historical process, and as in any other case of historical explanation the truth is (as Oscar Wilde said) rarely pure and never simple. One can no more expect a simple answer than one could to the question: what was the origin of the first world war? Any answer has to be either complex or hopelessly oversimplified.

As regards the role of science, the important thing to emphasise is that it is to support rather than to initiate. The best analogy is not to parenthood but to nursing the baby. Science is not so much the mother of innovation as nursemaid to it. It does not usually originate or trigger innovation; rather it supports innovation by providing things like manpower, techniques and advice.

Further evidence for this comes from a study by Gibbons and Johnson (1974) on inputs to technical problem-solving during the development of innovations. This study got right away from the idea of a single origin: how far away is indicated by the fact that on average 30 inputs per case were identified. For the 30 innovations studied there was therefore a total of 900 inputs, and of these at least 100 were classified as science, admittedly by source rather than by content.

Nursemaids have never, of course, enjoyed uniform work loads. At particular periods in particular areas, the science-technology interaction is particularly intense. Thus Gazis (1979), in his comments on research at IBM, suggests that the novelty of the technology is an important factor. When the technology is revolutionary rather than evolutionary it is more likely to depend on and to impact on science. The need to push back the physical limits of a technology, or to overcome serious problems encountered while making engineering changes, provides incentives to explore the underlying scientific principles and phenomena.

247

I might add, though the point seems obvious, that a nursemaid shares the benefits of the technological conveniences of her employers. As a provider of tools, technology is indispensable for science.

Conclusions

My two main conclusions, then, are:—

(1) The knowledge base for innovation includes science as well as technology. The amount of overt basic science depends on the strictness of the definition of 'basic' and it may be small, but much is already embodied in technology, in techniques and in people.

(2) The supporting role of science seems to be more important that the initiating role. Science is part of the infrastructure for innovation rather than a trigger for it.

Is this evasive? Is it too nebulous to convince Treasury hawks and sceptical politicians of the value of supporting science? True, it is not as clear-cut as one would like. But the alternative is worse. It is to agree to play a game we can't win. Requests keep on coming to make things simple by finding examples of 'pure' discoveries which have triggered innovations. But Oscar Wilde was more accurate than he knew when he said that the truth is rarely pure and never simple. To take up that challenge is to fall into a trap, because it seems to concede a view of the role of science which hardly ever applies. Science is not the mother, or the father, it is more like a nursemaid. Or perhaps it is a mother, but only in the sense of A. P. Herbert's ballad:

> Other people's babies—
> That's my life.
> Mother to dozens
> And nobody's wife.

Acknowledgements

I am grateful for the help of Professor J. Ronayne and Professor R. D. Johnston, and owe special thanks to the former for letting me see the manuscript of his forthcoming book *Science in Government*.

Professor S. BLUME (*Professor of Science Dynamics, University of Amsterdam*):

UNIVERSITY RESEARCH AND TECHNOLOGICAL CHANGE: A PROBLEM AND ITS STUDY

In the last few years it has become clear that the governments of industrialised Western nations have come to agree on the importance of technological innovation as an element in economic strategy. New technology, in fields like computers, communications, biotechnology, materials science, is widely coming to be seen as the most likely source of future economic growth (and, more debatably, of new employment) in high-cost Western countries. Drawing on the literature, and on my own research, I shall try in this paper to sketch out something of the kind of contribution (university) research can be expected to make to technological change. How can the universities best contribute, through their research, to technological progress which serves the economic and social aspirations of our societies?

Theoretical Perspectives on Technological Change

What determines the rate and direction of technological change? Is it an inevitable consequence of advancing scientific knowledge, or is it a function of human needs expressed through market forces? These questions, which remain controversial, have been the subject of many studies in recent years.

Schmookler's seminal study *Invention and Economic Growth* was based on the examination of variations in the number of patents, both within individual American industries and over time. Patent data were thus taken as an indicator of inventive activity. The tendency of two sets of (historical) data—one representing patents, the other economic forces—to parallel each other, with that for patents lagging behind, led Schmookler to conclude that market forces determined the rate of invention. The state of the art in science and technology then has a limited role within this 'market pull' theory. It serves essentially to determine the *means* which the inventor uses in trying to develop what is required.

Others have argued that Schmookler much underestimated the importance of the 'supply' of science and technology. Rosenberg, for example, responds to Schmookler's comment that 'demand induces the inventions which satisfy it' with the rejoinder that

249

some demands do, 'but which and why?'. It is apparent from history that many human demands have failed to evince the required inventions. Rosenberg's argument is that economic forces can only operate within the limits set by the state of knowledge.

The question then remains of why, if economic demand is not paramount, inventive activity varies so significantly between the various sectors of production. In trying to answer this question Nelson and Winter have introduced two valuable concepts. The first of these is the notion of 'technological trajectory'. This reflects the clear tendency of technologies to 'evolve' according to some apparent 'internal dynamic' (as the history of any area of technological activity seems to show). The second concept introduced is the notion of 'selection environment'. Customers are constantly testing and evaluating the various technological options open to them, making selections, and so providing feed-back signals to the inventing firm.

It seems to me that one can distinguish between different *types* of feed-back processes upon which inventing firms act:
- propensity to innovate of different potential customer groups;
- interpretation of the values of customers in determining the direction in which technological change should be sought;
- the possibility of highly specified demands in areas in which customers are highly sophisticated (*e.g.* scientific instruments).

The work I have described suggests that, in the first place, the state of scientific knowledge determines the areas in which innovation is likely most easily to take place. Second, within those areas in which significant progress is possible state-of-the-art knowledge provides the most important *resource* for problem-solving. Empirical studies support this conclusion. However it does *not* imply that scientific knowledge plays a single unique role in technological innovation, even within a highly sophisticated industry. I can best illustrate this from my own present work on technological change in diagnostic medicine.

The Various Roles of Science in Innovation

Innovation in medical diagnostics seems to proceed by three quite distinct processes. One of these is the introduction of wholly new techniques. The pathway here seems to reflect the application to diagnosis of physical principles or properties not previously seen as having medical applicability. Far more common is the second process, which seeks to improve the instrument through which the principle is applied. Here we are speaking essentially of adaptive company research and development: the attempt to improve performance (relative to competing products) along selected dimensions. The third process involves a technique of proven value in one area being tested for other possible applications. Where successful, clinical research of this kind tends to feed back to the producers who typically seek to develop a model tailored to requirements of the new application. These three processes seem to be quite different, and to make use of different sciences and in different ways.

I want now to say more about the first of these three, for it is potentially the most important, and it has most in common with the search for new technological opportunities upon which so many present hopes are pinned. This application of new principles is well illustrated by current work on a nuclear magnetic resonance imaging device (NMR imager) for diagnostics. The NMR imager is being widely heralded as the 'ultimate' means of imaging within the body. Many large firms are spending huge sums of money on its development. Yet the fact is that initial attempts to image using NMR parameters developed within the academic world. Moreover, by the time industrial interest crystallised a number of academic groups (largely physicists, but also groups based in departments of chemistry and of medical physics) had largely succeeded in generating images of the whole human body. Largely speaking, industry picked up these ideas by tapping into this university expertise in a variety of ways. The point of the example (which I am elaborating in my own studies) is that this *radical* development in diagnostic technology took place largely under the impetus of academic curiosity, and in academic settings.

Changing Concepts of 'Usefulness'

I want now to change the focus of this discussion from *theories* of technological innovation to a particular aspect of *policy*.

The investment of public funds in the support of scientific research has always owed much to a view of science as a source of national prosperity. This was as true of the 1960s as it is today. But how are the potential rewards to be harvested? The view in the 1960s was essentially that success in exploiting science for practical purposes depended not on directing fundamental research in line with practical considerations but on ensuring that producers and users of knowledge were *aware* of each other's problems. In the 1970s the dominant conception of *how* university research was to be useful underwent a profound shift. The idea which developed, and by no means only in Britain, was that for university research to be useful it should be addressed to very clearly formulated 'customer requirements'.

In the 1980s a still further conception of usefulness is coming to be applied to university research, at least in the most industrialised countries. To a large degree this follows from the nature of the new technologies on which such hopes are pinned. It is not possible adequately to predict the range of the application of these technologies, the uses to which they are likely to be put. There is a sense in which, in the language of Nelson and Winter, we are speaking of the establishment of new 'technological trajectories'. Many highly sophisticated research-intensive firms are coming to recognise this—to recognise, in other words, that it is not in their interest for universities to be pushed too far in the direction of applied research or problem-solving. This does not mean that the 'golden age' of the lavish funding of the 1960s is returning. The tendency is likely increasingly to be to let fundamental scientists work as they will, but with generous support limited to certain fields of science and technology. There is a danger of implicit acceptance of the notion that there are 'useful' and 'useless' sciences.

University Roles

Much of the analysis of this paper has focused on certain sorts of technological innovations (*e.g.* NMR), or has implicitly related to the new 'technological trajectories' seemingly offered by biotechnology and the like. In presenting these examples I have suggested that university research is crucial, and that what is required is 'oriented' but basic research. But even for the most advanced countries industrial well-being cannot rest wholly on such radical new developments.

In other areas of technology, in relation to other and less sophisticated industrial sectors, the contribution which university research ideally makes to technological innovation is necessarily quite different. There are two points which I should like to make in this regard. The first is that there is very frequently a conceptual gap between the outcome of university research and the stage at which the majority of firms can pick it up. There is a sort of working-up stage which has to be accomplished before the fruits of university research can be picked up. Organisations particularly tailored to this role seem vital. The second point relates to the role of university research in relation to traditional and/or small-scale industry, typical of less industrialised countries and regions. Here, an effective university role seems to depend on a *holistic* approach, bringing together the variety of disciplinary competences found in the university. Moreover successful university links with emerging industry seem often to derive from prior involvement of the university in planning and infrastructure development. Research characteristically involved here is not physics or chemistry or engineering (though these may all contribute), but planning, geography, sociology . . .

It is not only that there are many roles for university research in relation to industrial innovation and development. It is also that the common tendency (on the part especially of policy-makers) to look only to certain sciences deemed 'useful' for the discharge of these roles is mistaken. In relation to the diversity, the complexity, and the indefinability of the problems which face all our societies, there are no useless sciences.

DISCUSSION

In general delegates were in agreement with the contention of Professor F. R. Jevons (Deakin) and Professor S. Blume (Amsterdam) that fundamental science nurses innovation and the advent of new technology, through the supply of manpower, techniques and state of knowledge, although economic forces, the necessity pull and customer requirements may play a significant role in triggering their emergence. The need to encourage and develop fundamental scientific research was stressed and it was felt that universities should seek to destroy the notion that fundamental research is useless as against applied research that has immediate utility.

While acknowledging the importance of fundamental scientific research, the need to build institutional bridges that would transform this research into a form acceptable by industry was considered to be equally important. Delegates were generally of the opinion that such institutional bridges are necessary, for while disciplines such as medicine and agriculture are endowed with practising environments, via the teaching hospital and the university farm respectively, to translate university fundamental research into this acceptable form, not all disciplines are similarly endowed.

Professor J. M. Ashworth (Salford) viewed as important the support of governments in encouraging universities to set up industrial consultancy companies which would act to bridge the gap between university research and industrial needs and hence facilitate the emergence of acceptable forms of new technology and innovation.

The value of non-technical sciences in promoting a successful university research role and the acceptability of new technology, particularly in less industrialised countries and regions, was emphasised. In clarifying this point, Professor Blume chose to illustrate how the multi-disciplinary

253

approach in research and fundamental non-technical sciences were applied to the development of northern areas of Finland in issues such as housing, the revitalisation of existing industries and other problems faced by the population. Dr. R. C. Tress (Leverhulme Trust) stressed this importance further by saying that if new technology were to be introduced, or technology transfer were to be brought about, the choice, management and acceptability of this technical change must be considered in terms not only of what would be scientifically possible but also of what would be technically and socially acceptable within the context of the region or country in which this technical change would be applied.

Several delegates, realising the importance of fundamental science and its relationship with technological innovation, expressed concern over the lack of preference among the better students for courses in basic sciences. Although it was pointed out that this might not be true of the UK, it was true in other countries where at best preference appeared to oscillate between basic sciences and the technical subjects; and in the less-developed countries basic sciences almost always became the last choice. Fears were expressed that under such a condition mediocrity would set in in the fundamental sciences which would eventually lead to a state of knowledge and expertise so low as to be unable to nurse or support new technology, technological innovation and even technology transfer effectively.

Delegates acknowledged that the lack of preference for basic sciences related to a large extent to the reward that would accrue from the job market and the ability of the job market to absorb science graduates. In countries where industries are at infancy science graduates would find difficulty in securing rewarding jobs and hence students are discouraged from doing science.It was felt that countries having little or no industry should deliberately devise an industrial policy to encourage industrialisation as this would have a catalytic effect on the growth of scientific manpower which would in turn bring about development.

Sub-Topic 4 (b)

UNIVERSITIES AND GOVERNMENT IN THE CONDUCT OF SCIENCE AND TECHNOLOGY

Chairman: Professor J. M. ASHWORTH
Vice-Chancellor of the University of Salford

Rapporteur: Professor K. J. HANCOCK
Vice-Chancellor of Flinders University of South Australia

Tuesday, 16 August

Professor W. J. KAMBA (*Vice-Chancellor, University of Zimbabwe*): Over the last two decades or so the question of the relationship between universities and government generally or in regard to any particular aspect has generated a great deal of heated and sometimes bitter debate. The world recession, the deterioration of the world economic situation and the concommitant damaging effects on national economies have forced governments not only to reduce, but to reduce substantially, their financial support to universities. This state of affairs has soured the atmosphere in which the debate has been, and continues to be, conducted.

Central to such debate is, as it must be, the discussants' conception of the role or functions of a university.

Role of a University

In his plea for the forging of closer links between universities and the real world Sir Henry Chilver, in his article in the latest issue of *The Times Higher Education Supplement,* states: 'In Britain it is a not uncommonly-held view that practical and professional relevance are not so much central as peripheral to higher education policy.' 'It is,' he continues, 'often argued that excellence in the practical arts and professions can be achieved by the spin-off effects of more rarefied and "purer" studies in higher education.'

This view, in essence, encapsulates the ideal of higher education for which universities were founded. According to this ideal the primary two-fold aim of a university is teaching and research, or,

255

to put it in academic parlance, the discovery and dissemination of knowledge—but the discovery and dissemination of knowledge for its own sake.

Someone once remarked that a university is a place where nothing useful is thought or taught. For a long time the almost exaggerated emphasis on the pursuit of knowledge for its own sake elevated the university to an 'ivory tower' almost detached from the community in which it existed—observing society from up there. For as long as universities were reasonably self-sufficient financially, *i.e.* did not depend on the state for their sustenance and continued existence, this traditional view was possible to maintain. But the increasing financial pressures and general shortage of resources, the rapid and intensive socio-economic and political changes, the gigantic technological advances during the last four decades or so, have led to a shift of emphasis and re-ordering of priorities and to a new relationship between universities and the state.

In Britain the recognition of the need for high levels of education in the areas of professional and practical relevance, such as medicine, engineering, and other fields of technology, bears testimony to this shift. The plea I referred to earlier, by Sir Henry Chilver, is not simply for universities to come down to earth, but for them to develop even closer links with the real world. A decade ago the Grimond report urged: 'a university cannot stand aside from the moral issues and problems of society . . . it must be committed to the persistent and enlightened exploration of problems for the common good'.

Role of Universities in Commonwealth Developing Countries

The universities of the Commonwealth share a common heritage—in their origin and, in many respects, in their continued general structures and orientation. They imported, and continued to be influenced in varying degrees by, the British university model with all its attendant elements. In the 'newer' Commonwealth, if I may be permitted to quote our Secretary General, who so aptly put it, 'the universities were not only mirror images of British universities; they were heavily dependent on them for leadership, staffing at all levels, academic and administrative, for validation, for general "ethos" and philosophy of education, and for effective training and development of their local junior academic staff.' But the contexts in which these universities operate differ and in a number of respects differ substantially. These contexts have affected what universities can do.

You have the 'older' Commonwealth industrialised countries which are also 'multi-university'. You have the 'newer' Commonwealth which consists almost entirely of countries in the third or developing world (with a small number described as 'newly industrialising countries' (NICs)). The great majority of these countries are also single-university countries in which the one university is seeking, and is expected, to do what is done in Britain, for example, by 44 universities and, in some respects, by a substantial number of polytechnics.

Over the years it has become quite clear that in the developing world, and particularly in the one-university countries, the pursuit of knowledge for its own sake by universities is a luxury the countries cannot afford. Universities are expensive institutions to establish and run. In a single-university country the university is a heavy drain on the country's scarce resources. The state and the community are, therefore, entitled to expect returns which contribute, and can be seen to contribute, to national development, *i.e.* to the improvement of human conditions—to the improvement of the quality of life of the people.

The university is seen as an important, nay, a key instrument of national development. It must render public service to the country. In its teaching and research it must contribute to development. It must produce high-level manpower to man the civil service, commerce and industry—it must produce men and women who are capable of generating new ideas in all spheres of life and knowledge.

Research in Science and Technology

The role of the university thus conceived provides a somewhat different atmosphere in which research by universities is undertaken. It is to the universities that the government and the community look for answers to their problems. In the circumstances universities are expected to place emphasis on applied research—research directed at seeking solutions to problems that affect the ordinary man and woman; research directed at identifying and investigating developmental problems. This is bound to involve a great deal of research in *science and technology*.

Yesterday we heard of the symbiotic character of science and technology—basic/fundamental/pure research on the one hand and technology on the other. But if by basic/fundamental/pure research we mean research for new knowledge intended not for application to any scientific end but as a contribution to the conceptual development of our understanding of nature, then there is a severe limit to what universities in one-university countries can do. In the many cases in which it is not possible to draw a clear and unambiguous line of demarcation between basic research and applied/technology the universities have a crucial role.

Universities and Governments

Governments and universities in both industrialised and developing countries accept that science and technology are indispensable to development now and beyond, but governments and universities recognize or must recognize that their resources limit in varying degrees what they can do. The industrialised countries can to a greater degree do more in the area of fundamental research while the developing countries would focus much more on applied research.

Relationship between universities and government. Progress in science and technology call for close co-operation between government and universities. Governments articulate plans for national development and set out what they consider to be national priorities. Because of their high-level manpower training and research capability, universities have a crucial role to play not only in the progress towards the realization of national goals but also in the formulation of national priorities. It is, therefore, necessary for there to be both dialogue and cross-fertilization of ideas between universities and governments.

In the area of science and technology the developing countries have, for the most part, had to rely on imported technology with local efforts focused on acquisition of skills, adaptation of the technology to suit local conditions. Innovation has tended to be generally confined to the developing of appropriate technology, particularly in respect of rural areas. In all this the universities have, and must play, a crucial role.

There is always potential conflict, which will now and again erupt into real conflict, between university and government. The nature of the relationship between university and government ultimately depends upon, and is in fact conditioned by, the socio-economic and political context in which the university exists and operates. The presentation of the relationship as one of conflict—almost inevitable conflict—without a differentiation of the context, has not been particularly helpful.

It is necessary to emphasise that the university must enjoy a good measure of autonomy because its contribution depends substantially on the ability of its academics and students to discuss, evaluate, re-evaluate, criticise and investigate ideas, and thus make available to the policy-makers and the community possible options. The need for closer communication between universities and governments is, therefore, not intended to mean a complete abandonment of university autonomy.

The creation or the existence of effective machinery (*a*) for funding the needs of the university in general and research (science and technology) in particular, and (*b*) for determining research priorities in science and technology, will facilitate the forging of a good, balanced relationship between university and government. There are a number of types of machinery, with which we are familiar, which operate currently regarding the funding of universities in general. I do not propose to say any more in this respect.

National Council for Science and Technology (NCST)

As regards the funding of research in science and technology and the machinery for determining priorities, I would recommend the creation or strengthening of national councils for science and technology. Such councils would be charged with:—

(1) the formulation of national policies for the development of science and technology and the co-ordination of research activities;

(2) the mobilisation of funds for financing science and technology development as well as allocating these funds to the university and various research institutes in order to enhance the country's development;

(3) the drafting of a national plan for science and technology to be integrated into the development plans of the country;

(4) the collection and dissemination of scientific and technological information among various research and development institutes;

(5) the monitoring of scientific and technological developments outside the country with a view to utilising them;

(6) the co-ordination of activities of various research and development institutes so as to avoid unnecessary duplication and waste of human and financial resources;

(7) the making of recommendations to government in relation to science and technology needs of the country;

(8) the monitoring of the implementation of science and technology plans and advising the government accordingly;

(9) the organising of seminars for natural scientists, technologists, and social scientists so that natural sciences and technology do not develop in isolation from social realities and socio-economic goals, and also that social sciences do not develop in isolation from the realities of the process of material production.

259

It would be also desirable to establish some specialized institutes to operate within the umbrella of the NCST.

The effective participation of the university in such a structure is essential.

An aspect of university contribution which is not being fully utilized in the developing countries is that of consultancy. Vast sums of money are lost each year by engaging consultants from outside the countries. Africa is spending one billion US dollars a year on consultants. Yet in a lot of instances what happens is that outside consultants come into the country and spend time consulting the university people whose advice is then not acknowledged or rewarded.

I certainly would urge an aggressive approach on the part of universities to secure government consultancies.

Foundations

In conclusion I wish to emphasise that foundations or trusts have a vital role to play in supporting research activities at universities. My own University is a beneficiary of much of such support. I wish to take this opportunity to publicly acknowledge the support we have received from one such trust represented here—Leverhulme Trust.

*Professor E. G. HALLSWORTH (*Universities of Sussex and Adelaide*): The needs of the universities of the Commonwealth are, to a greater or lesser degree, dependent on government for support. To the extent to which they are dependent on government finance, and in part to the extent to which there exists in the country a tradition of freedom for the universities, the university may be under pressure from the government to modify its academic programme along certain lines.

In examining the question of how well to meet the needs of government and at the same time to maintain the widest degree of independent control, it is worthwhile outlining the reasons why governments are willing to provide finance to the universities. A government requires a university to do three things:—

*Professor Hallsworth being unable to attend the Congress, his paper was read by Sir Denys Wilkinson.

(1) to provide a source of trained personnel for government services, the professions and industry; this was the first requirement of the universities—to provide the theologians and lawyers required by the state;

(2) to maintain the quality of their scholarship, by continuous learning—and in more recent times this has meant continuous research;

(3) to be able, on request, to give advice to the government.

In terms of the discussions at this meeting all these are relevant. The extent to which each can be offered depends upon the total resources available to the university system. Even assuming that all governments of the Commonwealth are willing to support the university sector to the same proportionate extent, it is obvious that the number of centres of excellence that can be maintained in a country depends on the total resource available. Several of the Commonwealth countries with a larger financial base can maintain centres of excellence in all or most of the fields on which government may need advice. Those with less cannot, and the problem of meeting the needs of the situation for research and technological innovation has for the smaller countries some added difficulties.

The provision of trained personnel in the relevant fields is in the first instance both the most essential and in some ways the most difficult. Without adequately trained personnel in government—and government service—the transfer of ideas from one side to the other becomes much less effective. The difficulty facing the universities is consequently to decide in what fields of science and technology they will provide training. Since resources are not limitless, this immediately results in a diminution of the authority of a university. Either a group of universities acting together will agree on the distribution of courses, particularly in technology, between their institutions, or presumably the government will force the issue by withholding funds, specifying the areas for which funds may be utilised.

This process of increased development of research in certain areas can be assisted by the manner in which the grants for research are allocated by research committees. A secondary problem arises here in that the smaller the group of 'wise men' in the field concerned, the more difficult it becomes to obtain from the 'wise men' that constitute the research council a totally unbiased view of the advances in science and technology, and of the needs to sustain them. In the ultimate, the very ability of the few top people may result in resources being directed to their own fields of interest, with the resultant neglect of other possibilities. It is on this aspect that the system of dual funding of university research is so important. It is essential that a young man with ideas peripheral to and out of the main stream of current thought should have the opportunity to pursue his ideas for at least a period. The pattern of the Medical Research Council, of allocating some 13% of the annual budget to relatively short-period (3 years) grants to allow the prosecution of such research, is one that could be followed more widely.

One interesting example of co-operation between universities in provision of a special course is that now being given at the International Centre for Insect Physiology and Ecology, Nairobi, and attended by students from Ibadan, Makerere, Nairobi and other African universities. The degrees, however, will be awarded by the universities to which the students are attached. This is an idea that deserves wider consideration.

Some Approaches Adopted

With regard to the provision of advice on science and technology from university to industry, several different approaches have been adopted. According to Rothwell (1983) the literature overwhelmingly emphasises the key role played by personal or informal communication during innovation. This is at the technology-in-industry level. Precisely the same pattern has been found in the diffusion of good agricultural technology, where the decision-makers—the individual farmers—adopt the new techniques more effectively when there is almost weekly face-to-face contact with the person transmitting the knowledge of the innovation—even although in this context the possessor of the innovative knowledge may be skilled only in that particular portion of the field (Hallsworth, 1983).

The approaches made by universities to bridge the gap in communication with industry have included industrial liaison officers, university innovation centres, university companies, and prototype production at the university. 'The role of the liaison officer varies between a formal data base and an informal go-between. At the worst the single liaison officer acts as a window to the university and is particularly useful to the managers of small firms' (Rothwell, 1983). The National Science Foundation in the USA concluded that innovation was inseparably linked with entrepreneurship. As a result, innovation centres have been set up with NSF support, which were encouraged to derive income from their activities. Although this system appears to have had some success it has not been widely followed. Although for many years universities have supplied consultants to industry, it was probably not until 1959 that a university in the Commonwealth set up a company to provide answers to some of the problems of industry. This was the University of New South Wales which set up 'Unisearch' to promote the aims of the University. Others have been set up since then, some concentrating on a single technology and others with a wide range of services.

An Alternative Approach

All of the mechanisms adopted so far have tended to preserve the uncommitted approach to industry that has been traditional in the maintenance of university independence. There have been exceptions—as, for example, the University of Leeds, which had initially a large proportion of its teaching and research activities deliberately geared to the needs of the leather and textile industries, out of which Astbury, Speakman and others produced first-class fundamental research.

In the more difficult times of the present it is perhaps worth looking for some mechanism which will provide a more direct linkage between the operations of university personnel for industry and government and their own financial well-being. This is the half-funded appointment, where a man is appointed university lecturer but draws only half the normal university salary for his age and grade from the central university salary funds. The other half he obtains as a component of the research grants offered by research councils, industry itself and government departments. As long as he is working in an area of high relevance to industry, etc., there should be a ready flow of grant money. In the event that his originality, perseverence or relevance declined, his ability to compete for contracts would decline, but at no point would his income fall to less than half the normal salary. In at least one of the Brazilian universities the university component of salary remains the same after the normal retiring age has been passed, and becomes the officer's pension, for which he needs to do no more teaching or research. The man with ideas that industry or grants committees find of interest will continue to be able to compete.

The combination of the half-salary recently adopted in the Science Policy Research Unit at Sussex, and the Brazilian arrangement of continuing the salary as a pension on retirement, seems to go some way towards providing a solution to the maintenance of an active personal involvement in the university—industry link,

and at the same time leave the question of 'early retirement' in
the hands of the officers concerned.

Dr. C. J. Maiden (*Vice-Chancellor, University of Auckland*): My
contribution to this topic will be to present a case study centred
around the activities of the New Zealand Energy Research and
Development Committee and the Liquid Fuels Trust Board. Both
these bodies were formed by the New Zealand government in
response to the severe impact of the oil shocks of the 1970s on the
local economy. Also both bodies are primarily concerned with
science and technology and involve the New Zealand universities
and government.

The NZ Energy Research and Development Committee

In 1972, prior to the first oil shock, New Zealand imported
virtually all its liquid fuel requirements in the form of oil or its
products. At this time such imports represented about 60% of
New Zealand's primary energy requirements and cost less than
5% of the country's export earnings. After the first oil shock the
cost of liquid fuels jumped to between 20% and 30% of export
earnings and thereby severely weakened the New Zealand economy. One of the responses of the government to these events
was to form, in 1974, the New Zealand Energy Research and
Development Committee (NZERDC). The Committee was to be
funded by government and was to contract for research and
development on energy matters of national importance. The original constitution of NZERDC was three members from government, two from the private sector and four from the universities.
The secretariat, consisting of an executive officer and support staff,
was housed at the University of Auckland, the home of the
chairman of the Committee. Thus from the beginning there was a
strong university influence on the operation and activities of the
Committee.

The broad policy of the Committee was to fund contracts for
energy research, development and demonstration directed towards
understanding and meeting New Zealand's future energy requirements in ways best suited to meet the national interest economically, socially and environmentally, and which made wise use

264

of the country's energy resources. Within this broad policy the Committee decided to support a balanced programme of research, development and demonstration under the following priorities:—

(1) energy use;
(2) energy conservation and substitution;
(3) resource assessment;
(4) management of energy systems;
(5) technologies for energy production and use;
(6) specific social and environmental studies.

Since its inception the Committee has implemented its policy by using the resources of universities, research associations, consulting groups and industry and by maintaining a close liaison with concerned government departments.

In addition to letting research contracts, the Committee has organised a number of task force studies involving its own professional staff and individuals from the private sector, government departments and universities. These studies have been of particular value in defining areas of future work. Significant studies include:—

• energy scenarios for New Zealand
• the potential for energy farming for transport fuels in New Zealand
• coal in New Zealand.

This is not the occasion to provide a detailed review of the research undertaken by NZERDC although I will later report on one area of interest. However I would like to point out that the Committee has been very successful in extending the number and range of people involved in energy research in New Zealand. Also it has been effective in promoting co-operation between staff in the universities, research associations, government departments, consultant offices and industry. The 150 or so NZERDC reports show that the Committee has been successful in having research pursued and published.

The impact of NZERDC on the New Zealand universities has been substantial. Of the 336 contracts let to date, 148 have been with universities and, in the financial year 1982–83, some 61% of contract expenditure was with universities. In addition university staff have contributed to demanding reviews of contracts and to the task force studies mentioned earlier. Incidentally, contract reviews have been a most important aspect of the work of NZERDC. Normally all contracts in a particular category are reviewed sequentially on the one day, with the audience consisting of all principal investigators, NZERDC staff, as many Committee members as are able to attend and other invited participants.

Many of the NZERDC contracts have led to policy initiatives by government and follow-up actions in the private and public sectors of the economy. One particular success story is the implementation of compressed natural gas as a transport fuel in New Zealand. I would like to discuss this subject because it relates also to sub-topic 4 (e)—*i.e.* the implementation and exploitation of new technology and analysis of its social impacts.

The Implementation of Compressed Natural Gas (CNG)

In late 1977 NZERDC funded a research project with the Wellington Gas Company to investigate the technical, economic and environmental aspects of the use of CNG as a vehicle fuel. This project was completed by late 1978, just before the second oil shock. The impact of the second oil shock on New Zealand was severe and carless days were introduced early in 1979. About that time the minister of energy asked NZERDC to produce a plan, as a matter of urgency, for the implementation of CNG as a transport fuel. A task force was set up by the Committee and, within a matter of weeks, a report was provided to government. The report outlined all the aspects which would need to be considered if such a programme were to go ahead successfully, *e.g.* goals, co-ordination of the programme, gas reticulation, refuelling stations, vehicle conversions and testing, standards and regulations, publicity and public relations, financial incentives and further research requirements. Almost all the recommendations in the NZERDC report were followed, at least to some extent.

The status of the CNG programme in New Zealand at present is as follows:—

(1) Government has set a goal of 200,000 vehicles operating on CNG by 1990. (This is about 14% of the New Zealand automobile fleet.)

(2) At present about 40,000 vehicles operate on CNG—this corresponds to about 4% of vehicles in the gas reticulated areas of New Zealand.

(3) The price of CNG is about half that of petrol and there are other financial incentives for the motorist, fleet users and developers of refuelling stations.

(4) Some 240 CNG refuelling stations are in operation or under development. The diffusion of this 'new technology' into the marketplace is being followed with interest. In the early days it was the 'innovators' who were converting their vehicles to CNG. Now the programme has encompassed the 'early adaptors' and the promotion and marketing activity is being directed towards

the 'early majority'. With the innovators and the early adaptors successfully using CNG the stage is set for a wider acceptance. Already the CNG programme has resulted in significant foreign exchange savings for New Zealand and there have been no reports of adverse social or environmental impacts.

The Liquid Fuels Trust Board

Because of the severe impact of the cost of imported oil on the New Zealand economy the government formed the Liquid Fuels Trust Board (LFTB) in late 1978. The primary function of the Board is 'to promote, encourage, finance, undertake, and co-ordinate any activity that has as its purpose or one of its purposes the reduction in the use of imported fuel for transport purposes in New Zealand'. The LFTB is funded by a $0 \cdot 1$ cent per litre levy on all sales of petrol and diesel fuel.

The Board's function is more directed than that of NZERDC and, consequently, the university contribution has been less. However the chairman of the LFTB is a university person and its second technical director was seconded from the University of Auckland for two years. Most LFTB investigations have been contracted to other organisations with about 20% of all contract dollars being spent in universities.

The initial thrust of the Board was to investigate how New Zealand's very large natural gas reserves might be used to produce transport fuels. In late 1979 the government accepted the recommendation of the LFTB to build a gas to gasoline plant, based on Mobil Oil technology, to produce 500–600,000 tonnes/year of synthetic petrol per year. The Board pointed out that with such a facility New Zealand could become about 50% self-sufficient in transport fuels in the middle 1980s. This self-sufficiency would be made up as follows: 25% from condensate (a light oil) which is separated from natural gas flows at the wellhead; 17% from synthetic petrol; about 5% from CNG and LPG; and about 3% from New Zealand's only commercial oilfield.

The work of the LFTB, like NZERDC, has been most effective. In 1973–74 New Zealand imported 4,257,000 tonnes of oil or its products, in 1981–82 this figure was reduced to 3,257,000 tonnes and the forecast for 1986–87 is 2,370,000 tonnes of imports, *i.e.* about half that of 1973–74. New Zealand is presently on target to be about 50% self-sufficient in transport fuels in 1986. The synthetic petrol plant is under construction and is ahead of schedule and within budget. Also, as I indicated earlier, the CNG programme is going well.

Conclusion

The energy programme in New Zealand is a very good example of the co-operation of 'universities and government in the conduct of science and technology'. The economic benefits to the country will be large, relieving our balance of payments deficit by many hundreds of millions of dollars annually. Also I believe that the stature of the New Zealand universities in the community has been enhanced by their contribution to solving a problem of national importance.

The key elements in the success of NZERDC and LFTB have been:—

(1) a mix of university and non-university members of both bodies;

(2) a small but very high quality permanent staff;

(3) the use of in-house and task force studies to define areas of future work and priorities;

(4) most research, development and demonstration contracted to outside bodies, including universities;

(5) a vigorous and demanding system of contract reviews.

The contribution of the New Zealand universities in all these areas has been substantial. I do not believe that this 'injection' of applied research into the universities has been sufficient to deflect their primary long-term responsibility to carry out basic innovative research that adds to the growth of scientific knowledge.

DISCUSSION

This session was introduced by the papers of Professor W. J. Kamba (Zimbabwe), Professor E. G. Hallsworth (Sussex and Adelaide) and Dr. C. J. Maiden (Auckland). (Dr. Maiden had agreed, at short notice, to give a paper which described special programmes developed in New Zealand in the 1970s in response to the rising price of imported fuel).

At the inception of the discussion the Chairman identified major themes which emerged in the papers. Foremost among these was the contest between centralism and decentralization in the promotion and guidance of university activities. At the one extreme, governments sought—through ministries, councils and related mechanisms—to determine the directions of scientific enquiry, relying upon their control of funds to secure compliance with their policies. At the other, governments allowed the universities to develop relations with both governmental agencies and private enterprise for the execution of research upon mutually attractive terms. The Chairman suggested that although these were polar models (with most real-world cases lying between them) the contrast was a useful basis for discussion. It appeared that the less developed countries were closer to the former extreme than to the latter. For developed countries the decentralized model was more applicable, although the New Zealand experience described by Dr. Maiden was an exception. The Chairman further suggested that the decentralized model was often associated with indirect methods of government assistance—for example, paying subsidies to support projects negotiated between universities and companies. It was also associated with a reluctance to embark upon any form of manpower planning: universities were relatively free of specific directions or guidance and tended to concentrate on research which led to 'enabling technologies'. From those broad technologies industries could develop specific commercial applications.

Many of the contributions from persons associated with the universities in the less developed countries seemed to support the Chairman's analysis. Delegates pointed out that governments in these countries had immediate and pressing priorities which led to perceptions of pure and curiosity-oriented inquiry as a luxury which they could hardly afford. Indeed the first priority with respect to universities was the provision of high-level manpower with specific skills. This gave the research function a lesser role than in the developed countries. Illiteracy, for example, was a major impediment to development and governments were concerned that universities should acknowledge their role in its alleviation. Governments *were* concerned that universities apply themselves to identified research needs and this concern led to a directive approach on the governments' part.

Several of the comments reflected the tension which exists in the less developed countries between the priorities of governments and the aspirations of academics to adhere to norms of autonomy which characterize government—university relations elsewhere. Some speakers suggested that the tension was exacerbated by instability of government, which frequently brought to the fore political leaders unconversant with and unsympathetic to the traditional goals of academics. A different and useful perspective was given by a delegate who is both a university pro-chancellor and a politician. This delegate observed that politicians regard universities as being 'in orbit': unless they descend from their 'dizzy heights' pleas for autonomy and freedom will fall on deaf ears and financial stringencies will intensify.

Several speakers pointed out that in the developed countries, as well as the less developed, economic adversity typically alters the balance between centralism and decentralization in favour of the former. Presumably this is due to universities' dependence upon public funds. One speaker illustrated the point by reference to the UK. Although there is now a government which is ideologically committed to the free market it has been uniquely interventionist with respect to the universities.

Some delegates also discussed the adverse effect upon governmental attitudes of the perceived gap between much of the universities' research and the immediate needs of government and industry. An Australian vice-chancellor said that governments, when confronted with research needs, tended to regard the Commonwealth Scientific and Industrial Research Organisation, rather than the universities, as the appropriate body to deal with them. Another delegate suggested that informal relations could often be developed with industry which, in time, would engender more sympathetic governmental policies.

There were several suggestions that improved communication and public relations could contribute nationally to better understanding; and one delegate commented that efforts of this kind were more likely to succeed at the informal level, for public discussion tended too often to become confrontational.

Sub-Topic 4(c)

INDIGENOUS DEVELOPMENT OF TECHNOLOGY BASED ON THE IDENTIFICATION OF LOCAL NEEDS

Chairman: Sir KENNETH ALEXANDER.
Principal and Vice-Chancellor of the University of Stirling

Rapporteur: Professor A. J. EARP
President and Vice-Chancellor of Brock University

Tuesday, 16 August

In introducing this session the Chairman suggested that we would now be moving towards more specific modes of innovation. We had been reminded by Professor W. J. Kamba (Zimbabwe) that a basic requirement was the universities' acceptance of their responsibilities and that the education and training function was as important as the research role which had been emphasized in the discussions. Sir Adrian Cadbury had said in his keynote address that the attitude of a country's élite was crucial to its economic and social development. A high degree of commitment and enthusiasm was needed in the universities. How do you encourage those who have it? A teacher's enthusiasm rubs off on his/her students and if the academic's eyes are focused only on the stars and he 'doesn't give a damn for the drains' this will affect the graduates' attitude to development. Earlier, Professor J. M. Ashworth (Salford) had contrasted the relationships to the applied sector in agriculture and medicine in the UK with those in engineering. In the morning session we had been discussing university/government relations. Developing countries tend to have centralized structures, which may be appropriate enough for determining policy decisions and resource allocation, but may be inappropriate for extending links with producers (diffusion). We must bring the third partner, the producer, into the picture. Our focus on local needs provides the opportunity to do so.

Professor P. V. INDIRESAN (*Indian Institute of Technology, Madras*):

271

As generally understood, the term 'academic' means something not practical. Then, should the work of an academic be practically useful? Like the fashion in women's skirts, the interest academics take in utilitarian problems tends to go up and down. Currently it is high and with some academics would beat any miniskirt that might have been designed. In the developing countries the academic has little or no choice, as the stock of qualified people is so small that one and all have to take up as much responsibility as possible. One would then be tempted to conclude that the universities in the developing countries would be inevitably closer to their societal problems compared to those in the developed countries who can concentrate on more 'academic' pursuits. Interestingly enough, this is not true.

The type of work done in the universities of developing countries is so similar to that of their counterparts in the developed world that they are often of little interest to their own society. For instance, it has been pointed out that the centre of gravity of Indian science lies in the United States. It is possible that the same is true for most other developing countries also. At the same time Schumacher, with his fascinating slogan 'small is beautiful', has been a counter-attraction. This is a new religion and as such has attracted both proponents and opponents who stake their faith (or lack of it) with the utmost fervour. But, all said and done, Schumacher's philosophy has not had any greater impact than to generate academic debates and esoteric discussions in international conferences. This was brought home in an interesting manner to a Western do-gooder in Thailand. After listening carefully to a fascinating exposition on appropriate technology, the wily Thailander asked the expert: 'Do you use it yourself?' To explain that what is good for an Englishman may not be appropriate for a Thailander is the same as saying that the latter is an inferior type of person—may be true, but psychologically unacceptable!

To the academic in a developing country Mecca is still in the West; the recognition he seeks is according to the standards of the West; his ambition is to publish in journals published in the West and on problems originated by and relating to the questions raised by Western researchers. It is doubtful whether 'appropriate technology' is taught even in one engineering degree course anywhere in the developing countries. In fact far more work on appropriate technology is going on in the West than in the developing countries. After all, the rich man does not lose face to ask for something cheaper; for the poor man such a question is a reminder of his failure. In consequence, appropriate technology has remained virtually an academic question.

For the past four years I have pleaded with my colleagues to take to the technological problems that abound in our own environs: problems like waste disposal, the siltation of the local river, building designs for the tropics, vehicles for the rural roads, conservation of water, etc.; without avail. In the city of Madras the precipitation is enough to supply the whole city; yet 90% of this water is allowed to waste into the sea even while the city suffers from unprecedented water shortage and water is supplied only once in three days. Yet no one is interested to take up the challenge. The previous British Deputy High Commissioner, wise in the ways of our people, told me once: 'Professor, get some British experts to come to Madras to advise that these problems are worthy of investigation'. Perhaps I should.

To be fair, there are several reasons why our academics do not entangle themselves with such local or down-to-earth problems. First, such work does not get them recognition in the international community—as, for instance, a place to go to during sabbatical leave. Secondly, these problems are often far removed from the expertise an academic normally has. Thirdly, the academic's intervention is generally resented by the concerned authorities. It is also true that to tackle such real-life problems requires great courage. Failure in an academic situation may be covered up by writing another scholarly paper. In the practical world there is no escape route; one has got to find a workable solution.

Returning to the question of technology: however romantic one may be about the past, and whatever one's view on what the proper economic wisdom ought to be, the fact remains that most of the new investment, even in developing countries, is in modern, Western-based technology. Bullock carts may still carry a heavy burden, but far more money is invested to buy new trucks than on new carts; in any case they cannot carry all the burden and, if they do, there will not be enough food for the people unless most of them are killed by typhoid and other diseases associated with the overpopulation of cattle. Time moves only one way and all countries have to move forward only.

Much of what a university can do, particularly a technological one like ours, is through local industry. Even in the West the relationship between industry, which is the ultimate repository of technology, and the universities, who may be said to be the begetters of new technology, is often not as close as desired. In developing countries the gap is far wider. Considering the various stages of development of technology, starting from the basic idea arising out of basic research, the extension of such an idea to experimental use through applied research, the introduction of

273

new processes by development, the design of new products, their manufacture through production technology, and, finally, the maintenance and servicing of the products sold in the market, the universities are best equipped for basic analysis and experimentation only. On the other hand, in the developing countries, the technological requirements are almost entirely confined to the last phase of maintenance and servicing with probably a little bit of production thrown in. In the developed countries the industries themselves have well-established laboratories for development, for applied research and even for basic research. So there is a possibility of a dialogue; for instance, a university don can converse with a scientist in the ICI. But in a developing country a professional interaction between a teacher and an engineer in industry is virtually impossible unless the teacher can include such expertise as repairing a television set or operating a power press among his accomplishments.

If this yawning gap is to be filled the university has to take on itself responsibilities normally far outside its scope and be prepared to develop in its entirety a manufacturable product and get involved not only in education but also in product development, design, establishment of a production system and perhaps even in manufacture. In a way this is not entirely unusual; even in the West, technology parks do all these things in areas where the industry is not advanced enough.

I have been fortunate enough to tackle this problem successfully a few times. This I could do only by inducting an engineer from the user-agency as a full-time member of our development team. Organisationally, the induction of such an engineer is not simple; developmental work takes years to fructify, and to keep the user-agency interested all this time, and to persuade it to provide not only money but its best man for years, is a greater problem than any technical difficulty one may come across. But this external professional input is absolutely essential. The university may have the invaluable wealth of talented students; but these students are like butterflies; they flit from flower to flower, from problem to problem and it is the presence of the user's agent which provides a constant direction and the essential motivation for the project to survive. In my personal experience, where the user is not interested enough to spare his own man the project collapses.

Secondly, it is necessary to take up a product that cannot be purchased for some reason or other. The tendency is to forget that the university exists the minute a technology is available for sale. In any case a university cannot and probably should not compete with anything that other agencies can provide; its speciality should be that it can produce something novel, something no-one else can. However this novelty need not be global; it is enough if it is novel only to its own environment.

Assuming that the university should contribute to its society by encouraging the introduction of new techniques, the Indian Institute of Technology, Madras, is introducing, from this year, a new master's-level programme in entrepreneurship. In this programme teams of two or more master's-level students will be trained to establish an industry, and, in addition, the extensive experimental and fabrication facilities as well as wide-ranging expertise available in the IIT will be placed at their disposal to develop a suitable product or process for manufacture. At the same time banks will be involved to fund the investigations and also to provide the finance when, as is hoped, the students will go on to establish their own industry. Among other things these students will be taught the basic aspects of government regulations (very important for us), financing, labour management, production control, etc., from experienced experts drawn from among practising professionals. It is hoped that this will be one more way the IIT can act as a catalyst for the introduction of new technology into the country.

Should universities be involved in the actual implementation of developmental projects and if so to what extent, can be a debatable issue. No doubt there is a need in all societies for the totally detached academic who plods in his own solitary path to acquire knowledge for its own sake. At the same time such a total isolation of the Town and Gown is unlikely to benefit both, certainly not the latter. In developed countries the gap between what the society wants and what a university can give is probably not difficult to bridge. But in a developing country, struggling far behind the frontiers of knowledge, this is not a gap but a chasm. Particularly because this gap is so large, it has got to be filled. In this connection, the Mountain is not going to come to Mohammed, so Mohammed himself has got to go to the Mountain.

Professor A. O. Adesola (*Vice-Chancellor, University of Lagos*):

I. *Technology in a Developing Economy*

Chambers Twentieth Century Dictionary lists science as knowledge ascertained by observation with experiment, critically tested, systematised and brought under general principles. Technology on the other hand is defined as the practice of any or all of the applied sciences that have practical value and/or industrial use. In other words, whereas science tells us what to do technology proposes how to get it done in practical terms. Success at improving both length and quality of life invariably depends on effectiveness of technology in solving the daily problems of one's environment. To this extent, history of civilization is by and large history of technology.

After all, technological superiority has inevitably meant military and economic dominance. The world scenario today projects technology only too clearly as the determinant as to which countries are powerful, weak, domineering, oppressed, developed or under-developed. Technology, we also know, divides the North from the South, the rich from poor, the producing from the consuming nations, and the leaders from the led. Surely the importance of technology does not escape any political leader, more so in developing countries where many have come to realise the pervasive nature of technology in national development. In fact, with technological capability, a nation's greatest asset could be its human resources when fully mobilised and effectively utilised, as amply demonstrated by the performance of Japan. The story of Africa, on the other hand, shows that, irrespective of whatever national resources may be abundant, without adequate technological capability the nation would always be relegated to the background.

Whereas it did not take developing countries time to identify technology as the missing catalyst in their national developmental chemistry, it has nonetheless taken them a very long time to find out how to acquire this catalyst. At one time some thought it could be purchased along with imported machinery; others believed that it was passed down along with the educational system left behind by their colonial masters. Many eventually found that imported technology invariably needs to be adapted to the conditions of the host country, hence the metamorphosis from terminologies like 'technology transfer' to 'intermediate technology' through 'appropriate technology' to 'adapted technology'.

II. *The Nigerian Experience*

Perhaps it would be instructive to illustrate some of the activities that have occurred in my country, Nigeria, in her effort to popularise technological capability. In particular, we need to examine the activities of the prime movers of such technological revolution. History points to government, the educational system and

276

private entrepreneurs as the usual agents for such change. The federal government of Nigeria identified the need for development of technical manpower as a first and necessary step for the economic development of the country. The government was also cognisant of the close relationship between the capability to produce indigenous scientific and technological manpower and the enactment of enabling educational policies. Indeed, prior to 1976 most of the universities and higher institutions mainly offered courses in liberal arts and social sciences as opposed to science or technology-based disciplines. There were six engineering faculties graduating a total of 360 students annually. The picture for middle-level manpower was more depressing in that the annual output of middle-level technicians was about the same as the annual total output of engineers from the nation's universities. This gave the ratio of about one engineer to one technician as opposed to the desirable and appropriate target ratio of one engineer to 8–10 technicians. In fact a survey conducted by the National Council for Science and Technology estimated the total stock of scientific manpower as at 1975 at about 20,000 which was 120,000 short of the very liberal minimum target of 140,000 set by Unesco for a developing nation of its size. Thus by early 1976 the country was suffering not only from an acute and general technical manpower shortage but also by what was aptly referred to as 'misuse of limited manpower'. Whereas the manpower shortage was general, it nonetheless had the curious pattern of being an inverted pyramid in that the country seemed to be starting technology from the top. To correct this there was need to train many craftsmen and technicians so as to widen the technological base by producing personnel who would service and maintain the fairly modern, sophisticated and sometimes unproven technologies and equipment that were being imported on a large scale into the country.

Rather than be drowned by the depressing and disabling scenario of technical impotence, the government embarked on a two-pronged attack. On the one hand the government invited foreign consultants and contractors to execute the capital projects and on the other hand a crash programme was inaugurated to develop middle-level technical manpower. A clear indication of level of commitment of the government to the latter is given by the fact that within 1977–80 a total of 7031 students were enrolled in the programme for a disbursement of roughly US $100 million in foreign exchange.

In spite of misgivings about the technical manpower crash programme, the ultimate test of its effectiveness is how well the trainees perform on the job. Reports to date indicate that many of them question the relevance of their training to the tasks they have to perform on their return home. They find the working environment in their home country so different and the support facilities so skeletal as to make many of the skills they have acquired irrelevant and unprovable within the Nigerian context. Their frustrations have helped to focus national attention on the necessity to view and understand technology in terms of historical location, time and environment and not as something that can be easily transported or transplanted from one place to the other.

III. *Endogenous Technology*

This realization led to phasing out the crash programme and brought about a shift in emphasis from foreign to local institutions for the promotion of technical skills and manpower. This shift in emphasis was initially framed in generalities like self-reliance and self-sufficiency but only to find ultimate articulation in the terminology of endogenous technology.

Unfortunately most of the inhabitants live in rural settings and receive very little or no benefits from such programmes as the aforementioned technical manpower crash programme. For a fairly long time to come at least 2/3 of the population in Africa will reside in rural areas and for any meaningful technological transformation to take place within the continent the rural dwellers must have easy access to and be involved in the development of such technology. For endogenous technology to have maximum impact, areas of primary interest must be farming, irrigation, housing and water resources projects. Such technologies, as argued by Schumacher, should be relatively small, simple and capital-saving, such as to meet the needs and modest resources of rural communities.

As educators we must ensure that any proposal to popularise endogenous technology is designed and evaluated from a framework that adequately answers the following questions. Who should be taught? Who is to teach? What is to be taught? How should it be taught? In particular, if a nation's greatest asset is to be its human resources then as many people as can be trained should be trained, even if specialised institutions have to be set up to cater for those who have either missed or not followed the orthodox school career. In this regard, it would be useful to examine the trend of our national manpower development with regard to technological orientation.

For the period 1973 to 1976 we find that on the average about 43% of all graduating students were in science-based disciplines. It was at the end of this period that government intensified efforts to popularise science and technology by starting several polytechnics and an additional set of universities with emphasis in the area of science and technology. It would therefore be interesting to see how successful government efforts have been in promoting science-based disciplines. Using figures available from my University, the indicators are quite unsettling. In particular, whereas the total number of science graduates has increased steadily from 199 in 1974 to 510 in 1981, they have formed a smaller percentage of their graduating class, from 40% in 1975–76 to 26.8% by 1981. If this is a true reflection of the pattern in other universities then the conclusion appears inevitable that in spite of the national effort since 1976 the national manpower profile seems to be getting less science/technology oriented. This has serious implications for the question: who should be taught?

We now consider the question of who is to teach or how well trained are teachers in engineering and technology? The present pattern indicates that most of our university teachers were educated in the Western hemisphere. Their training and research interests mirror the aspirations and problems of the societies in which they were trained. Most of their research work is pitched close to the frontiers of technology and thereby difficult either to transplant or to translate into their home country environment. Since academicians generally teach what they know best, there has therefore been a general tendency for the curriculum and teaching in developing nations to duplicate those in Western universities.

The reluctance of engineering faculties in developing countries to make adequate adjustment in their curricula has been seen by outside bodies as irresponsible resistance to the wheels of progress. Perhaps outside opinion would be less critical if those bodies realised that reluctance by engineering faculties to accept innovative ideas in the area of endogenous technology emanates more from the feeling of inadequacy and ill-preparedness rather than the desire for political confrontation over academic freedom. There are several ways of bridging this gap. For example, at the University of Lagos we have a training scheme whereby all fresh PhDs are entitled to one-year postdoctoral industrial training. Perhaps in continuing with this scheme deliberate effort should be made to ensure that our young teachers have part of their professional exposure/immersion in some of the more advanced third-world countries where the idea of endogenous technology is more firmly entrenched within the society. Furthermore, there is need to re-orientate part of our academic research to the problems of our society. After all, technology is a way of life with cultural and traditional ramifications and in order to ensure growth and development engineering educators must seek to place technology in their cultural environment. The African Network of Scientific Technological Institutions (ANSTI) programme is one of the organisations that attempts to meet this goal through the training of graduate students within the continent of Africa. It also hopes to organise on a regional basis orientation programmes for young teachers in the engineering profession so as to familiarise them, especially those trained outside Africa, with endogenous technology materials.

The issue of engineering curriculum review and development within the third-world economy is one that is best left to experts in the field of engineering. However, I should just emphasise the point that engineering education and training must cater for the needs of the community which it serves and whose labours through taxation provides its support; for this reason it is inevitable that endogenous technology must necessarily be an essential part of the curriculum.

Technology cannot be taught in isolation from the social setting of the consumer market. Before any effective innovation can be introduced into the community there is need to be familiar with the traditional technologies used in agriculture and craft industries. Experience shows that a new technology that is seen as child of the old one is generally more acceptable than one that is a replacement of the old technology. There should therefore be room in engineering curricula to train students to contemplate the socio-political consequences of technical decisions and designs. There is also need to inculcate in our youngsters the dignity of labour and discourage their obsession with status as opposed to achievement. These were some of the common criticisms employers frequently made of some of our graduates. Partly in reaction to this, our faculty of engineering introduced in October 1976 a four-year post-'A'-level programme in place of the erstwhile three-year programme, in which some of the extra year is devoted to additional practical training giving graduates better 'hands on' ability and confidence than their predecessors. The feedback on this modification of the curriculum has been encouraging.

Perhaps the area that would provoke the most prolonged debate is that of deciding how endogenous technology is to be taught. Suffice it to say that the method to be adopted depends largely on the background of the student population and the recipient community. There is common agreement on the scarcity of resource material for teaching endogenous technology. Perhaps engineering teachers could organise workshops on a regional basis for the planning, organisation and production of resource material on this subject. International organisations can be the catalyst by providing the umbrella for such a collaboration.

The issue of cost effectiveness has usually plagued all technical programmes designed for third-world economies. Engineering training programmes are necessarily highly capital intensive and the case can be made for joint sponsorship of many of the training programmes. Some developing nations can ill afford technological universities but perhaps could wisely invest in co-sponsoring one on a regional basis.

Considering the problem of energy and capital shortages in most developing countries, it appears that in order to maximise the use of limited resources and minimise cost of engineering training there may be need to develop new teaching methods for our engineering institutions. It is very unlikely that all or even most of the ideas discussed above can be incorporated into our educational systems as they are today without first initiating radical structural changes.

The introduction of endogenous technology into our society should also involve interaction between the technological arm of our higher institutions and the local entrepreneurs. The task of working with local entrepreneurs is not likely to be an easy thing. For one thing they are hard to find and sometimes difficult to recognise within an incapacitating environment. Secondly, it is not usually easy to divert their interest from trading into primary or secondary production since the returns in the service sector are invariably higher than those in the production sector. Thirdly, a local entrepreneur may need to be taught more than technology before you will be able to guarantee his business success and thereby sustain his interest. Invariably they will need to be taught elements of business management. It is gratifying to note that not only have a few organisations accepted such a challenge but also that within a decade they are beginning to have a remarkable impact on the small industries within their countries. There is need for the encouragement and support of such institutions and a leading role should be played by universities in conjunction with government.

In summary, I have tried to make the case that the endorsement of endogenous technology as a tool for national development is inevitable for the developing countries. There is need to take a hard look at the educational system as a whole so as to realign it with the dynamic realities of a developing economy. While we

281

continue to train our students for tomorrow's technologies we must not be oblivious to the pressing realities of today; after all, today was yesterday's tomorrow.

DISCUSSION

After the two papers had been presented, the Chairman suggested that there were four issues: one, the difference in emphasis between those doubtful of the need for an intermediate role and those who would stress its importance; secondly, there were the questions related to teaching; thirdly, there was the question of relationship with specific industries (gearing); and fourthly, the suggestion that ACU itself might stimulate research in this area.

In the ensuing discussion Sir Clifford Butler (Loughborough) pointed out that agriculture in the UK was exemplary in terms of technology transfer largely because the government had been wishing to spend money on both research and an advisory development service; technologically, agri-businesses are up to date. Transfer of technology is not just a one-way process: information is brought back to the researchers. And in medicine professors are also practitioners, a concept which might also be applicable to engineering, perhaps through the use of joint appointments. The University of Salford was reported to be moving in this direction successfully. At Loughborough sandwich courses were one way of achieving a closer relationship between university and industry since close contact was required for the integration of the industrial and academic experiences; this gets supervisory faculty into the plants and industry, in turn, is involved in student projects.

Dr. R. Subbayyan (Bharathiar) cited some practical examples from his University in the development of electrical motors for local needs. A co-operative training centre for technicians was proving highly satisfactory and was only one of the many spin-offs.

Sir Arthur Vick (Warwick) supported Sir Clifford Butler's position and gave two additional examples: at Queen's, Belfast, agriculture teachers also hold joint appointments; teaching companies, of which there are three at Warwick, enable graduates in engineering to come back on a part-time basis and study the problems of their industries.

Dr. D. Mordell (Commonwealth Engineers' Council) pointed out that the UK engineering curriculum had been developed for UK needs and there had been development over 150 years. Educational technology should be used for the transmission of information. Third-year physical engineering syllabuses, for example, might be much the same the world over, but the *projects* could and should be of a local nature. There was an urgent need for software for a united Commonwealth effort. Detailed proposals for this had recently been published and were being distributed.

282

SUB-TOPIC 4 (c): INDIGENOUS DEVELOPMENT/LOCAL NEEDS

Professor J. Aminu (Maiduguri) suggested that there were no differences in the technology: rather, it was the application that varied according to locality. He doubted whether there was such a thing as indigenous technology: the technology of Japan, for example, could not be described as indigenous. What was required was a more equitable distribution of resources and ACU might urge this.

Dr. E. O. Akinluyi (Lagos) observed that in India the banks appeared to be helpful in backing technology transfer, whereas in Nigeria they operated on the colonial principle of believing they were doing you a service by being there. No government was in a position to fund everything itself.

Dr. A. A. Kwapong (United Nations U.) reminded us that, thus far, we had been overlooking one essential ingredient, namely *social discipline*. The socio-economic environment was an important factor. Social discipline had been a key to success in Japan and Singapore. Private jets and deposits in Swiss banks do not assist development. Can the universities help to raise standards of public morality?

A speaker from India stated that modern technologies were applied in widely different contexts; in the less developed countries the need was not so much for low-level technology as for high-level skills. ACU could help in bringing about a greater diffusion of information.

Professor F. O. Kwami (Kumasi), in response to a previous suggestion, told us of their technology consultancy centre for small-scale industries, which provides opportunities for craftsmen and technicians to improve their technology and techniques—in the words of the Chairman, 'an outpatient science park'.

Sub-Topic 4(d)

INTERNATIONAL TRANSFER AND ADAPTATION OF IMPORTED TECHNOLOGY TO MEET LOCAL NEEDS AND RESOURCES AVAILABLE

Chairman: Professor S. WIJESUNDERA
Vice-Chancellor of the University of Colombo
Rapporteur: Professor J. F. SCOTT
Vice-Chancellor of La Trobe University

Thursday, 18 August

Professor S. B. SAUL (*Vice-Chancellor, University of York, UK*): Transfer of technology, either within a firm or multi-national or between firms and countries, is essentially an economic and commercial problem—one of costs and markets. Obviously an initial technical evaluation is of the highest importance, and the process of adaptation and modification may well require a high level of technical sophistication, but we are not here talking of initial breakthroughs; we are looking for the rationale behind important decisions which may take a very long time in the making. I am not an engineer, but I find it hard to believe that much effective instruction can be given on what is very much an ad hoc one-off situation, but I may be quite wrong.

I must presume that I was asked to take part in this section of the conference because I have written on the economic factors behind technological change both in historical perspective and in the contemporary world. Certainly I have no qualifications whatsoever for saying how students of engineering should be taught to respond to the problems of technological transfer in a technical sense. I am however emboldened to proceed along my own line by some words of Lord Flowers: 'It is sometimes a struggle, especially when money is short, to convince our scientists and engineers that their students should be more aware of social and economic factors than they are themselves. It is, however, essential, especially to those who are likely to achieve managerial positions'.

Technological transfer itself is as old as history of course, but the developments occurring from the eighteenth century on made the process more rapid and purposeful. Many process inventions could not be bought or copied easily. The outstanding case was the Bessemer steel process which for some years could not be made to work by anyone else, since without knowing it Bessemer had by chance used ore with a low phosphorus content. The iron-making process of the industrial revolution—puddling—depended wholly on the skill of the man who stirred the iron and finally removed it from the furnace—the puddler. Stealing a look at the process in South Wales did not help much, and skilled men were tempted away across the Channel and the Atlantic by a variety of incentives, though the best stayed in Britain where the wages were highest (the process was in fact never successfully mechanised). The Japanese learned of the process from books brought in by the odd Dutch traders before Commodore Perry opened up international relations in 1853 but book knowledge was not enough for them ever to work it successfully.

Efforts were made to limit the outflow of technological know-how, most of all the legislation prohibiting the export of machinery. In the short run it was not unsuccessful, but the law was widely evaded. The most remarkable example was Samuel Slater's astounding feat of carrying in his memory all the details of an Arkwright spinning frame and establishing his own mills in New England with the machines he constructed. Technological transfer was inhibited by the limitations imposed by both labour and capital, and it is interesting to note Habbakuk's comment that objection to new techniques was more serious in Britain because by and large they were used to save labour, whereas in the US they were used to employ the same labour more intensively. There has been much argument about the alleged shortcomings of British businessmen in the face of new technologies, and the debate is too complex to be followed through here. Suffice it to say that there are a number of examples where a transfer of technology was slow to take place simply because the market was different. The outstanding example is the slow take-up of ring spinning in the last quarter of the nineteenth century—even though the machinery was extensively exported from Lancashire. The reason was that automatic spinning was best suited to low counts of yarns which were relatively unimportant for British industry. That the situation was to change radically after world war I is something that British cotton masters could not have anticipated, and their decision to stick to the older mule spinning technique was justified. Whether British industry was justified in ignoring fuel-saving techniques because fuel was very cheap is quite another question.

This brings out one other important point about technological transfer—that the coming of a new technology often results in major efforts to improve the old which will in fact inhibit the transfer. There are innumerable examples: improvement in coaching services when the railways arrived; great changes in the Leblanc soda technique to combat the new Solvay method. This is an important matter, for the economic criteria for adopting a new technique and scrapping an old one are really very severe. Assuming equal qualities, total cost per unit of output of the new must be lower than the variable cost of the old (since the capital costs of the old have to be carried anyway).

But we are now right up against the vexed and difficult question of factor costs which have been mentioned in relation to third-world technology but are just as relevant to transfer between more advanced countries. It is fairly obvious that countries with relatively high labour costs will welcome above all technologies which save labour. But this does not mean that they only welcome such technologies—not by any means. It is not difficult to come across capital intensive technologies that are economic, whatever the level of labour costs. Furthermore, capital intensive technologies may be necessary because skill is unavailable—even though labour in general is cheap.

Turning now to more general issues, there are two extreme views on the process of technological innovation and transfer. One is that it is largely an exogenous variable—almost an uncontrollable factor. In recent times the outcome of much detailed research has offered the opposite view—that invention not only actively responds to economic factors but could almost be explained entirely in those terms. Almost certainly this goes too far. The relevant patterns of technological innovation are primarily physical and only secondarily socio-economic. Understanding the inner dynamics of technological change is fundamental to appreciation of the nature of technological transfer. Certainly concentration on heroic individual advances is exaggerated. One characteristic is that technological development seems inevitably to lead to the formation of a system which sets boundaries to further development. Often one gets bit by bit modification of a design that remains unchanged in its essential aspects over extended periods of time. The basic breakthrough becomes a guide-post, and very often one or two early models of a technique stand out in the history of a technique—the first Ford tractor of 1917 is a case in point.

One of the problems of technological change is what we may call technological insularity or lack of transmittability. Technological know-how is largely product and plant specific, and its transfer is a lacklustre and toilsome affair. The flow across system barriers is littered with obstacles—subject to delays in time, and it is never a toll-free operation. There are costs involved in searching for a technique—finding out what is available. There are costs for adaptation, costs which are certainly experienced within multi-national firms themselves. There are long time lags and not infrequently there is no assurance of success in technological transfer—and always the possibility of drastic improvement of the old in the face of the new has led to postponement or at least slowed the rate of diffusion of an innovation. The road to follow is not always certain. Even so, the historical truth is that cost reductions by *improvement* in major innovations have by and large been greater than those associated with their initial introduction. A firm undoubtedly needs an organisational pattern geared to coping with such problems—a problem-solving diagnostic capacity at top management level, a search and acquisition capacity, and a research and development capacity to make further individual progress.

As regards transfer and diffusion of a technique in general, the most vital factors seem to be:

(*a*) the advantage of overall profitability—often difficult to calculate as may need to take account of complementary developments;

(*b*) extent of uncertainty associated with the use of the new technique and speed of its reduction;

(*c*) the attitude of management to new technique;

(*d*) access to capital—the capital market being very imperfect.

The size of firm is not necessarily vital: big firms have more research and development, more sophisticated managerial organisation and easier access to capital, but just as often the small seem to play an important role—it is the attitude of management that is vital. The optimum degree of specialisation is hard to determine. Specialists are good at improving, refining and modifying a product, but weak at devising or taking up the eventual successor to the product.

Adoption of technology might depend on a minimum efficient size below which (or maximum above which) its use is not optimal. The adoption of an innovation may depend on the extent to which it can be tried out on a limited basis. It is sometimes asked if firms consider the transferability of a technology in working towards its development. Firms with a limited home market inevitably must have this in mind; with a big home market, less so, though in some industries—agricultural machinery, for instance—the existence of shows and trials forced manufacturers to bear the question firmly in mind.

The use of new technique is a matter of learning—it requires new work methods, upgrading of production skills, modification in plant layout and design. It has a ripple effect and can only come gradually. Learning is a key factor in determining the scope for utilisation of a technique and of course there are the productivity gains derived from 'learning by doing' when the design has been established, especially in high technology industries where human capital is important. Research and development is important but only as part of learning by experience which depends on *all* investment.

There are two key determinants of technological progress and transfer: the process of learning and the process of scaling or patterning of the system to perform the desired tasks. Learning is central in the evolution of a technique in the first place. The process of scaling is inherently an uncertain activity because beyond a certain point quantitative changes in the scale of an object are inevitably transformed into changes with profound implications for its functional and structural properties.

Another feature important for transfer is the fact that technical know-how lacks the monolithic nature of pure scientific knowledge. It is acquired in bits and pieces and is often compartmentalised. Even in clearly related fields the development of one technique leaves the state of many others unaltered. Far from being a maid-of-all-work, it is in no small measure tied to the system within which it is generated.

A second point to bear in mind is technological insularity—lack of spill-over, despite what defence industries claim. Transfer is inherently prone to errors. True, there have been some glamorous successes of inter-industry transfers—electron microscopes, numerically-controlled machine tools—but the failures are just as common. Transfer may be a most fruitful source of technical innovation but the time element may be long.

Finally one ought to make to students two general points. The fear that transfer of technology will lead to a decline of foreign trade and to unemployment in the transferring country need be no more real than it was for Britain 150 years ago provided new technologies are constantly being generated. The modern problem may be that diffusion is becoming faster, helped by the activities of multinationals and general improvement in communications so that the reaction time will be limited. The second point is of great relevance to transfer to developing countries but is also of general application. A country can often successfully leapfrog stages of development by a judicious choice of technology in some sectors, but the converse is also true. There is a severe penalty attaching to an indiscriminate choice of technique because such choices continue to affect the course of subsequent development and cannot easily be repealed.

Maybe contrary to what is sometimes thought, in all contexts the prime criteria for choice is not labour or capital intensity but amenability to modification and upgrading through learning.

And a final word from the heart. Just as war is too serious a matter to be left to generals, so technological innovation cannot be left to engineers and economists. What we need urgently is an independent science of technology which would form the basis of an obligatory course for all engineering students.

Professor AMLAN DATTA (*Vice-Chancellor, Visva-Bharati*):

THE NEED FOR NEW PERSPECTIVES FOR THE UNIVERSITIES

Science is principally concerned with knowing; technology with doing or changing things materially. Universities have generally been concerned with the advancement of science considered as universally valid knowledge. But they have also been interested in technology, which develops in response to necessity or concrete human needs, and these are relative to time and space.

At a colloquium held at Tokyo in 1982 Hendrik Casimir, former President of the Royal Netherlands Academy of Sciences and Letters, drew attention to the change in the relationship between pure science and technology that has taken place in the last two centuries or so. Casimir said:

'If we look back on the development of technology and science, we see that technology at first went ahead without much support from basic scientific thinking . . . with the Renaissance we begin to see signs of more quantitative and experimental things . . . At first this study did not yet make a contribution to technology. In the 19th century . . . scientific discovery went ahead of undreamt-of technological development . . . A very characteristic phenomenon of modern science . . . [is] the science-technology spiral. Scientific work inspires new technology [which] is used for even more profound scientific research'.

Leo Esaki, a Nobel Laureate from Japan, responded by pointing out that Casimir's perception of the situation did not reflect the Japanese experience.

'In Japan', said Esaki, 'we think not of science and technology but tend rather to put the two together in the combined notion of scientific technology . . . when Europeans speak of science and technology, we have the feeling that priority or the precedence is given tacitly to science rather than technology . . . Dr. Casimir himself seems to give unconscious priority to science rather than to technology, and I think we generally say that science is firmly established as an indispensible component of Western civilization. As opposed to this, science per se has not come to occupy such a basic position in Japanese civilization'.

Esaki was right about his own country. It is not an overwhelming desire to know the universe which drew Japan towards Western science, but an urgent material task, first and foremost the necessity of defending the country against the foreigner with his superior weapons, which prompted Japan to learn and use Western science and the technology that went with it. Nor is this something entirely peculiar to Japan. Men everywhere have cultivated science from two principal urges: wonder and the pursuit of power.

This is not to deny either the truth or the importance of Casimir's observation on the history of development of Western science and technology. In any case Esaki would not deny the phenomenon of what Casimir described as the 'science-technology spiral'. Just as this has had tremendous consequences for the organisation of modern society so it has also deeply influenced our system of education. We shall come back to that a little later. We have to set the general perspectives right before that.

While Japan borrowed heavily from the technology of the West, this was not simply a process of copying or imitating. Japan's resource endowments were notably different from those of the leading Western countries. Japan was deficient in natural resources, including land, while the size of population relatively to area was much larger. It was, therefore, necessary to adapt techniques of production to the peculiar factor proportions of Japan.

This is, of course, only a particular illustration of a more general truth. Technology has two aspects. On the one hand it is, in the modern age, rooted in scientific knowledge which is universal. On the other hand it must express itself through a medium of skills and resources which have a widely varying local base. Science today is the finest example of a co-operative human effort all over the world. There is a growing stock of scientific knowledge which is today, or ought to be, the common inheritance of all mankind. Any country wishing to move forward must borrow from this common stock. But no country can make effective use of that knowledge without giving it a form and direction specific to its own needs and resources.

The distinction between pure science or theory, on the one hand, and invention, innovation and development, on the other hand, is useful in this connection. Till the end of the eighteenth century most of the major inventions were made by people who were artisans or craftsmen, rather than scientists who were responsible for major scientific discoveries. So long as the science-technology spiral had not established itself and inventions arose chiefly from the ranks of the practising craftsmen, training in industrial skills could take place in the main within families and craft guilds without much support of a systematic scientific education. This was equally or even more true of agriculture, where hereditary and family-based transmission of skills was the rule. The change which we have described above made all this out-of-date and impracticable. With the growth of modern technology the need arose for a technical cadre which was trained not within the family but in colleges of engineering, institutes of technology and universities. To be sure, universities as such are chiefly concerned with science, that is, the advancement of learning, rather than technology and industrial development. Also a great deal of scientific research, particularly development-oriented research, is undertaken within industry and in government-supported scientific laboratories. But those who work in these institutes and laboratories are themselves products of universities. Thus universities have played a role of great importance not only in creating, storing and disseminating universal knowledge, but also in advancing modern technology. This is something of which the universities can be proud. But it is also a matter which needs today to be assessed critically.

In the underdeveloped countries of the world the development of modern technology has been strikingly wanting in uniformity. What we have in these countries is familiarly called a dual society or a dual economy. There is a traditional sector and a modern sector, and the relationship between the two leaves much to be desired. To a certain extent the two sectors of the economy and the society make each other sick. The modern sector is concerned typically with export trade and industry, some forms of modern transport and defence, and the big cities with people employed in the higher levels of the administration. Universities along with the beneficiaries of higher education belong to this sector. The traditional sector covers the great majority of the population living in villages. Its material support is provided by traditional technology. This technology has itself evolved over a very long time through an extended process of trials and errors.

As the modern sector started developing in predominantly traditional societies, it was expected that that sector would play a leading, progressive and beneficial role and its influence transform and strengthen the whole economy. The new education would filter down from the élite to the common people. New ideas of justice and liberty would spread, reorganising and uplifting the depressed classes of society. But much has gone wrong. And it is important to try and understand how it has gone wrong. Within these changing societies the gulf between the traditional sector and the modern sector has not been bridged as was expected. The one, instead of strengthening and rejuvenating the other, has upset and disorganised it and made it sick. The new education in the city and the power and position they give have not so much spread through the country as drawn away the more talented and ambitious people from the villages and so left them weaker and impoverished. The new technology and the industry it has created have not so much given rise to a wider and ampler circulation of wealth throughout the country as led to the disintegration of traditional handicrafts and so upset the pre-existing balance between agriculture, industry and various services in the villages. The lopsided development of medicine and public hygiene has cut down death rates without reducing birth rates and so aggravated the problems of poverty, unemployment and underemployment. A stream of underemployed people from the villages has only served to aggravate the social situation in the city without improving it elsewhere. Our universities and institutions of higher technical training have not helped solve the problem. Rather they have, in their own way, added to the complexity of the problem.

To the extent that the universities have tried to represent the spirit and the pursuit of universal knowledge, this is something admirable, for if the universities do not do it who else will! But that is not all that there is to this matter. In a dual society and a dual economy the main role of the universities has been, unfortunately, not to bridge the gulf between the two worlds but, if anything, to widen it. This should be a matter for deep concern for all of us. Do the universities have a constructive role to play here? What can that role be?

I come from a university called Visva-Bharati which was founded in the early years of this century by Rabindranath Tagore, the great Indian poet, philosopher and educationist. He quite deliberately set up his educational institution in a rural district, although he himself came from Calcutta. He wanted to build up at Santiniketan a university conceived in the largest humanist spirit. He chose for his institution a Sanskrit motto which, if literally translated, reads: 'where the world becomes a single nest'. He wanted Visva-Bharati to be hospitable to the cultures and the sciences and the creative ideas of all parts of the world and to offer here a model of unity in diversity. There can be no question about the universalism of Tagore's conception. However, I am not concerned here with all aspects of that conception. I am rather concerned with one particular aspect. Living in an age of religious revivalism in India, Tagore was unequivocally on the side of science. Among other things, he wanted science for rural development. The antagonism that he wanted to overcome was not only that between the East and the West, or science and the humanities, but also that between the city and villages. The villages have not been able to generate from within themselves all the science that they need. But if the science that the city has to offer is to be used for the greatest good of humanity, it must consciously and by a deliberate effort put itself in close and continuing touch with the villages where the great majority of mankind continue to live to this day. Science must travel from all over the world and find a nest in the villages, and the universities should play a role in facilitating this process.

The different parts of the world have been rapidly drawn together and made physically close to one another in the last two hundred years. It is in this general atmosphere of annihilation of distance that the universities have functioned over those years. But side by side with this diminishing importance of physical distance a new trend has already set in and made itself felt in movements and patterns of thought all over the world. There is an increasing appeciation of the value of the distinctive cultures and identities of small communities away from the anonymous crowd. No statement of the new horizons of thought and aspirations of mankind in the coming age, or what we may describe as the next phase of evolution of human society, will be complete without a reference to this new trend. This sets a new task for humanity. Science and technology must, soon or late, be called upon to adjust itself to this new task. Every country and every community must continue to borrow knowledge and technology. But without an adaptation of that knowledge and technology to the new aspirations of humanity, leading it away from that concentration of power and wealth in

293

the metropolis and great cities of the world, which has been a characteristic of the age in which we live but against which a reaction has already unquestionably set in, the world will not be at peace with itself. It is in this context of a new task for humanity that universities all over the world must strive to plan their programmes for the future.

When the less developed countries started borrowing technology they wanted the technology without losing the distinctiveness of their cultures. This was, in a sense, unrealistic. New technology was bound to affect and change other aspects of culture as well. Willingly or unwillingly, new cultural traits had to be accepted along with a new technology. But the old problem has now come back in a new form. It is no longer a question of preserving the old culture. It is rather a question of saving mankind from the effects of overcentralisation of power and the destruction of those familistic and community bonds which most people appear to need even to preserve their basic humanity. But this involves a new task for the world as a whole in terms of re-ordering human society. It equally involves new perspectives and a new task for technology, which the universities must take into account if they are to continue to play a significant role in future.

The task that confronts a new generation is not that of creating a world-wide industrial society with gigantic institutions, bureaucracies and anonymous crowds kept in a state of animation by mass production of consumables and pleasureable stimuli, oddly consorting with devices of mass destruction. Rather what needs to be built up, however slowly and haltingly, is a great human confederation of small communities, small vibrant nests of people, secure and yet open to the wide sky of the world outside, not altogether self-sufficient but largely so, avoiding uniformity and striving for equal relations among men, not dominated by high technology but open to science and the spirit of freedom and adventure that it represents. If this gives some indication of the aspirations of the new age, it will be unimaginative and arrogant on the part of the universities not to try to be in tune with these emerging aspirations.

Even where science as technology has chiefly an instrumental value, the universities by virtue of their capacity for a critical review of social objectives should, even against some odds, help make science an instrument of higher objectives than those the dominant interest groups of society would like to prescribe and promote. Finally, the universities must also be ready to turn their critical powers against themselves. For universities, like all institutions, are prisoners of history and of tradition. They must have the spirit and the will to break out of that prison by their own effort.

DISCUSSION

Professor J. Manrakhan (Mauritius): I entirely agree with Professor Saul's concluding remarks. I have tried to institute such a course. When I did so the engineers said it was crazy; perhaps it was, because I am not an engineer myself. Professor Datta suggests that the critical powers of universities should be turned inwards to themselves. This I have also tried in order to develop new and better courses, but the result was virtually the same courses and the same research as before. A general complaint in universities is that shortage of funds stops research, but in my experience good research in applied science always gets funded.

Professor J. C. West (Bradford): May I comment on the last paragraph of Professor Saul's paper, speaking as an engineer. War and technology have it in common that they are both regarded as dirty crafts and in consequence are left to the generals and the engineers. It must be realised that if engineers are trained to be more able, then they become more powerful. The necessary changes in courses for engineers should provide training in management, safety and health, labour relations and so on. Equally, we should try to make economists, historians, medical students and others take complementary courses in engineering and be able to undertake the appropriate management roles in technology themselves, not let the engineers do it for them.

It has been said that necessity is the mother of invention and technological transfer. But case studies are carried out over too short a time-base. Let me give an example. Before 1914 the rapid increase in aviation produced the need for parachutes. Since the material had to be light-weight, strong and easily packed, it became apparent that silk was appropriate. During the last war it was just not possible to produce enough silk for parachutes. This led to the rapid introduction of the new synthetic material, nylon. During the war existing textile machinery was used to make parachutes, but in the 1950s computer-controlled special machines were introduced. The output rate went up from 3,000 m.p.h. to 300,000 m.p.h. By 1966 there was over-production of nylon and similar synthetics. Then came the oil crisis and the prices of all oil-based synthetics soared. Synthetic yarn was as dear as natural fibre. Now the demand for silk is blossoming. In 50 years the technology has come full cycle. The point I want to make is that technological transfer is a dynamic process and never, unlike fairy tales, a 'happily ever after' phenomenon.

Professor A. K. De (IIT, Bombay): India has imported over 700 technologies and will continue to have to do so. Until 1976 investment in research and development was encouraged by the government, but this state of affairs no longer exists. Countries like India cannot, in general, compete with the rest of the world. A major factor determining this is the lack of skills in marketing. Technology students have to study sociology, economics and science. At my institute they spend 14% of their time on such studies.

Professor M. A. Aziz Khan (Chittagong): The mechanisms of technological transfer are extremely complex. It is what might be called the Pasteur effect: simple to the successful individual, but very complicated to everyone else. In the receiving country a minimum level of science and general education is necessary. Thus appropriate training is required and knowledge of the technology, but development is so fast that this is a problem. Social structures and economies also change rapidly. Developing countries wanting to receive new technologies must be prepared to accept changes in the social and economic conditions. Undoubtedly mass production of goods will have this effect. Unless countries receiving new technology are prepared to develop a scientific base they will not gain the benefit from the new technology.

Professor J. Aminu (Maiduguri): The transfer of technology in the private sector is a matter of markets and costs, as Professor Saul indicates. What is involved is a transfer of skills. Unfortunately it is not the engineers who have taken over but the politicians. It is governments in developing countries who sign contracts, not engineers. Governments talk to each other in philosophical terms not in practical realities. Private enterprise is only interested in selling goods. Technological transfer can only satisfactorily take place when there is a cadre of persons of a high degree of education. If transfer takes place too quickly there is a real chance that the nation may become poorer rather than richer as a result.

Dr. C. G. Okojie (Ibadan): I am a politician and so speak from a viewpoint different from those of my colleagues. Technological transfer needs proper funding and so must be dependent on politicians' attitudes. In the developing countries universities tend to have the same background and aims as in the tradition of the developed countries, and are of little relevance to the needs of the country. The gap between universities and the real world is immense and the universities have a responsibility to bridge it. Universities, to be effective, must learn to lobby politicians successfully.

Professor A. O. Adesola (Lagos): I agree with Professor Saul that market conditions play an important role. However consumers may not have much choice if the country is poor, or where imported products only affect them on the fringe or where political allegiances make only certain countries acceptable trading partners. It is the duty of universities to teach students an understanding of the needs of the country through, for example, a study of the social sciences. The relationship between rural dwellers in villages and inhabitants of cities varies from country to country. Frequently we find that, for example, $100 million spent on technological transfer provides $90 million on air-conditioners to make the élite in cities more comfortable.

SUB-TOPIC 4 (D): INTERNATIONAL TRANSFER/ADAPTATION

Technology needs local modifications to cater for local needs, but at present few can advise on this since university curricula are not necessarily relevant. Advisers need to know what is happening in local communities and can only come from the receiving country itself. May I speak for a moment on medical education, my own field. Traditional medicine, using herbs, incantations and so on, has many supporters but there is a genuine role for co-operation with practitioners of Western medicine. It is essential for Western-trained doctors to study traditional medicine and to understand its methods.

Dr. N. K. Boardman (CSIRO, Australia): Among all technological transfer, that in agriculture is the most important. In this connection I should mention the Australian Centre for International Agricultural Research. The major problem is to identify the needs of developing countries, and so it is essential to have collaboration with receiving countries to define those needs. This is the basis of the Centre's work. The social structure of a developing country must be known, hence the need for co-operation.

Professor P. V. Indiresan (IIT, Madras): Developing countries do not usually use university links to encourage transfer of technology but go to the major business companies.

I have always thought there are four stages in the development of engineers: (i) when they wish they had been taught how to do things; (ii) when they wish they had been taught more mathematics; (iii) when they wish they had learnt about economics and psychology; (iv) when they wish they had learnt philosophy. The education given to an engineer today has to last him 30–40 years. It is unwise to give too much emphasis to indigenous technology in his training for that reason, since it will inevitably change over that time-scale. It is not appropriate for universities to get involved in the very large projects.

Often factories are put up in developing countries with great fanfares, although they manufacture products not really needed. Fifteen years later the product is in great demand but the factory has deteriorated and cannot be adapted because the developed countries have moved on to a newer technology. This is when the existence of an indigenous technology can be valuable: it can step in and bring the factory up to date, provided it has the self-confidence to exercise this role.

Dr. B. C. L. Weedon (Nottingham): There are some questions to which I would like the answers. How can the universities in the developed countries help? Do the arrangements for secondment of staff help? Are bilateral links between universities helpful? Often specific postgraduate courses for students from developing countries are mounted: are these useful? It is essential that we recognise the pride of achieving development by their own efforts in developing countries.

Dr. P. P. M. Meincke (Prince Edward Island): I feel we have neglected the transfer of 'know-how'. It is essential, in the long run, to make things work. In order to sprout, seed must fall on fertile soil. I believe universities in developed countries can help identify the fertile soil. Ultimately it is individuals who make things happen. In technological fields such individuals may be labelled 'entrepreneurs'. Universities can play a part in developing an entrepreneurial spirit in graduates. At my university fourth-year students have a project in which they have to identify and plan enterprises that do not as yet exist on the Island. It is interesting to note that, out of 100 such projects, 25 have led to the establishment of new businesses; a surprisingly high proportion. We must never forget that problems are opportunities in disguise.

Dr. E. T. Brash (Papua New Guinea): My government always appoints an internal counterpart to any external consultant. For example, in a major development of a copper mine the government gave academics a role in the relevant environmental impact study, calling where necessary on Australian universities for additional expertise. Governments need advice from academics when drawing up contracts. We should never forget that the big multinational firms have some of the best and most acute brains in the world and are very tough negotiators.

Professor S. B. Saul (York): I should have learnt from experience not to make dramatic statements at the end of my paper! The transfer of technology is not trickery, but it is very difficult. In training engineers it is no use just adding a nominal amount of social science to the course. The object is to teach him to understand in what areas he lacks knowledge. We need an integration of the problems of transfer, engineering and the social sciences.

Sub-Topic 4(e)

THE IMPLEMENTATION AND EXPLOITATION OF NEW TECHNOLOGY AND ANALYSIS OF ITS SOCIAL ASPECTS

Chairman: Dr. J. W. O'BRIEN
Rector and Vice-Chancellor of Concordia University

Rapporteur: Dr. D. J. E. INGRAM
Vice-Chancellor of the University of Kent at Canterbury

Thursday, 18 August

Professor E. BRAUN (*Head of Technology Policy Unit, University of Aston in Birmingham*): It has become customary to use the term new technology as if it applied to a particular closed group of new equipment, more particularly to all machinery and devices which have been radically changed by the use of computer techniques and microelectronic circuits. Although it is true, of course, that microelectronics has developed very rapidly since its inception a quarter of a century ago, and has radically altered many everyday products and much production technology, it is equally true that no technology stands still and the process of implementation is a continuous one. This simple but painful truth has been amply demonstrated in many of the older industries, such as steel, shipbuilding and motor vehicles. Either the product or the process or both may change drastically from time to time and there is no hope for a manufacturer who stays behind. The first rule of the industrial game is never to rest on one's laurels. The corollary to this is that each manufacturer must at least keep informed about developments in his sphere of activity. Perhaps not everybody needs to be innovative in the pioneering sense, but to ignore the new and not to innovate in the adaptive sense is tantamount to opting out of future existence.

Technological innovation is a large subject but as far as we are concerned here we need only distinguish three qualitative aspects of innovation and two quantitative ones. Qualitatively innovation

299

is concerned with the design of new or improved products, with the development of new or improved processes, or with the introduction of new manufacturing methods. Although the last of these categories may be regarded as the diffusion of a new product, such as a numerically controlled machine tool, it poses truly innovative problems as the machine is new to the organisation introducing it. Quantitatively we may distinguish between radical and incremental innovations. Without much sophistication this is merely to indicate that some innovations are technically difficult to achieve while others involve only quite small advances. The economic evaluation of innovations may be quite different from the technical one and simple ideas, like the cat's eye for road marking, may be economically much more significant than highly complex ventures such as the hovercraft.

One of the important aspects of a radically new product is that it is generally necessary to produce it by radically new methods. Radical product innovation often requires radical process innovation. A classic example is microelectronics, where process innovations largely determined the shape of the product. In the early part of the life cycle of a radically new product, when the product itself is in need of development and no production machinery is available for off-the-shelf purchase, the innovator depends upon the availability of a large network of resources. Highly trained, educated and skilled personnel, research and development facilities, specialist technical services and supplies, not to mention legal, commercial and financial services, are all of the essence. At this stage the stakes are high—much is to be gained by success and much lost by failure.

As the product advances through its life cycle the problems become quite different. Generally speaking, the specially developed new production machinery will become available to all comers with the necessary cash. Product know-how will have accumulated and licences may be obtainable. It sounds thus as if anybody with the necessary capital could set up a plant to manufacture yesterday's revolutionary product which today may still be near the forefront of technical development and may still have considerable growth potential. Several things militate against this simple notion.

First and foremost, the systems nature of industrial production means that each manufacturing unit depends upon a whole host of suppliers who provide anything from humble office equipment to sophisticated parts and materials. Without close liaison between the manufacturer and his suppliers and without adequate safeguards for quality and reliability of supplies, the manufacturing process becomes a nightmare. But even if we are not so ambitious

300

as to wish to manufacture an entirely new product and merely wish to introduce the latest generation of production machinery to produce old products by old processes, a procedure we have elsewhere called manufacturing innovation, the problems are formidable.

Unless the manufacturer is somehow protected from national and international competition, he will have to be constantly watching for weaknesses in his manufacturing chain. There may be many different weaknesses: wasted materials or energy, excessive stocks of finished or semi-finished products, inadequate quality or consistency of production, excessive labour requirements; all adding up to poor factor productivity. The weak link in the chain is not usually an absolute but a relative weakness—relative to what is achieved elsewhere or what is currently regarded as best practice. Having diagnosed the weakness the manufacturer must seek a remedy. This may consist of organisational arrangements, of training, of technical measures, or of a combination of these. If the remedy consists of the introduction of new machinery or equipment, without substantial alteration to the product or the process, we speak of manufacturing innovation.

In many cases this will involve the purchase of some novel machinery, say one or several industrial robots. To apply such machines successfully requires a whole constellation of propitious circumstances which need to be arranged. The first difficulty is the choice of machine. It may be too novel, untried and unreliable, or it may be unnecessarily complex and expensive, or it may otherwise not fit the task it is intended for. But even if the chosen robot is perfectly good, it will only fulfil its task if the application engineer and robotics expert work closely together, if the staff and workers operating the robot are well-trained and co-operative, if there is adequate service back-up, and if the robot is properly integrated into the manufacturing system. There are enough ifs here to give many a manager a thorough headache.

The obvious question arises whether the university system can help to ease the successful adoption of new technology and perhaps one might even ask the heretic question whether it should ease the process if it could. Let us take the easy question first, although I must confess to the unfashionable view that the role of universities in the process of technological innovation and even of adoption of new technology is rather limited and consists mainly of the training of competent graduates and some support by basic research and consultancy. The main requirements in innovation are flexible open minds, open communications, and enthusiasm unhampered by rigid structures. These are attitudes which should be self-evident to a good education system. Part of the open communications requirement is, of course, that university teachers and students should be aware of the latest developments in their subject. It is only when a subject has grown to considerable size and importance that specialist courses become possible, first at postgraduate and then at undergraduate level. Courses in computing, in microelectronics, in information systems—to name but a few—are examples of how the universities can and must adapt to new technical developments. Yet even the best education system must lag somewhat behind the most innovative technologies and techniques. To pioneer means, almost by definition, to be out of one's depth.

What of the much more vexed question of the extent to which new technology should be supported? The answer clearly depends not only on what social consequences we expect the new technology to have, but also on what social change we may regard as desirable. I can do little more here than to point out some of the issues involved and to refer the reader to more extensive treatments of these matters.

We must ask what the individual and society want and may reasonably expect from technology. In my view the individual may expect the fulfilment of four needs: (i) provision of the basic requirements of life, such as food, clothing, shelter, health and personal safety; (ii) the easing of necessary tasks, particularly the removal of strenuous physical work; (iii) the provision of pleasurable toys; (iv) the provision of a degree of personal autarchy. Society may additionally expect technology to provide the necessary means of production to achieve the satisfaction of individual needs for all its members and the provision of the technical needs of a vast social infrastructure. This term spans a wide range of services— transport, telecommunications, water supplies and waste disposal, police, fire-fighting, external defence, education, legal and administrative services. Very obviously a densely populated modern state cannot survive without technology, let alone provide for its citizens some of the satisfactions which they hope for.

Unhappily technology has come to serve as a substantial tool in a miscellany of power aspirations. For on the one hand technology is a creator of wealth and thus a servant of the wealthy and powerful, and on the other hand it provides economic and military might with obvious implications for power politics of every kind. Perhaps equally unhappily, excessive or unwise use of technology has become associated with the exhaustion of natural resources, with pollution and with the destruction of nature. Neither of these associations should be cause for the wholesale condemnation of technology, but both should cause much thought and heart-searching and political debate on suitable social controls for curbing the unbridled use of technology, and much research on alternative and better means of safeguarding the environment in the broadest sense.

So far we have only mentioned the easing of burdens, the lightening of necessary tasks, the extension of man's powers, the provision of autarchy for him. But much as we desire autarchy and independence, we also need a sense of belonging and a feeling of contributing to the well-being of our society. In modern industrial societies the main conscious link, the major cohesive force, is provided by work. It is therefore vital that we strive to regain full employment, strive to give people a fair share of obtainable technological wealth and a sense of doing their bit for their society. Although there are alternative ways of obtaining social cohesion, most of these are fraught with dangers as they usually involve banding together against an enemy.

I do not believe that technology will eliminate work. There is enough to do in this world even if we use the most sophisticated machinery to help us. It is a task for policy-makers to see to it that technology is not used to eliminate work but to create more well-being. There are real dangers of making a lot of people useless by eliminating the skills they can provide. There is no way in which changes of skills with changing technology can be avoided, but again it is a task for policy-makers and for engineers and everybody else to make sure that people are employed as humanely and with as much use of skills as possible. Technology can do it, provided the social forces which direct technology make these concerns their own.

Professor D. M. NOWLAN (*Vice-President (Research and Planning): University of Toronto*):

THE ROLE OF UNIVERSITIES IN THE IMPLEMENTATION OF NEW TECHNOLOGIES

In secondary school we used to tell ourselves that to pass physics it was necessary to know two things: $f = ma$ and you can't push on a rope. When thinking about the introduction and spread of new technologies, I am easily reminded of our inability to push on a rope. New technologies are not implemented by virtue simply of the existence of new inventions or discoveries. Innovation or implementation is a complex social process that depends on specific decisions, interests, and institutions. This process draws new technologies into use, like pulling on a rope. The high-school physics maxim helps remind us that the speed at which new technologies are introduced, their distribution and social implications, cannot be determined solely or even principally by the technical characteristics of the underlying inventions.

The decisions that do lead to the development of new technologies rely heavily on commercial incentives, aided—or, in some cases, supplanted—by government action. By and large, universities have not been major actors in the process of technological innovation, although their role in different countries at different times cannot be vouchsafed by a single description. As a generalisation, universities in low-income, developing countries have been more regarded in recent decades as significant direct agents of technological and institutional change than have universities in North America. For much of the post-war period universities in North America have defined themselves as centres of learning and teaching with research roles that have emphasized the importance of free inquiry and conceptual (as opposed to immediately applicable) results. With the main exception of clinical areas of medical research, which has been conducted usually in association with teaching hospitals and strongly oriented towards application, the primary role of universities with respect to the introduction of new technologies has been indirect: basic research provided the discoveries upon which innovations elsewhere were based and courses of instruction provided both general and professional backgrounds for high-level manpower throughout society without special regard for the current state of the labour market.

This insouciant disregard for the immediate applicability of university learning and discovery has now been replaced in many large North American universities by aggressive product marketing. Courses of instruction are tailored explicitly to apparent market demand and heavily advertised; research capacities are touted and research liaisons sought with both the private and the government sectors. For better or worse, we are bent on becoming significant partners in the social process of technological change.

This is not happening in opposition to the views of governments and industry. Indeed, the change has occurred in part because of the inability of universities to resist a mood within society that is less tolerant of the cloistered academy. This finds expression through government policies that press upon universities to match graduates more closely with current job-market needs and that redirect research money towards government-defined areas of strategic interest. As well, our growing interest in research and development expenditures as a solution to flagging productivity growth and the heightened public attention that is being paid to frontier research on topics such as biotechnology, microelectronics, robotics, communication technologies, toxic substances and new energy forms have provided an agreeable setting for the creation of numerous enterprises that involve universities in corporate research partnerships with industry and government.

The development and implementation of new technologies is above all a risky process. In consequence the private sector seeks high returns and short payback periods for successful innovations as compensation for the high proportion of inventions that fail in the market place. Governments alone are able to gamble with the resources of all of taxable society in the support of technological change. Without the discipline of the market, governments can take a longer view of change than the private sector; but without this discipline governments have only ambiguous criteria for the selection of new technologies and often limited rationale for the technologies they do support.

Whether through governments or the private sector, the process of developing and transferring technologies is somewhat alien to a university whose strength lies in a willingness and ability to undertake intellectual not financial risk, and whose attitude to large-scale technological change must be analytical and enquiring, not promotional. Universities are becoming closer partners in the development of new technologies, but the relationship is not yet settled and their role far from clear. Out of the frustrations and tensions that have accompanied the changes in this relationship over the recent past, there may however have emerged some guideposts that, although murkily defined, can help mark our future course. From my own observations and our collective experience at the University of Toronto, there are four aspects of the university's role in new-technology implementation upon which I might offer some brief comment: (1) manpower training; (2) the university's contribution to university-industry-government partnerships; (3) the creation of new knowledge about the social effects of new technologies; and (4) the importance of the university as an originator and repository of public knowledge about new discoveries.

Without a doubt universities are and have long been important producers of trained manpower, but there has not always been agreement on the best way to exercise this function. With the social awareness that now exists of the significance of technical change to the career of a working person, there may be something approaching consensus that the best education that can be had currently is education for change itself. This perspective is consistent with the university's own image of its manpower-training role, but it is nonetheless frequently challenged by government policies that are strongly influenced by the immediate market situation. My own reading of the evidence is that the gradual but very noticeable change in the distribution of resources and students among the various disciplines in North American universities over the past decade or two has been more efficiently responsive to social needs than any policy-induced change would have been based on the erratic, short-run market readings that tend to dominate government thinking. I realize that in a highly developed economy with a range of post-secondary institutions embracing polytechnical schools, community colleges and universities it is easier to take a longer and more fundamental view of the university's role in manpower training than it is in a country with a less structured post-secondary sector; but the university's perspective on manpower needs in the face of today's technology is relevant even in low-income countries. The issue in all countries is not how to ring the bells and toot the whistles of new products; it is how to create and manage change.

The most obvious manifestation of the university's new flirtation with the processes of innovation and applied research has been the creation of corporate research or development ancillaries, often in partnership with industry or government or both. At the University of Toronto we established a few years ago a wholly controlled Innovations Foundation which essentially has the right of first refusal over the further development and exploitation of university inventions, except those the ownership of which lies elsewhere as a result of contractual undertakings. This corporation is our primary vehicle for the commercial development of the products of primary research, which it does either in partnership with venture capitalists or in conjunction with companies that might themselves be interested in the ultimate exploitation of new inventions. Although the Foundation is not yet very active, the effect of having this linkage between the inventive results of university research and their commercial exploitation is already noticeable; some research has become more responsive to commercial interests. This of course is an efficient way of establishing a feed-back loop between social

306

need, as measured by the market place, and university research; it also has in it the potential for inefficiently diverting university research that would have its social payoff beyond the relatively short time horizon of commercial interests.

Like other universities, we have also been developing more specifically focused research ancillaries to take advantage of the financial and other benefits that a close relationship with industry or government can provide. In partnership with the government of Ontario we have recently incorporated an Institute for Hydrogen Systems and are about to establish a Microelectronics Development Corporation with federal government support. The hydrogen institute, which won government backing largely through the enthusiasm and influence of one of the University's professors, will undertake detailed studies of the technological and social aspects of a hydrogen-based energy economy. A formal agreement between the new Institute and the University constrains the Institute to spend a certain minimum percentage of its research budget on basic as opposed to applied research. Through the Institute we are able to participate in the development of a wholly new energy technology in a way that would not be possible without special government backing or without the close support of industry, which is represented on the Institute's board, but at a balance of benefit or cost to the University that will be apparent only over a longer period.

In considering the creation of other ancillary corporations we are concerned, as we were in the case of the Institute for Hydrogen Systems, to ensure that there will be an advantage to fundamental or basic research. Also there has been some interest in building into new enterprises as an explicit objective the analysis of social effects where that appears relevant and feasible. For example, a proposed centre for the study of toxicology which we and the University of Guelph are developing in conjunction with governments and industry includes the area of risk assessment among its research agenda. Another example is the loosely-knit Co-operative on Information Technology which with Waterloo University we have organised to bring together scholars from both institutions interested in social, humanistic and technical aspects of a microelectronic information society. In general, however, the study of social and economic effects of new technologies requires a level of disciplinary skill and commitment that makes it difficult simply to add these areas to the agenda of an enterprise devoted to the development and implementation of some new technology. The social issues are fundamental and not just peripheral add-ons to the process of implementing new hardware.

307

Let me turn by way of final comment to the important role to be played by universities as originators and repositories of public knowledge. As increasingly active partners in the process of technological development, universities are forced to think fundamentally about their attitude towards the ownership of the new ideas, new products and new processes they are helping to create. Commercial gain rests frequently on proprietary knowledge; in consequence, universities are and will continue to be pressed by their private-sector partners into confidentiality agreements that breach customary standards. (From the fact that government agencies seem frequently to want a surprising degree of proprietary right over the results of research they sponsor, one must assume that in the public sector as well exclusive knowledge has institutional value.) Because open learning and discovery is such a cherished attribute of universities, this pressure—requirement, almost—to become accomplices in proprietary research is of course resisted.

The desirability of preserving openness in universities goes beyond the issue of institutional integrity; there are compelling social benefits to be gained from the existence of public, non-proprietary knowledge of technology's new products and processes. The exploitation and diffusion of new technologies is not a particularly rational process; it rests, as I noted at the outset, on a complex social structure of ownership rights and responsibilities (whether private or public). As new techniques in biotechnology or new microelectronic products are drawn into use, some individuals and groups in society will benefit and others will be harmed. Among our greatest concerns is that the gain to be realized by innovators will not take into account the costs incurred by, for example, technologically displaced or unemployed workers. Society's primary defence against the resource misallocation that this might entail is to maintain high levels of investment and new-job creation throughout the economy. One of the best ways of encouraging this to happen is to ensure that a wide variety of individuals and institutions, small as well as large, have access to the knowledge required to exploit the new technologies. Through their unique commitment to openness universities have a special responsibility in a rapidly innovating society to encourage this access.

DISCUSSION

At the end of his introductory paper Professor D. M. Nowlan (Toronto) made a very definite plea that universities should be more 'open' in their research activities, and be very reluctant to allow too much confidentiality of 'proprietary knowledge' to their sponsors or commercial collaborators. This point was taken up immediately the discussion period opened, several speakers congratulating Dr. Nowlan on making this stand and supporting his plea. Professor L. S. Bark (Salford), for example, stressed that the very essence of university work was that this should be to increase knowledge for all, and we had a definite responsibility to 'tell people what we know'. There was, moreover, the very practical question of promotion of academic staff which, to a large measure, depended on published work. Too much confidentiality was therefore bound to hinder the fair working of any promotion exercise.

There were, however, some expressions of caution in some of the comments which followed. Whilst agreeing with the general principle, it was pointed out by several that the necessary financial support required to continue and develop some research programmes could only be obtained if the sponsors were guaranteed some commercial confidentiality or proprietary rights. Thus, Dr. N. K. Boardman (C.S.I.R.O., Australia) suggested that at the development stage fairly large sums of money might be required, and these were not going to be provided from industry unless some possible pay-back could be foreseen. In the discussion which followed on this point it was suggested that there might need to be a difference of approach between the 'early pure research stage' and the 'development stage' of an idea which clearly had practical applications.

Dr. B. C. L. Weedon (Nottingham) also raised two practical questions: how could 'first refusal' be guaranteed to the University of Toronto's Innovations Foundation when the rights of all the academic staff were involved; and what actual benefits did the University allow to the individual inventor himself?

In replying to these and other points, Dr. Nowlan explained that the idea of 'first refusal' had received a surprising degree of support and consent amongst the University academic staff and this may have been partly due to the good financial incentive that was offered—50% of the net proceeds were allocated to the individual inventor himself, the other 50% being distributed to the department and central funds. He explained that they were also very careful to retain publication rights (even, if necessary, with a certain amount of delay) when any proprietary rights had been assigned.

Dr. Nowlan suggested that some of the greatest difficulties in agreeing financial arrangements often arose with government departments and agencies, and he felt that universities might do much better in such cases if they joined forces and acted together. It was also suggested during the discussion that approach to those 'at the top' in government departments on these issues could often be very helpful, as the lower echelons were often afraid to take any initiatives.

In response to queries on specific examples of how universities might have benefited financially in the past from the development of their discoveries, Dr. Nowlan said that until recently it had often only been in the way of 'goodwill'. The discovery of insulin was one such example from his own University, but in recent years universities had adopted a more commercial approach, and Pavlon (a serum for children) was an example which had produced some financial pay-back.

Another major point that was taken up early in the discussion and referred to several times later was the suggestion in the paper by Professor E. Braun (Aston in Birmingham), that, to some extent, universities should remain aloof from the detailed application of innovative technology, and that the role of the universities in the process of technological innovation was 'rather limited'. A query on this point was first raised by Dr. E. O. Akinluyi (Lagos), and in his reply Professor Braun explained that he did not wish to imply that it was the wish of universities to remain 'aloof', but that there must, in essence, be a limit to what they can actually do as technological innovators. The real work of innovation has to be done 'at the coal face'—and universities would cease to be universities if they became too enmeshed in the actual business of innovation. Moreover they should be able to stand back and take a 'critical look' at what was taking place, and therefore must not become too involved themselves.

This view was somewhat criticised by Professor M. Yeates (Queen's, Kingston) who maintained that, with their different faculties and subject spreads, universities should be 'crucibles of society', and probably only they could view such developments with as broad a view as was necessary.

There were some comments towards the end by Professor S. Blume (Amsterdam) and Professor K. J. Hancock (Flinders, South Australia) suggesting that not enough attention had been paid to precisely what the social sciences themselves could do in trying to analyse the problems and implications of technological development. Thus new technologies must always have social impacts and were never neutral. In their very essence they must transfer power and wealth from one section of society to another, and universities were the only places at which any objective study of this could be undertaken. Professor Hancock said that it must be remembered that the social sciences had a large number of other complex problems to tackle at the moment, and that, moreover, the assessment of technological change was a very complex and difficult problem.

When picking up these points in his summary reply at the end, Professor Braun stressed his own interest in some of the social impacts of technological change, and of those relating to unemployment in particular. In this connection he picked up an earlier comment that the 'work ethic' was necessary to the individual rather than to society at large. He was sure that some form of 'social cement' was more than ever necessary in our modern societies and put forward the suggestion that the idea of a 'work-link' rather than a 'work ethic' was important. This would give a coherence to society which, if lost, would have to be replaced by another kind of 'social cement'—such as a 'common enemy', which would be much more dangerous.

SUB-TOPIC 4 (E): IMPLEMENTATION AND EXPLOITATION

In trying to advise developing countries on what they might gain from the experience of the West, he began by quoting the story of the Irishman who, when asked the best way to get to Dublin, replied: 'It would be much better to start from somewhere other than here'. He felt that developing countries might indeed have the opportunity of 'starting from somewhere other than here' and learn from the experience of the developed countries which paths might be worth following and which were better avoided.

Topic 4

THE DEVELOPMENT AND TRANSFER OF TECHNOLOGY

Co-ordinating Chairman's Commentary on the Group's Discussions

Final Plenary Session
Friday, 19 August

Sir Denys Wilkinson (*Vice-Chancellor, University of Sussex*): The interdependence of the universities of the Commonwealth was vividly illustrated by Colin Maiden's account of the important role played by the universities of New Zealand in that country's successful development of substitutes for petrol. This success resulted in a reduction of oil imports from Nigeria and a corresponding lessening of funds available for Nigerian universities. This result, that I quote as a parable, had presumably not been directly intended and I mention this case to emphasize a recurrent theme of Topic 4, namely that technological developments often have unforeseen impacts, by no means always beneficial. I also mention this case because it is one of the very few examples of universities making a significant contribution to the solution of a major national problem. This is related to another recurring theme of Topic 4: that universities can and must continue to engage in fundamental research, can and must continue to recognize and consciously seek for the applicability of that research, can and must continue to provide the diverse 'enabling technologies' that have to be woven together in any specific innovation, can carry out or assist in development perhaps even to the prototype stage but have little or no role to play in the final commercialization and marketing. But even more important than any primary role in invention and development is their responsibility for providing appropriate education. And, as Aziz Khan told us, the most important technological transfer might indeed be that of education itself.

312

But to begin. Most people who have ever lived are dead; most scientists who have ever lived are alive: most of our history is in the past; most of our science is in the present. It is this disparity between the time scale of the evolution of our culture and the break-neck time scale of the evolution of our science and technology that poses the most formidable problem for the development and transfer of technology. The impact of technological change on society, particularly in its cultural dimension, is enormous; its benefits can be enormous, its destructive effect on our culture can be enormous and yet we have no time to think, no way to bring about a proper match between the evolutionary time scale of ordered and responsible cultural change and the rushing imperatives of the technological age.

And what is the genesis of those imperatives? Almost always it is the not-too-attractive combination of consumer demand and the profit motive. Rarely does technological development stem from a primary desire to better man's largely miserable lot. And even when it does, it often misses what ought to be its mark. As Amlan Datta illustratively, if sadly, informed us: 'Students graduating from the colleges of medicine in India feel at home in Australia, Canada or England. . . It is in the villages of India that they feel lost'.

Two hundred years ago, in the dawn of the industrial revolution, the distinction between science and technology was clear: science, *scientia*, was knowledge; technology, *tekhne*, was arts and crafts. *Scientia* and *tekhne* flourished side by side but their interactions were scant. Abraham Darby, whose Ironbridge monuments we visited during this Congress, in his development of the coke-smelting of iron that effectively brought about the industrial revolution, could have no debt to the then non-existent University of Birmingham, but his debt to the entirety of the pre-existing formal scholarship of the world was little more. In those days *scientia* knew; *tekhne* did. Today science and technology are no longer side by side but rather are inextricably intertwined in a loving embrace or a vicious circle depending on your perceptions and taste. The distinction between science and technology now lies more in purpose and attitudes than in content; it certainly does not lie in intellectual challenge which, if anything, tends to be greater on the 'applied' side where your problems are given to you than on the 'pure' side where you can choose them for youself. Perhaps the clearest distinction, implied by P. V. Indiresan, now resides in responsibility: if your theory proves wrong you can think up another one but if your bridge falls down that is bad news of a different order. I am happy to recall that the Royal Society's toast still is: 'Arts and Sciences'.

In the less developed countries (LDCs) highly-trained manpower is very scarce and resources are scanty. It is there particularly important to understand the science/technology symbiosis. If this is not understood there is a danger either that technological development is regarded as too costly so that scientists retreat into the ivory tower or that it is decreed that only developmental work of the most evident and immediate applicability can be considered, because of societal needs, and that pure science is an irrelevance. Thus it is that in some countries of the developing world the universities are even further from societal problems than are those of the developed countries whereas in other LDCs their work is over-tightly geared to immediate local needs.

Today's science/technology symbiosis, indeed symphysis, means that you will not be able best to appreciate the benefits of a technology unless you understand enough science to know how the technology works and to modify it to suit the local environment, physical or cultural. Any country must have scientists at home at least competent, as Fred Jevons put it, 'to dip into the international pool'.

It seems to me that whether or not an LDC has a significant programme of endogenous technological development, it must have scientists (including social scientists) capable of independent evaluation of the technologies that it might be proposed to transfer to it from advanced countries. This local evaluation must be from all points of view including that of the need for adaptation of the technology to fit the local scene (and how will this be done?) and of its future development for changing needs or to incorporate later advances (and how will this be done?). LDCs must not be told what technologies are good for them; they must decide this for themselves through their own scientists, most of whom would be best placed in their universities. Of course a country needs more than a proper evaluation of a technology: if transferred, that technology must be implemented. This involves technical manpower at all levels and the provision of that manpower is a critically important matter, as Akin Adesola stressed in telling us of Nigeria's discouraging experiences in seeking to acquire training of middle-level technical manpower in advanced countries. Without local evaluation and implementation transfer of technology remains, as one of our more pessimistic participants told us, only 'trickster words': 'technology transfer does not take place—only sale of goods'.

Institutional collaboration between LDCs and advanced countries, which already takes place to some degree, should be encouraged in relation to these problems. As Basil Weedon insisted,

314

the universities of the advanced countries still very much want to help but without infringing the rights and duties of those of the LDCs.

This brings me to another aspect of the technological imperative: the problem of the 'appropriate technology'. It is clearly impossible to reject the blandishments of high technology although that seduction must be paid for by a heavy investment of scarce money and even scarcer manpower. I should not enter into psychological and financial reasons for this except to comment that the fine print of heavy loans associated with high technology transfer too often entrains the purchase of unwanted or unnecessary products. Berrick Saul had it that: 'One of the most successful mechanisms of technology transfer has always been piracy'; unhappily the list of crimes extends to rape. But the inevitable acceptance of high technology should not inhibit the parallel, much cheaper and, at least in the medium term, much more valuable introduction of appropriate technologies that can significantly assist or even revolutionise indigenous agriculture, crafts and industries. It seems to me that this would fortify the cultural base of a country against the impact of the high technologies and increase the chance that those high technologies would themselves benefit and sustain local values rather than erode them. I see no conflict in the parallel study and implementation of high and appropriate technologies but I do hold strongly that both are of great importance and must be considered side by side.

This reinforces another conclusion of Topic 4, namely that it is essential that the countries concerned should specify their own needs for technological change with the help of, but emphatically not the unquestioning reliance upon, external advisers. In this respect it seems to me that too many governments turn too soon and too fully to foreign consultants, either by-passing advice available in their own universities or not eliciting that advice in respect of the appropriateness, in the national context, of the external recommendations.

I hope that I have not given the impression that Topic 4 regarded technological development as Bad; although one of our members did say that: 'War and technology are regarded as dirty things'.

Of course, much technological development betters mankind, although so far chiefly in the developed countries; the LDCs have benefited little to date. And, of course, there is so tremendously much good that technology can obviously bring; it cannot and should not be stopped, but we must recognize the dangers and, above all, learn to manage it, learn to manage change. This was perhaps the most important conclusion of Topic 4.

There was agreement that universities should study change itself so as to analyse the likely social and cultural impact of new technology and that this was the more important for transferred technologies that had arisen in response to the needs or demands of one cultural milieu and were being transplanted into another. University training should be more oriented towards change and its management for the future. It was indeed argued that the best university education now to be given was not that of today's specialisms, that would be obsolete tomorrow, but rather education for change itself, the preparing of a flexible and responsive mind, well grounded in basic principles and other assorted eternal verities, but not narrowly committed to particular technical responses to particular technical problems. In this I must say that, as someone who has spent seventeen years in Cambridge and nineteen in Oxford, I found a wry reminder of the classical 'training of the mind' of yesteryear.

Somewhat more immediately: it was suggested that specialist practitioners in one field, say engineering, should be made aware of factors relevant for society in the application of their specialism. This was not to say that an engineering course should be lightly overlarded with half-a-dozen formal lectures on economics and half-a-dozen on sociology, which would be worse than useless; but rather that engineering students should be taught what it is that they do not know and the importance of those things for society in the application of their work.

I have laid stress on the 'rushing imperatives'. What might be the attitude of governments to the time scale of change? On the one hand governments have their own re-election as their dominant consideration and therefore are chiefly concerned with matters involving time scales commensurate with their elective periods; on the other hand, as David Nowlan reminded us, governments should be better able to take the long view than profit-dependent corporations that are disciplined by the rod of high and quick returns. The answer to my question is obviously linked, in any particular country, to the breadth of its political spectrum and to its political stability. A related question is the relationship of government to the universities in the process of change. It seems that, everywhere, when times are good money flows freely from government to universities and that when times are bad governments reduce the funding of their universities but simultaneously demand that the universities combat the economic crisis. Walter Kamba's thoughtful contribution was helpful to us here. There is an incommensurability of time scales. Governments and universities are trying to do different things and to that degree there is no conflict between them, but in most countries all but a tiny part of the cost of the universities is borne by government which naturally wants to call the tune and to specify the time signature of that tune. But it is difficult to tootle a hornpipe upon a tuba: governments usually fail to appreciate the processes and possibilities that the intellectual and cultural mechanisms of universities must represent. Central planning never works unless those to be affected by that planning are involved in its formulation; this does not happen nearly enough in the relationship between governments and universities. Topic 4 agreed that ACU-like meetings could profitably include a few (carefully) invited politicians.

I have mentioned the LDCs which, with the newly industrializing countries (NICs), in our Commonwealth context we might define collectively as our 'post Statute of Westminster' members. They cover a tremendous, a wonderful, range of cultures but for us at this Congress they have in common that they are at the receiving end of technological change just as centuries ago they were, not always very happily, at the receiving end of political change. And there are dangers today as then.

You will recall Adam Smith's 'Invisible Hand' that providentially brought about a reciprocity between the motive of private gain and the end of public good. This has never seemed to work very well in international affairs and indeed Adam Smith himself in the context of the colonialism of his day wrote: 'The savage injustice of the Europeans rendered an event, which ought to have been beneficial to all, ruinous and destructive to several of those unfortunate countries'. From time to time in Topic 4 I felt that there was danger of this happening again today, not in the crude form of neo-colonialism, despite muted dark references to the alleged wickednesses of the multi-nationals, but in the more insidious and ultimately more destructive sense of an incompatibility between modern technology, no matter how sensitively transferred and appropriately adapted, and precious ways of life. There is little point in espousing a technology that gives you the leisure to enjoy a way of life that that technology has destroyed. I do not fully share this pessimism but we must not ignore it. At our Vancouver Congress in 1978 I entered a plea for the more conscious preservation by our universities of the living cultures of their countries. I would re-enter that plea today and extend it to lay upon our universities the responsibility for a deep study of the consequences for our cultures, our most wonderfully-varied cultures, of their being overlayed by modern technology; it is an overlay that could suffocate.

It was interesting that in our dozen hours of discussion we

scarcely mentioned the technology whose development we deplore and whose terrible swift transfer we most fearfully dread: that of defence. In the context of this week such discussion would, of course, have been inappropriate but the tremendous investment of such money and effort by almost all countries, including those beyond the Statute of Westminster, must form a back-drop to any meeting such as ours. Let us remember that even the US Secretary of Defence after whom one of the world's most powerful engines of destruction is named testified that: 'It is infinitely cheaper to defend ourselves by economic means'.

As is evident, Topic 4 produced no consensus as to any universal role or roles that universities should play in the machinery of technical innovation leading to the appearance in the market place, fields or factories of new determinants to be reckoned with in our changing world. Those important roles must depend on the country concerned and appear, as at present perceived, to differ significantly not just between developed and developing countries but from one country of a given economic complexion to another of that same complexion in a way that has no clear rationale and that must be due to social, cultural, political and psychological factors. But whatever the differences in national perceptions and practices, there was universal agreement as to the correlation between education, at all levels, and economic and social development; between education and the enhancement of the quality of life in a more equal and a juster world.

So whatever our differences of condition and perspective we would all endorse H. G. Wells' dictum that: 'Human history becomes more and more a race between education and catastrophe'.

Group Discussions

TOPIC 5

CONTINUING EDUCATION

Co-ordinating Chairman: Dr. J. H. HORLOCK
Vice-Chancellor of the Open University (UK)

Chief Rapporteur: Mr. K. E. KITCHEN
Registrar of the University of Manchester

For index to names, see p. 427

Sub-Topic 5(a)

REQUIREMENTS OF MODERN INDUSTRIAL SOCIETY

Chairman: Dr. J. H. HORLOCK
Vice-Chancellor of the Open University (UK)

Rapporteur: Mr. I. T. SNOWDON
Registrar of the University of Waikato

Monday, 15 August

Sir GEOFFREY ALLEN (*Director of Research and Engineering Division, Unilever plc*):

1. The main characteristic associated with the modern industrial society is the speed of change:—

(i) For scientists and engineers the subject matter and the skills they learn in their undergraduate courses rapidly become obsolete. Continual practice of their discipline is the only way to remain completely up to date. It is worth remembering, however, that the basic principles, the laws of nature, etc., do not change; and the methodology of problem-solving always remains a valuable asset.

(ii) For managers the general skills do not change, but the tools (for example, information technology) and to some extent the social and industrial attitudes, are changing at a rate hitherto unknown. So much so that in an industrial society familiar with the: 'need to teach technologists management skills' there may well be a less familiar: 'need to teach non-technical managers about technology'.

(iii) For any candidate for a professional or skilled-craftsman post who has had a vocational tertiary education, the window within which he can obtain a first job may well be diminishing.

2. At its most basic, the one requirement of a tertiary education needed to keep its beneficiary in good stead in modern industry is that it should instill an awareness and a facility for continual learning. Indeed it is very desirable that this facility for continual learning becomes an integral part of secondary education.

When the student leaves college, polytechnic or university to take his first post he is likely nowadays to be faced with an induction course. This may vary from a day to a year and range from the most general to particular aspects of the work.

3. Most large companies now have induction courses for new employees which will give a flavour of the company culture, its range of business activities and its expectations from newcomers. In some cases training in techniques specific to the company may be given.

In the UK some companies are beginning to pay more attention to more prolonged structured induction courses which may amount to a postgraduate course in its own right. It may, for example, contain elements directly related to the requirements of professional institutions, for example the engineering institutions. In my own company, which has central research and engineering activities providing development projects and technology for the 500 operating companies which are Unilever, we are trying to devise a two- to three-year planned graduate career development for newly recruited engineers and some scientists. Each young engineer would have a carefully planned mix of work in the centre and also in a company. Short courses will probably be used to increase his stock of knowledge. We are still forming the programme.

The Science and Engineering Research Council (SERC) already has several 'integrated graduate development' schemes in action. These allow the new graduate to do roughly the equivalent of a master's degree during the first two or three years of his career with a firm. The firm forms a partnership with a nearby university or college from which the part-time teaching can be given. The job done by the graduate in his firm usually becomes his 'postgraduate project'. There is clearly considerable scope for this kind of activity and the experience gained by the academies taking part should have considerable impact on future academic curricula.

When one tries to plan comprehensive induction courses of this kind for new recruits to industry, several things become apparent:

(*a*) the student often takes more readily to the scheme than do the tutors;

(*b*) many recruits, particularly those going along a technical management path such as production, want to have early real responsibility and not continue with too many courses;

(*c*) the need to find industrial managers who are competent and sufficiently patient to be tutors is paramount, but often a considerable difficulty;

(*d*) the academic has to be prepared to be flexible in the presentation of material and the ordering of the curriculum to

meet the company objectives and careful dialogue is needed to
establish the course content.
However, difficult though it may be to initiate these courses, the
evidence is that they are taking off with reasonable satisfaction.

4. Continuing education for scientists and engineers who have
already had some considerable time in industry is much discussed.
We all see the need but we all experience considerable difficulties.
Others will dwell on this at length. I will make a few observations
of my own experience in the UK based on the SERC and the
Open University.

The essential problem is to provide courses which up-date
technologists whilst they carry on with their job. The Open University has achieved international acclaim with its undergraduate
courses. So why not some postgraduate courses, say, of one
or two years' duration, which would also allow in self-taught
technologists of an adequate standard?

It sounds simple, and I thought in 1981 I had laid the foundations
of such courses sponsored by SERC with the Open University. It
has taken a great deal of time to agree on subjects, *e.g.* computer
technology, production engineering, and even longer on the course
content—the latter because the spread of student experience is
much wider than for internal university courses. The methods of
distance learning may well have a difficult mix. Tutors from the
companies to which the student belongs would clearly strengthen
the scheme. Finally a network of regional colleges and universities
would be needed to provide some of the tuition at these advanced
levels. It is not too difficult to see that the role of the Open
University might be to devise the course structure, provide the
material by using national experts and then orchestrating the
network of regional polytechnics and university departments. Of
course this might result in some lack of enthusiasm from conventional institutions, and may indeed be one aspect of the difficulty
of setting up such a course. I remain convinced not only that such
courses are feasible but that they will be extremely valuable.

5. In sections 3 and 4 we have talked about courses or development schemes for science and engineering graduates. It is equally
important that managers with non-technical backgrounds have an
awareness of the problems of managing technology-based firms
and indeed an awareness of modern technology. So far little
attention has been paid to this problem. The Industry, Technology
and Engineering Committee of the Royal Society have taken note
of this problem and have discussed it with several business schools
in academe—so far without any real progress. However, it appears
that by co-operation with other groups in the UK this may

get under way. Certainly some members of the newly-formed Engineering Council see this particular need.

I am not aware of any major project of this kind. Perhaps the best that one can do is to suggest that the Open University history of science project be asked to extrapolate further forward and run courses on the direction of future science and technology!

6. Conventional universities and polytechnics acting in their current styles have not been successful in providing *all* the post-university needs for modern graduates in a modern industrial society; nor should this be a first priority. However, Open University-type supplementation *acting in concert* with conventional institutions could provide, on a national scale, much of the shortfall.

Professor T. A. BRZUSTOWSKI (*Vice-President, Academic, University of Waterloo*):

Introduction

These remarks deal with new requirements for continuing education at the university level in the modern industrial society of the late twentieth century. They are limited to the continuing education, as distinct from postgraduate education, of those who already have university degrees.* More narrowly still, they are confined to the situation as it is emerging in the developed countries.

The principal point to be made is that continuing education is rapidly evolving from a marginal activity of the conventional universities to one of their principal responsibilities. The pressure for this evolution comes from the widespread and rapid change in many aspects of society, but particularly from the explosive growth of information and the technologies available for processing it. This evolution will probably require many structural changes within the universities, with some effects which could prove to be problems and others which might turn out to be of benefit.

---

*For present purposes, the distinction will rest on the fact that this kind of continuing education does not lead to the award of advanced degrees.

The Pressure of Change

It is becoming conventional wisdom that the modern industrial society is undergoing rapid and fundamental change. Much has been written, by scholars and popular writers alike, about the 'post-industrial society', or the 'information society', or even the 'knowledge society' into which industrial society is being transformed. Many contend, in fact, that the transformation is complete, and only the recognition of it is lagging.

The universities deal in knowledge, and their graduates are involved in generating it, transmitting it, and putting it to use. The number of workers who process information is increasing, while the number of those who work with material goods is steadily declining. That trend is undoubtedly more pronounced among university graduates than for the population at large. Moreover it is in the area of information that technology is changing most rapidly. This compounding creates a special pressure for change in the ways that the universities discharge their twin responsibilities of teaching and research—a pressure not just for change, but for accelerating change.

There is already plenty of evidence of accelerating change in university teaching. Handbooks and textbooks now often require revision after one printing, not after several, and more and more courses in the technical areas evolve so fast that the delay in producing textbooks renders them obsolete. University faculty in engineering, mathematics and science routinely incorporate in undergraduate courses subject matter which they themselves encountered only in postgraduate studies, or in the course of their subsequent scholarly work. Curricula in the social sciences and the humanities increasingly include introductory courses which teach computer skills, and increasingly take such skills for granted in advanced courses—even in some of the traditional disciplines. Computers are used as a tool of the scholar—as in the preparation of concordances, and as the medium for original scholarship—as in the writing of software for interactive language instruction.

The people in universities are also changing. Students entering the universities from the high schools in successive years exhibit a growing familiarity with computers, and an increasing sophistication in putting them to use in the university. Faculty members who still treat computers as big remote machines for solving equations in research now must catch up to students who treat them as familiar everyday tools for creating files, producing graphical displays, solving coursework assignments, printing their essays, and playing games which require the hand-eye co-ordination of the young. Faculty members who continue to have no first-hand

325

familiarity with computers find themselves increasingly isolated among students and colleagues who use words which sound like English, but speak another language.

At the administrative level this widespread and accelerating change exerts an enormous and continuing pressure on university budgets to buy new equipment for research and teaching, and particularly new computers and communication links. This equipment is needed not just to continue traditional activities more effectively, but also to support worthwhile new academic activities which the new information technology has made feasible.

It would be tempting at this point to leap to the rosy conclusion that this is 'the age of the university', that the university is 'the institution whose time has come', that modern information technology will at last make it possible to develop and teach programmes which will provide university students with all the modern knowledge they need to pursue modern careers in the modern industrial society. In fact a very different conclusion seems much more realistic. Universities have traditionally claimed that the ability to continue learning independently and the commitment to a life-long process of education are the attributes of successful university graduates. For these people a university education provides both the motivation and the tools for acquiring new knowledge. The information technology available to the modern industrial society has not rendered that motivation misguided, nor the tools redundant. On the contrary the modern university graduate must, in addition, have the ability to learn how to use new tools for learning.

In terms of a mathematical metaphor, the universities and their graduates must be concerned not just with knowledge, and its first derivative with respect to time, but also with its second derivative. Even then the first three terms of this time series will suffice only for shorter and shorter time spans as the accumulation of knowledge accelerates.

The Case for a New Form of Continuing Education

Traditionally university curricula have incorporated new knowledge into course materials. Since the curriculum was to be of a fixed duration, the growing body of knowledge had to be condensed by abstraction. In many disciplines detailed examples were provided to explain the most recent advances. The graduates of such curricula obtained up-to-date knowledge of relatively broad fields of study.

326

However, it seems that the universities can no longer keep up to the rate at which new information is being generated. The assimilation of new knowledge and the development of new paradigms, which embrace the new and the old and make both accessible to students, continues to be a slow process, enhanced relatively little by the advances in information technology. As a result it seems that university graduates of the future might not be exposed to knowledge which is relatively either as broad or as current as might have been the case in the past. Indeed there may be great pressure to focus the fields to study far more narrowly in order to keep them current.

Traditionally the universities provided their graduates with the basis for continued learning by 'stressing the fundamentals'. Today it is no longer clear which fundamentals are to be given emphasis. For example, much of today's industrial and business activity involves a technology (microelectronics) which is less than two decades old and is based on science which is only slightly older than that. Moreover it is increasingly likely that much of the knowledge which will be used by this year's university graduates for the rest of their lives doesn't even exist today. No amount of curriculum development can address that problem.

Demographic and sociological considerations are also affecting university education. The populations of most developed nations are getting older, and many nations are moving to eliminate the mandatory retirement age. This means that careers will be longer, with university graduates continuing to be active for nearly half a century after the completion of the baccalaureate. In addition it appears that at least the North Americans are now expecting to move more frequently from one job to another. Taken together these trends suggest that the population of university graduates will experience a much larger number of career changes than has been traditional. Furthermore those are the people whose jobs largely involve the processing of information, bringing them into contact with the most rapidly advancing of all technologies. This means that university graduates will have to acquire new knowledge increasingly frequently during their working lives.

All these factors combine to define an emerging need for a new form of continuing education in the universities.

The New Form

For all of the reasons discussed above the universities should consider it their responsibility to add programmes of a new form to their existing activities in continuing education. Let them be called 'updating' programmes.

These new programmes should serve to update the knowledge of university graduates in relation to the changes in their careers.* They will have to be intensive, transmitting a large amount of knowledge during relatively short periods of instruction.† They will have to be accessible in content, approach and format at various stages in the working life of a university graduate. And they will have to be very much up to date.

Some precedents already exist. The department of electrical engineering at the Massachusetts Institute of Technology announced last year that it was assuming the responsibility for developing such a programme for its own graduates.‡ The associate student programme of the Open University also seems to be an updating programme in the present sense. It is probably not a wild exaggeration to suggest that the updating programmes could grow to become the most important responsibility of the universities in the area of continuing education.

The development of these programmes of periodic updating of the education of university graduates presents many challenges. The pedagogical challenges alone are formidable. The student population will be very different from the undergraduate population, and far less homogeneous in age and experience. By and large they will be successful individuals, economically secure, motivated to learn but discriminating and demanding at the same time. Some will be interested only in specialized knowledge on topics they have identified, but others will be seeking new knowledge in a broader context. Many of these students will be older than the professors who teach them, and will be in positions of authority in their organisations. Coming from business and industry, where the balance between form and content in the presentation of technical information is generally very different from that in the universities, they will be very sensitive to the quality of the communications in the course. They will be prepared to pay the full cost of their education, but they will demand 'a quality product'.

The selection of faculty members for such programmes will be a difficult task. The ideal candidates will be active scholars who have earned recognition as authorities in their disciplines, are effective teachers and communicators, and have sufficient breadth

---

*Note that continuing education for updating the knowledge required to pursue *the same* career is not new. Medical doctors have had such programmes for a long time. However there are few university programmes even of this type.

†In contrast, for example, to the more leisurely pattern of studying part-time for several years in order to obtain an MBA which is related to a graduate mid-career shift from technical responsibilities to management.

‡Admittedly it is not altogether clear what balance will be struck in that programme between the medical model and the present definition of updating.

of knowledge to see their own field in a broad context and be aware of both its importance and its limitations. Such people are already very busy and much in demand. It is unlikely that they could assume a demanding role in continuing education in addition to their normal duties. For the faculty involved in it, the new form of continuing education might have to become a major commitment of time, probably at the expense of regular on-campus teaching. The effect of such trade-offs on the university could be far-reaching.

A greater challenge still will be the development of the curriculum. It is most likely that existing courses from the regular undergraduate or postgraduate degree programmes would not be appropriate for the purposes of the proposed approach to continuing education. As has already been pointed out, the students in this programme will be people with post-university experience in business, industry or government. They would have learned that knowledge required to solve real problems transcends the boundaries of academic disciplines, and they would not likely be ready to accept a rigid disciplinary structure of any programme of continuing education which claims as its purpose the updating of knowledge they need to pursue their careers. Therefore it will likely turn out that the new multi-disciplinary courses which integrate knowledge from several disciplines will be required, in addition to a rich menu of narrowly-focused specialist courses which have a practical emphasis. The preparation and teaching of such multi-disciplinary courses by teams of professors from a variety of departments may become an essential feature of continuing education.

The universities might be wise to seek counsel in this process from outside organisations, particularly the professional associations and the technical societies. Each university's own alumni association might play an important role in the development of updating programmes of continuing education, all the more if the university identifies a particular responsiblity to its own alumni in all forms of continuing education.

The Impact on the University

It is entirely conceivable that by the turn of the century there might be some universities (still called conventional) in which the effort is divided equally among three responsibilities: undergraduate education, research and postgraduate education, and continuing education.

Consider one such university—the young but well-known U of X—in greater detail. U of X derives one-third of its income from fees for continuing education. The fees are high, and cover all direct and indirect costs attributable to continuing education. About half of the students in continuing education are enrolled in updating programmes, and more than half of them are alumni of U of X.

The alumni association of U of X is a vigorous organisation, deeply involved in many university activities, including the development and monitoring of programmes in continuing education. Alumni of U of X describe their relationship with their alma mater metaphorically, using terms such as 'maintenance', 'check-up', and 'recall' reminiscent of the relationship between the purchaser of an automobile and its manufacturer. Prominent alumni readily lobby and campaign on behalf of the university, and annual alumni giving has grown by two orders of magnitude since the 1980s.

The administration of U of X has grown much more complicated since the days when most of its budget came from government grants. Many faculty positions are supported entirely from research grants and contracts and from tuition fees in the continuing education programmes. Until recently these funds had been called 'soft money', but with the recent sharp decline in the population of age 20 and less, together with the increasingly large swings in the policies of successive governments which have been unable to come to terms with the sudden demographic shifts, it is the grant portion of income which is beginning to be thought of as soft. Nevertheless many academics are grumbling that the marketing of continuing education is exerting excessive influence on plans and decisions in the university.

Scheduling is becoming a problem. The various demands of the continuing education programmes create constraints on the scheduling of lectures and teaching tasks in the regular programmes. The U of X is managing to reconcile the various needs only by grouping more of the decreasing number of undergraduates into classes in which the students follow essentially fixed programmes. Nevertheless the registrar devotes a great effort to developing optimal scheduling algorithms.

The academic departments, once the seats of distributed power in the U of X—since they represented administrative and budget centres, academic programmes, disciplines, and physical facilities all in one organisational unit—are now less influential. The multidisciplinary programmes in continuing education have created interdepartmental flows and groupings. Moreover status and rewards for faculty members are now much more closely related to the goals of U of X than they are to external recognition by the disciplines.

Needless to say, U of X at the turn of the century differs in many ways from the universities of today. The picture is not altogether rosy; not all of the differences are obvious improvements which benefit the university, but some are. The role of continuing education in determining the course of the university is large and important, particularly in its new form, the updating programmes.

Some will call this picture of a changed university exaggerated and unrealistic, and insist that nothing more profound will occur than some slight growth in the existing programmes of continuing education, and the application of some new communication technologies in the existing activities in distance teaching. Perhaps. But there are so many signs of change in the modern industrial society, and so many qualitative trends already unmistakeable, that it is much more probable that the view of a placid evolution of the universities, an evolution limited to minor quantitative changes, is the one which will turn out to be fanciful.

DISCUSSION

Discussion revolved around the two main themes of this session:—

(*a*) the needs of industry and commerce for more and better continuing education for scientists, technologists and managers;

(*b*) the pressures on universities to meet these needs and the effects on traditional university activities and organisation of responding to these pressures.

In introducing his paper Sir Geoffrey Allen (Unilever) drew on his own experience, first as a university teacher, then as chairman of the Science and Engineering Research Council, and most recently as Director of Research for Unilever. During these transitions he had become very much aware of the increasing need for continuing education in industry, commerce and the professions. The accelerating pace of change and the greater complexity of both research and management had served to emphasise two needs: (*a*) for scientist and technologist to have frequent updating, and (*b*) for managers to have a better broad understanding of technology and for scientists to learn more about management skills.

There were no dissenting voices on the view that the accelerating rate of technological innovation led to a need for frequent updating of what had been learned as part of full-time university education. Universities could and should play a major role in specialist topping-up of this kind and indeed had now gained considerable experience in this activity. In the view of many present, however, there was considerable scope for further expansion of this activity. The group expressed great interest in the recent public commitment of the department of electrical engineering at the Massachusetts Institute of Technology to take responsibility for future updating of all its graduates. Some members admired this as a brave statement but others drew attention to the implications of such a commitment in terms of resources.

It was pointed out that in the United Kingdom specialist updating activity was expected to be self-financing. This led to a wider discussion in which many expressed the view that such activity should increasingly be a partnership between universities and industry both in respect of assessing teaching needs and fulfilling them. Sir Geoffrey Allen commented that he believed senior managers in industry were now taking specialist updating much more seriously and that this provided universities with a challenge which they should meet. Several speakers emphasised the need to involve professional associations in all aspects of the updating process.

Discussions turned to Sir Geoffrey Allen's second major theme—that of cross-fertilisation of understanding between scientists and engineers on the one hand and the many managers who had been trained in the humanities on the other. Most speakers accepted that meeting this need was important but that attitudes developed by students in both school and university frequently made the task a difficult one. Professor Brzustowski referred to experiences at his own university where engineering students who took courses in the humanities generally performed well but where arts students showed little desire to take courses in technology, not even preliminary courses in the principles of design. Several speakers commented that the inhibitions of arts students went back into their previous schooling and some suggested that early specialisation was to blame. Sir Geoffrey Allen took the view that it was largely a pedagogic problem in that there were too few technologists capable of teaching technology to students with insufficient background in the basic principles.

This type of cross-fertilisation of knowledge was described by some contributors as 'awareness' education. Questions were asked about whether universities really had a role to play in this form of continuing education. The general conclusion was that a wide variety of agencies, including commercial organisations, professional associations and other branches of higher education could all contribute. Universities should be selective in what they undertook in this field. Many believed that 'distance education' had a role to play and that organisations such as the United Kingdom's Open University were in a good position to provide high quality courses of this kind.

The group had noted Professor Brzustowski's views on the likely effects on conventional universities of the increasing demand for continuing education. He foresaw the possibility that by the turn of the century some universities would have three roughly equal activities: (a) undergraduate education; (b) postgraduate education and research; (c) continuing education.

A number of speakers were of the opinion that there would be widespread resistance from existing staff to any sudden or substantial change in this direction. Staff already felt under heavy pressure and many still believed that some aspects of continuing education were not a proper function for universities. Some saw this reluctance as a modern phenomenon and drew attention to the proud history which many universities had of providing forms of continuing education in their formative years. It was thought that external pressures on universities to expand their continuing education activities would continue to grow in the rest of the decade but that unless accompanied by extra resources and a changed system of rewards they could well lead to internal dissension and division. Existing university staff would themselves need some up-dating and re-training if they were to meet this new teaching challenge effectively. In particular it was suggested that periodic second-ment to industry was highly desirable for those teachers who would be heavily involved in continuing education for scientists, technologists and managers.

In conclusion the Chairman thanked the speakers for raising many interesting points which he was sure would be followed through in later sessions of the Congress.

Sub-Topic 5(b)

REQUIREMENTS OF DEVELOPING COUNTRIES

Chairman: Dr. J. H. HORLOCK

Vice-Chancellor of the Open University (UK)

Rapporteur: Mr. C. E. JACKMAN

Registrar of the University of the West Indies

Tuesday, 16 August

Professor G. J. AFOLABI OJO (*Vice-Chancellor, National Open University, Nigeria*):

Background to Continuing Education

In many parts of the developing countries facilities for formal education were, until recently, specifically designed for youths of the school-going age. Admission to the schools was exclusively reserved for non-adults. Before the time when precise ages of children were recorded, any child seeking admission was made, in parts of southern Nigeria, to put his hand over his head to touch the ear on the other side of the head. If the other ear could be reached in that rule-of-thumb age determination, then he was considered old enough to enter the first year of the primary school. At first only children who were not of proven assistance in domestic or farming chores were 'dashed out' to the schools. The hard-working children were scrupulously tied to the apron-strings of their parents or relatives to learn the profession or trade of their mentors with a view to perpetuating the name and status of their respective families.

Throughout the first few decades of contact with formal education, little or no facilities were provided for the formal education of adults who were beyond the school-going age, the terminal end of which was dependent on, among other things, the degree of educational awareness of the adults, the occupations in which they were currently engaged, and the potential non-traditional jobs available for them to aspire towards. For instance the early missionaries, who were anxious to raise converts for the church, made it a point of duty to encourage adults interested in their proselytization endeavours to learn to read and sometimes write in the evening hours. Colonial administrative officers were similarly interested in equipping clerical assistants of various grades with the type of education that would enable them to perform. Details of such early attempts at what may be described as continuing education in Nigeria have been succinctly articulated in a wide range of literature on the subject (Michael Omolewa, (*a*) 1981 *Adult Education Practice in Nigeria* (Evans Brothers Ibadan); (*b*) 1982, 'Historical Antecedents of Distance Education in Nigeria', in *Adult Education in Nigeria,* The Journal of the Nigerian National Council for Adult Education, vol. 7, Dec. 1982).

Worth emphasizing in the various accounts is that by 1929 a Nigerian had used the distantly-based facilities of informal education to obtain an external degree of the University of London, and the number of such Nigerians reaching what may be described as the apex of continuing education (in terms of the degree qualifications acquired) went up as the years rolled by. The Nigerian story is virtually paralleled in English-speaking West African countries and other territories of British colonial contacts.

Another point worth underscoring is that in most of these developing countries continuing education, elastically defined, continues to be highly regarded as a desirable aspect of the educational developmental process. At successive stages of the process the emphasis of continuing education has shifted from an unsystematized and haphazard promotion of literacy to what may be described as formalized adult education sustained especially by a number of educational institutions set up to foster, in the main, the educational interests of the youths from primary through secondary to tertiary educational levels, and, more recently, to the early stages of the provision of facilities for life-long education. The trends of the shifts of emphasis given to continuing education are well documented, in the case of Nigeria, in the successive national policies on education, the most recent of which, dated 1977, crisply enunciated the commitment of the nation to continuing education as follows: 'the Federal Government shall undertake to make life-long education the basis for the nation's educational policies' (Federal Government of Nigeria, 1977, *National Policy on Education*, page 7, section 2). With this unambiguous resolve on the part of the federal government, it can be safely concluded that continuing education has come or is already coming to stay. This general statement is fairly applicable to most developing countries, albeit at varying degrees of certitude.

Trends in Technological Innovation for Continuing Education

In most developing countries the initial stages of continuing education were bereft of any technological backup. Not only in the vast field of education, both formal and informal, but also in the various sectors of the economies, technological innovation was conspicuously absent in the sense that erstwhile traditional technologies held sway and resiliently resisted change. The earliest continuing education classes or programmes were the cut-and-dried informal versions of formal education rendered in the regular educational institutions.

It was not too long after the initial attempts of establishing continuing education that it became generally recognized that the use of simple audio-visual aids was a booster to securing the interests of adults for continuing educational programmes. Especially in the urban areas, apart from using pictures and photographs as illustrative materials, slide projectors and movie-projectors were introduced to bolster up the programmes. Where practicable the rural areas benefited from this category of simple audio-visual techniques when mobile cinema programmes were run. The enlightenment unit of the ministries of information and social welfare of the various countries featured prominently in extending the use of basic technological innovations, especially for purposes of political education and also for developmental programmes in general. More often than not the use of such technological innovations has been occasional, indeed a flash-in-the-pan experience for the adults, and not a feature integrated with their educational exposure. Worse still, most educationists of the time acted as if they reckoned that only the lower levels of educational endeavour required audio-visual support, and that the tertiary level in some subjects (for instance commerce, economics and history) could be learnt or taught without audio-visual resources. As such, the concern for promoting continuing education was not for most of the early times impregnated with a desire for technological linkages, a situation which could hardly have been different in view of the prevailing technological inadequacies then.

Over the years some positive changes were noticeable as each additional input of technological innovation has meant a leap forward in fostering continuing education at many levels. In many parts of Nigeria the first item of major technological innovation for continuing education was the wireless radio. Its spread through the country was gradual but steady: at first in a leap-frog style of diffusion from the national capital to the regional headquarters and next to the provincial or divisional headquarters. At the next phase of expansion it spread to almost all the rural areas where only those who could pay the monthly 're-diffusion fees' took advantage of the innovation, mainly for entertainment and information and less so for education. Battery-operated radios followed closely in the trail of the wireless radio while those dependent on electricity supply were confined until recently to the urban areas. By and large the radio technological innovation for educational programmes has been limited to a few pockets of advantage in both urban and rural areas. Till now not every one or household can afford to own and operate radio sets. Furthermore the value of radio technology for educational programmes has not been fully exploited to reach the rural areas where more than 80% of the population reside, especially because centralized broadcasting which is currently in vogue is not normally designed to get to the vast majority of rural inhabitants in dispersed locations. For further details on the current limitations of educational broadcasting in Nigeria refer to A. A. Moemeka, 1983, *Broadcasting as Tool for Rural Education* (ABU Press Ltd, Zaria).

Recent Reinforcement of Technological Inputs in Continuing Education

As continuing education becomes more established at many levels it has also become increasingly obvious that it has to depend on multi-media resources for the transmission of knowledge, including correspondence, broadcasting, audio-visual aids such as sound and video cassette playbacks, home experiment kits, packaged programmes, and face-to-face occasional teaching. As many of these as are available in any particular teaching and/or learning situation may be employed in a complementary rather than substitutive or repetitive way. It goes without saying that the use of these multi-media techniques has a reinforcing effect on teaching and learning, and that their use in appropriate mix, depending on the particular situation, is most desirable. Unfortunately this is a desire easier expressed than implemented in many developing countries because of the numerous inbuilt constraints to the use of such resources, especially those which require technological support systems.

Indeed it was primarily the fear that the technological infrastructural facilities in present-day Nigeria might be inadequate to sustain an open university system in the country that was most frequently articulated by the senate of the National Assembly in stepping down the Bill for establishing the institution for eighteen months. Some of the senators argued that a so-called 'university of the air' will be virtually grounded by irregular power supply from the National Electric Power Authority, by unreliability and slowness of handling mails by the Posts and Telegraphs, by the inadequacies of the Nigerian Television Authority (NTA) and the Federal Radio Corporation of Nigeria (FRCN), and by the sheer fact that nothing technological (telephone, transport, computer, etc) works effectively for most of the time in Nigeria.

Admittedly anyone familiar with the realities of the technological situation of Nigeria cannot lightly dismiss these reservations. All that could be upheld in the defence put up by the planning committee on the Open University of Nigeria was that the institution was going to be a special brand of open university system closely tailored to the technological circumstances and realities of Nigeria. The committee stressed that, until such time as the efficiency of the public services was improved, the Open University would depend mainly on correspondence materials; it would develop its own courier service for the distribution of printed materials and the collection of assignments; it would install adequate stand-by independent electricity generating capacity at its headquarters, regional offices and local study centres where audio and video tapes of lectures would be made available to students; and it would in time develop its own independent capability in the broadcasting and telecasting fields.

Certainly the planning committee has expressed many pious hopes which can be better and more realistically assessed in the years ahead. As of now, the present technological situation of Nigeria eloquently illustrates the incontrovertible point that continuing education in the country, especially as from university level onwards, stands in need of the injection of up-to-date and modern technological resources that will guarantee efficient and maximum output. Until such a change takes place, it must be assumed that the type of continuing education that can be fostered must be related to the existing relatively low technological level of the country. The same understanding is applicable to developing countries at similar levels of technological development. In this context it must be mentioned that many existing open university systems in the developing countries, for instance Allama Iqbal University in Pakistan, have adopted this stance and have been making worthwhile and meaningful contributions in continuing education.

Technological Challenges Ahead of Continuing Education in Developing Countries

Every traditional university institution in the developing countries can be assumed to be aware of its responsibilities in respect of continuing education. The various records of efforts they have made to reach beyond their campuses speak glowingly of their concern for continuing education. Some have laid on special extra-mural programmes in administration, law and management on a part-time basis for adult learners. Others have provided evening courses (intra-mural) for workers who can afford to come to the institutions to study part-time. There are also many varieties of extension services which enable the institutions to reach out to workers who cannot pursue their studies full-time. In short, the challenges for sustaining continuing education are being acknowledged and responded to by most institutions within the limits of their resources. The variegated picture for the West African English-speaking countries was vividly painted in early October 1982 during a West African Conference on University Outreach, co-sponsored by the University of Ibadan and the State University of New York, Empire State College.

Two major relevant points emanating from the conference deserve consideration here in order to highlight some requirements of developing countries in technological innovation in continuing education. First, it is becoming increasingly realized that alternative models of education which emphasize continuing education are desirable not only because of the current crises which grip traditional universities but also because of the increasing opportunities which abound for alternative models of education. Hence there are, of course, increasing pressures to technologize education, even to de-school or de-formalize education, and most particularly to emphasize life-long education through continuing education. Especially in the developing countries, the need to stress the desirability of education from cradle to grave so as to make it more relevant and functional cannot be over-emphasized. It seems that this objective can be more readily attained if technological innovation is made to permeate continuing education so as to, among other things, enhance its accessibility.

Secondly, there is need for outreach programmes, particularly in developing countries, if teaching and learning enterprises have to be maximally fruitful. In certain fields such as agriculture, medicine, technology and engineering, emphasis has to be not only on the practical dimensions but also on the frequent changes being brought into these fields through technological changes. Only

339

education with a continuing dimension which is actively responsive to technological innovation can make developing countries reap the benefit of these fields of learning. In particular, the West African outreach conference emphasized over and over the need for educational institutions in developing countries to turn attention to the fact that they have to engage in a herculean task to keep such institutions at a level of efficient operation by paving the way for technological innovation in continuing education.

Conclusion — Hope for More Technological Innovation in Continuing Education

Developing countries cannot afford to gloss over the technological constraints which could hamstring continuing education. Such constraints seem to be inbuilt aspects of developing countries. It is therefore necessary for concerted efforts to be made to identify these constraints and to find ways and means of countering them. In the process one of the worthwhile steps to take is the harnessing of suitable local technological resources so as to reduce as far as practicable dependence on the technological capital and set-up of developed countries which could pose intractable problems if imported or transferred. Special courses should be mounted in educational institutions of developing countries on the identification and utilization of local technological inputs. Hope for development can only be assured when this movement towards technological independence becomes a reality.

Ideally the universities in developing countries should not allow this challenge to pass them by. Universities have a unique role, in developing countries, to blaze the trail to integrate education with technology. The departments of educational technology in the universities must see themselves in a role much wider than being the users of technologies of other countries in solving their own national educational problems. They must rise up to engineer the ideal situation for blending local technology with education, taking into consideration the social and cultural milieu of developing countries. While the developing countries have an eye on the numerous developments in communication technology which have enriched continuing education in the developed parts of the world, they must be constantly aware of their own peculiarities which include a heavy proportion of rural inhabitants who cannot readily belong to the world system of modern educational technology without appropriate adaptations and modifications.

DISCUSSION

Professor Afolabi Ojo (National Open University, Nigeria) explained to his audience the context in which his paper had been written and dealt with the Nigerian experience that led to the planning of the National Open University of Nigeria which was now in the process of being established.

Professor Ojo said that the federal government of Nigeria had made clear its commitment to continuing education and that Nigeria was trying to move gradually towards informal systems of education since formal education in some instances (of which he gave examples) appeared to be divorced from the real world and to have little or no relevance to the customs and habits of Nigerians. Professor Ojo stated that the reaction in Nigeria to the idea of an open university or a university of the air had been unexpectedly violent because Nigerians felt that a system of education of this kind, dependent as it was on the use of technology, could not work in a country which was not yet ready for widespread technological innovation: but Professor Ojo pointed out that in the course of establishing distance teaching in Nigeria or any other developing country it was necessary to use technological devices which were compatible with the various infrastructural limitations of the country concerned, and that such devices must be simple, easy to maintain and easy to repair.

Professor R. N. Trivedi (Ranchi) indicated that continuing education in a developing country had to be looked at in a different light from continuing education in a developed and highly industrialised society. He said that education of this sort had two functions in a developing country:—

(i) it provided educational opportunities for persons who had not had the means or the opportunity to obtain a university education; and

(ii) by making educational opportunities available which were more flexible than the conventional university education, it freed universities from the task of trying to fit into a stereotyped pattern persons for whom conventional education was not suited.

Professor Trivedi warned that in making arrangements for the establishment of continuing education developing countries should not seek to rely exclusively on the models of developed countries, but should rather seek to devise special models; and that, since all developing countries could not be fitted into the same mould, these models should be flexible and should be so designed as to be capable of operating effectively in the particular local circumstances that obtained.

During the subsequent general discussion, the following points were made:—

(i) In developing countries there was frequently an expectation that the continuing education provided by universities should meet the needs of an exceedingly wide range of customers. In some countries where university education was regarded as something for the chosen few there was pressure on universities to provide 'education for the masses' and the concept of continuing education was seen partly in this context. This was often reflected by the view that universities should play an important part in basic literacy programmes. Such universities were also often under pressure to provide the more conventional continuing education services of professional updating and adult education at university level. Unless the universities' role were to be distorted it was important that continuing education tasks should be carried out by the most appropriate medium, including industry and commerce as well as other parts of the educational system.

(ii) Frequently continuing education was seen as an alternative to employment and even developed countries had to face the reality of people seeking to enter higher education primarily because they had failed to find employment. In developing countries this phenomenon often added to the difficulty of defining and developing the role of universities in continuing education.

(iii) Distance teaching was a most important aspect of continuing education and had a major role to play alongside and parallel with conventional teaching. However in establishing distance teaching many developing countries could not expect to use television and computers and other modern technological devices to the same extent as developed countries. The answer would often be concentration on simpler devices such as audio-tapes. Moreover the technology must not be allowed to dominate and must not exceed the infrastructure available in the country concerned.

(iv) There was general agreement that universities in developed countries could play a vital role in providing centres at which staff from developing countries could receive training for continuing education work.

(v) There was general agreement that the discussion on continuing education in developing countries had highlighted the need for the most careful analysis to identify in any society the specific needs and their relative priority, the most appropriate type of institutional provider and the most effective and feasible teaching methods.

Sub-Topic 5(c)

ROLE FOR DISTANCE EDUCATION

Chairman: Dr. R. H. PAUL
Vice-President, Learning Services, Athabasca University

Rapporteur: Mr. K. E. KITCHEN
Registrar of the University of Manchester

Tuesday, 16 August

Professor F. R. JEVONS (*Vice Chancellor, Deakin University*):

THE ROLE OF DISTANCE EDUCATION: TOWARDS PARITY OF ESTEEM

My Thesis

The role of distance education (DE) is being restricted by outdated attitudes towards it, not by students but by authorities. The thesis I want to nail to the church door, therefore, is that for mature students DE deserves parity of esteem with the traditional face-to-face mode. My Lutheran analogy is chosen not for its theological content, nor to commemorate the 500th anniversary of Martin Luther's birth, but for the historical parallel to a major reformation which arose within established orthodoxy, gave rise to many ramifications and involved disputations which seem more than a little esoteric to outsiders. The only indulgence I attack is that of assuming that the face-to-face mode is necessarily the best for all students in all circumstances. I hope that a thirty years war can be avoided but it looks as though it will be some decades before distance educators can follow their faith without any stigma of second-class status.

My view is that it is time people stopped asking which mode is better. That question is hopelessly oversimplified: it is like asking which is better, books or lectures. Some DE is good, some bad: just like the traditional mode. Airing prejudices about the intrinsic

343

superiority of one mode or the other is not as useful as trying to improve standards in both. Unfortunately educationally archaic views are still prevalent. For instance in Australia the Ralph report on management education (1982), which dealt essentially with master of business administration programmes, expressed the view that DE is not good enough for an MBA.

A Bewildering Nomenclature

A major difficulty is the variety of educational practices related to, or capable of being confused with, DE. This is reflected in a bewildering nomenclature. The confusions are not only terminological but also concern issues of substance.

External is still the official name in Australia but it is not loved in the fraternity, partly because it carries vibes of the old London external system which provides examinations but not teaching.

Correspondence is widely used but also disliked by many in the fraternity. Commercial correspondence colleges are a mixed bag; some are respectable but others are not. Also, modern DE systems are multi-media, though print remains the principal medium in most.

Open has a number of meanings, most of which have no necessary connection with DE.

Off-campus has the virtue of brevity but not of rigour and its popularity in Australia is not widely shared elsewhere.

Extramural means DE in New Zealand but elsewhere it has a broader meaning, like *extension*, which can but need not employ DE.

Intentionally or not, the implication often is that they are not taken as seriously as proper university courses. Similarly in one usage DE is taken to be a variety of *non-formal* education (Ansere, 1982). The view does exist in Australia that students choose DE merely for its convenience and that the choice reflects lower commitment. This rests on a conceptual confusion: commitment is not measured by the time spent travelling. If there were a good objective way to measure commitment I believe that, in my University at least, DE students would score better than traditional students. In completion and success rates they do as well if not better (Jevons, 1982).

Features of DE Systems

Against this confused background it is important to be clear what the essential features of a DE system are. The distinguishing feature is the separation of teacher from learner for much of the learning. Stripped to its bare essentials a DE system must have:—

(1) An institution providing learning materials. DE is not the same as private study.

(2) Media or communication technologies to link learner and teacher.

(3) Support services. The communication is two-way. Usually there is some opportunity for face-to-face contact, maybe compulsory but often not. Some students don't make use of such opportunities, maybe by choice but sometimes by necessity, and the ideology of DE in its pure form demands that they should have an equal chance of success. Counselling should be available, whether via media or face to face.

DE systems are evidently complex. They involve greater division of labour and are often called 'industrialised' (Peters, 1973).

The various media used by some institutions have been tabulated by Rumble and Keegan (1982). Print carries most of the educational content in most cases. In institutions which aim at the highest quality the printed material is prepared not by individuals but by course teams. It is not adequately described as 'lecture notes' because it uses devices such as intext questions and exercises to promote interaction of students with the text. Editorial and design input makes it not only more attractive but also more effective as learning material.

The Company They Keep

The tensions surrounding questions of definition and status are illustrated by the recent turbulent history of the way DE is organised internationally.

The International Institute for Distance Learning (IIDL) was formed in 1978 at the initiative of Lord Perry, then the Vice-Chancellor of the UK Open University, to bring together the small band of institutions, publicly financed, which teach exclusively or mainly by DE. It excluded commercial institutions. It also excluded a large number of institutions which have DE wings because it was felt that these wings are often small and not taken very seriously. Deakin University squeezed into the magic circle, but only just: even now, whether we have a preponderance of off-campus or on-campus students depends on whether you count heads or equivalent full-time students.

IIDL was seen as élitist and aroused intense antagonism. It voluntarily self-destructed at Vancouver in 1982 in the light of developments at the world conference on distance education there.

The International Council for Correspondence Education, after emotional debate, agreed to change its name to International Council for Distance Education. It is now felt to be more respectable, the influence of commercial institutions no longer being unduly great.

Nevertheless the fear remains among the most committed DE institutions that they will be judged by the company they keep and that the DE mode as such will suffer: with friends like that, who needs enemies?

A Comparative Approach

When the two modes are compared it is easy to forget the thousand ways in which traditional education is imperfect or can go wrong and that DE has advantages as well as disadvantages. Here are four which seem important to me as intrinsically educational advantages, quite apart from the flexibility of DE which eases access for adults.

(1) The student is freer to approach the ideal of the independent or autonomous or self-directed learner.

(2) The interface with employment is more intimate. DE shares this with part-time on-campus education but in the latter case the geographical constraint is even tighter than for full-time education.

(3) DE offers the opportunity of cumulative improvement in pedagogic quality. DE materials, especially print, have a permanent physical existence, unlike lectures, which disappear into thin air the moment after delivery. They are objective knowledge in Karl Popper's sense and subject to criticism and improvement through criticism (Popper, 1979). In my view a major challenge now facing DE is to make the most of that opportunity: to turn DE systems into *learning* learning systems. Lectures, by contrast, though conscientiously revised year by year, are not, I believe, better on average than they were thirty years ago.

(4) Related to the previous point is the staff development effect of work in course teams. Few who have worked seriously in a course team have escaped unscathed by new ideas and approaches, not only about the subject matter but also on presentation, pedagogy and assessment.

Criticisms of DE often focus on the need in some subjects for laboratory or studio work and on the lack of an affective or socialising element. True, many things cannot be done at a distance. Laboratories in study centres or home experiment kits are ways to ameliorate the difficulty of the dependence of experimental sciences on hardware. But there are also ways to turn the problem on its head. For instance, in the Deakin graduate diploma in computing the home micro-computers which are used partly as stand-alone instruments can also be linked via the telephone system to the big computer on the Deakin campus. Here the hardware provides its own answer to the tyranny of distance (for non-Australians I should explain that 'the tyranny of distance' is a well-known phrase describing a dominant factor in Australian history and the title of a book by the historian Geoffrey Blainey).

The importance of affective or socialising elements is not the same for mature students as for school-leavers. Many DE students prize highly the opportunity for contact with staff and other students which summer schools, weekend schools or tutorials give them; others feel no such need either for learning or for social purposes.

Cost Comparisons

DE has large infrastructure and course initiation costs but the marginal cost per student is lower, so above a certain number of students it is more cost effective. That number is certainly substantial, even if we take with a pinch of salt the estimate by Keegan and Rumble (1982) that it is in the range 9000–22,000.

Cost comparisons are fraught with conceptual difficulties because the cost structures of DE and traditional education are not only different but complex in each case. The outcome depends on what mix of activities and what levels of quality of materials and support services DE institutions choose to aim at. I therefore view with some alarm the frequent claims that DE is cheaper to provide. They are two-edged swords: fine for persuading governments to set up DE systems but not so good when the system is in place and has to be run on the cheap. They could set DE back on the road to parity of esteem.

National Policy

The question of costs leads me to the national-level issue of the best mode of provision. The basic alternatives are autonomous or mixed institutions, autonomous in this context meaning a DE institution operating in its own right as distinct from the DE wing of a conventional institution.

Keegan and Rumble (1982) list reasons for preferring autonomous institutions; they derive mainly from economies of scale, because there is usually a single such institution per country, and from the view that the didactic structure of DE, and therefore the

347

administrative structure needed to back it, differs radically from the traditional. As a matter of history there can be no doubt that the credit for the recent rise in the status of DE belongs to the autonomous institutions of the 1970s: the great public relations success of the UK Open University — so great that within a very few years some US educators were claiming it as a mark of distinction *not* to have visited it; the rapidity with which the Universidad Nacional de Educación a Distancia in Spain established itself; the theoretical underpinning provided largely by Otto Peters of the Fernuniversität in West Germany. However I doubt whether those institutions will maintain their monopoly or near monopoly positions in those countries in which they have it, if only because of their inability to cover enough subject areas. For instance, in the UK, Strathclyde is about to offer an MBA by DE.

Mixed institutions, on the other hand, usually lead to DE systems which are too fragmented. In New Zealand Massey, though mixed, has a qualified monopoly, but in Canada, by Keegan and Rumble's count, 20 universities have correspondence or DE departments; in India 23 universities have correspondence directorates; in France 18 out of 75 universities have centres de télé-enseignement universitaire; in East Germany 30 out of 54 universities offer degrees at a distance; and in the USA 64 independent study departments were affiliated in 1981 to the Independent Study Division of the National University Extension Association (Keegan and Rumble, 1982).

The inquiry on *Open Tertiary Education in Australia* (1975) found that the most controversial issue facing it was whether to create a new national institution completely dedicated to DE. Recognising the advantages, it nevertheless recommended against. There is substance in the reasons but they cannot in my view justify the 32 institutions, 12 universities and 20 colleges of advanced education, which in 1982 provided higher education by DE in Australia. The numbers come from yet another inquiry, that by Johnson (1983), which has reported so recently that it is too early to say what action, if any, will result from it. The national policy options considered by Johnson are:—

(1) The Commonwealth Tertiary Education Commission to create a national co-ordinating agency.

(2) To build on the systems already operating in some states — for instance, Victoria has designated 'general' and 'specialist' providers.

(3) To create a National Institute of Open Tertiary Education — a 1975 proposal which lapsed.

(4) To do nothing and let market forces prevail.

(5) The providers themselves to set up a mechanism to foster collaboration.

As I see it, the question is not to decide whether central intervention is appropriate but only to judge the degree and manner of it. Successes in inter-institutional collaboration so far have been limited in scale. There has been Queensland-Deakin collaboration in developing MEd courses; the partial success of this joint venture has been evaluated by Gillard et al (1983). An alternative approach is illustrated by the putting together of a major sequence in women's studies from courses contributed by several universities. But these are no more than drops in the ocean. Institutional inertia and protectiveness, and the 'not invented here factor' — the reluctance to use materials prepared elsewhere — have proved formidable hurdles in the past. Adam Smith's 'invisible hand' will need to be made a little more visible if Australia is to arrive at the kind of oligopoly, with cartel formation encouraged, which I believe would best suit its needs.

Conclusion

In conclusion I appeal again to the Lutheran analogy to illustrate that schismatics don't have it easy, if only because it is difficult to accommodate all the various kinds of dissent within a single body. But I do see DE as having come of age. The Vancouver conference of 1982 showed that, despite enormous variations between institutions providing DE, there is now a substantial body of common principles. I predict with confidence that DE will move towards the parity of esteem which in my view it already deserves. My main reasons for confidence are:—

(1) It offers greater flexibility to adult students, who are likely to increase in numbers relative to school-leavers because of the need to update and because of greater leisure to fulfil the ideal of lifelong learning.

(2) The educational disadvantages are already balanced by advantages, and foreseeable developments in communication technology will swing the balance further in favour of DE.

What I find difficult to predict is the speed of the trend. I hope we can find ways to hurry history along.

DISCUSSION

In introducing his paper Professor F. R. Jevons (Deakin) referred to the problems of nomenclature and the progress which was being made towards international agreement on the use of the term 'distance education'. In order to assist the discussion he gave his own definition of distance education, arguing that it should have the following features:

(*a*) an institution must provide high quality learning materials: distance education is not just private study;

(*b*) media or communication technologies are used to link learner and teacher;

(*c*) there are support services usually including some face-to-face contact and counselling.

A major question underlying the discussion which followed was that of parity of esteem between distance education and traditional face-to-face methods. It was clear that there were lingering doubts among traditionalists about the quality of education achievable by the former. Professor Jevons argued forcefully that the notion that distance education was inferior should be finally put to rest. He believed that the debate should be about the differing qualities of each method and how and when each could be used to best advantage. He argued that quality in distance education could be assured in a number of ways, for example by involving traditional university staff in course planning and external examining. Moreover the opportunities for cumulative improvement in pedagogic quality in distance education were considerable.

Discussion next turned to an examination of the concept of distance education in terms of clientele and educational purpose. Several main points emerged as follows:—

(*a*) In general it was thought that 18- to 22-year-olds are likely to prefer the traditional full-time face-to-face methods of higher education which, at their age, can be far more than a narrow educational experience. Evidence was quoted to support the view that mature students frequently prefer distance education. Their motivation can overcome its shortcomings and they can maintain career and home commitments. Interfacing with employment can be closer and there is evidence to show that such students perform as well and sometimes better when using distance education methods.

(*b*) In terms of function it was argued that distance education is ideal for broadly-based general education. There was, however, support for the view that it may be much less suited to initial training in those professions where extensive practical work is vital although it can be an excellent medium for updating those professionals in later life. One related and very topical question raised was how far distance education could be successful in technician education, although there were doubts about how far this should in any case be a university function.

(*c*) Discussion also took into account that distance education would be used for different purposes in different countries. For example, members from India reported that they were using distance education for 18-year-olds, as well as for those who had missed out, in order to ease the pressure of numbers for orthodox institutions.

Turning to costs it was agreed that high-quality distance education was not a cheap alternative and that politicians must not be permitted to think of it as such. Capital and development costs were high, even in countries where relatively simple technology was involved. There was, nevertheless, some advantage in the low marginal costs of adding extra students once courses were developed.

The issue of costs led to consideration of pressures towards establishing single national institutions for distance education in order to maximise returns on investment. In the United Kingdom and Nigeria such policies had clearly been important. In Canada, India and Australia, however, it was reported that very many conventional universities were rapidly moving into distance education.

Some suggested that a monopoly in distance education was unhealthy and that the pressures on universities generally to provide continuing education would break any monopoly.

In conclusion the group agreed that there was an immensely varied pattern of development in distance education. This was seen as a healthy state of affairs in what is undoubtedly an area of rapid growth across both the developed and the developing countries, and which is bound to be encouraged by technological advance.

Sub-Topic 5 (d)

IMPACT OF COMMUNICATIONS TECHNOLOGY ON DISTANCE LEARNING

Chairman: Sir James Redmond
Member of Council, Brunel and Open Universities (UK), and
former Director of Engineering, British Broadcasting Corporation

Rapporteur: Mr. A. Rowe-Evans
Secretary and Registrar, University of Warwick

Thursday, 18 August

Professor R. C. Smith (*Pro-Vice-Chancellor (Continuing Education),
Open University, UK*):

1. *Introduction*

My interpretation of the title is to share with you the impact of
changing communications technology on distance learning and to
structure this in the form of, first, looking at the hardware options
now becoming available. Secondly, I will look at the implications
for the creators of the software for videotapes, videodiscs, computers, etc., which has implications for not only distance learning
institutions but also more conventional universities, which are
contemplating a modicum of development in this area. Thirdly, I
will consider the sociological factors which are likely to have a
significant influence on the rate at which new ideas are taken up.

Before doing so, however, it will be helpful to examine, in the
distance learning context, typical courses and how students' time
is allocated since in practice decisions about the use of new
technology are taken in the context of needs of particular courses.
There are two examples. The first is a typical postgraduate technological updating course on software engineering. Half the student's
time on such a 100-hour course is spent with learning text, about
10% in using audio-visual materials and 10% on assessed work.
The remaining 30% is spent undertaking practical work, in this
particular case using a home-based microcomputer which can

352

access the University's computer by telephone, if required. On the other hand, for a management education course there is a requirement for a considerable proportion of face-to-face and group activity—40% of the time including a residential school. Another 40% is spent with the learning texts and 10% of time goes on respectively audio-visual work and assessment. In another management education course concerned with personnel selection and interviewing, the video component, including interaction on-line work, has its percentage increased considerably. The main points to be drawn from these examples are that print remains the major carrier of the education messages and that the level of involvement of the different technologies must be determined by the needs in the individual courses.

2. *Relevant Hardware Development*

2.1 *Broadcasting.* Despite the increasing number of celestial and terrestrial channels becoming available, there is a general tendency for a decreasing use by educationalists. The main reasons are that the number of viewers per programme is not high in the ratings, alternative and more flexible means of conveying the audio-visual messages are becoming available, and the cost. Nevertheless it continues to be a powerful stimulator to educational activity. Notable exceptions to this are satellite systems which are made available for large rural areas—tropical and arctic. Narrow band channels on these can be used for tutoring and tele-conferencing. Newer satellites are requiring less costly ground stations to receive their signals.

2.2 *Cables and wires.* The gradual extension of cable television to more countries is a development which is likely to be of considerable interest to conventional universities. The capacity (number of channels) on cables is likely to increase, particularly with the introduction of optical fibres; their ability to interact with the viewer is also likely to increase, and their cost to decrease. Their main disadvantage is their slowness in gaining access to the whole population, even in an urban area, and the expectation that in the long term only 50% of the population (mainly in non-urban areas) will be connected. Another disadvantage could be that unit production costs would need to fall to fill the greater programming requirement and quality may suffer. Nevertheless the next few years, in the UK perhaps in particular, will see considerable scope for experimental and local programming which could advantage local universities, and greater student choice of viewing times in these localities.

The telephone is another wired system which is improving the quality of its signals. This will provide increased access to digitalised computer stores (which could contain a wide variety of library information) and a higher level of interactivity on a group basis. This implies that teleconferencing, which has successfully been used in Canada and the USA for some time, will become more widely available. The ability to undertake teleconferencing through tutorials on visual display units, *i.e.* electronic blackboards, will increase and the CYCLOPS experiment in an Open University region has pointed up how these can be used.

2.3 *Computers* are the fastest growing component of new communications technology. For some time large mainframe computers such as PLATO have been available for educational purposes. Microcomputers are more portable and are more flexible. They control videodiscs for educational programming; they are used by home-based students on courses at Deakin University, several American universities, and are in planned Open University courses. They have been introduced widely in UK schools which will produce for universities, in a few years' time, students who will be very familiar with them as an everyday tool. The hardware price is halving every 18 months or so which is increasing their accessibility.

2.4 *Storage devices.* Audiotapes are still one of the most widely used storage devices being cheap, reliable and effective. Videotapes, like audiotapes, are re-usable but less easy to access in a random fashion. Videodiscs read by lasers, especially those controlled by microcomputers, have a greater potential in the educational armoury. Computer programmes can be transported on audiotapes or floppy discs.

2.5 *Accessibility.* Given a wide range of developments in communications technology, one of the fundamental questions which needs to be addressed is how accessible new equipment is to the students. This is especially apposite in developing countries. As an example of how we analyse this in the Open University to aid the decision-making process, I have extracted some relevant figures from our annual analysis using a sample of over 9500 students.

Proportion of OU students with access to equipment listed (Nov. 1982)

	HOME %	ELSEWHERE %	TOTAL %
Microcomputer (maths.)	15	19	34
(Maths.)	(26)	(32)	(58)
Video-cassette player	20	22	42
Audio-cassette player	91	N/A	91
Telephone	94	N/A	94

3. *Implication for Software and Courseware*

3.1 *The nature of the student.* It is vital to analyse the student situation in the context of what medium to use, not least of which is the accessibility referred to in paragraph 2.5. In the Open University the lowly audio-cassette is often ranked as the second most useful component in the course after the correspondence texts. The features that appeal are their convenience and portability, the control students have over them since they can play them as many or as few times as they need, and their informality. Students often comment that cassettes are like having a personal tutorial in their own room.

A serious consideration in using teleconferencing (or tutored video instruction—TVI—which basically implies recording a face-to-face lecture with campus students and transporting it, without editing, to, say, an industrial location for use) is that the target audience should have some background knowledge of the subject and understand the jargon. Thus, these methods can be particularly relevant to updating professionals in their own field. The potential of many of the new technologies is to bring more of the control of the curriculum into the hands of the students, although one still needs a requisite amount of teacher-led activities.

3.2 *The nature of the content.* Different media have different prime educational benefits for most students. For example, books and learning texts tend to be essential components for learning new concepts (in conventional universities too). Lectures and television have the potential for stimulating creative activity. Laboratories, tutorials and computers are particularly apposite for mental and physical skill-training. Design of the courseware, therefore, needs, as I indicated in the introduction, an analysis of a course proposal in the context of the nature of the student and the content, to determine how much time should be spent on different activities and what particular medium should be used.

3.3 *Costs* of using the different media can be substantial and cash flow can become a problem in the sense that large initial investment may be required. Hardware costs are generally falling but the costs of producing the software much less so. The ratio of man-hours of professional (*e.g.* academic, audio-visual producer, editor, programmer) time needed to produce one hour of student time can be 100 : 1 for learning texts and television programmes, and even 200 : 1 for computer software, *e.g.* for controlling a highly interactive videodisc. For simply transferring an existing videotape to a videodisc, the cost is relatively small—it is the investment on a combination of professionals that produces the cost. There is one facet to be wary of in this exercise of using a

355

range of professionals. Each tries to undertake the new activity in his own image, *i.e.* a programmer modifying the educational process to fit computer technology, an academic trying to convert his present practices using new media and so on. Judicious use of teamwork can overcome this.

4. *Sociological Controls*

The development and introduction of communications technology into conventional institutions, particularly, will depend on the reactions of three primary constituencies. First, the educational institutions and staff who will be concerned about its impact on work practices and their status. Secondly, on the students who may have expectations of changed methods of learning. The third is the expectation in the community at large and amongst future employers of the students from our system. Detailed limiting cases of optimistic and pessimistic scenarios have been deployed in a recent book by Professor D. G. Hawkridge of the Open University. (Hawkridge, D.: *New Information Technology in Education*. Croom Helm, 1983). Essentially, the optimistic forecast sees students spending a greater proportion of their time at screens with full access to library collections in many forms. For example, arts students will be able to compare master performers in the arts in action (*e.g. Twelfth Night*), compare scholars' views and so on. Academics will spend more of their time creating and transferring information than on direct lecturing. Adults will be drawn in more to the university sector as geographic location becomes less important than previously. Campuses will be used by them at weekends.

The pessimistic forecast sees continuing cuts in education budgets; a pruning of existing library resources, let alone broadening to new ones; the average age of academic staff will be increasing, their status in society will decrease, they will resist changes which will appear to lead to further staff reduction. Industry will deplore the irrelevance of the educational process to what they need; central government will exert more control to maintain quality and so on.

The reality is likely to be somewhere between these two extremes and there are some pointers towards the optimistic scenario, particularly from some universities most heavily under threat. What I believe we must do in the higher education sector of the education industry is to ensure that the quality of provision from the student's viewpoint is maintained, if not increased (and particularly perhaps in the conventional universities); that we do as academia invest more time in creating new forms of *relevant* courseware to supplement lectures and tutorials which have the potential for both *improving* learning and providing it to an *increased* number of students. Since the increase is likely to arise from the continuing education sector, this last point is especially important.

*Professor P. D. GUNATILAKE (*Vice-Chancellor, Open University of Sri Lanka*):

THE CASE OF DEVELOPING COUNTRIES

This paper attempts to describe the 'state of play' in the use of communication technologies in learning-at-a-distance programmes in the developing countries and to understand their impact on distance learning.

Communication Technology

Through the invention of moveable type by Gutenberg in the mid-fifteenth century a dramatic expansion of learning was made possible. It was not until the late nineteenth century, however, that print was used as a way of communication from teacher to students. Today the printed word is the most commonly used mode of communication in learning-at-a-distance programmes. The advent of the communication revolution in the twentieth century has resulted in a variety of non-print communication technologies, too, being used to carry educational material to students. Among these are:

(*a*) the radio, which has been used as an inexpensive way to reach isolated rural students;

(*b*) audio-cassettes, which have been used to complement learning-at-a-distance programmes;

(*c*) educational television, which provides the advantages of both audio and video features for learning;

(*d*) developments in interactive television, which can improve the instructional effectiveness of the video material;

---

*Although Professor Gunatilake was unable to attend the Congress, copies of his paper were available to those participating in this Group Discussion.

(*e*) teleconferencing, which links students in various centres for discussions and seminars;

(*f*) communication satellites, which provide uniform national or regional educational services; and

(*g*) developments in videodiscs, videotex and microcomputers, all of which offer increased opportunities for those learning at a distance.

Distance Learning

The term 'distance' in the expression 'distance learning' should be viewed as geographical as well as psychological and both types contribute to isolation. Both create distance between learner and the learning resources. Whatever the cause or condition of isolation, it influences the motivation to learn as well as the mode and frequency of the delivery of educational material and services. As to 'learning': the effectiveness or success of learning-at-a-distance programmes depends not only on the communication technologies for the delivery of educational material but also on such things as the pedagogical quality of the material, the learning process itself, and on the cultural and situational context. When a choice of several different communication technologies is possible, then the appropriate matching of learning objectives with each technology is crucial. Such issues need to be considered in any attempt to understand the impact of communication technology on distance education.

The Printed Word

With a few exceptions in the industrialised countries, the international explosion in distance learning services during the early 1970s was based almost exclusively on the print medium. Print allows individuals who possess basic literacy skills to access it most readily and control the time, location, pace and manner of learning. Furthermore printed material is adaptable to many different learning environments. It is useful for providing content where a good deal of ground needs to be covered or where the subject matter needs to be dealt with in depth, or where certain skills (analytical, mathematical, conceptional) need to be developed. It has traditionally been considered a central aspect of pedagogical planning, especially in relation to assignments and assessments. Printed material is an economical way to deliver information and can reach into every home if there is a decent postal service. It has been and, in the foreseeable future, will undoubtedly continue to be the most important component in the distance learning services in the developing countries.

Radio

Radio is the appropriate technology for meeting some of the educational needs in the developing countries, since it is generally available throughout the country, even in small villages, and is considerably less expensive both in capital and programming and maintenance costs as compared to other electronic communications technologies.

The popularity, availability and low cost of radio make it a convenient and practical medium for use in programmes for distance learning. The radio can overcome problems associated with illiteracy and is useful in reaching isolated rural audiences quickly and relatively inexpensively. The chief disadvantage of the radio broadcasts is the necessity for requiring students to listen at fixed broadcast times. But through the use of audio-cassettes greater flexibility in the use of material prepared for radio broadcasting is possible.

Though radio provides some of the educational needs in the developing countries at the elementary, secondary and post-secondary levels, its potential for learning at a distance has yet to be realised.

Audio-Cassettes

The audio-cassette recorder is inexpensive, simple to operate, durable and portable. This medium is an economical way of providing information in audio format for learning-at-a-distance programmes. The ability of individuals to control the time when information is delivered and heard is only one advantage; being able to cater to local and regional characteristics by using relevant examples is another. In addition individuals can pace themselves and can review the learning materials by replaying the cassette as often as needed. Furthermore the audio-cassette allows the learner to receive individual comments and permits a degree of privacy and confidentiality that is not possible on public audio broadcasts.

Audio-cassettes allow for mastery of learning, explanation and discussion of graphical, tabular and printed conceptional material, practice in problem-solving and exercises in mathematical processes. Audio-cassettes can be used for providing resource material, such as discussions, interviews, case-study material, language use, for analysis by students, and for step-by-step analysis and discussion by the unit author.

In general the audiotape programme has a rather low preparation cost and can be used in relationship with print and visual materials to provide a more powerful perceptual mix. Like radio, however, the creative potential of audio-cassettes has yet to be fully explored.

Television

Television offers one of the easiest ways of reaching learners at a distance. Its main advantage is its accessibility—it reaches every home—and it can be entertaining and attractive. It is therefore important for recruitment and motivation. It can also make available to the learner educational resources that would be difficult to provide in any other way—such as film of overseas countries, ingenious and expensive graphics, access to world leaders in politics and education, etc. Broadcast programmes can provide an overview of subject matter dealt with in more detail in texts.

With the production of such educational television programmes as 'Sesame Street', 'Civilization' and 'The Ascent of Man' in the West, educators were encouraged to attempt to use television to provide new types of quality instructions to a wider audience than had heretofore been possible. The use of television for instructional purposes is now increasing. However, there is the danger that the use of television in developing countries, basically an urban medium promoting a metropolitan lifestyle, may undermine the traditional values of rural society if used for education in rural areas.

Cable television has increased the number of opportunities for television programming in the industrialised countries and has provided a number of interesting experiments that have important educational implications. Other developments, such as the use of telephone lines for slow scan television and use of optical fibres for interactive programmes, have also been employed in a number of projects. But the impact of these communication technologies on distance learning in the developing countries has yet to be felt.

Video-Cassette

Video-cassette is a useful medium in learning at a distance programmes. This technology incorporates the advantages of audio-cassette and video-based media. It can serve as an important medium for illiterate students who depend on the spoken word and on visual images for communication. At the other extreme, video-cassette can assist the application of the more abstract and analytical ideas covered in print to the more concrete and complex real world. It can provide models or bridges to understanding, by giving concrete examples or visual models of abstract ideas. Broadcast television can also do this, but video-cassette is more suitable because of the increased control and repetition available to the student.

It will be a long time before a majority of students in the developing countries will have video-cassette machines in their own homes and one cannot therefore expect video-cassette to be in widespread use in distance education within the next few years. However, where a distance education system depends on students attending local study centres, as is the case in some developing countries, the video-cassette provides an effective medium for presentation of educational material and for teaching of skills to students.

Teleconferencing

Teleconferencing permits interactive group communication through an electronic medium that carries audio, video or text signals, and three main types of teleconferencing have been identified: audio-teleconferencing, video-teleconferencing and computer teleconferencing. Audio-teleconferencing is the most commonly used of these in learning-at-a-distance institutions and relies on telephone lines for transmission.

While telephone teaching is proving to be popular with both tutors and students, there are still many problems. Some of the developing countries do not have a telephone system widespread enough or reliable enough to be useful for distance education. Even where there is good national coverage line quality is often a problem. In others telephone teaching is prohibitively expensive because of problems of distance. It is also clear that special skills from tutors and discipline from students are required for teleconferencing.

Communication Satellites

Recent developments in satellite communication technology have provided educators with new opportunities for assisting those who must learn at a distance. The advances made in both microelectronics and launch vehicles have significantly reduced the cost of communication by satellite. As a result it is now possible for remote areas to have up-to-date communication services in television,

361

radio and telephone through the use of satellites and this, of course, presents new opportunities for the delivery of new educational programmes to these areas.

In 1975–76 some 2300 villages in India participated in the SITE (Indian Satellite Instructional Television Experiment) project which the Indian Space Research Organisation had formulated with the National Aeronautics and Space Administration (NASA). Hundreds of thousands of villagers viewed television for the first time and saw programmes on agriculture, health and family planning.

Satellite communications have had several uses in developing countries: to provide pre-diploma courses to students; to disseminate information from university and development agency sources to key development personnel in participating countries; and to provide continuing education programmes to extension workers, health paraprofessionals, primary school teachers and community development workers. There has been a wide range of satellite demonstration projects with educational applications in some developing countries and others, like India, have established the structures to provide educational programming via satellite on a permanent basis.

Satellite communication is particularly advantageous for serving scattered populations in widely dispersed areas, populations who are one of the main target audiences for learning-at-a-distance programmes. Since the cost of providing satellite communication is not related to distance, remote communities can be served as cheaply as communities in more central locations. Remote locations can be provided with communication services without incurring such costs for stringing wire, laying cable or building repeater stations across difficult terrain. Moreover communication can be provided to communities in order of priority of need. This is in contrast to the use of land-based equipment where the nearest and most accessible communities are normally served first.

The satellites offer some of the best opportunities for learning at a distance. The rapid, world-wide growth in the use of satellites for communication, combined with the decreased hardware costs for the consumer, suggest that the next few years will witness an increase in the opportunities for learning at a distance using this technology.

Videodisc, Videotex and Microcomputers

Videodisc is a relatively new technology. The opportunities of this technology for learning at a distance have yet to be fully realized, but it has the potential for becoming a sophisticated, interactive medium that may provide educators with highly effective delivery system.

Videotex is a generic term for a two-way information delivery system which uses telephone lines, coaxial cable and other modes of transmission to carry the consumer's request for data to computer and to relay the requested material back to the consumer. Most videotex applications are still in trial phases. The potential opportunities for the use of videotex as an interactive medium for learning at a distance are far-reaching.

The increasing availability of microcomputers offers major new opportunities for learning at a distance and is becoming a powerful tool for education.

One does not, however, expect these technologies to be in widespread use in distance education in the developing countries within the next few years.

Looking to the Future

Most of the distance education systems in the developing countries rely almost entirely on correspondence teaching backed up by face-to-face tuition in groups, or they rely on broadcast series backed up by printed material and possibly some face-to-face tuition. Now the range and combination of media available is suddenly bewildering. Nevertheless it is possible to pick out some features that enable one to estimate what will be most useful over the next few years, accepting that varying socio-economic and geographic factors will result in differences in what will be more important to one system than another.

The first feature is accessibility. What media are likely to be available—or can be provided economically—in most students' homes over the next few years? Accessibility will also be influenced by the extent to which a distance education system is dependent on the use of local centres—more expensive equipment can be provided in local centres, where shared use is possible. The second is convenience. Can the student use the medium when and where it suits him, and without extra training? The third is academic control. How easy is it for the teacher to design and prepare the material himself? How much training will be required? The fourth feature is the extent to which the medium provides a 'human' touch—to what extent can the learner relate to the tutor or teacher through the medium? And lastly, what is available now that can be used?

Using these criteria one begins to see that print materials, radio and audio-cassettes will continue to be the most important components in the distance learning services in the developing countries. As to the other electronic communication technologies, the costs are legendary. While they may be justified by a far-sighted social policy as media of general public education, where potential audiences and the potential for modifying public attitudes and tastes are vast, it is hard to justify the cost where potential audiences are so much smaller and where it must mainly be a cost additional to that of providing the other instructional material that remains essential to the activity of the serious student. The question may seem to be almost churlishly iconoclastic, but isn't it at least possible that only a small proportion of the cost of writing, producing and delivering a series of television programmes would be far more effectively deployed in improving the library facilities available to serious students and in mounting opportunities for them to gain face-to-face access to teachers and specialized equipment and materials during weekend seminars and the like. Is this not a similar situation to that discussed many years ago by Charles Carter, who argued that it would be substantially cheaper to transport his senior physics students at Lancaster to the linear accelerator in Manchester by gold-plated Rolls Royces, three times a week, throwing in luxury hotel accommodation and champagne dinners to boot, than to establish a linear accelerator on campus at Lancaster? It appears that the new innovations in electronic communication are unlikely to prove themselves in the developing countries within the next few years when the modes they could displace are presently more cost-effective and had evolved over many hundreds of years.

DISCUSSION

The discussion brought out strongly the need for discrimination in the use of media. The academic, economic and cultural setting in which a course is conceived, prepared and delivered is complex, and each factor can vary over an enormous range and the technology used must be tuned to the environment. While there was a keen desire to take advantage of new opportunities, there was caution in the face of the very large investment required per course by some media, and some saw academic and cultural dangers in their use. It was agreed *nem. con.*, however, that sooner or later, and for better or worse, academic life will have to adapt itself to the new techniques, which would have their effect not only in continuing education but also in the main stream of higher education.

The academic environment varies according to the subject, the level, the purpose of the course (*e.g.* awareness or updating), the size and accessibility of the audience, and so forth. The Open University still relies mainly (65–70% of student time) on written material for most courses, even though the whole range of new media is being vigorously pursued; the entire replacement of the book is not envisaged, even by the least conservative teachers. (Enquirers about the OU's methods of assessing student reaction to distance learning material, and assessing student performance, were directed to published material, and the means of providing for student interaction were also discussed.)

Some speakers regretted the very broad definition given to continuing education in the first session of the topic, which posed a bewildering variety of academic situations and problems. Nevertheless it was recognised that the university had a part to play at all levels and not only (as some would have it) in the updating of professional knowledge and skill. One speaker wondered whether academic thinking about distance teaching was not too much conditioned by the tradition in orthodox degree work, that the teacher should have complete control over the curriculum. In distance teaching, with a tendency to centralised production of materials, there was an apparent reduction in the teacher's autonomy, and perhaps a danger of a standardised, undemanding encapsulation of the subject. Furthermore, would not the habits of the mass media tend to produce 'stars', to whom individual university departments and teachers would become subservient? On the other hand, the new techniques should allow the student to control his own studies better—far from being simply lectured at in the media he should eventually be provided with more interactive facilities and have much broader opportunities for browsing among great quantities of call-up material.

Much of this discussion was centred on the videodisc development which was demonstrated during the day. Professor Smith had pointed out that the production of a disc would cost up to £100,000 (mostly in staff time) and therefore this technique would be suitable only for courses with large numbers of students, or the disc would have to remain in service for a long time, to keep unit cost within reason. This led to a discussion on the cost-effectiveness of centrally-produced material, and the relationship of cost to quality. High-cost methods, it was reiterated, are not necessarily the most effective. The enormous amount of staff time required to produce video material, greater by a huge factor than that required to prepare a lecture, was necessary to secure a standard of presentation high enough to impress and to hold an audience; the medium, in this respect, being far more demanding than a classroom. Simply to record a classroom event would be cheap, but the failure rate would be high.

Costs of the use of various media (*e.g.* television, telephone) vary widely from country to country, and will be a factor in determining which media will be used. Also to be considered is the availability and reliability of such media and their accessibility to the student group in question. In developing countries print will be the most reliable medium, followed by radio and audio-cassettes as these facilities develop. Cultural attitudes, in both teachers and students, will affect their willingness to use new media; such attitudes can change quickly, particularly among the young, so that what now seems difficult and unfamiliar becomes commonplace. (The 16–22 age group in the UK is increasingly 'playing' with microcomputers rather than pop records.) By the discussion of this question, it was perceived that the new media could be used in many different ways, as can reading; it is up to the teacher and student of our time to make intelligent use of them.

At this point speakers returned to the question in many minds—how far should their universities invest now to equip themselves for the new techniques, and could not a beginning be made without too much financial risk? For example, could not video-tapes be made in classrooms during lectures, without the need for a studio and professional television approaches and facilities? It appeared that 'tutor-video instruction' (TVI) was used by the Open University and had been quite extensively used at Stanford with some success. The dangers lay in producing by this simple means material that was simply dull, or unsuitable for the audience addressed. In general the technique was best for addressing a specialised audience on a topic with which they were already familiar—say, for updating professional expertise; but it would not do for awakening a wider audience to awareness of a topic generally alien to it.

There was some discussion of the need, and the techniques required, for addressing an audience wider than that of students following a specified study. It was stressed that, however wide the aim, the audience, the level and the aim must be clearly defined before any material is produced, or even before any decisions are to be made about media. Awareness can hardly be achieved if the approach is not through a simple, easy and familiar medium.

In conclusion the Co-ordinating Chairman (Dr. Horlock) thanked the contributors and referred again to the broad definition of continuing education with which he had opened the topic. No doubt the discussions in the next and final session *Prospects for the Future,* would further reflect on the pros and cons of adopting such a wide scope of discussion.

Sub-Topic 5 (e)

PROSPECTS FOR THE FUTURE

Chairman: Dr. J. H. HORLOCK
Vice-Chancellor of the Open University (UK)
Rapporteur: Mr. F. T. MATTISON
Registrar of the University of Hull

Thursday, 18 August

Dr. S. GRIEW (*President, Athabasca University*):

CONTINUING EDUCATION AND THE UNIVERSITIES: IMPEDIMENTS AND PROSPECTS

Earlier contributions to this symposium have dealt with a wide range of topics. We have heard of the needs of modern technology-based industry and of those often more basic requirements of developing countries. It has been argued that universities should upgrade the status of continuing education so that it becomes a principal rather than a marginal activity; and in one case it has been conjectured that by the turn of the century a third of a typical university's teaching activity will be devoted to upgrading professionals. A strong and compelling plea has been entered that distance education should be accorded parity of esteem with other more conventional modes of delivery; and it has been argued that distance delivery is a particularly appropriate means of meeting needs in continuing education. We have heard a good deal about modern communication and computer-based technology as a further means of improving the effectiveness of the continuing education enterprise.

Whether we like it or not, continuing education is already one of the universities' principal activities. Most jurisdictions that record such data now report that post-secondary enrolments in non-credit courses significantly exceed enrolments for degree credit.

367

Yet, as our participation increases, so it seems does the uneasiness of the consumer about our performance and that of the universities themselves with their involvement. Dissatisfaction has not been far below the surface in much of what we have heard this week. If we are to talk about the future prospects of continuing education we must try, I think, to understand this dissatisfaction, and I should like to address this topic today.

As I understand it, continuing education has its roots in the broader adult education movement that dates back to the first half of the nineteenth century and which derived its impetus from the largely ideological persuasion that emancipation was mainly to be found in education, which had thus to be regarded as a fundamental right of all citizens. Since, at that time, universities were geared mainly to the preparation of a professional and social élite it is not surprising, perhaps, that continuing education early came into conflict with the traditional purposes and values of universities.

Hand in hand with this ideological thrust, early proponents of continuing education seem to have derived additional support from those who believed that, by insisting on scholarly standards and a traditional curriculum, universities showed an unacceptable indifference to the real needs of those who most needed their services. The cry for 'relevance' in the middle of the nineteenth century focused on the proposition that the form and content of the curriculum should be specified by the consumer and not by the academic working from his isolated and privileged cell in the ivory tower.

It is really not surprising that the continuing education movement failed from the outset to strike the universities as an activity of much importance or value. At best it threatened to be a distraction from the 'proper' work of a university; at worst it was perceived by some as being little more than a vehicle for a takeover by those both unfitted and unsuitable for the benefits of a university education.

I am not suggesting for a moment that the kinds of attitudes that I have been caricaturing exist widely in their pure forms today. The world has come a long way since the establishment of the first Mechanics' Institute in England in 1825. We now support the notion that we should be involved. It makes a lot of political sense to do so. If governments were more forthcoming in their financial support of our efforts we should, I suspect, be even more supportive, since then it would make economic sense too. However, is our involvement really beyond the level of window dressing? I suspect that some, at least, of the dissatisfaction that I perceive can be traced directly to our failure properly to deliver on the commitments that we so often seem to be making. Alienation can so easily result from the raising of expectations that fail to be met.

To answer this question honestly demands a candour that is far from comfortable. Leaving aside a few glowing examples of successful participation, how many universities really do more than pay lip service to their declared concerns to meet responsibilities in the field of continuing education? In recent years the name of the continuing education game has increasingly become professional enrichment and upgrading. One does not have to look far to find objections within universities to assuming responsibilities such as these that bear remarkable similarity (at least verbally) to those advanced over a century ago. First, one is told that by fulfilling such demands one risks the dilution of standards and, in the recipients of courses designed to serve such needs, a specious belief in an enhanced command that will only be dangerous. Secondly, the ideology is turned on its head and objections are raised on the lines that such people as qualified engineers, experienced managers and successful family doctors (examples of those who are said to require opportunities for professional upgrading) can hardly be regarded as disadvantaged, and thus should not be seeking help from institutions that should be committed to increasing equality of educational opportunity rather than the consolidation of the privileges of professional élites!

It is tempting to assume that this reflects little more than the elegant if rather infuriating capacity for rationalization for which the academic mind is so well known. Academics tend to dislike any calls on their time and energy that divert them from pursuing the disciplinary-based callings for which they were initially prepared. And this inherent disinclination to move, even temporarily, out of the comfortable academic rut is more than adequately legitimized in most universities by an incentive system that offers little inducement to do so to those who might otherwise be prepared to devote time and energy to such fringe activities as continuing education. There are few prizes in universities for those who are willing to give substance to their institution's declared intentions to play its parts in advancing knowledge and skill and expanding the intellectual horizons of casual students. Rather, in very many universities there are not-so-subtle penalties for doing so.

Is it very surprising, therefore, that we more characteristically expend a far greater proportion of our time and energy either in developing persuasive arguments why we should avoid involvements; or in reducing the matter to the level of a faculty board debate, devising red herrings that will successfully divert us from the need to try, or so confuse the issue that no-one really knows the usually quite simple form in which it was first raised.

And the potential consumer is not entirely innocent. His declared needs are often so ill-defined that in trying to interpret them the putative instructor will frequently appear almost capriciously to be missing the point. Often the consumer's demand is for unnecessarily and unrealistically sophisticated a course, where a comparatively brief session of familiarization with new techniques would meet the case perfectly. Often consumers display just as great a predilection for the ivory tower as they traditionally accuse the universities of, and there surely is a limit to the extent to which the pot should call the kettle black. Not infrequently they seek help from universities when other kinds of institutions would be more appropriate sources for help. In doing so they can all too easily, if inadvertently, exacerbate the feelings of irritation they, and the universities, feel when it becomes clear that negotiations are bogging down.

I confess that I have detected a tendency in our discussions so far to evade some of these more central issues and to place more value in some of the peripheral questions that lurk around at the edges. For instance, there has been a lot of talk of technology. I admit that I find our preoccupation with advanced technology rather a pity. While I do not doubt the capacity of technology to contribute significantly to our delivery of useful courses, technology is only a *means* to an end and I am often saddened by our tendency at times to be so beguiled by the means that we frequently treat them as ends in themselves. However sophisticated the technology, it is the curriculum that will ultimately make or break any particular activity in the field of continuing education.

By much the same token, I have a feeling that distance education occupies a place in the list of means and must not be regarded as an end in itself. I know that my old friend, Professor Jevons, will agree with me and I hope that he will understand the slight anxiety I have that some may have obtained from his paper a misplaced confidence in the power of distance delivery somehow in itself to solve some of the more intractable problems in this field. My colleague, Ross Paul, put it very nicely some time ago, in commenting upon an initiative to which all of us at Athabasca University were enthusiastically committed, without really knowing why. 'It is very much', he commented, 'a solution in search of a problem'. Perhaps a little provocatively, may I comment that continuing education abounds in potential solutions but that many of them seem to me to be only marginally relevant to the real problems that plague us.

What, then, do I regard as the real problems that impede our successful participation in this enterprise? What follows will come as little surprise since I have already exposed most of my prejudices quite openly.

For a start, I think we should recognize that to a significant extent the early discomfort felt by universities about embracing continuing education as a major activity is never far beneath the surface in those councils that decide policy and priorities in such matters. Unless we are prepared to encourage a radical move away from the traditional values that give universities their distinctiveness, this discomfort will always be present. If, then, we are serious about making continuing education a major activity, I suggest we must separate it, conceptually, structurally and administratively, from those more central activities that are at the core of a university's purpose. If we do not, then both traditional and new activities will continue to compete for esteem, recognition and resources, and the new, given the nature of power within universities, will continue to flounder. A necessary condition for the success of continuing education within universities is, I believe, its organisational, economic and indeed moral separation from the institution's core activities. Those responsible for shaping and delivering programmes will, under these circumstances, have the authority and independence to implement developing plans without having, at every critical juncture, to refer back to university-wide boards of study or whatever. Of equal importance, different and more appropriate incentive systems will be negotiable so as to persuade academics who might otherwise fear than an involvement will jeopardize their careers that their participation can be pursued without danger.

Next, despite the burgeoning of steering, advisory and all kinds of other committees, the actual communication between the universities and their consumers in the continuing education field remains, I believe, largely ineffectual. I have a feeling that this is at least partly due to reservations that both sides harbour about the possibility of maintaining their autonomy and control if they agree to meet each other for committed dialogue. Obviously one cannot legislate trust and commitment, but this hurdle has somehow to be overcome and I should like to think that the separation of continuing education from a university's core activities would help substantially by providing its leaders with the authority and confidence they need if they are to talk realistically with potential consumers.

Thirdly, I enter the strongest possible plea for the reinstatement of substance as the overwhelmingly important item that should guide all discussions of courses and programmes in continuing education. I have already exposed my feelings about our tendency too often to prefer to move far too quickly to talk about delivery. Unless needs and a syllabus have been agreed in detail, discussion of delivery should be forbidden. If it is not, then in more cases than would give any of us comfort the syllabus will be changed to accommodate a preferred delivery system and there will be yet another vaguely disenchanted group of consumers to contend with. An old professor of mine, whenever a continuing education need had been defined, always urged that the next step should be to find a book that prospective students would be advised to read and that more elaborate delivery mechanisms should be eschewed until all were convinced that no appropriate book was available. I do not seriously suggest this as a guiding principle, but we do tend too often to forget that most people attend to their continuing education without realizing it, simply by reading books. Perhaps we should not feel ashamed when we find that our best advice should be to read such and such a book.

It follows that the actual shape of any specific activity will depend upon the nature of the particular need it is designed to meet. Too often we attempt the Procrustean task of accommodating offerings within a very limited number of formats that have evolved largely for the sake of administrative or logistic convenience: the semester course of one evening a week; the weekend residential seminar; the three-credit home-study package; all are examples. In doing so we again run the risk of delivering a product that is once more shaped by delivery process rather than by the needs of the consumers.

As statesman-like a posture as is available is that which allows one to admit when one cannot help. Too rarely are we in the universities prepared to admit that anything is beyond us, and often we persevere in trying to produce courses which we know could be developed with much greater ease and effectiveness by other bodies, sometimes by the consumers themselves. Our schools of medicine and law and architecture are peopled by part-time, often honorary, staff, without whom they would rapidly come to a standstill. Upon what basis do we assume that we are ordinarily better equipped to attend to the continuing education needs of such professionals than those who already occupy secure positions within the professions? Perhaps we should more frequently act as brokers when approached for help in the continuing education area, bringing together people who we know or suspect will interact to each other's benefit. Brokering is as old and as honourable a calling as any, and one, I predict, that will be increasingly espoused by universities in the years to come.

Finally, I should like to offer a few more general comments about the discussion which we have heard this week. The whole thrust of this symposium has been that continuing education is a 'good thing' and somehow bound to help universities to make their rightful contribution to technological innovation and economic prosperity and thus to regain their rightful places in the sun. Frankly, I am surprised that this assumption has not been challenged once.

Sir Adrian Cadbury, on our first morning here, made the point that innovation is not amenable to direction. Perhaps throughout this symposium we have all been aware of this and have harboured private doubts as to whether the massive involvement in continuing education that some advocate for the universities will really make very little difference to a society's capacity to stimulate technological innovation. I have no doubt that the demand for our involvement will continue unabated and that the suggestions that I have offered, if followed, would enable us to face the prospects with much greater optimism than I think is justified at the moment. However it is possible, I believe, that our advocacy this week has been more a function of our realization that universities are currently under fire and must respond in ways that appear likely to improve their capacities to contribute to technological innovation. Perhaps this, at least partially, explains our inability, during our discussions, to retain a firm hold on issues of substance.

Secondly, I have more than once been impressed by the similarity of what I have heard with things that I have been hearing ever since I entered universities nearly thirty years ago. Sir Geoffrey Allen's prescription of what is needed by a modern industrial society is, frankly, identical to what was being prescribed in the early 1950s when I started my career in the field of industrial training. I confess that this discomfits me. When precisely is 'modern'? Have things really changed in the meantime?

Thirdly, had I had the benefit of hearing the discussion before I drafted my original contribution to it I think that I would have underscored my point about the appropriateness of ascribing to universities, as such, the range of continuing education functions that we tend to assume for them. Sir Geoffrey's contribution was very refreshing in mentioning many other sectors as vital actors; and I was impressed by a contribution early in the week that drew attention to the success of the New Zealand Correspondence College at the trades and technical levels.

Finally, our Chairman set the stage for this week's discussion in an article entitled 'Keeping up with the New Industrial Revolution' which was published in *The Times Higher Education Supplement* on

12 August. In his second paragraph one reads: 'Much of the knowledge acquired during formal education will not retain its relevance twenty years later. It is by making an immediate impact on mature adults through continuing education courses that we have a chance of keeping abreast of new developments.'

While we have all been aware for a long time that the increasing obsolescence of formal education is one of the most alarming considerations demanding attention by curriculum planners, we do not often enough, I think, face one obvious corollary to the suggestion that continuing education must be regarded as an increasingly vital activity in reducing the impact of obsolescence. Perhaps in accepting that knowledge acquired during formal education will not retain its relevance twenty years later, we should recognize that it becomes even more pressing that we keep our first degree and basic training courses as non-specialised as possible; genuinely trying first and foremost to provide our full-time degree students with the intellectual powers and disciplines upon which later to build and develop. Every sword is double-edged, and this seems to me to be the other edge of the sword that we have been wielding this week.

DISCUSSION

In introducing his paper Professor Griew (Athabasca) related it to the discussions held at the first four sessions. He found an irony in the situation that the increasing interest in continuing education was accompanied by increasing dissatisfaction. Continuing education was socially inspired but felt to be inimical to the central purpose of the university, being regarded as a fringe or frill activity. Lip service only was paid to the need to become involved. This was demonstrated by the emphasis on peer judgement in the assessment of academics rather than an evaluation of their contribution to institutional objectives.

He noted that there had not been any input from the consumer during the week, and there had been a concentration on the process or delivery mechanism in continuing education at the expense of content. Excitement with the new technologies was understandable, but technologies, no matter how beguiling, were only a means to an end.

There was an urgent need to separate continuing education organisationally from the core functions of the university and to provide the former with its own system of rewards. There had to be a dialogue with the consumers, and a discussion of curriculum. Delivery methods had to be shaped to the needs of the situation and, if necessary, the universities should recognise that they were not omnicompetent and could sometimes operate to best advantage by acting as brokers putting consumers in touch with appropriate external teaching agencies from the wide range available.

He concluded by expressing a polite impatience with university attitudes to continuing education: particularly those that regard it as the means by which universities could recover their place in the sun. As Sir Adrian Cadbury had pointed out in the first plenary session of the Congress, innovation was not amenable to direction. Finally, they must recognise that the progressive and distinctive contribution of universities was precious.

The ensuing discussion centred around four main themes: the meaning of continuing education, its organisation, its consumers and the prospects and limitations of technology.

Various speakers referred to the problem of defining continuing education and to the fact that many differing definitions had emerged during the discussions of the week. It was noted that the British University Grants Committee had recently adopted the following definition: 'any form of education, both vocational and general, that is resumed after an interval following the end of continuous initial education'. It was agreed that this broad definition was a useful starting point and emphasised the great breadth of activity which came under the heading. Discussions had shown that activities as disparate as the involvement of universities in basic literacy programmes on the one hand, through to the commitment of the department of electrical engineering at the Massachusetts Institute of Technology to provide a lifelong updating for its graduates on the other, all came within the definition. One speaker compared the problem to that faced by a convention of anthropologists which attempted, without success, to produce a definition of man, but did not find the absence of a definition a disadvantage.

It was generally agreed that an autonomous organisation was needed for some of the tasks associated with continuing education. For other tasks it seems best to involve conventional university departments. One speaker suggested that it was useful to consider the following pattern of relationships between tasks and choice of teaching agency:—

A. Agency: autonomous continuing education department acting alone
   Tasks: traditional adult education, of the 'extra-mural' and 'extension' type
B. Agency: conventional discipline-based departments acting alone
   Task: academic updating for specialists
C. Agency: continuing education departments and discipline-based departments acting in partnership
   Tasks: (i) appreciation courses for non-specialists—e.g. computers for managers or industrial relations for engineers; (ii) first degree work for mature students; (iii) adult education supporting human self-fulfilment and citizenship

D. Agency: discipline-based departments in partnership with external employers or professional associations

Task: Post-experience education.

Parallel to the discussion of optimal organisational arrangements there was some discussion of the organisation of material. Some learning was best undertaken on an experiential basis, whereas other material required systematic teaching. Some members of the group expressed disappointment at the comparative paucity of discussion on the subject of the organisation of material in curricula and the special factors operating in the field of continuing education.

Particular stress was laid upon the expanding role of the external department of the University of London. Reports of its demise were premature, to say the least. It was moving away from a purely examining role and was expanding to provision of correspondence material and other 'learning packages'. In summary, it was alive, kicking and reaching out to the future.

Considerable attention was given to the consumer of continuing education. For the industrialised countries a major problem was the reluctant professional, who was not willing to volunteer for updating. It was estimated that no more than 20% were willing to undertake updating courses, although this rose to 30% if courses were based on private study techniques. For the rest there could only be the sanctions of failure or, as was the policy in some countries, the risk of loss of the licence to practice.

In developing countries, the situation was very different in all respects and the nature of the task for continuing education, in its many ramifications, was quite staggering. If half the population were illiterate, if millions had no educational opportunity at all, universities had to assume some special concerns. Such special concerns would often have an impact on the university teacher, who needed an amalgam of skills to enable him to escape the handicap of being purely a specialist.

The development of teaching technology was a challenge and an opportunity for continuing education. Capacity for reaching the student was increased and even the more sophisticated forms of educational technology provided substantial opportunities for developing nations. On the other hand, it should not be overlooked that the costs associated with some forms of technology were formidable and could lead to a narrowing of breadth and experimentation in continuing education. For example, the whole world could probably support only one videodisc on veterinary ophthalmology. The omnipresent danger with educational technology was that it would be seen as an end in itself when it should be seen as no more than a means.

Professor Griew, in summing up his impressions of the discussion; made four principal points:—

1. The need for a focus: an autonomous group which could act as broker, even going to the extent of identifying an agency external to the university as the most effective operator.

2. Consumer needs must be defined in the light of the needs of society.

3. The importance of persuading the professional of the need for updating.

4. A slight note of sadness that there has been no identification of suitable rewards and reward mechanisms for staff engaged in continuing education work. In his view the universality of assessment by peer review, as against assessment by extent of contribution to the objectives of the institution, did not bode well for continuing education.

Topic 5

CONTINUING EDUCATION

Co-ordinating Chairman's Commentary on the Group Discussions

Final Plenary Session
Friday, 19 August

Dr. J. H. HORLOCK (*Vice-Chancellor of the Open University, UK*): Definitions of continuing education (CE) are many and varied and the CE discussion group struggled hard during the Congress to find a definition that adequately reflected the wide range of provision that is evident throughout the Commonwealth. I began the week by proposing that we consider CE as constituting 'post-formal or post full-time education'. Subsequently I was persuaded to adopt a more precise definition and opted for that used by the University Grants Committee in the UK, namely 'any form of education, both vocational and general, that is resumed after an interval following the end of continuous initial education'. By the end of the week it was apparent that many still felt this definition to be less than comprehensive and I suspect that what we were searching for was a commitment to life-long education in its broadest sense.

But we also had to bear in mind the conference theme, *Technological Innovation: University Roles*. We interpreted this in two ways:

(*a*) the contribution which CE can make to the development of the technological society;

(*b*) the help which new technology can give to the teaching of CE.

Guided by our conference theme, we began by considering this first area of CE, vocational education for modern industrial society. We started with the generally accepted proposition that the growth of information and the rate of technological advance in modern industrial societies was now so rapid that the knowledge and skills acquired in initial education were no longer adequate to meet the needs of adults during the full course of their working lives. We therefore concluded that continuing education had an important role to play in bringing working adults up to date with new developments in their field. We went further and defined a need for three types of provision. First, we felt that there was a requirement for 'awareness' courses, making managers, amongst others, aware of new technological and other developments in their business or profession without necessarily making them expert in a new field. Second, we saw a need for 'broadening' courses, enabling specialists and others to become knowledgeable and authoritative in a new subject or a new technology which did not appear in their undergraduate courses. Finally, there was a need for advanced technology courses which make available the latest developments to those already expert in the field.

We then turned to the requirements of developing countries. Here the needs were found to be much more wide-ranging. 'We need all the vocational education we have talked about but we need much more', said one speaker. In essence, there was a need both to build upon the existing initial educational provision, through the updating of professionals such as doctors and engineers, but also to compensate for the lack or inadequacy of effective periods of formal education—a need, in other words, for CE to provide a wider educational base in those countries to prepare for the new technological society. The needs which CE was expected to serve were therefore many and varied, from the teaching of basic literacy skills through technical courses in farming and business skills to first degree education for adults and, beyond that, to the updating courses referred to above.

We moved next to the question of how to provide CE. We looked first at distance education—not simply private study but the provision of high quality correspondence texts and learning materials, integrated, where appropriate, with media and communication technology and backed up by strong academic support services (tutoring and counselling). We felt that distance education had a particular role to play in teaching adults, and particularly working adults, although we noted that it was also being used in some developing countries, notably India, to ease the pressure of demand on conventional universities. Some felt that distance education was perhaps less suitable for younger students and for training in areas where extensive practical work was required or where student numbers were likely to be small (as, for example, in some specialist updating courses). This raised the question of whether distance teaching should be integrated with or separate from conventional teaching. In several countries it was apparent that many conventional universities were rapidly moving into

379

distance education and in developing or sparsely populated countries in particular, where students have to travel long distances to a residential campus, there were attractions in combining periods of distance teaching with periods of conventional teaching.

Within this broad question of how to provide CE we touched on the second aspect of the conference theme—the ways in which new technological developments can assist in its provision. Sketched for us was a glittering array of new technology—television by satellite and cable, video-cassettes and videodiscs, teleconferencing and telewriting, micros for computer-aided learning—and their associated costs. Yet our discussion brought out strongly the need for discrimination in the use of the media and we concluded that the technology used had to be matched to the nature of the course, to the needs and capabilities of the students, and to the infra-structure available in the country (*e.g.* the reliability and pene-tration of public services such as electricity supply and broadcast-ing). We agreed on the adoption of the simpler, more accessible and easily available technology first (such as radio and audio-cassettes) but we stressed above all the continuing primacy of print as the principal and least dispensable form of communication.

Finally we addressed the question of who should be responsible for CE. We were agreed that the universities, with their academic expertise, teaching experience and traditional concern with adult education had a significant role to play. But we were conscious also that there was a need to collaborate closely with client groups, to ensure that provision was attuned to national or local needs, and with other providers, to ensure the optimum use of existing resources. As to responsibilities within universities, we felt that there was an important and continuing role for extra-mural depart-ments in the general area of adult education and in the provision of awareness courses within the vocational area. But we felt that the existing discipline-based departments had a bigger role to play in the vocational area, particularly in providing broadening and updating courses in specialist fields. As to the relative importance to be attached to CE in the universities, we were left with a new picture of university departments in the year 2000 AD with three equal commitments: to degree teaching; to postgraduate training and research; and to CE.

In summary, the main points arising from these stimulating and enjoyable discussions were:—

(1) A firm acceptance of the role of universities in providing vocational CE for technological development and innovation.

(2) The importance of a wider role for CE in general adult education, to provide the educational base in developing countries.

(3) The importance of distance education in both vocational and general adult education, but not always on its own: distance and conventional teaching will complement each other.

(4) New technology will have a major effect on distance teaching, but it must be matched to types of courses, to student needs and public services available in particular countries.

But, as was stressed during the week, universities cannot do all they are asked to do without adequate resources. The economics of the introduction or development of CE requires careful study of the market and probable student numbers, of the appropriate delivery systems, of capital and recurrent costs and of fee income. CE is not always cheap. And costs have to be equated with educational effectiveness. There is little point for the student if a superb technological delivery system transfers second-rate material. As in all university education, the quality of the curriculum and the effectiveness of the teaching are of prime importance.

Topic 5

OTHER CONTRIBUTIONS

Among the other papers brought to or circulated at the Congress were those mentioned below, which related to this Topic.

Dr. R. C. SHUKLA (*Vice-Chancellor, Bhopal Vishwavidyalaya*), in a paper on 'Continuing Education Programmes for the Teachers', described the development and operation 'through the medium of correspondence-cum-contact and other distant learning techniques' of professional BEd courses and in-service teacher education programmes.

Dr. (Mrs.) JYOTI H. TRIVEDI (*Vice-Chancellor, S.N.D.T. Women's University*) contributed a three-part paper* of which the first two parts dealt with, respectively, 'Distance Learning—Correspondence Course—Open University' and 'Distance Education through New Communication Technology'. The first describes the nature and characteristics of correspondence education and gives brief state-by-state details of correspondence and open university courses in Indian universities; the second examines the need for and components of distance and correspondence education, the contribution of educational technology, the choice of media, and the methods and effectiveness of distance learning/teaching.

See also end of section on Topic 2.

SECOND PLENARY SESSION AND
CONGRESS BANQUET
Friday, 19 August

At the Second Plenary Session the five Topic Chairmen reported on the week's discussions relating to their Topics. (Each Chairman's commentary on the work of his group appears at the end of his own Topic's section of this Report.)

The close of the Congress was marked by a Banquet at which the Toast to the Universities of the Commonwealth was proposed by the Rt. Hon. Sir ZELMAN COWEN, AK, GCMG, GCVO, QC, DCL (*Provost of Oriel College, Oxford, and former Governor-General of Australia*). Sir Zelman said: My wife and I thank you warmly for your generous invitation to join the Congress in Birmingham for this occasion. For both of us it is a *return* to the fold. We came first to a Quinquennial Congress on home ground in Sydney in 1968, when I was in my early days as a vice-chancellor. The Australian Vice-Chancellors' Committee had some special responsibilities for the arrangements for that Congress, and, even if my memory is a little rose-tinted, I recall a very good and happy occasion. It was, I fear, the last of its kind in offering an attractive complimentary smorgasbord of post-Congress tours. Then five years later we came to Edinburgh. Over the intervening five years universities in many places had gone through difficult times and there was some discussion in the conference of the impact and the longer-term significance of that experience. Edinburgh provided a splendid setting, and nature was extraordinarily kind, and our debates and deliberations were nicely balanced with generous hospitality and the many attractions of Edinburgh in festival. For my wife and for me it is a pleasure to come to this great English city which fittingly accommodates this thirteenth Congress.

Since the very first of the Congresses in London in 1912, the pattern has been set, and Eric Ashby gave an account of that event, to which representatives of fifty-one universities came.

'. . . There was a very full agenda of papers and discussions. To occupy the leisure moments of the delegates a Reception Committee prepared an impressive array of entertainment including a government lunch, dinners by City Companies, scientific exhibits, music, and a torchlight tattoo and mimic assault entitled "The Storming of the Sultan's Palace at Tlemcen" . . . There was also a giant Conversazione with 2000 guests, illuminated by Japanese lanterns. It makes one a little nostalgic to read that the caterer's estimate for refreshments at the Conversazione was about 1*s*. 3*d*. per head.'

Lord Ashby recorded that in *Community of Universities,* his history of the first fifty years of the Association, published in 1963.* If one shilling and threepence looked modest to him then, he would need a very powerful glass indeed to see what it would provide twenty years on. No doubt each planner in his generation found the problem of costs appalling.

My last attendance as a worker at an Association meeting was in Malta, when the Council met there in 1977. I knew then that I was to be proposed as Governor-General of Australia, and I assumed that office and left the university world late in 1977. So I missed the twelfth Congress in Canada, and other meetings besides. Throughout my years as Governor-General, however, I attended and took part in a very wide range of Commonwealth meetings in Australia. At the summit there was the meeting of Commonwealth Heads of Government in Australia in October 1981, and there were many meetings of a specialised character. All of this gave me a vivid picture of the range of Commonwealth activities and of the practicality of so much of its work. It also underlined a *style* which you, in these meetings, will recognise easily. Sonny Ramphal put it characteristically and well when he said that it is a Commonwealth of dissimilarity that seeks understanding not uniformity, a Commonwealth that welcomes accord where it is possible, respects disagreement where it is not, and can be relaxed about contrariety. It is a Commonwealth that is a sample of the world community, a Commonwealth which must be concerned with all the great problems of mankind because there is no area of global concern that does not touch some Commonwealth country intimately and directly.

I specially mention one event of those years. At an assembly in Melbourne at which the Secretary General of this Association was present, I gladly accepted an invitation to present the Symons Medal for distinguished service to the Association to Professor Sir David Derham, Vice-Chancellor of the University of Melbourne. It was a great pleasure to make an award which bore the name of Tom Symons, a friend who has rendered long and devoted service to the Association, to another old friend and colleague, one of our lot, who has been an outstanding Association and university man.

*Cambridge University Press for the Association of Universities of the British Commonwealth, o.p.

There are many here who know him and we all regret deeply that ill health has compelled his premature retirement.

This is a special occasion, a special Congress; an eightieth and a seventieth anniversary in the history of the Association. In his jubilee history Lord Ashby told of the 'remarkable' initiative of a member of the House of Commons, Gilbert Parker, which brought together representatives of thirty-one universities drawn from what we would now call the 'old Commonwealth' in 1903. That conference looked forward to the development of a closer and intimate relationship, to the promotion of exchanges and interchanges between these universities. It took a little time for the ideas to be developed further; it was not until 1912 that representatives of fifty-one universities, including universities in the Indian sub-continent, met in conference. This is numbered as the first of the Quinquennial Congresses. G. R. Parkin, the organising secretary of the Rhodes Scholarship Trust (and this year, 1983, we have celebrated the eightieth anniversary of the Rhodes Scholarship in Oxford), played a notable role as a catalyst. He saw the universities as engaged in a common task, but as lacking the means for 'common and concentrated effort for the comparison of experience and for the ready exchange of ideas'. To remedy this he proposed the establishment of a Bureau to promote a variety of useful functions which included the publication of a Yearbook. The proposal commanded ready assent; the historian tells us that 'there was no opposition. Three Australian delegates spoke in favour of Parkin's proposal and the session closed'.

The Bureau was established inexpensively and modestly in 1913, and this year we commemorate the seventieth anniversary of its founding. Styles and descriptions have changed to accord with more modern notions of Commonwealth; so it was that in the late 1940s the Bureau was restyled the Association of Universities of the British Commonwealth. In 1958 the first Quinquennial Congress to be held outside the United Kingdom met in Canada; in 1963, which was its fiftieth anniversary, the Association was granted a Charter as the Association of Commonwealth Universities, and in that year the membership of 117 universities reflected the growth and diversity of Commonwealth, a Commonwealth aptly described by an Asian leader a few years earlier as multiracial, multicultural and multilingual. Yet with all the change there was and there is a capacity to communicate in a common tongue. Within the Commonwealth, as the present Commonwealth Secretary-General reminds us, the English language remains as the precious legacy of an imperfect past. And I believe that in this Association, distinctively though not uniquely, we speak a common language

385

in more senses than one.

In the twenty years since 1963 there has been great growth: the membership has more than doubled to over 250 universities drawn from all the areas of the Commonwealth in which there are universities, from the Indian sub-continent, from Africa, Asia, the Pacific, the Mediterranean, the Caribbean. For the most part the members share a common historic tradition, though as they have developed and grown many, if not all, universities which make up the membership of the Association have established other and broader links and connections reflected in the training, the degrees and the experience of their faculties and academic bodies, in their links and associations with universities and academic traditions outside the Commonwealth. The Commonwealth bond, however, remains enduring; in a well-known passage in *Community of Universities* Lord Ashby speaks of the universities as:

'one of the most powerful forces uniting the countries of the Commonwealth; for Commonwealth leadership is largely in the hands of graduates, and, by virtue of the cohesion among Commonwealth universities, graduates from as far apart as Singapore and Vancouver, Ghana and Aberdeen, find that they share common assumptions, common cultural traditions, common canons of criticism and facility in using a common language.'

We have to take account of happenings not always comfortable, and at times dreadful, which have taken place in the twenty years since those words were written, but these cohesive forces remain important, and great meetings such as this testify to their vitality.

G. R. Parkin in 1912 stressed the role of the Association in facilitating common and concentrated effort, comparison of experience and ready exchange of ideas and, as the Secretary General, Dr. Christodoulou, has said in a recent speech, the fulfilment of these objectives has been achieved through the various meetings of heads of universities, Congresses and the governing council, through a variety of publications, among which the *Commonwealth Universities Yearbook* has a world currency and reputation, through a staff recruitment service readily provided and extensively used by universities in both developing and developed countries, and through scholarship and fellowship schemes and travel award programmes. He concludes, and I am sure that he is right, that the main contributions have been the spread of information about universities and their activities, the exchange of ideas between them, and the promotion of the maximum possible movement of academic staff and students from one country of the Commonwealth to another.

Eric Ashby, in the history to which I refer for so much that captures the image of the Association now as it did two decades ago, speaks of the headquarters of the ACU as 'an open door for vice-chancellors, professors, lecturers, registrars and bursars from all over the Commonwealth'. From my personal experience, recent and not so recent, I know how true that is. Again, the work done in preparation for a wide variety of meetings, in the administration of scholarship and staff exchange programmes, is immense, and is conducted efficiently and with extraordinary economy. The *Yearbook*, which Parkin proposed as a main instrument for the provision of information about Commonwealth universities, was likened by Ashby to Tolstoy's *War and Peace* in two respects; one, it is about the same length; and the other in that it is a 'monumental achievement'. If it does not aspire to the literary distinction of Tolstoy's work, let me point out that the Association, through its secretariat, is not lacking in high literary skills. Many of us who have been responsible in Commonwealth universities for the appointment of academic staff have relied on the Association for the organisation of interviews and reports on candidates in the United Kingdom. In days of greater staff recruitment this was a heavy burden on the secretariat; it still remains an important activity, and within months of my return to Oxford I found myself on one such committee organised and serviced by Peter Hetherington. Lord Ashby's reference to a great work of literature prompts me to express the hope that one day we may have an anthology of Hetherington reports, appropriately edited, no doubt, to avoid embarrassment and trespass upon privacy. I think that I can say with some confidence that there is a world-wide body of *aficionados* of those elegant and quite distinctive writings.

In 1963, when the Association marked its jubilee and when its history was last written, it was a time of great promise and growth for universities in many parts of the world, in the Commonwealth as elsewhere. Clark Kerr wrote of the university as the secular cathedral of that time, an object of admiration and great promise which called for and received great support. That was specially true of the United States; it was true also, as I have said, of the Commonwealth. We think of reports like those of Robbins, of Murray, of Hughes-Parry and many others and of their assumptions about the role and value of the university. Universities were supported and grew on an unprecedented scale. The climate of our time is very different, and as the Secretary General, Dr. Christodoulou, pointed out in a notable speech in India early this year, universities face many and severe problems. There are financial stringencies which create great difficulties and which

387

produce consequences which I need not detail to you who live with them daily. It is not, however, simply a matter of financial constraint in a time of widespread economic difficulty. In the Secretary General's words:

'. . . If in many countries these were simply some of the disastrous consequences of economic recession, the universities might perhaps look for comfort in the hope of better things to come; what they see in reality are the outriders of a greater massing attack on a front much broader than that of cost reduction at a time of public penury. They face, rather, an enforcement of change and an exercise of ever more direct control over what they do and even of how they do it.

. . . not only governments but the wider communities which they direct and which universities are deemed to serve have begun to choose to look at their universities with an intensely critical eye, have challenged them to justify their curricula as well as prove their cost-effectiveness, to exhibit their relevance as well as their research, to justify not only their expenses, but in some instances even their very existence.

The major theme of this Congress, *Technological Innovation: University Roles,* and the specific applications as expressed in the individual Topics point to current and appropriate concerns of universities and the communities of which they are part, and I shall certainly wish to read the record of the discussions. Maybe there will be an answer in them to a question raised by a section at the Cambridge Congress of the Association exactly thirty years ago, which was devoted to a topic which, as Lord Ashby opines, must surely be the most tendentious title ever on the programme of an academic conference: 'What subject or subjects today are best fitted to fulfil the role played previously in the university curriculum by the classics?' Let me take you back for a minute to the account in the jubilee history:

'Classicists rallied to the rescue, of course. The Vice-Chancellor of Oxford (Maurice Bowra) . . . called the title of the session a "vicious or an improper question", to be compared with: "What person is necessary to fulfil the role previously played, up to today, by your wife?" In a speech which alone justified the organising committee's choice of title, Maurice Bowra uncompromisingly defended the classics. He would not even be satisfied with the classics in translation: "translation", he said, "is as interesting as any crossword puzzle—and about as important". Notwithstanding this and other spirited defences of the classics . . . the current of opinion at the meeting flowed in the same direction as the tendentious title. It was (as Maurice Bowra described it) like "attending a very distinguished and very elaborate funeral . . . with *pompes funèbres première classe* and with many valedictory and obituary orations delivered over the grave".'

I wonder whether such passions have been stirred in the debates of this Congress?

The continuing growth of and support for the Association testifies to the importance of consultation, exchange and experience to which I have referred. Dr. Christodoulou put it well early this year in saying that the need to exchange ideas, techniques and experience between university academic and administrative leaders who will play key roles as agents of change is much increased in our day and this, he says, is 'sheer pragmatism'. The Commonwealth heads of government expressly acknowledged this in their communique at the end of their meeting in Melbourne in 1981. 'Heads of Government reaffirmed that student mobility and educational interchange within the Commonwealth were important to the national development efforts of Commonwealth countries and to maintaining Commonwealth links'. Some of the impediments to mobility, such as high fees, were noted, and the Commonwealth Secretary-General has followed up the heads' expression of concern by practical working measures. There are some encouraging signs.

Arnold Smith, the first Commonwealth Secretary-General, wrote recently in *Stitches in Time* that a hundred years from now historians will consider the Commonwealth the greatest of all Britain's contributions to man's social and political history. It is a big claim; there have been times, in the last decades of rapid Commonwealth growth and of continuing bitter dispute, when it has been sorely tested and tried, but it has come through as a unique world organisation. In our university world it seems to me that the continuing growth of the Association is testimony to the vitality and the utility of a distinctive, world-wide association. The editor of the revived *Round Table*, a journal which has a distinctive place in the recording of Commonwealth history, thinking and aspirations, wrote earlier this year about 'a rich, diverse, active and expanding unofficial non-governmental people's Commonwealth' and I believe that he is right in stressing the importance of this aspect of Commonwealth association and activity. We, in the Association of Commonwealth Universities, are a long established, an active and a very useful part of this non-official Commonwealth structure. In such Congresses as these, moreover, we bring to the debate on university matters the experience and thinking not only of professional university men and women but also of lay people who have made contributions of great value to the support and the welfare of universities, and that is very important.

May I, as an Australian, say that I am pleased that you will come again to Australia for the next Congress, in 1988. That year will be the 200th anniversary of European settlement in Australia, and it will be an important occasion for a national stocktaking, a time for reflection on our development as a people and a nation, and for exploration of our future course.

Eric Ashby concluded his history of the first half century with the words: 'The Commonwealth family will continually diversify. It therefore becomes of prime importance to promote a free trade in ideas, and of men who specialize in ideas, between Commonwealth countries. This is most easily done through their universities. The Association's task, as it enters upon its second half century, is to facilitate this free trade'. Twenty years on into its second half century, in complex and often difficult and dangerous times, the Association remains strong and active, supported by its members and counsellors, and well and very ably served and supported by its administrators led by its Secretary General, all of whom we should acknowledge specially on this occasion.

I have spoken about the Association; it exists to serve the universities of the Commonwealth, and it is this great body of institutions whose good health I commend to you. The toast I propose is: The Universities of the Commonwealth.

Council of the Association
1982–83

Sir Alec Merrison (Bristol), *Chairman*
Professor A. O. Adesola (Lagos), *Vice-Chairman*
Professor T. H. B. Symons (Canada), *Honorary Treasurer*
Sir Douglas Logan (UK), *Honorary Deputy Treasurer*
Dr A. Z. Preston (West Indies), *Immediate Past President*

Professor Dato' Dr. Awang Had Salleh (National U., Malaysia)
Dr. L. I. Barber (Regina)
Professor D. A. Bekoe (Ghana)
Professor L. M. Birt (New South Wales)
Professor A. D. Brownlie (Canterbury)
Professor D. E. Caro (Melbourne)
Professor S. V. Chittibabu (Annamalai)
Professor W. J. Kamba (Zimbabwe)
Dr. Hardwari Lal (Maharshi Dayanand)
Professor Lim Pin (National U., Singapore)
Professor J. K. Maitha (Kenyatta University College)
Professor Sir Roy Marshall (Hull)
Dr. P. P. M. Meincke (Prince Edward Island)
Professor Ramesh Mohan (Central Institute of English & Foreign Languages, Hyderabad)
Dr. J. G. Paquet (Laval)
Professor T. Ratho (Manipur)
Professor Z. R. Siddiqui (Jahangirnagar)
Dr. A. E. Sloman (Essex)
Professor I. H. Umar (Bayero)
Professor R. L. Watts (Queen's, Kingston)
Professor R. F. Whelan (Liverpool)
Professor S. Wijesundera (Colombo)
Sir Denys Wilkinson (Sussex)

Dr. A. Christodoulou, Secretary General

Members of the Congress

PRESIDENT
H.R.H. The Princess Anne, Mrs. Mark Phillips, GCVO, Chancellor of the University of London

ROYAL VICE-PRESIDENTS
H.R.H. The Prince Philip, Duke of Edinburgh, KG, KT, OM, GBE, FRS, Chancellor of the Universities of Cambridge, Edinburgh and Salford

H.R.H. The Prince of Wales, KG, Chancellor of the University of Wales

H.R.H. The Princess Margaret, Countess of Snowdon, CI, GCVO, Chancellor of the University of Keele

H.R.H. The Duke of Kent, GCMG, GCVO, Chancellor of the University of Surrey

H.R.H. The Duchess of Kent, GCVO, Chancellor of the University of Leeds

H.R.H. Princess Alexandra, the Hon. Mrs. Angus Ogilvy, GCVO, FRFPS, Chancellor of the University of Lancaster

VICE-PRESIDENTS
CHANCELLORS OF UNIVERSITIES OF GREAT BRITAIN AND NORTHERN IRELAND

ABERDEEN
The Rt. Hon. Lord Polwarth, TD, FRSE, FRSA

ASTON IN BIRMINGHAM
Sir Adrian Cadbury

BATH
The Rt. Hon. Lord Kearton of Whitchurch, OBE, FRS

QUEEN'S, BELFAST
The Rt. Hon Lord Ashby of Brandon, FRS

BIRMINGHAM
Sir Peter Scott, CBE, DSC

BRADFORD
The Rt. Hon. Sir Harold Wilson, KG, OBE, FRS

BRISTOL
Professor Dorothy M. Hodgkin, OM, FRS

BRUNEL
The Rt. Hon. The Earl of Halsbury, FRS

CITY
Sir Anthony Jolliffe, GBE, The Rt. Hon. Lord Mayor of London

CRANFIELD INSTITUTE OF TECHNOLOGY
The Rt. Hon. Lord Kings Norton of Wotton Underwood, FEng

DUNDEE
The Rt. Hon. The Earl of Dalhousie, KT, GCVO, GBE, MC

DURHAM
Dame Margot Fonteyn de Arias, DBE

EAST ANGLIA
The Rt. Hon. Lord Franks of Headington, OM, GCMG, KCB, CBE, FBA

ESSEX
The Rt. Hon. Sir Patrick Nairne, GCB, MC

EXETER
Sir Rex Richards, FRS, FRSC

GLASGOW
Sir Alexander Cairncross, KCMG

HERIOT-WATT
The Rt. Hon. Lord Thomson of Monifieth, KT, FEIS

HULL
The Rt. Hon. Lord Wilberforce, CMG, OBE

KENT AT CANTERBURY
The Rt. Hon. J. Grimond, TD

LEICESTER
Sir Alan Hodgkin, OM, KBE, FRS

LIVERPOOL
The Rt. Hon. The Viscount Leverhulme, TD

LOUGHBOROUGH
Sir Arnold Hall, FRS, FEng

MANCHESTER
His Grace The Duke of Devonshire, MC

NEWCASTLE UPON TYNE
His Grace The Duke of Northumberland, KG, GCVO, TD, KStJ, FRS

NOTTINGHAM
Sir Gordon Hobday

OPEN
The Rt. Hon. Lord Briggs of Lewes, FBA

OXFORD
The Rt. Hon. M. H. Macmillan, OM, FRS

VICE-PRESIDENTS

READING
The Rt. Hon. Lord Sherfield, GCB, GCMG

ROYAL COLLEGE OF ART
Sir Hugh Casson, KCVO, PRA, RDI, RIBA, FSIAD (Provost)

ST. ANDREWS
Sir Kenneth Dover, FRSE, FBA

SHEFFIELD
Sir Frederick Dainton, CChem, FRSC, FRCP, FRS

SOUTHAMPTON
The Rt. Hon. Lord Roll of Ipsden, KCMG, CB

STIRLING
Sir Montague Finniston, FInstP, FBIM, FRSE, FRSA, FRS

STRATHCLYDE
The Rt. Hon. Lord Todd of Trumpington, OM, FRS

SUSSEX
The Rt. Hon. Lord Shawcross of Friston, GBE, FRCS, RCOG

NEW U. OF ULSTER
The Rt. Hon. Lord Grey of Naunton, GCMG, GCVO, OBE

WARWICK
The Rt. Hon. Lord Scarman, OBE

YORK
The Rt. Hon. Lord Swann, FRCPE, FRCSE, ARCVS, FRS, FRSE

MINISTERS OF THE CROWN

Secretary of State for Foreign and Commonwealth Affairs
The Rt. Hon. Sir Geoffrey Howe, MP

Secretary of State for Education and Science
The Rt. Hon. Sir Keith Joseph, MP

Secretary of State for Northern Ireland
The Rt. Hon. James Prior, MP

Minister of Agriculture, Fisheries and Food
The Rt. Hon. Michael Jopling, MP

Secretary of State for the Environment
The Rt. Hon. Patrick Jenkin, MP

Secretary of State for Scotland
The Rt. Hon. George Younger, MP

Secretary of State for Wales
The Rt. Hon. Nicholas Edwards, MP

Secretary of State for Trade and Industry
The Rt. Hon. Cecil Parkinson, MP

Minister for Overseas Development
The Rt. Hon. Timothy Raison, MP

HIGH COMMISSIONERS IN LONDON OF OTHER COMMONWEALTH COUNTRIES

BAHAMAS
H. E. Mr. R. F. Anthony Roberts

SINGAPORE
H. E. Mr. Jek Yeun Thong

SWAZILAND
H. E. Mr. G. M. Mamba

DOMINICA
H. E. Mr. Arden Shillingford, MBE

CYPRUS
H. E. Mr. Tasos Panayides

EASTERN CARIBBEAN STATES (ANTIGUA AND BARBUDA, ST. LUCIA, ST. VINCENT AND THE GRENADINES)
H. E. Dr. Claudius C. Thomas, CMG

GRENADA
H. E. Mr. Fennis Augustine

BARBADOS
H. E. Mr. A. W. Symmonds, GCM

SIERRA LEONE
H. E. Mr. Victor E. Sumner

INDIA
H. E. Dr. V. A. Seyid Muhammad

PAPUA NEW GUINEA
H. E. Dr. Alexis H. Sarei, CBE

THE GAMBIA
H. E. Mr. A. M. K. Bojang

SRI LANKA
H. E. Mr. A. T. Moorthy

VICE-PRESIDENTS

UGANDA
H. E. The Hon. Shafiq Arain

MALAWI
H. E. Mr. Callisto Matekenya Mkona

AUSTRALIA
H. E. The Hon. Sir Victor Garland, KBE

FIJI
H. E. Ratu Josua Brown Toganivalu, CBE

ZAMBIA
H. E. Lieutenant-General Peter D. Zuze

NIGERIA
H. E. Alhaji Shehu Awak

KENYA
H. E. Mr. Bethuel Abdu Kiplagat

JAMAICA
H. E. Mr. H. S. Walker, CD

TANZANIA
H. E. Mr. A. B. Nyakyi

GUYANA
H. E. Mr. Cedric L. Joseph

BOTSWANA
H. E. Mr. S. A. Mpuchane

LESOTHO
H. E. Mr. J. K. Mollo

BANGLADESH
H. E. Mr. Fakhruddin Ahmed

GHANA
H. E. Mr. K. K. S. Dadzie

NEW ZEALAND
H. E. The Hon. William L. Young

MAURITIUS
H. E. Mr. C. Obeegadoo

CANADA
H. E. The Hon. Donald C. Jamieson, PC

TONGA
H. E. Mr. S. Tu'a Taumoepeau-Tupou

MALAYSIA
H. E. Mr. M. H. Kassim

TRINIDAD AND TOBAGO
H. E. Mr. F. O. Abdulah

MALTA
Mr. Francis F. A. Cassar (Acting High Commissioner)

ZIMBABWE
Mr. M. S. Kajese (Acting High Commissioner)

REPRESENTATIVES OF THE COUNTY OF WEST MIDLANDS AND OF THE CITY OF BIRMINGHAM

The Lord Lieutenant of the County of West Midlands
The Rt. Hon. Lord Aylesford

The High Sheriff of the County of West Midlands
Mr. H. Kenrick

The Lord Mayor of the City of Birmingham
Councillor W. J. H. Sowton, MBE

The Chairman of the West Midlands County Council
Councillor Sir Stan Yapp

Participants nominated by Member Institutions

AUSTRALIA

ADELAIDE
Dr. E. H. Medlin, Deputy Chancellor
Professor D. R. Stranks, Vice-Chancellor
Professor D. M. Boyd, Professor of Geophysics
Dr. D. R. Hainsworth, Reader in History

AUSTRALIAN NATIONAL
Professor Sir John Crawford, AC, CBE, Chancellor
Professor P. H. Karmel, AC, CBE, Vice-Chancellor
Professor F. W. E. Gibson, Head of Department of Biochemistry, John Curtin School of Medical Research

DEAKIN
The Hon. Mr. Justice K. J. A. Asche, Chancellor
Professor F. R. Jevons, Vice-Chancellor
Professor A. M. Bond, Foundation Professor of Chemistry

PARTICIPANTS NOMINATED BY MEMBER INSTITUTIONS

FLINDERS, SOUTH AUSTRALIA
Professor K. J. Hancock, Vice-Chancellor
Professor B. Abrahamson, Professor of Mathematics
Dr. Ann D. Crocker, Senior Lecturer in Clinical Pharmacology

GRIFFITH
Sir Theodor Bray, CBE, Chancellor
Mrs. Daphne M. Buckley, Member of Governing Council
Professor F. J. Willett, Vice-Chancellor
Professor R. D. Guthrie, Emeritus Professor

JAMES COOK, NORTH QUEENSLAND
Sir George Kneipp, Chancellor
Professor K. J. C. Back, Vice-Chancellor
Professor R. S. F. Campbell, Professor of Tropical Veterinary Science

LA TROBE
The Hon. Mr. Justice R. E. McGarvie, Chancellor
Miss Patricia Kennedy, Member of Council
Professor J. F. Scott, Vice-Chancellor
Dr. J. G. Jenkin, Reader in Physics

MACQUARIE
Professor P. H. Partridge, AC, Chancellor
Professor E. C. Webb, Vice-Chancellor
Mrs. Ebba M. van der Helder, Lecturer in German
Dr. Sabine H. Willis, Lecturer in Politics

MELBOURNE
Rev. Dr. J. Davis McCaughey, Deputy Chancellor
Professor D. E. Caro, OBE, Vice-Chancellor and Principal
Professor L. R. Webb, Chairman of Academic Board and Pro-Vice-Chancellor
Mr. J. B. Potter, AM, ED, Registrar

MONASH
Professor R. L. Martin, Vice-Chancellor
Professor R. D. Brown, Professor of Chemistry
Mr. J. D. Butchart, OBE, Registrar

MURDOCH
The Hon. Sir Ronald Wilson, KBE, CMG, Chancellor
Professor F. M. G. Willson, Vice-Chancellor
Professor G. C. Bolton, Professor of History (and Head, Australian Studies
Centre, Institute of Commonwealth Studies, University of London)
Mr. D. D. Dunn, Secretary

NEWCASTLE
Sir Bede Callaghan, CBE, Chancellor
Professor D. W. George, AO, Vice-Chancellor and Principal
Dr. D. W. Dockrill, Senior Lecturer in Philosophy

NEW ENGLAND
Mr. E. J. Hilder, Member of Council
Professor R. C. Gates, AO, Vice-Chancellor
Professor W. F. Musgrave, Professor of Agricultural Economics
Dr. A. F. Horadam, Associate Professor of Mathematics

NEW SOUTH WALES
The Hon. Mr. Justice G. J. Samuels, Chancellor
Mr. R. A. Corin, Member of Council
Professor L. M. Birt, CBE, Vice-Chancellor and Principal
Professor D. M. McCallum, Chairman of the Professorial Board and Head of School of Political Science

QUEENSLAND
The Hon. Sir Walter Campbell, Chancellor
Professor B. G. Wilson, Vice-Chancellor
Professor M. W. Gunn, Dean of Engineering and Head of Department of Electrical Engineering
Professor R. L. Whitmore, Professor of Mining and Metallurgical Engineering

SYDNEY
Sir Hermann Black, Chancellor
Professor M. G. Taylor, Deputy Vice-Chancellor
Dr. R. I. Jack, Associate Professor and Head of Department of History

TASMANIA
Professor H. G. Gelber, Professor of Political Science

WESTERN AUSTRALIA
Mr. D. H. Aitken, Chancellor
Mrs. Dorothy E. Ransom, Member of Senate
Professor R. Street, Vice-Chancellor
Dr. G. A. Bottomley, Associate Professor (Chemistry)
Dr. J. Attikiouzel, Senior Lecturer (Electrical Engineering Science)
Mr. M. R. Orr, Registrar

WOLLONGONG
Professor K. R. McKinnon, Vice-Chancellor

BANGLADESH

BANGLADESH AGRICULTURAL
Professor A. K. M. Aminul Haque, Vice-Chancellor

BANGLADESH U. OF ENGINEERING AND TECHNOLOGY
Professor A. M. Patwari, Vice-Chancellor

CHITTAGONG
Professor M. A. Aziz Khan, Vice-Chancellor

JAHANGIRNAGAR
Professor Z. R. Siddiqui, Vice-Chancellor

PARTICIPANTS NOMINATED BY MEMBER INSTITUTIONS

RAJSHAHI
Professor Muhammad A. Raqib, Vice-Chancellor
Professor Makbular R. Sarkar, Professor of Applied Physics and Electronics and Former Vice-Chancellor

BOTSWANA

BOTSWANA
Professor J. D. Turner, Vice-Chancellor

BRITAIN

ABERDEEN
Mr. C. A. MacLeod, Chancellor's Assessor
Professor G. P. McNicol, Principal
Professor A. Rutherford, Senior Vice-Principal
Mr. T. B. Skinner, Secretary

ASTON IN BIRMINGHAM
Professor F. W. Crawford, Vice-Chancellor

BATH
Mr. R. M. Mawditt, Secretary and Registrar

QUEEN'S, BELFAST
Dr. P. Froggatt, President and Vice-Chancellor
Professor J. Braidwood, (Senior) Pro-Vice-Chancellor and Professor and Head of Department of English Language and Literature
Mr. A. H. Graham, Secretary to Academic Council

BIRMINGHAM
Sir Peter Scott, CBE, DSC, Chancellor
Dr. C. Beale, TD, Pro-Chancellor
Professor E. A. Marsland, Vice-Chancellor and Principal
Professor J. D. Fage, Pro-Vice-Chancellor and Vice-Principal
Professor J. M. Samuels, Pro-Vice-Chancellor

BRADFORD
Professor J. C. West, CBE, Vice-Chancellor
Mr. I. M. Sanderson, MBE, Registrar and Secretary

BRISTOL
Dr. R. Hill, Chairman of Council
Sir Alec Merrison, Vice-Chancellor
Professor R. T. Severn, Pro Vice-Chancellor and Professor of Civil Engineering
Professor K. Ingham, OBE, MC, Professor of History
Mr. E. C. Wright, Registrar and Secretary

BRUNEL
Sir James Redmond, Member of Council
Mr. H. W. Try, Member of Council and Chairman of Finance Committee
Professor R. E. D. Bishop, CBE, Vice-Chancellor
Mr. D. Neave, Secretary General and Registrar

CAMBRIDGE
Professor F. H. Hinsley, OBE, Vice-Chancellor
Mr. M. J. Allen, Director of Extra-Mural Studies
Professor M. D. I. Chisholm, Professor and Head of Department of Geography
Dr. A. D. I. Nicol, Secretary General of the Faculties

CITY
Dr. R. N. Franklin, Vice-Chancellor
Professor P. K. M'Pherson, Pro-Vice-Chancellor and Head of Department of Systems Science
Dr. A. H. Seville, Academic Registrar

CRANFIELD INSTITUTE OF TECHNOLOGY
Sir Henry Chilver, Vice-Chancellor

DUNDEE
Dr. A. M. Neville, Principal and Vice-Chancellor
Professor P. D. Griffiths, Vice-Principal
Mr. R. Seaton, Secretary

DURHAM
Professor F. G. T. Holliday, CBE, Vice-Chancellor and Warden
Miss Irene Hindmarsh, Pro-Vice-Chancellor and Principal of St. Aidan's College

EAST ANGLIA
Mr. T. J. A. Colman, Pro-Chancellor and Chairman of Council
Professor M. W. Thompson, Vice-Chancellor
Mr. I. D. Thomas, Senior Lecturer, School of Development Studies

EDINBURGH
Dr. J. H. Burnett, Principal and Vice-Chancellor
Mr. A. M. Currie, OBE, Secretary

ESSEX
Dr. A. E. Sloman, CBE, Vice-Chancellor
Mr. E. Newcomb, Registrar

EXETER
Mr. P. J. Chalk, Treasurer
Dr. H. Kay, CBE, Vice-Chancellor

GLASGOW
Sir Alwyn Williams, Principal and Vice-Chancellor
Professor A. S. Skinner, Clerk of Senate
Mr. J. McCargow, Secretary

HERIOT-WATT
Rt. Hon. Lord Thomson of Monifieth, KT, Chancellor
Dr. T. L. Johnston, Principal and Vice-Chancellor
Professor A. R. Rogers, Vice-Principal
Mr. D. I. Cameron, Director of Administration and Secretary

PARTICIPANTS NOMINATED BY MEMBER INSTITUTIONS

HULL
Mr. T. H. F. Farrell, TD, Pro-Chancellor and Chairman of Council
Mr. W. L. Black, Treasurer
Professor Sir Roy Marshall, CBE, Vice-Chancellor
Mr. F. T. Mattison, Registrar

KEELE
Rt. Hon. Lord Rochester, Pro-Chancellor
Dr. D. Harrison, Vice-Chancellor
Professor D. Thompson, Head of Department of Law
Dr. D. Cohen, Registrar

KENT AT CANTERBURY
Dr. U. H. B. Alexander, MBE, Treasurer
Dr. D. J. E. Ingram, Vice-Chancellor

LANCASTER
Sir Alastair Pilkington, Pro-Chancellor
Professor P. A. Reynolds, Vice-Chancellor
Professor A. I. MacBean, Professor of Economics and Pro-Vice-Chancellor
Mr. G. M. Cockburn, Secretary

LEEDS
Professor William Walsh, Acting Vice-Chancellor
Sir Edward Parkes, Vice-Chancellor Elect
Professor T. B. Hogan, Pro-Vice-Chancellor
Mr. J. J. Walsh, Registrar

LEICESTER
Mr. M. Shock, Vice-Chancellor
Professor J. E. Spence, Pro-Vice-Chancellor
Mr. J. W. Walmsley, Registrar Designate

LIVERPOOL
Mr. H. B. Chrimes, Pro-Chancellor
Professor R. F. Whelan, Vice-Chancellor
Professor P. W. Edwards, Pro-Vice-Chancellor and Professor of English Literature
Mr. H. H. Burchnall, Registrar

LONDON
Mr. J. R. Stewart, CBE, Principal
Dr. A. O. Betts, Principal and Dean, Royal Veterinary College
Professor B. H. Groombridge, Director, Department of Extra Mural Studies
Dr. B. B. MacGillivray, Chairman, Joint Medical Advisory Committee, and Dean, Royal·Free Hospital School of Medicine

IMPERIAL COLLEGE OF SCIENCE AND TECHNOLOGY
Rt. Hon. Lord Flowers, Rector

INSTITUTE OF EDUCATION
Dr. W. Taylor, CBE, Director (Principal Designate, University of London)
Professor P. R. C. Williams, Head of Department of Education in Developing Countries

QUEEN MARY COLLEGE
Professor M. A. Laughton, Dean of Engineering and Professor of Electrical Engineering
Mr. D. Jaynes, Registrar

UNIVERSITY COLLEGE LONDON
Professor D. W. James, Vice-Provost
Major-General I. H. Baker, CBE, Secretary

LOUGHBOROUGH
Dr. H. W. French, CBE, Senior Pro-Chancellor and Chairman of Council
Sir Clifford Butler, Vice-Chancellor
Professor D. J. Johns, Senior Pro-Vice-Chancellor
Mr. H. Brooks, Registrar

MANCHESTER
Mr. D. K. Redford, CBE, Treasurer
Professor M. Richmond, Vice-Chancellor
Professor D. S. R. Welland, Pro-Vice-Chancellor and Professor of American Literature
Mr. K. E. Kitchen, Registrar

MANCHESTER, INSTITUTE OF SCIENCE AND TECHNOLOGY
Mr. F. A. Russell, Chairman of Council
Professor H. C. A. Hankins, Acting Principal
Dr. J. Parker, Dean, Faculty of Technology, University of Manchester
Mr. D. H. McWilliam, Secretary and Registrar

NEWCASTLE UPON TYNE
Professor J. Ashton, Professor and Head of Department of Agricultural Economics
Mr. W. R. Andrew, Registrar

NOTTINGHAM
Dr. B. C. L. Weedon, CBE, Vice-Chancellor
Rev. Professor J. Heywood Thomas, Pro-Vice-Chancellor
Mrs. Meryl E. Aldridge, Lecturer (Sociology/Social Policy)
Mr. G. E. Chandler, Registrar

OPEN
Dr. J. H. Horlock, Vice-Chancellor
Professor R. C. Smith, Pro-Vice-Chancellor (Continuing Education)
Mr. D. J. Clinch, Secretary
Mr. M. A. Watkinson, Private Secretary to the Vice-Chancellor

OXFORD
Mr. G. J. Warnock, Vice-Chancellor
Dr. W. G. Richards, Lecturer (Chemistry) and Chairman, University and Industry Committee

READING
Professor J. Wrigley, CBE, Deputy Vice-Chancellor

404

PARTICIPANTS NOMINATED BY MEMBER INSTITUTIONS

ST. ANDREWS
Dr. J. Steven Watson, Principal and Vice-Chancellor
Professor F. D. Gunstone, Professor of Chemistry
Professor R. A. Stradling, Professor and Head of Department of Physics

SALFORD
Professor J. M. Ashworth, Vice-Chancellor
Dr. T. J. Lunt, Pro-Chancellor and Chairman of Council
Professor L. S. Bark, Dean of the Faculty of Science and Professor of Analytical Chemistry
Mr. S. R. Bosworth, Registrar

SHEFFIELD
Sir Frederick Dainton, Chancellor
Professor G. D. Sims, OBE, Vice-Chancellor
Mr. B. E. Coates, Senior Lecturer (Geography) and Vice-President, Non-Professorial Staff Association
Mr. R. F. Eddy, Academic Registrar

SOUTHAMPTON
Professor J. M. Roberts, Vice-Chancellor
Professor D. C. Jackson, Deputy Vice-Chancellor and Professor of Law
Mr. D. A. Schofield, Secretary and Registrar

STIRLING
Sir Kenneth Alexander, Principal and Vice-Chancellor
Professor D. W. G. Timms, Deputy Principal
Mr. R. G. Bomont, Secretary

STRATHCLYDE
Dr. G. J. Hills, Principal and Vice-Chancellor
Mr. W. Scott, Course Supervisor in Manufacturing Sciences and Engineering
Mr. D. W. J. Morrell, Registrar

SURREY
Dr. A. Kelly, Vice-Chancellor
Professor M. B. Waldron, Pro-Vice-Chancellor

SUSSEX
Mr. T. H. B. Mynors, Senior Pro-Chancellor and Chairman of Council
Sir Denys Wilkinson, Vice-Chancellor
Professor F. J. Bayley, Pro-Vice-Chancellor (Science)
Professor Margaret M. McGowan, Pro-Vice-Chancellor (Arts and Social Studies)
Dr. G. Lockwood, Registrar and Secretary

NEW U. OF ULSTER
Sir Robert Kidd, KBE, CB, Pro-Chancellor and Chairman of Council
Professor P. J. Newbould, Acting Vice-Chancellor
Mr. W. T. Ewing, Registrar

WALES
Rt. Hon. Lord Edmund-Davies, Pro-Chancellor
Dr. C. W. L. Bevan, CBE, Vice-Chancellor
Mr. E. Wynn Jones, Registrar

UNIVERSITY COLLEGE OF WALES, ABERYSTWYTH
Mr. B. G. Jones, CBE, Vice-President
Dr. G. Owen, Principal
Professor H. Carter, Vice-Principal and Professor of Human Geography

UNIVERSITY COLLEGE OF NORTH WALES, BANGOR
Mr. G. R. Thomas, Acting Registrar

UNIVERSITY COLLEGE, CARDIFF
Professor K. S. Dodgson, Deputy Principal (Science) and Head of Department of Biochemistry
Dr. L. A. Moritz, Vice-Principal (Administration) and Registrar
Dr. A. Cryer, Senior Lecturer (Biochemistry) and Chairman of Non-Professorial Staff

UNIVERSITY COLLEGE OF SWANSEA
Professor B. L. Clarkson, Principal
Professor J. Dutton, Vice-Principal (Administration) and Professor of Physics
Mr. V. J. Carney, Registrar

WALES, INSTITUTE OF SCIENCE AND TECHNOLOGY
Mr. H. W. Morris, Hon. Treasurer
Dr. A. F. Trotman-Dickenson, Principal
Professor M. J. Bruton, Vice-Principal and Head of Department of Town Planning
Mr. F. Harris-Jones, Registrar and Secretary

WELSH NATIONAL SCHOOL OF MEDICINE
Mr. T. R. Saunders, Registrar and Secretary

SAINT DAVID'S UNIVERSITY COLLEGE, LAMPETER
Dr. R. Bowen, President
Rev. D. P. Davies, Dean of the Faculty of Theology
Mr. K. G. Ford, Secretary

WARWICK
Sir Arthur Vick, OBE, Pro-Chancellor and Chairman of Council
Mr. J. B. Butterworth, CBE, Vice-Chancellor
Mr. A. Rowe-Evans, Secretary and Registrar

YORK
Professor S. B. Saul, Vice-Chancellor

CANADA

ACADIA
Dr. J. R. C. Perkin, President and Vice-Chancellor

PARTICIPANTS NOMINATED BY MEMBER INSTITUTIONS

ALBERTA
Mr. J. L. Schlosser, Chairman of Board of Governors
Dr. M. Horowitz, President

ATHABASCA
Mr. J. P. C. Elson, Chairman of Governing Council
Dr. S. Griew, President
Dr. R. H. Paul, Vice-President, Learning Services

BRITISH COLUMBIA
Dr. K. G. Pedersen, President
Dr. C. B. Bourne, Professor of Law and Advisor to the President
Dr. D. T. Kenny, Professor of Psychology
Professor R. M. Will, Dean of the Faculty of Arts

BROCK
Professor A . J. Earp, President and Vice-Chancellor
Mr. T. B. Varcoe, Vice-President, Administration

CALGARY
Dr. P. J. Krueger, Vice-President (Academic) and Professor of Chemistry
Dr. T. H. Barton, Dean of the Faculty of Engineering
Dr. R. H. Carnie, Secretary to General Faculties Council and Professor of English

UNIVERSITY COLLEGE OF CAPE BRETON
Dr. W. M. Reid, President
Dr. D. F. Campbell, Professor of Psychology

CARLETON
Dr. W. E. Beckel, President and Vice-Chancellor

CONCORDIA
Dr. J. W. O'Brien, Rector and Vice-Chancellor
Mr. G. Martin, Vice-Rector, Administration and Finance
Professor J. H. Whitelaw, Associate Vice-Rector, Academic

DALHOUSIE
Dr. W. A. MacKay, President and Vice-Chancellor
Professor A. J. Tingley, Registrar and Professor of Mathematics

GUELPH
Dr. W. E. Tossell, Dean of Research

LAVAL
Dr. J.-G. Paquet, Rector
Professor G.-B. Martin, Professor of Food Science and Technology

LETHBRIDGE
Professor J. H. Woods, President and Vice-Chancellor

407

McGILL
Mr. H. G. Hallward, Chairman of Board of Governors
Dr. D. L. Johnston, Principal and Vice-Chancellor

McMASTER
Dr. A. A. Lee, President and Vice-Chancellor
Dr. L. J. King, Vice-President, Academic
Dr. A. C. Frosst, Assistant Vice-President, Research Services
Dr. A. C. Heidebrecht, Dean of Engineering

MANITOBA
Dr. A. Naimark, President and Vice-Chancellor

MONTREAL
Professor P. Lacoste, OC, Rector

MOUNT SAINT VINCENT
Dr. E. Margaret Fulton, President

NEW BRUNSWICK
Mr. J. F. O'Sullivan, Vice-President (Finance and Administration)
Dr. F. R. Wilson, Dean of Engineering

OTTAWA
Rev. Dr. R. Guindon, Rector and Vice-Chancellor
Dr. A. D'Iorio, Vice-Rector (Academic Affairs)
Dr. J.-M. Beillard, Secretary

PRINCE EDWARD ISLAND
Mr. D. M. Stewart, Chancellor
Dr. P. P. M. Meincke, President and Vice-Chancellor
Professor F. J. Ledwell, Dean of Arts

QUEEN'S, KINGSTON
Professor R. L. Watts, OC, Principal and Vice-Chancellor
Professor D. W. Bacon, Dean of the Faculty of Applied Science
Professor M. Yeates, Dean of Graduate Studies and Research

REGINA
Mrs. Lorraine Thorsrud, Vice-Chairman of Board of Governors
Dr. L. I. Barber, OC, President
Dr. D. E. Shaw, Vice-President

RYERSON POLYTECHNICAL INSTITUTE
Dr. B. Segal, President

SAINT MARY'S
Dr. K. L. Ozmon, President

SASKATCHEWAN
Mr. R. G. Klombies, Chairman of Board of Governors
Dr. L. F. Kristjanson, President

408

PARTICIPANTS NOMINATED BY MEMBER INSTITUTIONS

TORONTO
Professor D. M. Nowlan, Vice-President (Research and Planning)

TRENT
Mr. J. Matthews, Director, International Program
Professor T. H. B. Symons, OC, Vanier Professor

WATERLOO
Dr. D. T. Wright, President and Vice-Chancellor
Professor T. A. Brzustowski, Vice-President, Academic
Mr. A. B. Gellatly, Vice-President, Finance and Operations

WESTERN ONTARIO
Professor D. Smith, Dean of Social Science

WILFRID LAURIER
Dr. J. A. Weir, President and Vice-Chancellor

WINDSOR
Professor C. MacInnis, Dean of Engineering

WINNIPEG
Dr. R. O. A. Hunter, Chancellor
Dr. R. H. Farquhar, President and Vice-Chancellor
Dr. A. R. McCormack, Vice-President (Academic)

YORK
Dr. H. I. Macdonald, OC, KLJ, President and Vice-Chancellor
Dr. W. C. Found, Vice-President (Academic Affairs)
Dr. T. H. Leith, Associate Professor of Natural Science, Joseph E. Atkinson College
Dr. Jane Couchman, Chairman of Senate, and Chairman of Department of French, Glendon College

GHANA

CAPE COAST
Professor K. B. Dickson, Vice-Chancellor

GHANA
Dr. D. A. Bekoe, Vice-Chancellor
Dr. G. Benneh, Associate Professor and Head of Department of Geography
Dr. R. D. Baeta, Senior Lecturer, Department of Physics
Mr. E. A. K. Edzii, Registrar

KUMASI, U. OF SCIENCE AND TECHNOLOGY
Professor F. O. Kwami, (Interim) Vice-Chancellor
Professor J. Owusu-Addo, Dean of the Faculty of Architecture
Mr. A. S. Y. Andoh, Registrar

GUYANA

GUYANA
Ms. Cecilene L. Baird, Pro-Chancellor
Dr. G. Walcott, Acting Vice-Chancellor

HONG KONG

CHINESE U. OF HONG KONG
Dr. Ma Lin, CBE, Vice-Chancellor
Dr. Y. W. Lam, Dean of the Faculty of Science
Dr. F. C. Chen, Secretary

U. OF HONG KONG
Sir Albert Rodrigues, CBE, ED, Pro-Chancellor and Chairman of Council
Dr. The Hon. R. L. Huang, CBE, Vice-Chancellor
Professor L. K. Young, OBE, Pro-Vice-Chancellor

INDIA

ALIGARH MUSLIM
Professor Saiyid Hamid, Vice-Chancellor

ANDHRA
Mr. K. Koteswara Rao, Member of Syndicate
Mr. B. Krishna Mohan, Dean, Faculty of Law, and Member of Syndicate
Mr. S. B. Satyanarayana Rao, Member of Syndicate

ANNA
Professor V. C. Kulandai Swamy, Vice-Chancellor

ANNAMALAI
Professor S. V. Chittibabu, Vice-Chancellor

AWADHESH PRATAP SINGH VISHWAVIDYALAYA
Professor H. L. Nigam, Vice-Chancellor

BANARAS HINDU
Professor Iqbal Narain, Vice-Chancellor

BANGALORE
Dr. M. N. Viswanathaiah, Vice-Chancellor

MAHARAJA SAYAJIRAO U. OF BARODA
Professor B. C. Parekh, Vice-Chancellor

BHARATHIAR
Dr. R. Subbayyan, Vice-Chancellor

BHARATHIDASAN
Professor P. S. Mani Sundaram, Vice-Chancellor

BHOPAL VISHWAVIDYALAYA
Dr. R. C. Shukla, Vice-Chancellor

PARTICIPANTS NOMINATED BY MEMBER INSTITUTIONS

BIRLA INSTITUTE OF TECHNOLOGY AND SCIENCE
Dr. C. R. Mitra, Director

BOMBAY
Professor S. V. Ghatalia, Member of Executive Council and Senate

BURDWAN
Dr. R. Mukherji, Vice-Chancellor

CALICUT
Professor N. Purushothaman, Pro-Vice-Chancellor

CENTRAL INSTITUTE OF ENGLISH AND FOREIGN LANGUAGES
Professor Ramesh Mohan, Director

COCHIN
Dr. K. Gopalan, Vice-Chancellor

DIBRUGARH
Dr. S. D. Gogoi, Vice-Chancellor
Professor K. C. Barua, Head of Department of Physics

GANDHIGRAM RURAL INSTITUTE
Dr. M. Aram, Vice-Chancellor

GAUHATI
Professor J. M. Choudhury, Vice-Chancellor

GORAKHPUR
Professor B. M. Shukla, Vice-Chancellor

GUJARAT AGRICULTURAL
Professor R. B. Shukla, Vice-Chancellor

GUJARAT
Professor K. S. Shastri, Vice-Chancellor
Dr. P. P. Mehta, Member of Executive Council

GURUKULA KANGRI VISHWAVIDYALAYA
Mr. G. B. K. Hooja, Vice-Chancellor

GURU NANAK DEV
Dr. J. S. Grewal, Vice-Chancellor

HYDERABAD
Professor B. S. Ramakrishna, Vice-Chancellor

INDIAN INSTITUTE OF TECHNOLOGY, BOMBAY
Professor A. K. De, Director

INDIAN INSTITUTE OF TECHNOLOGY, DELHI
Professor N. M. Swani, Director

411

INDIAN INSTITUTE OF TECHNOLOGY, KANPUR
Professor S. Sampath, Director

INDIAN INSTITUTE OF TECHNOLOGY, MADRAS
Professor P. V. Indiresan, Director

JADAVPUR
Professor M. M. Chakrabarty, Vice-Chancellor

JAMMU
Professor M. R. Puri, Vice-Chancellor

JAWAHARLAL NEHRU
Professor M. S. Agwani, Rector

JAWAHARLAL NEHRU TECHNOLOGICAL
Dr. G. L. Narayana, Vice-Chancellor

KAKATIYA
Professor T. Vasudev, Vice-Chancellor

KALYANI
Dr. S. Mookerjee, Vice-Chancellor

KASHMIR
Professor W. U. Malik, Vice-Chancellor

KERALA
Dr. K. Gopalan, Acting Vice-Chancellor (Vice-Chancellor, University of Cochin)

MADURAI-KAMARAJ
Professor J. Ramachandran, Vice-Chancellor

MAGADH
Mr. F. Ahmad, Vice-Chancellor

MAHARSHI DAYANAND
Dr. Hardwari Lal, Vice-Chancellor
Dr. J. C. Sharma

MANIPUR
Professor T. Ratho, Vice-Chancellor

MYSORE
Professor K. S. Hegde, Vice-Chancellor
Mr. S. Anand

NAGARJUNA
Dr. K. R. R. Mohan Rao, Vice-Chancellor

NORTH-EASTERN HILL
Dr. B. D. Sharma, Vice-Chancellor

412

PARTICIPANTS NOMINATED BY MEMBER INSTITUTIONS

OSMANIA
Mr. Syed Hashim Ali, Vice-Chancellor

PANJAB
Professor R. C. Paul, Vice-Chancellor

PATNA
Dr. G. P. Sinha, Vice-Chancellor

POONA
Professor R. G. Takwale, Vice-Chancellor

PUNJABI
Dr. S. S. Johl, Vice-Chancellor

RAJASTHAN
Professor T. K. N. Unnithan, Vice-Chancellor

RANCHI
Dr. A. K. Dhan, Vice-Chancellor
Professor R. N. Trivedi, Professor and Head, Department of Political Science,
  and Director, Postgraduate Correspondence Courses

SARDAR PATEL
Professor K. N. Shah, Vice-Chancellor
Professor N. M. Parikh, Member of Executive Council

SAURASHTRA
Professor S. R. Dave, Vice-Chancellor

S. N. D. T. WOMEN'S
Dr.(Mrs.) Jyoti H. Trivedi, Vice-Chancellor

SRI VENKATESWARA
Professor M. V. Rama Sarma, Vice-Chancellor
Professor G. N. Reddy, Professor of Telugu

TAMIL
Dr. V. I. Subramoniam, Vice-Chancellor

VIKRAM
Dr. K. K. Kemkar, Vice-Chancellor

VISVA-BHARATI
Professor Amlan Datta, Vice-Chancellor

KENYA

NAIROBI
Dr. J. G. Kiano, Chairman, University Grants Committee, Kenya
Professor J. M. Mungai, Vice-Chancellor
Mr. E. N. Gicuhi, Registrar

KENYATTA UNIVERSITY COLLEGE
Professor J. K. Maitha, Principal
Mr. L. M. Mungai, Registrar

LESOTHO
NATIONAL U. OF LESOTHO
Dr. C. B. Mackay, Member of Council
Professor R. W. Steel, CBE, Member of Council
Mr. A. M. Setšabi, Vice-Chancellor

MALAWI
MALAWI
Dr. D. Kimble, OBE, Vice-Chancellor
Mr. R. B. Mbaya, Registrar

MALAYSIA
U. OF AGRICULTURE, MALAYSIA
Professor Nayan bin Ariffin, Vice-Chancellor

MALAYA
Royal Professor Ungku A. Aziz, Vice-Chancellor
Haji Sulaiman Abdullah, Lecturer (Faculty of Law) and Member of Senate

U. OF SCIENCE MALAYSIA
Y. B. Datuk Musa bin Mohamad, JSM, PKT, Vice-Chancellor

MALTA
MALTA
Dr. A. Galea, President of Council
Professor G. P. Xuereb, Rector
Mr. D. Darmanin, Head of Faculty of Management Studies
Mr. L. Ellul, Registrar

MAURITIUS
MAURITIUS
Professor J. Manrakhan, Vice-Chancellor

NEW ZEALAND
AUCKLAND
Dr. R. H. L. Ferguson, Chancellor
Dr. C. J. Maiden, Vice-Chancellor
Professor J. H. Percy, Professor and Head of Department of Mechanical Engineer-
ing
Mr. W. B. Nicoll, Registrar

414

PARTICIPANTS NOMINATED BY MEMBER INSTITUTIONS

CANTERBURY
Miss Jean M. Herbison, CMG, Chancellor
Professor J. F. Burrows, Head of Department of Law
Mr. W. Hansen, Registrar

LINCOLN COLLEGE
Mr. S. M. Hurst, Chairman of Council
Professor Sir James Stewart, Principal
Mr. G. A. Hay, Registrar

MASSEY
Dr. L. R. Wallace, CBE, Chancellor
Dr. T. N. M. Waters, Vice-Chancellor
Professor E. L. Richards, Head of Department of Food Technology
Mr. A. J. Weir, Registrar

OTAGO
Mr. J. A. Valentine, Chancellor
Dr. R. O. H. Irvine, Vice-Chancellor
Mr. A. J. Geare, Senior Lecturer, Department of Management
Mr. D. W. Girvan, Registrar

VICTORIA, WELLINGTON
Dr. W. I. Axford, Vice-Chancellor

WAIKATO
Mr. D. E. Southwick, Pro-Chancellor
Dr. D. R. Llewellyn, Vice-Chancellor
Dr. M. D. Carr, Reader in Chemistry
Mr. I. T. Snowdon, Registrar

NIGERIA

AHMADU BELLO
Professor A. Abdullahi, Vice-Chancellor

ANAMBRA STATE U. OF TECHNOLOGY
Professor C. A Onwumechili, Deputy President

BAYERO
Professor I. H. Umar, Vice-Chancellor

BENIN
Professor A. Baikie, Vice-Chancellor
Mr. B. O. Akwukwuma, Registrar

FEDERAL U. OF TECHNOLOGY, AKURE
Professor T. I. Francis, Vice-Chancellor

FEDERAL U. OF TECHNOLOGY, BAUCHI
Professor A. O. Adekola, Vice-Chancellor
Alhaji A. Aliyu, Director of Administration and Secretary to Council

FEDERAL U. OF TECHNOLOGY, MAKURDI
Professor G. Igboeli, Vice-Chancellor

IBADAN
Dr. C. G. Okojie, OFR, Pro-Chancellor and Chairman of Council
Chief I. Ekanem-Ita, Registrar

IFE
Professor A. O. A. Adenuga, Deputy Vice-Chancellor
Dr. E. O. Adetunji, Registrar and Secretary

ILORIN
Professor S. A. Toye, Vice-Chancellor
Mr. O. Daramola, Registrar

JOS
Professor E. U. Emovon, Vice-Chancellor
Mr. G. T. Korgba, Registrar

LAGOS
Professor A. O. Adesola, Vice-Chancellor
Professor V. O. S. Olunloyo, Dean of Engineering
Dr. E. O. Akinluyi, Director of Planning

MAIDUGURI
Professor J. Aminu, Vice-Chancellor
Mallam D. Bobbo, Registrar

PORT HARCOURT
Professor S. J. S. Cookey, Vice-Chancellor
Professor C. U. Ikoku, Dean of the Faculty of Engineering

RIVERS STATE U. OF SCIENCE AND TECHNOLOGY
Professor T. N. Tamuno, Pro-Chancellor and Chairman of Council
Professor T. T. Isoun, Vice-Chancellor
Mr. M. B. Mieyebo, Acting Registrar

PAPUA NEW GUINEA

PAPUA NEW GUINEA
Dr. E. T. Brash, Vice-Chancellor

PAPUA NEW GUINEA U. OF TECHNOLOGY
Mr. L. Romaso, Deputy Vice-Chancellor

SIERRA LEONE

SIERRA LEONE
Dr. A. T. Porter, MRSL, Vice-Chancellor
Mr. P. L. Tucker, Deputy Chairman of Court

416

PARTICIPANTS NOMINATED BY MEMBER INSTITUTIONS

SINGAPORE

NATIONAL U. OF SINGAPORE
Dr. Lau Kieng Hiong, BBM, Member of Council
Mr. Lim Kee-Ming, Member of Council
Professor Lim Pin, Vice-Chancellor
Professor E. Thumboo, Dean of Arts and Social Sciences

NANYANG TECHNOLOGICAL INSTITUTE
Dr. Cham Tao Soon, President

SOUTH PACIFIC

SOUTH PACIFIC
Professor L. F. Brosnahan, Vice-Chancellor

SRI LANKA

COLOMBO
Professor S. Wijesundera, Vice-Chancellor

SWAZILAND

SWAZILAND
Professor S. M. Guma, Vice-Chancellor

TANZANIA

DAR ES SALAAM
Mr. N. A. Kuhanga, Vice-Chancellor

UGANDA

MAKERERE
Mr. J. Bikangaga, Chairman of Council
Professor A. Wandira, Vice-Chancellor

WEST INDIES

WEST INDIES
Dr. A. Z. Preston, Vice-Chancellor
Professor L. E. S. Braithwaite, Pro-Vice-Chancellor and Principal, St. Augustine Campus, Trinidad
Dr. K. D. Hunte, Deputy Principal, Cave Hill Campus, Barbados
Professor G. M. Richards, Pro-Vice-Chancellor and Deputy Principal, St. Augustine Campus, Trinidad
Professor L. R. B. Robinson, Pro-Vice-Chancellor (Planning) and Director, Development and Planning Unit
Dr. S. R. Wray, Dean of the Faculty of Medicine
Mr. C. E. Jackman, Registrar

ZAMBIA
Dr. J. M. Mwanza, Vice-Chancellor

ZIMBABWE
ZIMBABWE
Professor W. J. Kamba, Vice-Chancellor
Dr. N. T. Chideya, Information Officer

Representatives and Guests

Executive Officers of Commonwealth National and Regional Inter-University Bodies

AUSTRALIAN VICE-CHANCELLORS' COMMITTEE
Mr. F. S. Hambly, Secretary

ASSOCIATION OF UNIVERSITIES AND COLLEGES OF CANADA
Dr. A. K. Gillmore, Executive Director

INTER-UNIVERSITY COUNCIL FOR EAST AFRICA
Mr. E. K. Kigozi, Executive Secretary

COMMITTEE OF VICE-CHANCELLORS OF UNIVERSITIES IN GHANA
Mr. A. T. Konu, Secretary

ASSOCIATION OF INDIAN UNIVERSITIES
Professor Jagdish Narain, Secretary

NEW ZEALAND VICE-CHANCELLORS' COMMITTEE
Mr. B. P. Hampton, Secretary

COMMITTEE OF VICE-CHANCELLORS OF NIGERIAN UNIVERSITIES
Mrs. A. F. Sanwo, Acting Secretary

COUNCIL OF ONTARIO UNIVERSITIES
Dr. E. J. Monahan, Executive Director

CONFERENCE OF RECTORS AND PRINCIPALS OF QUEBEC UNIVERSITIES
Mr. R. Pérusse, Director General

REPRESENTATIVES AND GUESTS

COMMITTEE OF VICE-CHANCELLORS AND PRINCIPALS OF THE UNIVERSITIES OF
  THE UNITED KINGDOM
Mr. G. K. Caston, Secretary General
Mr. B. H. Taylor, Executive Secretary and Secretary General Designate
Mr. D. Anderson-Evans, Senior Administrative Officer
Mr. A. M. A. Powell, Senior Administrative Officer
Miss Jenifer Dover, Senior Administrative Officer
Miss Mary L. Morgan, Senior Administrative Officer

Commonwealth University Grants Committees or Equivalent Bodies

COMMONWEALTH TERTIARY EDUCATION COMMISSION, AUSTRALIA
Professor D. N. F. Dunbar, Chairman, Universities Council

UNIVERSITY GRANTS COMMISSION, BANGLADESH
Professor M. A. Bari, Chairman

UNIVERSITY GRANTS COMMITTEE, BRITAIN
Sir Edward Parkes, Chairman
Mr. N. T. Hardyman, Secretary

UNIVERSITY GRANTS COMMISSION, INDIA
Mr. R. K. Chhabra, Consultant

UNIVERSITY GRANTS COMMITTEE, KENYA
Dr. J. G. Kiano, Chairman

UNIVERSITY GRANTS COMMITTEE, NEW ZEALAND
Dr. A. T. Johns, CBE, Chairman

NATIONAL UNIVERSITIES COMMISSION, NIGERIA
Alhaji Yahya Aliyu, Executive Secretary

UNIVERSITY GRANTS COMMITTEE, UNIVERSITY OF THE SOUTH PACIFIC
Mr. Tamesar Bhim, CBE, Chairman

Other Organisations within the Commonwealth

CAMBRIDGE COMMONWEALTH TRUST
Professor D. A. Low, Treasurer

CANADIAN HIGH COMMISSION
Mr. M. J. Hellyer, Academic Relations Officer

CANADIAN INTERNATIONAL DEVELOPMENT AGENCY
Dr. L. Perinbam, Vice-President, Special Programmes Branch

COMMITTEE OF DIRECTORS OF POLYTECHNICS
Professor L. Barden, Director, Newcastle upon Tyne Polytechnic
Mr. G. Holroyde, Director, Coventry (Lanchester) Polytechnic

COMMONWEALTH ENGINEERS' COUNCIL
Dr. D. Mordell, Chairman, Commonwealth Board on Engineering Education and Training

COMMONWEALTH FOUNDATION
Mr. S. Mahendra, Deputy Director

COMMONWEALTH SCHOLARSHIP COMMISSION IN THE UNITED KINGDOM
Sir Michael Walker, GCMG, Chairman

COMMONWEALTH SCIENCE COUNCIL
Dr. M. N. G. A. Khan, Deputy Secretary

COMMONWEALTH SCIENTIFIC AND INDUSTRIAL RESEARCH ORGANIZATION, AUSTRALIA
Dr. N. K. Boardman, Member of Executive

COMMONWEALTH SECRETARIAT
H. E. Mr. Shridath S. Ramphal, Commonwealth Secretary-General
Mr. M. Malhoutra, Commonwealth Assistant Secretary-General
Chief R. E. O. Akpofure, OFR, Director, Education Programme, Human Resource Development Group

COUNCIL FOR NATIONAL ACADEMIC AWARDS
Dr. A. Goldman, Assistant Chief Officer

DEPARTMENT OF EDUCATION AND SCIENCE, UNITED KINGDOM
Mr. R. H. Bird, CB, Deputy Secretary, Higher and Further Education and Science

DEPARTMENT OF EDUCATION FOR NORTHERN IRELAND
Mr. N. Morrison, Chief Inspector

DEPARTMENT OF SCIENCE AND TECHNOLOGY, AUSTRALIA
Dr. R. M. Green, Deputy Secretary
Dr. A. Jostsons, Counsellor (Atomic Energy)

DEPARTMENT OF SECRETARY OF STATE FOR CANADA
Dr. D. R. Cameron, Assistant Under Secretary of State

FEDERAL UNIVERSITY OF TECHNOLOGY, ABEOKUTA
Professor C. Ikoku, Vice-Chancellor

JOINT ADMISSIONS AND MATRICULATION BOARD, NIGERIA
Mr. S. Angulu, Registrar

LEVERHULME TRUST
Dr. R. C. Tress, CBE, Director

NIGERIAN HIGH COMMISSION
Alhaji A. G. Mukhtar, Director, Nigerian Universities Office, London

420

REPRESENTATIVES AND GUESTS

OVERSEAS DEVELOPMENT ADMINISTRATION
Dr. R. O. Iredale, Principal Education Adviser
Mr. M. D. Francis, Education Adviser

TECHNICAL CHANGE CENTRE
Professor Sir Bruce Williams, KBE, Director
Miss J. A. Bryan-Brown, Personal Assistant/Research Assistant to the Director

TIMES HIGHER EDUCATION SUPPLEMENT
Mr. P. Scott, Editor
Ms. Ngaio Crequer
Mr. J. O'Leary

UNITED STATES—UNITED KINGDOM EDUCATIONAL COMMISSION
Mr. J. O. A. Herrington, Executive Director

ZAMBIAN HIGH COMMISSION
Mr. E. N. Phiri, Senior Education and Recruitment Attaché

International Organisations
(including those with a partial Commonwealth membership)

ASSOCIATION OF AFRICAN UNIVERSITIES
Mr. N. A. Kuhanga (Vice-Chancellor, University of Dar es Salaam)

INTERNATIONAL ASSOCIATION OF UNIVERSITIES
Professor M. Meyerson, Acting President (President Emeritus, University of Pennsylvania)
Professor J. F. Ade Ajayi, Member, Administrative Board (Professor of History, University of Ibadan)
Dr. C. E. Young, Deputy Member, Administrative Board (Chancellor, University of California, Los Angeles)
Mr. D. J. Aitken, Secretary-General

LIAISON COMMITTEE OF RECTORS' CONFERENCES OF MEMBER STATES OF THE EUROPEAN COMMUNITIES
Dr. A. M. Neville (Principal and Vice-Chancellor, University of Dundee)

STANDING CONFERENCE OF RECTORS, PRESIDENTS AND VICE-CHANCELLORS OF THE EUROPEAN UNIVERSITIES
Miss Alison Browning, Assistant Secretary General

UNESCO
Mr. F. F. Papa-Blanco, Director, Division of Technological Research and Higher Education, Science Sector

UNITED NATIONS UNIVERSITY
Dr. A. A. Kwapong, Vice Rector

Organisations outside the Commonwealth

ASSOCIATION OF AMERICAN UNIVERSITIES
Dr. W. H. Danforth, Chancellor, Washington University in St. Louis
Dr. M. A. Eggers, Chancellor, Syracuse University
Dr. J. C. Olson, President, University of Missouri
Dr. J. W. Ryan, President, Indiana University
Dr. C. E. Young, Chancellor, University of California, Los Angeles

BERNARD VAN LEER FOUNDATION
Sir Hugh W. Springer, KCMG, CBE, former Trustee

COMMITTEE OF HEADS OF IRISH UNIVERSITIES
Professor M. P. Mortell, Executive Officer (Registrar, University College, Cork)

SWISS RECTORS' CONFERENCE
Professor Dr. A. Miller, Secretary General

Special Guests of the Association of Commonwealth Universities

Professor H. E. Duckworth, OC, President and Vice-Chancellor Emeritus, University of Winnipeg
Sir Hugh W. Springer, KCMG, CBE, Former Secretary General, Association of Commonwealth Universities

Congress Speakers and other Participants
(not named elsewhere in these lists)

Sir Geoffrey Allen, Director of Research and Engineering Division, Unilever plc
Professor S. Blume, Professor of Science Dynamics, University of Amsterdam
Dr. S. L. Bragg, Regional Broker. Eastern Region, Science and Engineering Research Council
Professor E. Braun, Head of Technology Policy Unit, University of Aston in Birmingham
Dr. D. M. E. Curtis, Lecturer, Institute of Local Government Studies, University of Birmingham
Professor K. J. Davey, Professor of Development Administration and Associate Director, Institute of Local Government Studies, University of Birmingham
Mr. C. N. Devas, Lecturer, Institute of Local Government Studies, University of Birmingham
Professor G. Deniélou, President, Université de Compiègne
Mr. H. Dickinson, Senior Lecturer, School of Engineering, University of Edinburgh
Professor G. J. Afolabi Ojo, Vice-Chancellor, National Open University, Nigeria

Congress Committees, Officers and Secretariat

CONGRESS ORGANISING COMMITTEE

The Rt. Hon. Lord Hunter of Newington, *Chairman*
Dr. C. W. L. Bevan (from 26.3.81)
Dr. S. A. S. Galadanci (until 31.10.82)
Professor D. W. George
Sir Douglas Logan
Sir Alec Merrison (from 4.11.81)
Dr. C. R. Mitra
Professor R. W. Steel (until 4.3.81)
Professor T. H. B. Symons
Dr. J. Steven Watson

Sir Hugh W. Springer, *Secretary General, ACU* (until 30.9.80)
Dr. A. Christodoulou, *Secretary General, ACU* (from 1.10.80)
Mr. H. Harris, *Secretary, University of Birmingham*
Mr. A. J. Prior, *Assistant Secretary, University of Birmingham*
Mr. T. Craig, *Editor of Congress Proceedings (Assistant Secretary General, ACU)*
Mrs. Blanche Gubertini, *Personal Assistant to Secretary General, ACU*

CONGRESS SECRETARIAT

Dr. A. Christodoulou
Mr. H. Harris
Mr. A. J. Prior
Mr. F. C. Albrighton, *Information Officer, University of Birmingham*
Mr. T. Craig, *Editor of Congress Proceedings (Assistant Secretary General, ACU)*
Mrs. Blanche Gubertini
Mr. P. B. Hetherington, *Assistant Secretary General, ACU*
Mr. E. E. Temple, *Assistant Secretary General, ACU*
Mr. J. A. Whittingham, *Finance Officer, ACU*
Miss Gillian B. Woolven, *Press Liaison Officer, ACU*
Ms. Alyson Barr (*ACU*)
Miss Isabella Peters (*ACU*)
Ms. Kathryn Sturtridge (*ACU*)
Miss Celia Wannan (*ACU*)
D. Wilde (*ACU*)

UNIVERSITY OF BIRMINGHAM

Assistance with the organisation of the Congress was given by:—

LADIES' COMMITTEE

Mrs. Eleanor Davis, *Co-ordinator*

Mrs. Angela Bedford

Mrs. Joy Garrett

Mrs. Augusta Hamlin

Mrs. Thelma Harris

Mrs. Audrey Hathaway

Lady Hunter

Mrs. Jo Marsland

Mrs. Diane McCleverty

Mrs. Valerie Samuels

Mrs. Pearl Shovelton

Mrs. Margaret Wade

The Committee was further supported by:—

Mrs. Betty Cross

Mrs. Jean Fage

Mrs. Jean Raynor

OFFICERS AND STAFF OF THE UNIVERSITY OF BIRMINGHAM

Mr. H. Harris, *Secretary*

Mrs. Anne M. Hutton, *Registrar*

Mr. J. H. Fathers, *Estates and Buildings Officer*

Mr. F. C. Albrighton

Miss Susan Bayley

Mr. R. Brown

Mrs. Elsie Denham

Mr. P. W. Denner

Mr. M. P. Everett

Mr. E. Farrar

Miss Susan Hill

Mr. R. E. G. Hughes

Mr. D. L. Irving

Mr. R. H. Jones

Mrs. Jennifer Lindley

Mr. T. McAvoy

Mr. P. R. Middleton

Mr. P. L. Milton

Mr. P. Neuteboom

Mr. R. A. Palmer

Mr. P. E. Plowright

Mr. A. J. Prior

Mr. F.E. Proctor

Mr. M. Rowe

Mr. R. N. Ruffle

Miss Gwen Smoker

Mrs. Julia Thomas

Mr. A. Todd

CONGRESS COMMITTEES AND STAFF

OFFICERS AND MEMBERS OF THE GUILD OF STUDENTS

Cheryl Scott, *Vice-President, Internal*
M. Hall, *Guild Secretary*
S. Mee, *Chairperson, External Affairs*
N. Smart, *Chairperson, Student Reception*
Mr. I. McCrae, *Permanent Secretary*
Mrs. Sheila Hughes

G. Audcent
J. Bachtler
Deborah Baker
A. Bakshi
Katherine Bangs
M. Bansal
Carolyn Barrow
H. Bone
Janet Bottle
A. Bowler
Helen Bramwell
M. Canny
Christine Chapman
M. Collie
Anita Davies
Julie Davies
Susan Davies
Marie Farrell
S. Ferris
Susan Floate
C. Gittins
Clare Gould
H. Graham-Brown
A. Head
Penny Hedge

Gaenor Hollingsworth
Bryony Johnson
Harbrinder Kang
Leena Keyworth
Sarah Kirk
Frances Laing
M.Lanchin
G. Lewis
K. Little
Fook Hoy Loh
Michelle Lowe
Hing San Man
Nicola Metcalf
D. Moon
Elizabeth Morgan
Lindsey Nicholas
Julia Nicholson
P. Peacock
Michelle Proudfoot
Charlotte Purchas
T. Raby
Susan Riley
S. Rist
Helen Rudd
P. Savvides
Angela Scoins
Noor Sham Chaari

Julie Showell
Margaret Sinclair
Elizabeth Smith
Susan Stearman
N. Stevenson
Kathryn Strawbridge
J. Sugrue
Apryl Thornhill
Carolyn Tilley
Tracey Tobin
Alison Turner
R. Wallington
Susan Ward
T. Weatherup
A. Williams
Jane Wilson
N. Worman

NAMES INDEX